LUFTWAFFE

In Chapters 5 and 6 the author considers production planning and problems from 1935 to the Munich crisis, emphasizing the many program changes due to bitter personal feuds in the Air Ministry and the aircraft industry, technological causes, and competition from other Nazi programs. Chapter 7 is devoted to an in-depth description and analysis of the industry in 1938—its size, strengths and weaknesses, profits, pricing policies, and research and development sector—while Chapter 8 deals with the period from the Munich crisis to the outbreak of war and seeks to weigh the role that Germany's obvious aerial superiority played in Hitler's decision to go to war in September 1939.

The final chapter assesses overall Nazi planning and execution of their aerial rearmament program, concluding that despite their rhetoric to the contrary, the Nazis had as much difficulty in developing and directing aerial rearmament as the other major powers did.

A professor of history at the University of Nebraska–Lincoln, Edward L. Homze is the author of *Foreign Labor in Nazi Germany* (1967) and, with Alma Homze, of *Germany: The Divided Nation* (1970) and *Willy Brandt* (1974).

ARMING THE LUFTWAFFE

Arming the Luftwaffe

The Reich Air Ministry and
the German Aircraft Industry
1919–39

Edward L. Homze

UNIVERSITY OF NEBRASKA PRESS
LINCOLN AND LONDON

Publication of this book was assisted by a grant from the University of Nebraska Foundation.

Library of Congress Cataloging in Publication Data

Homze, Edward L
    Arming the Luftwaffe.

    Bibliography: p. 269
    Includes index.
    1. Aircraft industry—Germany—History.
2. Germany. Luftwaffe—History. I. Title.
HD9711.G32H65   338.4'7'629133340943
ISBN 0-8032-0872-3   75-38055

To the memory of my father, John F. Homze—*he would have been proud.*

Contents

List of Illustrations

List of Tables

Preface

THE HISTORY of the German aircraft industry during the interwar period presents a unique challenge to the historian. From limited secret rearmament in the Weimar period to a full aerial development and production program under the Nazis, that industry represented a tangled interweaving of economic, technological, and military threads. How can this interweaving best be described? How typical of general Nazi economic planning was the handling of the aircraft industry? How adept were the Nazis at combining the managerial, technological, and military factors involved in this sophisticated field? What was the interrelationship between the formulation of grand strategy, Nazi ideology, and the ambitions and interests of the aircraft industry? How accurate a barometer of Nazi diplomatic intentions was the aerial build-up? What blend of personal rivalries, bureaucratic empire building, and changing ideological goals spurred the industry? These are my concerns in this description of the German aircraft industry.

During the research and writing of the book, I received advice and assistance from many individuals and institutions. I wish to express my thanks to Professors Robin Higham, Earl F. Ziemke, and Harry R. Fletcher for their suggestions in formulating and writing the study. I am grateful to Mr. Robert Wolfe and Mr. John Taylor of the National Archives, Washington, D.C., and Mr. Eugene M. Emme of NASA. In Freiburg, Bundesarchivrat Wolf Noack, Dr. Horst Boog, and Dr. Karl Gundelach of the Militärgeschichtliches Forschungsamt cheerfully helped supply my research requests. In London, the staff of the Imperial War Museum aided with the Milch papers. My thanks also to the Secretary of the Air Force for permission to use the archives at Maxwell Air Force Base and to the staff of that institution.

I wish also to thank the following agencies for the use of their photographs: National Archives, Audio-Visual Division; Naval History Division, Naval Photographic Center; and the 136st Photo Squadron, Aerospace Audio-Visual Service of the United States Air Force.

The National Endowment for the Arts and Humanities and the Research Council of the University of Nebraska provided assistance in the form of a grant for research in Germany and a semester's leave in Germany, respectively, making possible continuous work on the study. The skills of Mrs. Lois James and Mrs. Jackie Dittmer, who typed the manuscript, are greatly appreciated.

Last, I am deeply indebted to my wife, Alma, for her constant help and encouragement and to my children, Eric and Heidi, who have helped me build many model German planes. One further personal note. I wish to plead guilty to a fascination with airplanes. I am of the airplane, not the aerospace, generation, and I still look up when I hear an engine overhead.

I do, of course, assume full responsibility for the views and the shortcomings of this book.

E. L. H.
Lincoln, Nebraska

Abbreviations

BA/F   Bundesarchiv/Freiburg; Federal Republic of Germany's national archives at Freiburg.

DZ/MGFA Dokumentenzentrale des Militargeschichtlichen Forschungsamtes; Document Central of the Military History Research Office at Freiburg.

FDC   Foreign Document Centre, Imperial War Museum, London.

IMT   *Trial of the Major War Criminals before the International Military Tribunal,* 42 vols. Nuremberg: USGPO, 1947-49.

KDC/M Karlsruhe Document Collection, Maxwell Air Force Base.

NA   National Archives, Washington, D.C.

NCA   *Nazi Conspiracy and Aggression,* 10 vols. Nuremberg: USGPO, 1947-49.

RLM   Reichsluftfahrtministerium; German Air Ministry.

TA   Techisches Amt; Technical Office of the German Air Ministry.

USSBS United States Strategic Bombing Survey.

Arming the Luftwaffe

CHAPTER 1

Versailles to 1926

A FEW FEET from the Berlin Wall in the Invaliden Cemetery stands a simple tombstone with the name Richthofen carved in block letters. Beneath it lie the remains of Germany's great World War I flying ace, Manfred von Richthofen, the fabled "Red Baron," who was shot down on April 21, 1918. Richthofen's body had been buried in France but seven years after the Armistice was returned to the Reich for a state funeral. It lay in state for two days in Berlin's Gnadenkirche; then, on November 20, 1925, eight Pour le Mérite holders, including Ernst Udet, placed the coffin on a horse-drawn carriage. An army drum and fife band accompanied the carriage as it moved through the crowded, silent streets of central Berlin to the Fatherland's Invaliden Cemetery, followed by Richthofen's mother, the Baroness; his sister, Ilse; and his brother, Karl Bolko. Immediately behind them came an impressive array of dignitaries of the Weimar Republic, including the newly elected president, Field Marshal Paul von Hindenburg. The victors of World War I hoped that the German air force was as safely interred as its greatest combat hero.

The German aircraft industry which built a powerful air force during World War I had a modest beginning. In 1914, it consisted of ten aeroengine and fifty aircraft and parts companies of "glorified garage" dimension. The Imperial Army had 218 airplanes and 12 airships, while the navy's five-year plan called for an ultimate strength of 36 aircraft. Four years later, the industry consisted of twenty-six aeroengine and thirty-five aircraft companies with a monthly production of 2,000 aircraft and an employment list of thousands of workers. During the war it produced approximately 44,000 aircraft and 48,000 engines[1] and had firmly established itself as the airplane developed from the oddity of 1914 to the necessity of 1918. Everywhere military thinkers were keenly aware of the potential of the air weapon for the next war: that is why the victorious Allies sought to crush German aviation through the peace treaties concluding World War I.

The Treaty of Versailles, signed June 28, 1919, and effective January 10, 1920, prohibited for a short time the manufacture and import of aircraft, parts, and equipment. To oversee the provisions, an Inter-Allied Military Control Commission with its subsidiary, the Inter-Allied Aviation Inspection Committee, was organized with extensive powers of inspection and enforcement. One section of the treaty specifically dealt with German military aviation and another with civilian.

Pursuant to the military section of the treaty, which required the surrender of all military aircraft except for one hundred unarmed seaplanes and flying boats used exclusively in searching for submarine mines, Germany eventually turned over to the Allied and Associated Powers or destroyed approximately 15,000 aircraft, 28,000 aircraft engines, and 16 airships, and dismantled about 1,000,000 square meters of hangars.[2] All military flying equipment, aircraft, and training programs were prohibited to the 100,000-man German National Army, the Reichswehr, which was established March 6, 1919. The Imperial German Air Force was demobilized, although few fliers were transferred to or volunteered for the Reichswehr and the Sicherheitspolizei (Security Police), seeing action in the Baltic and Polish areas and helping to suppress revolts within the Reich before their air operations were ordered disbanded by the Allies.

The civilian section of the treaty prohibited civilian aviation production for a period up to six months from the day the treaty went into effect, that is, until July 10, 1920. In June 1920, at the London Ambassadors' Conference, the ban was extended—in contradiction of the treaty—until three months from the day all aeronautical material had been either delivered to the Allies or destroyed. In the meantime, a Junkers four-engined passenger plane and a Rohrbach passenger plane built during the period were confiscated and dismantled.[3] In the confusion that followed, German plants were still manufacturing aircraft as reparation for the Allies while some of their aircraft were being confiscated at home and abroad.

The Allies brought some semblance of order to German civilian aviation with the Paris Agreements of January 29, 1921, which reinforced the three-month prohibition on aircraft manufacture until the Inter-Allied Aviation Inspection Committee confirmed Germany's full compliance with the treaty. Concerned that the Germans were deliberately delaying implementation of the treaty, the Allies also reiterated their demand for a ban on flying units in the police. Through the awkward machinery of diplomacy, they laboriously attempted to force Germany to recognize "definitions" which would distinguish civil from military aircraft. For the next year, the Allies and Germany engaged in a legalistic chess match in which the Allies attempted to contain Germany's air potential through legal restraints that Germany assiduously tried to avoid. On February 9, 1922, the Allies notified Germany that the three-month ban would officially begin; and finally, on May 5, 1922, more than two years after the Versailles Treaty became operative, Germany was again allowed to design and produce aeronautical materials.[4]

Before the production of aircraft could be resumed, however, the Allies sought to limit the technical capability of the German aircraft industry. The highest organ of Allied control in Germany, the standing Ambassadors' Conference, outlined in a note to the German government Allied "definitions" regulating civil aviation, which were incorporated into nine rules. The most important limited German civil aircraft to a speed of 170 km. (105 miles) per hour, a payload of 600 kg. (approximately 1,300 lbs.), a ceiling of 4,000 m. (13,000 ft.), a range of 300 km. (approximately 186 miles), and a flight duration of not longer than two and one-half hours, all well below the standards of existing aircraft. Lists of all aircraft factories and their production, the technical capabilities of the aircraft produced, and the names of fliers engaged in civil aviation in the Reich were to be submitted on a regular basis to the Committee.[5]

The enforcement of the "definitions" was the task of the Inter-Allied Aviation Inspection Committee, appropriately renamed on May 5, 1922, the Aviation Guarantee Committee. It was agreed that the "definitions" would be reviewed every two years to conform with new aeronautical advances, but there was no revision until June 1925, when the Allies proposed slight increases in the allowable load and speed in exchange for additional rights over aircraft engine development. The Germans objected and little was accomplished.

The German response to the "definitions" illustrates the futility of the Allied legalistic approach and the difficulty of anticipating conditions in a rapidly evolving technological field. Article 314 of the Versailles Treaty had given the Allies the right to fly over Germany's sovereign air space, permitting them access to the lucrative eastern market. The Germans simply enforced the "definitions" on all airplanes forced to land on German soil. The operation of Great Britain's air routes to Central Europe and France's Franco-Roumaine line were thus particularly hampered. Thirteen of Franco-Roumaine's aircraft were forced to make emergency landings in Germany and were threatened with confiscation. By 1926, the Allies, under pressure from the airlines and as a part of the general rapprochement of the day, were ready to renegotiate air rights. The representatives of the German Traffic Ministry, Drs. Alfred Wegerdt and Wilhelm (Willy) Fisch, gained concessions from the Allies; and the Paris Air Agreement signed on May 21, 1926, after months of discussions, lifted the technological restrictions. Germany again promised not to build military aircraft or to support sport flying with public funds, although the agreement did allow seventy-two Reichswehr officers to participate in sport flying at their own expense. One-half of that number could be officers without any previous flight training, but only twelve could be trained annually.[6] After six years of Allied restrictions German civil aviation was freed from all its fetters.

GERMAN MILITARY THINKING

German military thinking in the 1920s was dominated by the experiences of World War I. As early as March 1916, Colonel Hermann von der Lieth-Thomsen,[7] organizer and chief of staff of the Imperial German Air Force, had written a memo suggesting that the flexibility and range of aircraft dictated the necessity of a single controlled unit.[8] The doctrine of a separate air force was not clearly defined in his memo, but the germ of that idea was present. Military planners in other countries were also developing their ideas of an independent air force. In April 1918, the British had organized the Royal Air Force as a separate independent service, but it was closely tied to their immediate plan of launching a strategic bombing offensive against Germany.[9]

The Germans had experimented throughout the war with the organization of their aircraft units. At first the flying units were a part of the Communications Force, where they were evenly distributed in batches of six aircraft to each army and army corps headquarters for reconnaissance and photography. By late 1915 the fighters were organized in distinct units and a year later all aircraft were grouped according to their function—fighter, bomber, or reconnaissance. Great things were expected from the bombing units, but the results were disappointing. The only strategic bombing offensive against England was a failure: in fifty-one raids with airships or Zeppelins, a total of 196 tons of bombs were dropped, but seventy-seven dirigibles were lost. The bombers did not fare much better. In fifty-two missions over England, they dropped only 73 tons of bombs—hardly enough to justify the expenditure of men and materials.[10] In contrast, the excellent and dramatic accomplishments of the fighters, close-support aircraft, and reconnaissance units were duly noted and appreciated. As a result,

German military air thinking after the war had a stronger tactical than strategic bent.

On May 18, 1919, in his first postwar memorandum, Captain Helmut Wilberg, a close assistant of Colonel Lieth-Thomsen in the Prussian War Ministry, argued the need for an air force in the new Reichswehr. He envisioned a force of sixteen air bases housing about 1,800 aircraft, including trainers, reserve, and liaison planes manned by 8,000 men from the army and 1,200 from the navy.[11]

When the Allies refused to allow the Germans any air force in their new army, the memo was filed but not forgotten by its recipient, General Hans von Seeckt, the ranking German military adviser to the Armistice Commission.[12] From 1919 to 1926, this enigmatic army officer was first chief of the Troop Office (Truppenamt), the Reichswehr's camouflaged general staff. (The Versailles Treaty had expressly forbidden the great general staff.) Seeckt, a brilliant and energetic officer of the old school, had achieved a reputation as chief of staff to Field Marshal August von Mackensen on the southeastern front during World War I and had distinguished himself also as a military diplomat serving successively with the armies of Bulgaria, Austria-Hungary, and Turkey. His education and broad service career made him the logical choice for the job of building the new Reichswehr. His immediate problem was how to rebuild a disciplined, spirited, loyal, and technically superior elitist army faithful to the Prussian tradition from the demoralized mass army that emerged from World War I.

Seeckt's basic assumptions were that after the devastating defeats of the German armies, Germany had to rebuild the psychological desire to rearm, to reexamine the entire theoretical basis of war strategy, and to select the personnel for the elite army which would be the cadre for a future mass army. From the time he entered office until he retired, he took every opportunity to exhort his fellow countrymen on the need to make Germany defense-minded (*Wehrhaftmachung*). With an enthusiasm bordering on spiritual dedication he worked unremittingly to preserve the Prussian military traditions in the Reichswehr, nurturing the concept of the army as the school of the nation and repository of the national heritage. In keeping with this image, Seeckt steered the army, as best he could, away from the vortices of politics in the Weimar Republic. The army had to be "above politics" to preserve its integrity and traditions.[13]

In military thought, Seeckt returned to the Prussian tradition of mobility. His service on the eastern front during World War I, where defenses were not as static as on the western front, convinced him that the war of the future would be one of movement. The superiority of offensive to defensive strategy became the basis for the Reichswehr training program which he clearly defined in the famous memorandum of 1921, "Basic Ideas for the Reconstruction of our Armed Forces" ("Grundlegende Gedanken für den Wideraufbau unserer Wehrmacht").[14] He argued that strategic mobility won wars; it was best achieved by the close coordination of all arms, the highest technical attainment, and superior military preparation. The paramount military objective of war was the destruction of the opposing army, and mobile armies supported by aircraft would greatly augment the striking power of the offensive over the defensive forces.

Seeckt's emphasis on the need for fresh, thorough study of tactics and strategy and his obsession with psychological rearmament are another example of how Allied treaty restrictions stimulated the Germans to turn adversity into advantage. The Allies prohibited aircraft and tanks to the Germans but could not control their planning. German military thought experienced a revival, and by 1924 men like Walther von Brauchitsch and Heinz Guderian were organizing maneuvers to test theories of using aircraft with armor. Seeckt's own interest in aerial warfare was more theoretical than practical, but by 1923 he was convinced that the future German air force should be organized into a separate, independent branch.[15] It was, however, in the areas of personnel selection for the Reichswehr and military organization that Seeckt's keen awareness of the potential significance of air power was immediately influential.

The selection of officers and men for the 100,000-man Reichswehr from the many thousands of applicants gave Seeckt the opportunity to fashion a disciplined, homogeneous, elite army. Over the objections of the army's Personnel Office, he ordered a select 180 flying officers, veterans of World War I, into the Reichswehr's officer corps of 4,000.[16] General Ritter von Haack, the last inspector of the Bavarian Air Force, served for a time as Seeckt's personal chief of staff and headed the officers in the Truppenamt,[17] who were assigned to the following agencies established by Seeckt on March 1, 1920. The Air Organization and Training Office, disguised under the title Truppenamt (Luftschutz), or TA (L), and commanded by Captain Helmut Wilberg, was the central office for the collection and dissemination of all information pertaining to military aviation. In the T 3, or Foreign Armies Department, was a "foreign air office" for the compilation and evaluation of information concerning foreign air forces. Under the Office for Weapons and Equipment (Inspektion für Waffen und Gerät, or In WG) in the Army Ordnance Office (Heereswaffenamt) was the Air Technical Office headed by Captain Kurt Student and charged with the responsibility of following the development of aeronautical technology abroad. The Air Armament Economics Office (Fliegerrüstungswirtschaftliches Referat, or WaWiL) under Captain Wilhelm Vogt collected and evaluated information about the aircraft industry abroad. Planned but never established because of Allied restrictions was a procurement office which was to work with the German aircraft industry.[18]

Teams of air officers were assigned to each of seven infantry divisions which also served as Military Area Headquarters (Wehrkreis-kommandos). Under the title special duty consultants, the officers coordinated troop training in aerial warfare and functioned as aerial photography officers for their districts. Initially, little actual flying was attempted with the troops, so the officers worked closely with civilian aviation groups to organize emergency flying patrols in the event of foreign invasion. They also did valuable service promoting aviation to the general public.[19]

The German navy had a disguised air office, comparable to the TA(L), which collected and disseminated information on foreign naval flying, published a journal, and actively promoted naval aviation. In 1923, special flying consultants were attached to the naval commands in the North and Baltic Seas, where they also served in aerial photography offices.[20]

SECRET REARMAMENT IN THE SOVIET UNION

The most successful attempt of the Germans to escape the watchful eyes of the Allied Control Commission and continue experimenting with military aviation occurred in Russia. The Versailles Treaty convinced many German diplomats and military men that the only realistic position was for Germany to strengthen her political and economic ties to the other pariah nation of Europe, Soviet Russia. The two had a common dislike of the victorious Western Allies, a common enemy in Poland, and a common desire to exploit the resources of other nations to regain their positions as great powers. As early as January 1920, Seeckt believed that a reconciliation between Germany and Soviet Russia was not incompatible with his own staunch conservative Prussian ideas. The memories of the war of liberation against Napoleon, the League of the Three Emperors, and the nineteenth-century informal bond of sympathy between the two eastern monarchies remained dear to many German conservatives. Even though much of the understanding between Russia and Germany in the nineteenth century was more fanciful than real, the myth exercised a strong influence on the thinking of many officers of the old Imperial Army.[21] Quite possibly as early as the summer of 1919, Seeckt was in contact with Karl Radek, the Bolshevik expert on German affairs imprisoned in Berlin, or with Moscow through an intermediary, the former Turkish minister of war and old friend and ally, Enver Pasha. Not much is known about the nature and results of these contacts, but the lines of communication between the Germans and Russians were open.[22]

Throughout 1920, the semiofficial diplomat Victor Kopp, a close collaborator of Trotsky, was in Berlin attempting to interest armaments plants in producing weapons for Russia. His efforts paid off by early 1921, when he reported that the Albatros, Blohm and Voss, and Krupp firms were prepared to produce aircraft, submarines, and artillery in Russia under German supervision. A group of German technicians, led by Major (ret.) Dr. Oskar Ritter von Niedermayer, were sent to Russia to continue the negotiations. Although he was not particularly impressed with the Russians, negotiations were resumed in Berlin at the end of September. Meeting in private, usually at the apartment of Major Kurt von Schleicher, Leonid Krassin, chairman of the Council for Foreign Trade, and Kopp represented Russia and Colonel Otto Hasse of the Truppenamt, the Germans.[23] The Russians were particularly eager to initiate contacts with the Junkers firm as well as continue talks with other armament plants. The major difficulty was financing German plants in Russia, for German industry was reluctant to invest heavily without guarantees from the Reich government. After some delay, the Reich Chancellor was able to overcome the financial difficulties by allocating 150 million marks to the army command. A special office in the Truppenamt, Sondergruppe R[ussia], under Major Veit Fischer, was organized to administer the funds and coordinate all Defense Ministry contacts with the Russians.[24]

Negotiations with the Russians from 1920 to 1922 were conducted simultaneously on three levels—the government, the Reichswehr, and private firms—with little or no cooperation among them. The Soviets sought immediate military aid, technological and financial help to rebuild their industries, and restoration of normal diplomatic and consular relations, in return for which they offered the Germans a renunciation of reparations, trade, and a chance to experiment with weapons prohibited by the Versailles Treaty. Although the Germans were divided in their acceptance of the Soviet proposition, the Reichswehr was most enthusiastic. The three levels of German contacts coincided neatly in 1922 when the diplomatic marriage of convenience, the Treaty of Rapallo, was signed between Germany and Soviet Russia. The treaty, by which Germany accorded Russia de jure recognition, created a favorable political atmosphere in which to conclude additional agreements. The Russians were willing to place military installations, equipment, and labor at the disposal of the Germans in return for credit, technical assistance, and a mutual sharing of military skills and experience.

Negotiations between the Reichswehr and the Russians continued throughout 1922 and 1923. During that period, the Germans organized a holding company, the Gesellschaft zur Förderung gewerblicher Unternehmugen, or Gefu, with a working capital of 75 million RM and offices in Berlin and Moscow, under the supervision of General von Borries and Major Fritz Tschunke. The Gefu oversaw the establishment of a Junkers airframe and engine plant at Fili near Moscow, three Krupp shell factories at Tula, Leningrad, and Schlüsselberg (Petrokrepost), and a poison gas factory at Samara. The Germans were to receive a portion of the production of these plants. A Moscow branch of Sondergruppe R, called Zentrale Moskau (ZMo), independent of the German embassy, was given administrative control over the military aspects of the secret agreements. Colonel Lieth-Thomsen, now retired from active service, was appointed head of the Zentrale Moskau and remained in that post from 1923 until 1928, when he was replaced by Major von Niedermayer. Zentrale Moskau reported directly to the army command (Heeresleitung) and remained relatively immune to civilian inspection and control. Its duties included the administration of the three most important training sites: the armored vehicles school near Kazan, the gas warfare school at Saratov, and the flying base at Lipetsk, a Russian resort town on the Voronezh River about 310 miles southeast of Moscow. The latter, the first operational training base of the German air force after World War I, was established in 1924 and equipped with an assortment of German aircraft either built in Russia or secretly shipped there. During the early years of its operation, however, the most numerous type of aircraft used there was the Dutch-built Fokker D.XIII, a single-engined one-place fighter. At the time of the French occupation of the Ruhr in January 1923, General Seeckt had requested from Reich President Friedrich Ebert that one hundred airplanes be purchased abroad for the army. The contract was given to the Fokker firm, which had served Imperial Germany so well during World War I, and was financed from the secret "Ruhr fund" collected by German industry.[25] The Fokkers were delivered too late to be of use to the Reichswehr, so fifty of the older models were sold to Rumania, while the others were sent to Lipetsk.[26]

Two German aircraft firms, the Albatros Works[27] and Junkers, were involved in the Russian agreements. In July 1921, Major von Niedermayer had inquired at Junkers about cooperating with the

Defense Ministry in Russia. An oral agreement was reached in November when General Ludwig Wurtzbacher and Colonel Otto Hasse visited the Junkers home office at Dessau. Junkers was to construct an aircraft and engine plant in Russia with funding from the Reich government. On March 15, 1922, Junkers and Sondergruppe R signed a preliminary contract which called for the payment of 40 million RM plus an additional 100 million RM as a capital sum, with no obligation of repayment.[28] The contract was to run twenty-five years, and production was to begin immediately in Russia. The Junkers firm would construct a regular metal factory, materials testing lab, engine workshop, and all equipment to maintain them.

The plant, constructed at Fili, operated from 1924 to 1927 with the cooperation of Moscow's ZAGI (Zentralny Aero-Gidrodynamitscheski Institut), headed by Andrei N. Tupolev. It trained a generation of Russian engineers and designers, including most of the famed Russian designers of World War II. Financial difficulties plagued it from the beginning; after the great inflation, the Reichswehr did not supply adequate financing, nor did the Russians place enough orders to maintain operations. By September 1925, the plant had lost 15 million RM, half of which was due to the insistence of the Dessau head office on debiting Fili with the interest charges and general costs of the whole Junkers firm. The plant was losing 50,000 RM for every aircraft built and was forced to close in 1927. Even though a variety of models, including the Ju 21, K 30, and Ju 22, were built there, the plant never reached its pianned annual capacity of six hundred aircraft.[29]

Prior to 1926, Germany's secret rearmament agreements with Soviet Russia were a mixed bag of accomplishments and failures. In Lipetsk, the Reichswehr had an operational center that would train the future top-echelon commanders of the Luftwaffe and allow experimentation with aircraft in cooperation with other combat branches. More important, it spurred military interest in aviation. The production of aircraft with the Russians were less successful. Apparently the Russians, after the immediate threats of the civil war and the battle with Poland were over, were very circumspect about aviation matters. They sought to use German technology as best they could but were determined to develop their own aeronautical industry.

CIVIL AVIATION

The years from 1918 to 1926 were extremely difficult ones for the German aircraft industry. The treaty restrictions, rampant inflation, and the chaotic political situation made normal business virtually impossible. Fokker, Pfalz, Gotha, and Friedrichshafen, active firms during the war, closed. Aviation departments of giant firms such as AEG (General Electric of Berlin) and Siemens-Schuckert were disbanded, and the few companies left had to develop branch offices abroad, diversify production, or establish airlines to use their products. Junkers opened a branch office, called Svensk Flygindustrie, in Malmö, Sweden, and another in Russia; Rohrbach one in Holland; and Claudius Dornier offices in Switzerland and Italy, while on December 1, 1922, in Warnemünde, Ernst Heinkel founded a firm to design aircraft produced by his licensee, the Svenska Aero A.B., in Sweden.[30]

The experiences of the Junkers firm in this period are typical. Hugo Junkers formed the Junkers Motor Works in 1913 and the Junkers-Fokker aircraft firm in 1917, the latter at the urging of the High Command, to produce all-metal military aircraft. After the war, Junkers organized his own aircraft plant in Dessau. In 1918, the Junkers plants had 2,000 employees; by the end of 1920, 720; and a year later, employment had shrunk to 200, even though on June 25, 1919, three days before the signing of the Versailles Treaty, Junkers had the first postwar airplane of German design, the F 13, flying. The F 13 was an all-metal, six-seat monoplane that became widely used as a transport and as a model for a generation of new transports. By 1929, there were 322 in service in twenty-four nations. Yet there was not a sufficiently large market for new airplanes, especially in countries that had war surplus aircraft. To create work for his plant, Junkers had to establish his own airline, diversify his production at home, build plants in Russia, and license subsidiaries in Sweden. These strenuous and ingenious efforts were still not enough as the Junkers firm teetered on the brink of bankruptcy throughout the 1920s.[31]

Commercial flying suffered from the same difficulties as the aircraft industry. The first airline in Germany was organized in 1917 by the Allgemeine Elektrizitäts Gesellschaft (AEG) and was called the German Air Transport Agency (Deutsche Luftreederei). During the war it operated a military post line; shortly after the war, on January 8, 1919, August Euler, director of the newly formed Reich Aviation Office (Reichs-luftamt), licensed the Luftreederei to operate as an air transport company. Its first undertaking was a post and passenger service line between Berlin and Weimar, where the National Constitutional Assembly was meeting. The airline proved its worth, especially during the general strike when normal communications between the government and the assembly were disrupted. The Junkers firm opened an airline between Dessau and Weimar in 1919, and the Rumpler firm a line between Munich and Vienna in 1920. The most ambitious new venture was the German-Russian Airline

(Deutsch-Russische Luftverkehr-Gesellschaft, or Deruluft), founded on November 11, 1921, which opened a 1,200-kilometer line from Königs- berg to Moscow on May 1, 1922. The airline business mushroomed, and within a few years over thirty companies were operating, most of them unprofitably.

By 1923 the combination of competition, over-extension of resources, shortage of capital, exaggerated desires of German cities for air connections, and extraordinary inflation brought about the inevitable merger of the airlines into two firms, the Deutsche-Aero-Lloyd and the Junkers-Luftverkehrs AG. Aero-Lloyd was formed from the Luftreederei and most of the smaller airlines with the financial backing of some of the largest banking, trade, insurance, and industrial corporations in the Reich, including the Deutsche Bank, Norddeutsche Lloyd, Hamburg- Amerika-Paketfahrt AG, and the Zeppelin, Albatros, Dornier, and Sablatnig firms. Both Junkers and Aero-Lloyd had subsidiaries abroad and operational agreements with foreign airlines, but both required subsidies to maintain themselves. Under pressure from Reich authori- ties, these two firms were eventually amalgamated into Deutsche Lufthansa on January 6, 1926. The Reich government held 26 percent of its stock and the various German states another 19 percent.[32] There has been considerable speculation about the military role in organizing Lufthansa. Richard Suchenwirth states that the Defense Ministry arbitrar- ily merged all civilian companies into Lufthansa, a position most Western writers take.[33] Karl-Heinz Völker argues, as do most other German authors, that competition between the two firms was uneconomical and did not serve the best interests of the Reich, so the Transportation Ministry forced the merger by threatening to withhold subsidies. He admits, however, that after 1933, under the directorship of Erhard Milch, second in command of the Luftwaffe, Lufthansa maintained a relationship with the Reichswehr that was "close and sympathetic."[34]

Indeed, the relationship was incestuous. After the war, a Reich Aviation Office was organized under the distinguished air pioneer August Euler. Captain (ret.) Ernst Brandenburg was assigned to this office as a deputy state secretary in December 1918. A Pour le Mérite flyer, commander of a bombing squadron, and first-rate air strategist, Brandenburg deserves, along with Seeckt, the appellation "founder of the future Luftwaffe." A reliable, skillful organizer, an excellent promoter of civilian and sport flying, and an ultranationalist, Brandenburg became the close collaborator of the military in this critical civilian agency.

In 1922, when Euler left the Reich Office for Aviation and Motor Transportation, Brandenburg was transferred to the Ministry of Transportation as a deputy state secretary in the Aviation Department. In

1924, through Seeckt's intervention, he was appointed chief of the department with a rank of ministerial director (Ministerialdirigent).[35] In this position, Brandenburg was able to fund secret aviation projects for the military, organize flight training for future officers, and provide adequate camouflage for much of the aerial rearmament in the 1920s. He also supported the merger of the airlines, although there was nothing sinister in this as some have argued.[36] Businessmen, military officers, and governmental officials of various political persuasions saw the necessity of organizing the airlines on a national rather than a private, competitive basis. The success of the national railroads was a natural model. Indeed, there was minimal disagreement concerning use of the airlines to evade Allied restrictions. The German commonality of interests combined good business practices with national aims of self-protection. A strong, centralized airline would rationally develop the internal market, provide an excellent base for expansion in the international air market, and, in cooperation with the army, operate as a secret air reserve until Allied restrictions were removed and Germany could once again rebuild her air force.

Sport flying offered additional possibilities for secret rearmament while it stimulated interest in flying among Germans. By 1923 the Allied restrictions on motorized sport flying were lifted, and the Germans prepared to utilize it fully. The French invasion of the Ruhr and inflation made progress impossible in 1923, but on January 1, 1924, with the currency finally stabilized, the Reichswehr organized Sport Fliers, Ltd. (Sportflug G.m.b.H.) under the direction of Fritz Siebel. Sport Fliers established ten flying schools, with at least one in each of the seven military districts. Active and inactive flight officers from the army received training to maintain their proficiency and a small group of civilian enthusiasts were given instruction. A number of private flying schools were established in the same period and their activities coordinated by the military. Funding for these schools came from the secret, or "black" budget of the Reichswehr administered through the Transportation Ministry. In 1925 the Reichswehr's aviation budget was 10 million RM, 3 million of which was marked for research and development, 2 million for the Russian bases, and the remaining 5 million for flying schools, maintenance of disguised aircraft units, and air-raid protection measures.[37]

Glider flying typified, in many respects, the state of German aviation in the early 1920s. So obvious a sport as gliding was not considered important enough to be banned by the Allies. The Germans, however, immediately perceived in it a means of instilling air-mindedness in German youth and advancing the science of aviation. Shortly after the war, Oskar

Ursinus, editor of the aeronautics journal *Flugsport*, initiated a glider competition in the Rhön region, a mountainous country between the upper reaches of the Fulda, the Werra, and the Franconian Saale. The area, selected because of the strong upwinds and thermal updrafts, had been used before the war by a number of glider pilots, including the famous aviation pioneer Otto Lilienthal.

The first of the legendary postwar Rhön contests was held in the summer of 1920. Two dozen enthusiasts gathered for the competition, won by Wolfgang Klemperer of the Aachen Academic Aviation Club with a record flight of 1,830 meters in 142 seconds. (Dr. Klemperer later became well known as a rocket scientist at the Douglas Aircraft Company.) In the next few years some of the best minds in German aviation participated in the Rhön contests: the future aircraft designer Willy Messerschmitt; the future commander of German airborne troops in World War II, Kurt Student, then a captain in the Reichswehr; the famous aircraft manufacturer Anthony Fokker; and the distinguished scientists Ludwig Prandtl and Theodore von Kármán. With competitors of this quality, progress was rapid. In 1924 a record flight of eight hours, forty-two seconds, was made, and by 1930, when the secrets of thermodynamics had been discovered, gliders were mastering long distances and record altitudes. In the sixteenth race at Rhön, in 1935, five gliders flew more than three hundred miles to Brno, Czechoslovakia, while three years later a record altitude of 6,840 meters and a record flight duration of fifty hours, fifteen minutes, were achieved.[38]

Gliding became a craze among German university students in the 1920s. As early as October 31, 1921, Captain Wilberg of the Truppenamt recommended to General Seeckt that the Reichswehr promote gliding as a means of stimulating air-mindedness and training pilots. Seeckt personally visited one Rhön contest and his officer in charge of the Air Technical Office, Kurt Student, was one of the most active participants.[39]

More important, gliding competition stimulated the development of German aviation. Just as Allied restrictions on powered flight acted as a powerful incentive to aeronautical research instead of retarding it, so did the channeling of talent into glider flying. As Theodore von Kármán has pointed out, glider flying sharpened German thinking in aerodynamics, structural design, and meteorology. Because of the aerodynamic advantages of the single long-span wing over the double- and triple-wing arrangements of World War I planes, the single span became a dominant characteristic of German gliders. The ultimate development was today's glider with a long, thin wing and a graceful, streamlined fuselage. Gliders taught Germans better ways to distribute weight and deal with vibrations through structural design and opened the entire field of meteorology to the dangers of hidden turbulence, the use of the jet stream, and of course, thermal currents. Von Kármán even asserts that glider flying advanced the science of aviation more than most of the motorized flying in World War I. Almost all of the experts agree that German designers profited enormously from their glider experiments.[40] The sleek, aerodynamically trim single-wing fighters and bombers of the 1930s can trace their lineage to the small, fragile gliders that soared over the windswept hills of the Rhön.

NOTES

1. For the prewar period, see John H. Morrow, Jr., "The Prussian Army and the Aircraft Industry, 1909-1914," *Aerospace Historian* 20, no. 2 (June 1973): 76-83; for the war, see General der Kavallerie Ernst von Hoeppner, *Deutschlands Krieg in der Luft* (Leipzig: Koehler, 1921). Production and aircraft figures are from Werner Schwipps, *Kleine Geschichte der deutschen Luftfahrt* (Berlin: Haude & Spenersche, 1968), pp. 69-71, 76-77; Hauptmann Hermann [pseud.], *The Luftwaffe: Its Rise and Fall* (New York: G. P. Putnam's Sons, 1943), pp. 55-56; and J. A. Gilles, *Flugmotoren 1910 bis 1918* (Frankfurt: E. S. Mittler, 1971), pp. 123-24, who estimates that 43,476 engines were produced during the war.

2. The figures for war materials turned over to the Allies or destroyed vary considerably. Heinz Orlovious and Ernst Schultze, *Die Weltgeltung der deutschen Luftfahrt* (Stuttgart: Fred Enke, 1938), pp. 9-10, give 14,000 aircraft and 28,000 engines; Moisy F. von Gandenberger, *Luftkrieg-Zukunftskrieg? Aufbau, Gliederung und Kampfformen von Luftstreitkräften* (Berlin: Zentralverlag, 1935), pp. 39-40, mentions 14,014 aircraft, 27,757 engines, and 2,500 anti-artillery; Otto Gessler, *Reichswehrpolitik in der Weimarer Zeit* (Stuttgart: Kurt Sendtner, 1958), p. 226, gives 14,000 aircraft and 27,000 engines; Hans Guhr, *Sieben Jahre interallierte Militär-Kontrolle* (Breslau: Korn, 1927), p. 15, gives 14,014 aircraft and 27,757 engines; Peter Supf, *Das Buch der Deutschen Fluggeschichte*, vol. 2 (Berlin: Klemm, 1935), p. 226, indicates 15,714 aircraft and 27,757 engines; Gilles, *Flugmotoren*, p. 123, says that 27,160 engines were destroyed and 2,600 delivered to the Allies.

3. Schwipps, *Kleine Geschichte*, pp. 82-83.

4. Karl-Heinz Völker, *Die Entwicklung der Militärischen Luftfahrt in Deutschland 1920-1933*, Beiträge zur Militär- und Kriegsgeschichte, vol. 3 (Stuttgart: Deutsche Verlags-Anstalt, 1962), pp. 129-30; and Richard Suchenwirth, *The Development of the German Air Force, 1919-1939*, USAF Historical Studies, no. 160 (Air University, 1968), pp. 7-8.

5. Völker, *Luftfahrt in Deutschland*, p. 130; Schwipps, *Kleine Geschichte*, p. 83.

6. Suchenwirth, *Development of the German Air Force*, pp. 14-15; Hermann, *Luftwaffe*, pp. 61-63; Robin Higham, *Britain's Imperial Air Routes, 1918-1939: The Story of Britain's Overseas Airlines* (London: G. T. Foulis, 1960), pp. 88-91.

7. Hermann von der Lieth-Thomsen was made chief of staff to the commanding general of the air forces (General Ernst von Hoeppner) on October 8, 1916. Later he was chief of the Field Flying Forces. A Pour le Mérite winner, he left

the service in 1919 but operated as an unofficial government adviser in Russia until 1929, when a serious eye ailment forced his return to the Reich. In 1935 he was appointed general in the new Luftwaffe and served as adviser at the High Command level until his death in 1942.

8. "Die Entwicklung der deutschen Auffassung über die Führung des Luftkrieges," unsigned draft copy in the von Rohden materials, code number 4376-353, in the Bundesarchiv/Freiburg, which henceforth will cited as BA/F.

9. Sir Charles Webster and Noble Frankland, *The Strategic Air Offensive against Germany, 1939-1945,* vol. 1 (London: H.M.S.O., 1961), p. 38.

10. John Killen, *A History of the Luftwaffe, 1915-1945* (London: Frederick Muller, 1967), pp. 27-30; Hilton P. Goss, *Civilian Morale under Aerial Bombardment, 1914-1939,* 2 vols. (Maxwell Air Force Base, 1948), vol. 1, chap. 1; Douglas H. Robinson, *Giants in the Sky: A History of the Rigid Airship* (Seattle: University of Washington Press, 1973), chap. 4.

11. Völker, *Luftfahrt in Deutschland,* p. 124.

12. A recent critical but sympathetic account of Seeckt is Hans Meir-Welcker, *Seeckt* (Frankfurt: Bernard & Graefe, 1967).

13. John Wheeler-Bennett, *The Nemesis of Power: The German Army in Politics, 1918-1945* (New York: St. Martin's, 1954), p. 100; Harold J. Gordon, Jr., *The Reichswehr and the German Republic, 1919-1926* (Princeton, N.J.: Princeton University Press, 1957), pp. 298-300, 304-6; F. L. Carsten, *The Reichswehr and Politics, 1918 to 1939* (Oxford: Clarendon Press, 1966), chap. 3; and Walter Görlitz, *History of the German General Staff, 1657-1945* (New York: Praeger, 1953), pp. 222-35.

14. Friedrich von Rabenau, *Seeckt—Aus seinem Leben, 1918-1936,* vol. 2 (Leipzig: Hase & Koehler, 1940), pp. 474-75.

15. Gordon A. Craig, *The Politics of the Prussian Army, 1640-1945* (Oxford: Clarendon Press, 1955), p. 396; Heinz Guderian, *Panzer Leader* (New York: E. P. Dutton, 1952), pp. 21-28; Rabenau, *Seeckt,* 2: 529; Völker, *Luftfahrt in Deutschland,* p. 137.

16. Telford Taylor, *Sword and Swastika* (New York: Simon & Schuster, 1952), p. 30; Carsten, *Reichswehr and Politics,* p. 148.

17. Alan Robert Thoeny, "Role of Separate Air Force in Nazi Germany" (Master's thesis, University of Wisconsin, 1963), p. 2.

18. Information taken from General der Flieger a.D. Hellmuth Felmy, "Luftfahrt Ausbildung in der Reichswehr," Teil I, B/I/1b, Karlsruhe Document Collection, Maxwell Air Force Base, henceforth cited as KDC/M; Generalleutnant a.D. Bruno Maass, "Organization der Fliegerstellen im RWM 1920-1933," A/I/2; General der Flieger a.D. Wilhelm Wimmer, "Stellungnahme zu Luftfahrt-Ausbildung in der Reichswehr von Hellmuth Felmy, Teil I." B/III/1a, KDC/M.

19. Wimmer, "Luftfahrt-Ausbildung," p. 4.

20. Ibid., p. 51; Völker, *Luftfahrt in Deutschland,* pp. 127-28, 131.

21. A good general account of the peculiar love-hate relationship between the two nations is Walter Laqueur, *Russia and Germany: A Century of Conflict* (Boston: Little, Brown, 1965).

22. Carsten, *Reichswehr and Politics,* pp. 70-71.

23. For more information on Krassin, see Lubov Krassin, *Leonid Krassin: His Life and Work* (London: Sheffington & Son, 1929), and Edward Hallett Carr, *The History of Soviet Russia,* vol. 3, *The Bolshevik Revolution, 1917-1923* (London: Macmillan, 1953).

24. Helm Speidel, "Reichswehr und Rote Armee," *Vierteljahrshefte für Zeitgeschichte* 1 (1953): 20-34; F. L. Carsten, "The Reichswehr and the Red Army, 1920-1933," *Survey* 44-45 (October 1962): 114-32; George W. F. Hallgarten, "General Hans von Seeckt and Russia, 1920-1922," *Journal of Modern History* 21 (1949): 28-34; Craig, *Politics of the Prussian Army,* p. 410.

25. Völker, *Luftfahrt in Deutschland,* p. 134; Karl-Heinz Völker, "Die geheime Luftrüstung der Reichswehr and ihre Auswirkung auf den Flugzeugbestand der Luftwaffe bis zum Beginn des Zweiten Weltkrieges," *Wehrwissenschaftliche Rundschau* 9 (1962): 540-49.

26. Felmy, "Luftfahrt Ausbildung," pp. 4-5; Wimmer, "Luftfahrt-Ausbildung," p. 4.

27. Founded in 1909, the Albatros Flugzeugwerke had considerable success during World War I designing fighters. After the war its chief designer, Robert Thelen, left the firm, and his successors produced military aircraft for the Red Air Force and the German base in Russia. The firm, in continual difficulty because its sport and commercial aircraft were not successful, was forced to liquidate, with Focke-Wulf taking over its physical plant to use as a repair shop. (Karl Heinz Kens and Heinz J. Nowarra, *Die deutschen Flugzeuge, 1933-1945* [Munich: J. F. Lehmanns, 1965], pp. 39-40.)

28. The details of the financial arrangement are not clear. Werner Baumbach, *The Life and Death of the Luftwaffe,* trans. Frederick Holt (New York: Coward-McCann, 1960), p. 3, and the von Rohden study on National Archives Microcopy T-971, roll 26, frame 954, mention 80 million RM, while Suchenwirth, *Development of the German Air Force,* p. 13, quotes General Felmy's 100 million figure. Carsten, *Reichswehr and Politics,* p. 138, cites from the Nachlass, Mentzel, No. 5, pp. 63-64, Bundesarchiv Koblenz, the contract from which are taken the figures used in the text. David Irving, *Die Tragödie der Deutschen Luftwaffe: Aus den Akten und Erinnerungen von Feldmarschall Milch* (Frankfurt: Ullstein, 1970), p. 38, mentions 9.7 million gold marks.

29. Generalingenieur a.D. Thomsen, "Junkers Flugzeugwerke in Fili, in der Nähe von Moskau 1924-1927," dated June 14, 1954, Lw 103/39, in Dokumentenzentrale des Militärgeschichtlichen Forschungsamtes, Freiburg, henceforth cited as DZ/MGFA. For the impact on Russian design, see A. S. Yakovlev, *Fifty Years of Soviet Aircraft Construction* (U.S. Dept. of Commerce, NASA TTF-627, 1970); Carsten, *Reichswehr and Politics,* p. 234. For a pre-Junkers view of the Fili operation, see Hermann, *Luftwaffe,* pp. 82-86.

30. W. H. Tantum and E. J. Hoffschmidt, eds. RAF, *The Rise and Fall of the German Air Force (1933-1945),* (Old Greenwich, Conn.: We Inc., 1969), p. 2; Suchenwirth, *Development of the German Air Force,* pp. 8-9.

31. Kens and Nowarra, *Flugzeuge,* pp. 337-38; Hermann, *Luftwaffe,* pp. 30-31, 68-70; R. E. G. Davies, *A History of the World's Airlines* (New York: Oxford University Press, 1964), p. 25.

32. Schwipps, *Kleine Geschichte,* pp. 85-87; Völker, *Luftfahrt in Deutschland,* pp. 152-53.

33. Suchenwirth, *Development of the German Air Force,* p. 14; Derek Wood and Derek Dempster, *The Narrow Margin* (New York: Paperback Library, 1961), p. 31; Hermann, *Luftwaffe,* 81-87; Tantum and Hoffschmidt, *Rise and Fall of the GAF,* pp. 2-3; Taylor, *Sword and Swastika,* p. 30.

34. Völker, *Luftfahrt in Deutschland,* p. 153; Schwipps, *Kleine Geschichte,* p. 87; Irving, *Milch,* pp. 38-40.

35. Rabenau, *Seeckt*, p. 529; Suchenwirth, *Development of the German Air Force*, pp. 9-10, based on Privy Councillor Wilhelm Fisch's interview of December 27, 1957.

36. Hermann, *Luftwaffe*, pp. 82-86, insists that Junkers was forced into the merger by a cabal of militarists and industrialists. The Reichswehr had failed to fulfill its pledge to Junkers, in return for building a Russian plant, to purchase of some of his aircraft and grant commercial trade concessions in the Reich and Russia. Threatened with bankruptcy, Junkers was forced to give up his airline. Curt Riess, "Die Junkers Tragödie," *Münchner Illustrierte*, Juli-August, 1955, is also convinced of this explanation. It is no accident that Riess wrote the introduction to Hermann's book.

37. Völker, *Luftfahrt in Deutschland*, pp. 144-45; Maass, "Organization der Fliegerstellen," KDC/M, p. 9; Karl Gundelach, Rudolf Koester, Werner Kreipe, "Ausbildung in der Fliegertruppe," B/III/1b, KDC/M.

38. For accounts of the Rhön contests, see Schwipps, *Kleine Geschichte*, pp. 90-101; Hermann, *Luftwaffe*, pp. 14-19; Theodore von Kármán, *The Wind and and Beyond: Theodore von Kármán, Pioneer in Aviation and Pathfinder in Space* (Boston: Little, Brown, 1967), pp. 96-103; *Frankfurter Rundschau*, May 30, 1970.

39. Völker, *Luftfahrt in Deutschland*, pp. 131-32; Suchenwirth, *Development of the German Air Force*, pp. 6-10.

40. Von Kármán, *Wind and Beyond*, pp. 102-3. C. G. Grey, *The Luftwaffe* (London: Faber & Faber, 1944), pp. 96-100; Generalleutnant Heinz J. Rieckhoff, *Trumpf oder Bluff? 12 Jahre deutsche Luftwaffe* (Zurich: Interavia, 1945), pp. 29-31; Baumbach, *Life and Death*, pp. 2-6, von Rhoden study, NA Microcopy T-971/26/953. For a detailed account of the Allied restrictions on German aviation see Eugene Emme, "German Air Power, 1919-1939" (Ph.D. dissertation, University of Iowa, 1949).

CHAPTER 2

From the Paris Air Agreement to the Third Reich

THE REICHSWEHR STRATEGY in the 1920 was based on the assumption that Germany could not fight a major war. The army was little more than a border police force and the international situation unfavorable for full rearmament. The major immediate threat was Polish intervention in the event of internal difficulties. Most of the secret rearmament measures were aimed only at Poland, since Germany knew she would be helpless against a major power like France. Moreover, with limited funds, the German government was reluctant to spend large amounts for secret stockpiling of arms, and consequently, the German aircraft industry was in deep trouble. Short of capital and unwilling to expand its production capacity, the industry was cautious about investing heavily in machines unless it was guaranteed production of a large series of aircraft. That was impossible as long as the government refused to stockpile. If there were to be any industrial preparation for war production, the Reich would have to pay.

The Reichswehr's solution to these problems was threefold. First, it trained existing units to form a superb cadre for a future mass army when conditions were more propitious. Second, the army began long-range plans for industrial support of the future mass army. Third, the army developed contingency mobilization plans for emergency situations such as the invasion of East Prussia by Poland; Lufthansa pilots and aircraft in cooperation with the secret reserves and the regular army would furnish the basis for the emergency army.

TRAINING EXISTING UNITS

Although Germany was denied military aviation, she obtained complete sovereignty in civil aviation. As the Allied Aviation Guarantee Committee phased out its activities beginning September 1, 1926, the Reichswehr gained considerable latitude in developing its air arm. At Allied insistence, Germany abolished public support of sport flying. Sport

Fliers, Ltd., supported by the Defense and Transportation Ministries, was disbanded and its assets assumed by the German Commercial Flying School (Deutsche Verkehrsflieger-Schule [DVS]), the Academic Flying Group (Akademischen Fliegergruppen [Akaflieg]), and the organization especially founded in April 1927 as a cover for military aviation activities, Aviation, Ltd. (Luftfahrt G.m.b.H.). For all practical purposes, these groups continued the work of Sport Fliers, Ltd., and operated as an unofficial air reserve for the army.

Shortly after the signing of the Paris Air Agreement, Helmut Wilberg, now a lieutenant colonel and the leading flying officer in the Truppenamt, began preparing a comprehensive air training program utilizing the civilian air groups. The service roster of the Reichswehr indicated that by 1926 only 100 of the 180 originally selected flying officers were still eligible for active flight duty. Retirement, illness, and advancing age had pared the group by nearly half, and Wilberg suggested the training of younger officers. After lengthy negotiations with the Transportation Ministry, a system was devised whereby forty officer candidates a year were to receive flight instruction at the DVS school in Schleissheim before entering the Reichswehr formally. The training lasted twelve months, and a select group of ten men was sent on to Lipetsk for an additional six months of advanced fighter pilot training. All forty of the trainees received pilot training in this course and earned their B-2 pilot licenses.[1] They were then taken on active duty but were required to attend a two- to four-week refresher course yearly. These officer candidates were called Jungmärker and their parents were sworn to secrecy over the nature of their training.

In addition to the forty Jungmärker, the Reichswehr selected active-duty officers known as Altmärker for flight training. About two-thirds of them had had prior flight instruction, while the others attended a year-long program with the Jungmärker. Most of these officers were trained as observers, during the winter at a secret Berlin school and during the summer at Staaken DVS school near Braunschweig. The better students were sent to Lipetsk.[2]

After a year of preparations, the Lipetsk base was operational by the summer of 1925, although the first six-month training course did not begin until April 1927. All of the instructors were civilians recruited largely from the private flying schools and Lufthansa. For security reasons they were paid in American dollars and served on a contractual basis. There were about sixty permanent German staff with another seventy to one hundred persons periodically engaged in other experiments. Between 1925 and 1933 approximately 120 fighter pilots and 100 observers were trained at Lipetsk. Observer training was discontinued in 1932, when the army decided it was more efficient and economical to train them at Braunschweig.[3] The Russians also had military air units at Lipetsk, but they were strictly separated from the Germans. Some Russian military and civilian personnel were employed as technical assistants by the Germans, but most of the repair and technical work was carried out by Germans.

The Lipetsk base gradually became more important as a testing center than as a military training base. Newly developed aircraft and armaments were shipped or flown there for tests impossible to conduct in the Reich. The Russians were always suspicious and difficult to work with, however, and their close surveillance of German personnel and materials caused endless delays. Russian pilots and technicians, who were permitted to inspect and fly German equipment, were particularly interested in the new models of the early 1930s such as the Heinkel He 46, a close-support reconnaissance aircraft; the Heinkel He 45, a daylight medium-range bomber and reconnaissance plane; the Arado Ar 65, a single-seat fighter; the Junkers K 47, a low-wing, all-metal two-seat fighter; and the Dornier Do 11, a twin-engined medium bomber. Radio and communications equipment, machine guns, and bombs were also tried out at Lipetsk. The Germans profited enormously from these field tests, especially from the winter testing of military equipment.[4]

The tactical lessons derived by the Germans from their Russian experiences were also valuable. In 1929 a group of fighter pilot instructors organized a training program and eventually compiled a fighter manual (Jagdfliegervorschrift) which comprised a complete schedule of training, including air-drill regulations, close- and open-formation flying, aerobatics, high-altitude flying, aerial combat tactics, and air-to-air and air-to-ground gunnery and bombing practice. Most of it was based on World War I experiences and from participation in Russian troop exercises, particularly in the Voronezh area, which was set aside for German use as a gunnery, bombing, and observation range. The Red Army's strong emphasis on close air support for ground forces impressed many German officers, and much of the later German thought about the use of fighter-bombers and assault aircraft can be traced to their Russian experiments.[5]

Germany's improved diplomatic status and the depression, not ideological differences, brought an end to the Russian experiment. The heavy budgetary drain of the Lipetsk base—nearly 3 million RM annually—and the possibility of establishing more open military training within the Reich dictated the gradual liquidation of the Russian bases. After 1930 the Reichswehr did not use the Voronezh maneuver area, and after the graduation of the 1931 class of observers at Lipetsk, the Russians were notified that no further observer training was foreseen there since the

Braunschweig school was by then fully operational. Testing was shifted to the Rechlin base in Germany with only fighter training remaining at Lipetsk. In October 1932 the Russians demanded that the Germans use the Lipetsk airfield as fully as previously by returning all the military aircraft that had been transferred to the Reich, but the Germans refused and further negotiations proved fruitless. The seizure of power by Hitler in January 1933 only hastened the disbanding of the air stations, much to the genuine regret of the Russians. In the summer of 1933 the army ordered deactivation of the Lipetsk base. The station's personnel were returned home with the best equipment, leaving stationary fixtures, older aircraft such as the Fokker D XIIIs, and much of the testing equipment behind.[6] An important chapter in the secret rearmament of the German air force was closed.

INDUSTRIAL PREPARATIONS FOR REARMAMENT

At a meeting of the Heerswaffenamt (Army Ordnance Office) on November 24, 1924, General Ludwig Wurtzbacher charged the Nachschubstab (Supply System Staff, later renamed Economic Staff, Wirtschaftsstab) with the responsibility of ascertaining the future military use of the country's industry.[7] The Economic Staff was to determine the war capacity of industry and develop overall production plans based on it after having established the necessary rapport with industrial leaders. They were to work in complete secrecy because the Weimar government had forbidden such activities. The basic planning was to determine the munitions, weapons, equipment, and supplies needed for an optimum sixty-three-division mobilized army with supporting navy and air force. A preliminary survey indicated, however, that that was far too ambitious for the industry's capacity, and in the spring of 1925 the size was revised to twenty-one divisions. By 1928 the Economic Staff deemed even this too large and settled for sixteen divisions, although twenty-one remained the basic figure for the ideal army. Only in 1933, after the Nazi assumption of power, was the sixty-three-division plan revived.[8] The governing concept in the Reichswehr was that rapid industrial mobilization was the key to success in the age of total war. Modern technology made armaments obsolete so quickly that it was uneconomical to stockpile the large quantities of weapons needed to supply a mass army. A better solution was to research and develop weapons vigorously and maintain preparations so industry could produce them when needed.[9]

On January 26, 1926, the Ordnance Office organized a camouflaged company, Statistische Gesellschaft (Stega), under the directorship of

Geheimrat Dr. von Borsig, to conduct a statistical survey of industry for rearming. Stega collected all important current data on firms, including names of owners and managers, location and description of plants with detailed maps, type and number of machines, and possible products which they could produce. With this information, the army planned for emergency conversion of firms. Stega's main office was in Berlin, but regional offices were established in each military district, staffed primarily by former officers with business experience and industrialists.[10] Stega found that many companies were not enthusiastic about rearming. Industrialists had few compunctions about violating the Versailles Treaty or cooperating with the army sub rosa—most felt it was only a question of time before the treaty restrictions were lifted and the government could openly support rearmament—but other concerns were uppermost in their minds. In the mid-1920s most of them were interested only in their business future and were unable to make financial sacrifices for secret rearmament. Industrial preparations would be costly and would have to be subsidized by the government. Some firms, like Krupp, were eager to cooperate, but others were not. The I. G. Farben firm, for example, was worried that their international prestige and connections would be impaired if news of secret preparations were leaked to the press.

Despite resistance from industry, the Reichswehr pressed forward with its plans. During the first phase, 1924-28, the emphasis was on planning prototypes of weapons which could be mass produced during the second phase, 1928-33. During the first phase both the army and navy had their own organizations for letting contracts under the loose supervision of the Ordnance Office, but in 1929 the separate armament programs were merged into a unified one, the Fertigungsprogramm (Production Program), based on the sixteen-division force with the ultimate goal of twenty-one divisions. A parallel Industry Program (Industrie-Programm) was designed to increase the basic industrial capacity of the country and prepare for rapid conversion to war production.[11]

Air force planning followed a similar course in these years but was handicapped by extensive administrative decentralization, the low rank of air officers, low priority of air rearmament, and need for tight security. Throughout the 1920s, military aviation matters such as personnel, tactics, and training were under the control of the Truppenamt, while aviation equipment was under the Ordnance Office. Disharmony existed between the two. Since the air arm was not an independent service branch with its own command structure, the air officers within the army invariably found themselves outranked. Thus, when Major Hellmuth Felmy was appointed Chief of Air Operations and Training on February 1, 1929, his requests for funds had to compete with those of colonels and generals. Some improvement came as a result of the recommendation made in 1928 by Major Albert Kesselring, efficiency expert of the Reichswehr,[12] that a separate air inspectorate be established. The army refused, pointing out it would provoke unfavorable foreign reaction, but did reorganize the various air offices under a single command on October 1, 1929. Brigadier General Hilmar Ritter von Mittelberger was made head of the Training Inspectorate (In 1) branch in the Reich Defense Ministry and its subbranch, Inspectorate 1 (L). These offices became the cover for German military aviation activities through their responsibility for tactical training, technology, budget, air defense, weather service, personnel, training schools, and general administration.[13]

A comparable fusion of scattered departments had occurred with the Ordnance Office on February 1, 1928, when procurement, production, development and testing, and industrial preparation were combined under the direction of Captain Helmuth Volkmann. Although there was to be frequent reorganization and considerable subdividing and expansion of these offices, the overall structure of aviation affairs was simplified and strengthened in the years from 1926 to 1933.[14]

To assist the aircraft industry in gearing up for rearmament, the Ordnance Office in 1926 established a dummy civilian corporation, Fertigungs G.m.b.H. (Production, Ltd.), which let contracts to aircraft plants. It was also to inspect and approve technical designs, drawings, and computations and help prepare the industrial firms for large-scale production in the event of an emergency. Fertigungs G.m.b.H. found the aircraft industry in a chaotic condition, without common industrial techniques, drawings, engineering standards, or even numbering systems. Standardization was the first order of business before firms could be shifted from individualized hand-crafted production to continuous-flow production. This was the absolute minimum requirement if designing firms were to license other firms to produce their aircraft. The magnitude of the task can be seen from the fact that one light aircraft with a weight of a ton required an average of 32,000 parts and 50,000 rivets. Nearly 10,000 DIN A-1 technical drawings would be needed for the manufacturing, repair, and licensing firms if it were to be mass produced.[15] Many firms which feared sharing their trade secrets with others and thereby strengthening their competition resented the activities of Fertigungs G.m.b.H., especially so long as the Weimar government's ban on stockpiling military aircraft precluded any sizable series production. The designing firms had to release all technical data to their licensed firms for preproduction conversion even though there was little prospect of actually producing the planes and profiting from their designs. Nor did the licensing firms want to invest in jigs, machines, and labor training without assurance of an immediate return on their investment. These problems were by no means unique to Germany, however; the British and Americans experienced similar ones.[16]

During the first phase of rearmament preparations, 1924-28, the Reichswehr contracted only for prototypes, usually on a single-airplane basis and from one or two invited firms. After 1928, military specifications were delineated by the Ordnance Office, and companies were invited to submit designs and cost estimates. The aircraft were then tested and the winning entry awarded a contract. The first prototypes were developed in 1927-28 to meet the tactical requirements established by Captain Student's Weapons and Testing Branch (WaPrüf 6 F) of the Ordnance Office. Student suggested that four basic types of aircraft be developed and tested to accumulate the necessary data for refinement into tactical-technical specifications for mass production. They included a single-engined daytime fighter with the code name Heitag (Heimatjagdeinsitzer); a single-engined, short-range daytime spotter plane called Erkudista (Erkundungsflugzeug); a combination night fighter and reconnaissance plane named Najuku (Nachtjagd-und Erkundungsflugzeug); and a long-range, high-altitude reconnaissance plane and bomber called Erkunigros (Erkundungsflugzeug Gross). From the Arado firm came the fighter Ar SD I with a Bristol Jupiter engine; the Albatros firm supplied the spotter L 76/77 and later the L 78 with a BMW (Bayerische Motoren-Werke) VI engine; the Bavarian Aircraft Works (successor to the Udet and Messerschmitt companies) furnished the Bf 22 as a night fighter; and Heinkel built the bomber, the He 41.[17]

The four prototypes were tested at either the Lipetsk base or the testing station near Lake Müritz at Rechlin, Mecklenburg. The Rechlin facility had been built during the war and, because of its inaccessibility, was virtually unknown to the outside world. After 1925, its camouflage name was Testing Station Rechlin of the Reich Formation of the German Aviation Industry. All military tests involving the dropping of bombs or use of weapons and all final acceptance tests were conducted at Lipetsk for security reasons. The navy had its own testing station at Travemünde. After the testing of the four prototypes, there was considerable refinement of the tactical-technical specifications before they were passed from the Ordnance Office to the aircraft industry.

This formulation of tactical-technical specifications was the first attempt to build the system that was finally used in the 1930s. The military tacticians of the Truppenamt established requirements for the development of aircraft types and submitted them to the Ordnance Office, which in turn converted them to technical specifications for industry. All too often, industry was not able to meet the specifications. Generally in the

1930s four years were required to develop an aircraft from design to series production, and slightly longer—five to seven years—for aircraft engines. By that time, the specifications usually had changed markedly.

The first four prototypes failed to meet the expectations of the Ordnance Office and were dropped from the development program because they were underpowered or had some unsatisfactory aerodynamic characteristic. New, reworked specifications were released in 1929 which retained the basic aircraft types but increased the speed requirement to 220 km./h. for bombers, 350 km./h. for fighters, and 250 km./h. for reconnaissance planes. By 1932 the industry met these specifications with the Heinkel He 46 and He 45 as short- and long-range reconnaissance planes; the Arado Ar 65, shortly replaced by Arado Ar 64 because of its better cockpit visibility, as the fighter; and the Dornier Do 11 as the bomber. These models were ready for production by the end of the year and, except for the Do 11, had already been produced in a small series of from five to eighteen. They were the first aircraft of exclusively military design for the new twenty-one division army.[18]

The inclusion of a bomber in the program was a significant move. The Truppenamt and the government were sensitive about using the term bomber in the 1920s; they insisted their aircraft were defensive only. A contingency plan for "emergency armament" was devised for the mobilization of Lufthansa planes as reconnaissance and bomber aircraft. A variety of obsolete and primitive machine gun mounts and bomb-release mechanisms were to be fitted on the civilian planes to convert them to military use. As a result, the air offices referred euphemistically to any large aircraft as a multipurpose reconnaissance plane rather than a bomber. After 1929 this artificiality was dropped in favor of the term night bomber, but it was not until 1935 that use of converted civilian planes as bombers was dropped from military plans.[19]

The German aircraft industry consisted of eight airframe and four engine plants in 1929. The leaders in aircraft productions were the Junkers, Heinkel, and Dornier firms, followed by the Albatros, Arado, Bavarian Aircraft Works, Focke-Wulf, and Rohrbach plants. Junkers and Bavarian Motor Works (BMW) were leaders in engine construction over Argus and Siemens. Although most of the engines used in the 1920s were foreign models either made abroad or built under license in Germany, there was some progress in engine development by domestic firms. In 1924 Captain Student commissioned BMW to build the Napier Lion and later in the 1920s the same firm built the Pratt and Whitney Hornet. Siemens built chiefly Bristol Jupiter and a few Gnôme-Rhônes engines.[20]

With the help of the Aerolloyd airline, BMW had developed the BMW IV, a 528-h.p. engine which evolved into the BMW VI, the firm's liquid-cooled, inverted twelve-cylinder standard engine. Inspectorate 1 (L) thought it absolutely necessary to increase the power of the BMW VI engine to the 800-h.p. range to compete with those of other countries, but the conversion would take five to seven years. In the autumn of 1930, the Reich Transportation Ministry, which had the responsibility for development of a standard engine for both civilian and military aviation, called for bids on a 30-liter displacement, liquid-cooled engine with the lowest possible horsepower-weight ratio. BMW and Daimler-Benz were both awarded development contracts with extensive financial backing from the Reich. BMW's design was a failure, but in 1936 the first Daimler-Benz DB-600 engines were ready.[21]

The Junkers firm had under development a diesel engine with lower fuel consumption which, despite its greater weight, promised to be ideal for long-range aircraft. In 1930 the company was also given a contract for the famous Jumo 210, a 20-liter nondiesel engine which was developed by 1936. The Argus firm was commissioned to build a 3,000-h.p. engine in the mid-1920s, but an operational engine of that horsepower proved to be well beyond its technological ability.[22]

In spite of the progress within the engine industry, engine development became one of the chief bottlenecks of the aircraft industry in the 1930s. There were many reasons for the slow rate of development. During World War I, for example, the Daimler auto and Benz-Werke firms accounted for approximately two-thirds of all the aircraft engines produced in the Reich.[23] After the war, the Benz-Werke, located in the demilitarized zone, had to give up production entirely, while Daimler turned to automobile engines. For nearly ten years these two leading manufacturers produced no aircraft engines. It was only after 1926, when the companies merged, that they returned to engine production, so that by World War II, the company was the Reich's chief aircraft motor manufacturer. Another indication of the low level of development was that by 1933 the Reich had only three aircraft engines in the 1,000-h.p. class suitable for modern military aircraft—the BMW VI, the BMW 132, and the Siemens SAM 22B. Two of the three were of foreign design: the BMW 132 was the Pratt and Whitney Hornet license, while the SAM 22B was the Bristol Jupiter.[24] It was not until 1936 that the first generation of engines of German design appeared.

The shortage of public funds hampered the pace of engine development. In the period 1929-32, the Reich government spent 175,032,950 RM subsidizing all forms of aviation, but only 21,105,000 RM for new development. Of this total, 4,855,000 RM was allocated for new engine development, compared with 13,250,000 RM for new aircraft development.[25] The government's attempts to establish a reliable group of engine plants to meet a national emergency also encountered difficulties.

The army, beginning to motorize its units, was a successful rival of the air offices in preempting manufacturers. Often the air offices had to settle for the smaller, less financially stable firms, which cooperated only with considerable funding from the government.

Nor was the reasonably good prevailing level of business activity in the period 1925-28 sufficient to support the engine industry expansion and development programs designed by the air branch of the Ordnance Office. The results before 1933 were meager, although the rapport which developed between the engine manufacturers and the air Ordnance Office paid rich dividends in rapid expansion after 1933.[26] The possibility of importing engines from abroad in the event of an emergency was discussed frequently by the Transportation Ministry but rejected for reasons of national security by the Reichswehr. Germany was committed to rebuilding its own aircraft engine industry.

When the depression struck, two of the four engine plants, Junkers and the BMW, fell into serious financial difficulties and had to be extensively reorganized in order to survive. The Daimler-Benz firm sharply curtailed its aircraft engine production but through its automobile line was able to withstand the crisis. Only the small Argus plant survived without difficulty. It had produced engines and, when forced to stop in 1919, had acquired the Horch-Werke and produced automobiles. In 1926 the company returned to the production of aircraft engines, specializing in light air-cooled models for sport and commercial planes. With the help of Transportation Ministry contracts the aero-engine line was successful enough that in 1930 the firm phased out its automobile production. In that same year it introduced the 500-h.p., eight-cylinder, air-cooled, V-shaped As 10 engine, which, along with its variations, became one of the most popular engines in its class. By 1939 over ten thousand As 10 series engines were produced.[27]

During the 1920s aeronautical research suffered from many of the same problems that plagued the airframe and engine industries: uncertain political conditions, inadequate financing, and wildly fluctuating economic activity. The national and state governments found it difficult to support the numerous university and college research institutes, the extensive Reich Institute of Applied Physics and Applied Chemistry, and the Kaiser-Wilhelm Institute with its thirty-seven subdivisions. In 1924 an attempt was made to establish with Reich funds a Central Research Institute for Aviation in Adlershof, but it had little success. In 1928 an umbrella organization, the German Aviation Research Council under Professor Ludwig Prandtl, was established to pool the talents of industry and the academic and special scientific institutes, but the organization was chronically short of funds. Although brilliant individual work, such as Prandtl's application of hydrodynamics to aeronautics at Göttingen and von Kármán's work at Aachen, was being done, German research lacked direction and focus. Germany had no single research center comparable to the United States' Langley Field and Wright Patterson, France's Chalois-Meudon, England's Farnborough and Teddington, Italy's Guidonia, or Russia's ZAGJ.

After 1926, with an improving economy and a more tranquil political environment, Reich funding for aeronautical research became more regular and Dr. Adolf Bäumker, a former officer, was appointed to direct a centralized program. Through the Transportation Ministry's budget, 7 percent of the total subsidy for aviation was channeled into research (table 1). Private industry supported some investigations, but its precarious financial condition precluded a substantial research program.

MOBILIZATION PLANS, 1925-33

The mobilization plans for the aircraft industry were interlocked with the existing capacity of the industry, the military planning of the Reichswehr, and the prevailing international and domestic political conditions. Generally, mobilization planning was done on three levels: immediate, intermediate, and theoretical, or long-range. In the twenties, the German army referred to the immediate level as Notrüstung, or emergency armament. It consisted of units capable of being operational within several weeks; for example, a crew might be assigned to a Lufthansa transport which could be converted into a night bomber within a few days. The intermediate level, developed more fully after 1927, was based on a complicated Mobilization Plan for a Wartime Army (Aufstellungsplan

TABLE 1

REICH SUBSIDIES FOR AVIATION AND AERONAUTICAL RESEARCH, 1926-32

Year	Subsidy for Aviation (RM)	Portion for Research (RM)
1926	46,850,000	2,050,000
1927	43,803,500	2,900,000
1928	55,534,395	4,650,000
1929	42,897,500	6,420,000
1930	46,992,550	2,500,000
1931	41,300,900	2,430,000
1932	43,842,000	1,985,000
Total	321,220,845	22,935,000

SOURCE: Dr. Adolf Bäumker, "Zur Geschichte der Luftfahrtforschung," Lw 103/61, DZ/MGFA.

einer Kriegswehrmacht, or A-Plan). A detailed timetable known as Calendar A was devised, and after the initial mobilization order was given, various units or programs were activated on the order date plus preparation time. Thus, a reserve unit might be activated on X plus seven days. The timetable for the aircraft industry might well extend over a year's duration. The theoretical level of mobilization planned for an ideal future force, or for the next four to eight years. Most of the planning at this level was hypothetical and based largely on General Staff estimates of the future needs of the military. A simplified illustration of these three levels of planning is seen in the plans for increasing the Reichswehr from its first-level size of seven infantry and three cavalry divisions to the intermediate level of twenty-one divisions. On the third level, there were numerous plans for building a mass army; for example, a 1925 study called for a field army of sixty-three-infantry and five cavalry divisions with comparable naval and air units.[28]

The planning and its terminology was overlapping and confusing. The terms "emergency armament" and "mobilization planning" became interchangeable by the end of the 1920s, while the concept of an ideal army of twenty-one divisions was used by agencies such as the Economic Staff to distinguish it from the more realistic emergency army of fifteen to sixteen divisions.[29] Planning for the aircraft industry was particularly difficult. The long lead time (interval between design and series production), technological complexity, and rapid obsolescence of modern aircraft telescoped the three levels of mobilization into one. Thus German planners often tried to dovetail current production into future mobilization programs. The results were confusing to both producers and planners.

Except for emergency armament, little planning was done in the early 1920s; but starting in 1925, the first of two four-year armament production programs was launched. The 1925-29 program aimed at designing prototypes for mass production and producing aircraft that could be used as a ready reserve, such as aircraft for the flying schools, the base at Lipetsk, and, above all, Lufthansa. These aircraft could double as fighters, bombers, and transports in an emergency. During the second period, 1929-33, industrial preparation for series production of the prototypes was scheduled and some limited series production of aircraft planned.

In the summer of 1927 the organizational branch of the Truppenamt submitted its first complete mobilization plan to the various offices for their consultation and approval.[30] Anticipating the request of the Truppenamt, the Ordnance Office had already completed an industrial cost survey, which was submitted on August 15. It would cost 38,478,600

RM, including 5,150,000 RM for industrial preparation, the first year of the four-year program to support an air force for a fifteen-division army. The air force would have 247 airplanes plus spare parts and supplies, 64 motor-drawn 88-mm. flak guns and 90 flak machine guns, 60 searchlights, and 30 directional hearing devices. The cost of the program would drop after the first year to an annual expenditure of 19,212,460 RM. There were no provisions for prototype development, since all the aircraft to be purchased were production models.[31] The Reichswehr was dissatisfied with this estimate, believing it inadequate for its intended twenty-one-division army.

In 1928, a long-range estimate was made of the theoretical maximum capacity of the aircraft industry. It was posited that in 1929 the industry could produce 7,006 airplanes for the army and 1,746 for the navy. These figures were illusory, however, for German plants were no longer accustomed to mass production, nor could the subsidiaries supply a fraction of this theoretical productive capacity. Nevertheless, on the basis of this estimate a program would be launched to enable the industry to produce annually 2,293 aircraft for the army and 750 for the navy at the end of the first phase.[32] The brief pseudo-prosperity of the late 1920s allowed the Reichswehr some latitude in developing this program. In fiscal year 1928-29 the Reichswehr budget rose to a peak of 827 million, up from 490 million RM in 1924.[33] Significantly, 27,263,000 RM was used in 1928-29 for industrial preparations and the lion's share, 12,445,000 RM, went for expansion of the aircraft industry.[34] The next year, because of the depression, the figure dropped to 9 million RM for the aircraft industry. Of that amount, Junkers received 2.0 million, Bavarian Aircraft 0.9, Dornier 1.6, Heinkel 0.7, Albatros 0.4, Rohrbach 0.3, Klemm 0.2, and the remainder went to the aircraft engine plants.[35] Völker estimates that from 1925 to 1933 a total of 80 to 100 million RM was spent on aerial armament or industrial preparations.[36] This figure was based on the 10 million RM annual secret budget of the air offices in the Truppenamt and does not include naval or civilian aerial expenditures. Dr. Bäumker, a high-ranking aviation official in the Transportation Ministry, the origin of most of the secret funds, estimated just over 321 million RM in subsidies for aviation from 1926 through 1932 (see table 1). Even allowing a generous half of that amount for purely civilian aviation (the subsidy for Lufthansa alone averaged 18 million RM annually), approximately 150 to 170 million was probably spent on secret air rearmament in this period.

The difficulties of arriving at a definitive account of the secret rearmament are many.[37] The documentation is incomplete and scattered, and intervening decades of controversy over the extent of the rearmament have obscured the issue even more. In the case of aerial rearmament, the most sensitive of all areas, the very nature of the aircraft industry precludes a definitive judgment. To a foreign investigator, the elaborate improvement of airport facilities and navigational aids, the extensive night and all-weather training of Lufthansa crews, and the comprehensive developmental program might seem to be an obvious part of the secret rearmament of the Reich. To a German they are normal business expenditures of an aggressively expanding industry. The best evaluation would be that Germany's level of technical proficiency in the aircraft industry was comparable to that of other great air powers, even though she did not possess an active air force by 1930. This was largely achieved through the secret rearmament policies of the government.

Some measure of the strength of German civilian air power can be seen in statistics for 1927 and 1928. German civilian transports flew more miles and carried more passengers than all the French, British, and Italian airlines combined.[38] The training, particularly in instrument flying; personnel; and equipment of the German airlines were on a par with those of the best airlines in the world. French military intelligence estimated that in 1931 Germany possessed 1,100 civilian airplanes, 400 of which had potential military use after a short conversion period of eight to ten days.[39] In addition, Germany's 40,000-member Luftfahrt-Verband (Aviation League) represented a sizable reserve of trained manpower that could be tapped in an emergency.

The conversion of civilian into military aircraft was a consideration of all countries in the 1920s, but it was not until the late 1930s that combat testing of converted civilian aircraft actually took place. For Germany, which was strong in civilian but weak in military air power, the appeal of conversion was obvious. Junkers's director general, Gotthard Sachsenberg, a distinguished commander of a naval fighter squadron during World War I, argued in two memos in 1928 and 1929 that everyone was aware Germany was evading military restrictions by building its civilian air fleet. He contended that the military ought to recognize and capitalize on this. Instead of ordering a variety of aircraft types from separate firms, the policy currently being followed, the Reichswehr should establish the basis for large-scale series production and concentrate on the construction of a big fleet of fast air transport-bombers built along the lines of Junkers's all-metal transports. A contract for one hundred transport-bombers would do more to stimulate production and the modernization of the aircraft industry, encourage the spirit of military flying at home, and impress foreigners than all of the tiny prototype programs combined.[40]

Sachsenberg's ideas were far too radical for the staid and conservative officers of the Ordnance Office. They were divided over the use of commercial aircraft as bombers and unconvinced of the superiority of a bomber force. Some dismissed Sachsenberg's suggestions as a crass attempt of the Junkers firm to salvage its deteriorating financial position with a huge contract from the Reich.[41] Ironically, Sachsenberg's memos anticipated the first large building program of the Third Reich, and his concentration on a single type of aircraft to develop the production capacity of the industry and to impress Germans as well as people abroad were to become the hallmarks of the early Nazi rearmament program.

While Germany's neighbors were concentrating on their own severe economic problems, and Germany's own aircraft plants were perilously close to bankruptcy, the full fury of the depression hit Germany. Only then did any immediate relief come from the Reich government. The ban on stockpiling purely military aircraft was finally rescinded at a top-level conference held on November 29, 1930, and attended by Reich Ministers Wilhelm Groener of Defense, Julius Curtius of the Foreign Ministry, and Theodor von Guérard of Transportation; Ministerial Director Erich Brandenburg of Transportation; and Brigadier General Hilmar Ritter von Mittelberger, chief of the Air Inspectorate.[42] The government was confident that another provision of the Versailles Treaty could be ignored. The stockpiling of combat-worthy aircraft, weapons, and equipment based on the prototypes developed since 1926 could be readied in depots for the provisional air units to be activated in accordance with the mobilization calendar.

Shortly thereafter, the first of three duty squadrons of four airplanes each was activated. They were to augment the existing Lufthansa reserve courier squadrons but drew their personnel from the training units previously stationed in Lipetsk. Given the cover title Reklamestaffeln, commercial skywriting squadrons, they ostensibly were owned by the private firm Luftfahrt G.m.b.H. but in reality were stationed and controlled by the district military headquarters at Königsberg, Berlin, and Nürnberg-Fürth. They were to participate in district military exercises, especially troop training for close air support.[43]

With the decision to lift the ban on stockpiling, the pace of planning and production increased swiftly. In February 1932, the Reichswehr reported that by April 1 it would have 228 aircraft—36 military and 192 converted civilian planes. The goal for the following year was 274 aircraft—82 military and 192 converted planes. The military recognized that the convertible aircraft were no substitute for regular military planes, but the goal was to activate the force, especially the bomber section. In the next armament period, 1933-38, the army's basic strategy was to develop plans for the mass production of military aircraft in the event of mobilization and to develop and produce a big bomber. Any hesitation about using offensive bombers was gone. Colonel Wilhelm Wimmer of the

Reichswehr Technical Office said that he had "not the least doubt that in the future, the only nations to have anything to say will be those that possess powerful air fleets built around an airplane that can, day or night, strike fear in the hearts of the enemy population."[44]

At the same time, February 1932, Felmy, now a lieutenant colonel, submitted a study for the creation of an air force to support the mobilization army of twenty-one divisions. He called for an eighty-squadron air force with 720 aircraft and 240 in reserve by 1938. It would consist of six long-range reconnaissance squadrons of 54 aircraft and 18 reserves, fourteen short-range reconnaissance squadrons with 126 aircraft and 42 reserves, eighteen fighter squadrons with 162 aircraft and 54 reserves, and forty-two bomber squadrons with 378 aircraft and 126 reserves. An additional 96 trainers would bring the grand total to 1,056 airplanes.[45]

Felmy's study was the basis for the much publicized Nazi "1,000-Aircraft Program" of 1933. The preponderance of bombers— forty-two of the eighty front-line squadrons, owes much to the inspiration of the Italian air theorist General Giulio Douhet.[46] Douhet had argued that the war of the future would be won largely by air superiority. The big bomber, capable of fighting its way through defensive fighters, would deliver the crushing strategic blow to the enemy's industrial and population centers and decide the outcome of the war within a few days. Felmy was aware that the French Air Force had adopted plans for four squadrons of big bombers of the AB 20 type with a range of 2,000 km., a bomb load of one ton, and an effective defense of nine machine guns. He apparently relegated his own fighter force to attacking enemy reconnaissance aircraft, and insisted that the first priority of his bomber force was the quick knockout of the enemy's air force. At the first moment of hostilities, the maximum offensive striking force had to be concentrated on destroying the enemy's air bases; the slightest hesitation could be fatal. Only after air supremacy was achieved through the destruction of the enemy's air force could the air force be used for further strategic employment. Although Felmy and others could later argue that the air force of the Reichswehr was designed exclusively for defense, his plans were clearly in the mainstream of military thinking which emphasized a strong offense as the best defense.[47]

In part, Felmy's strategy, based on the idea that "the bomber always gets through," reflected the state of aeronautical technology. From the end of World War I to the mid-1930s the speed of bombers had developed faster than that of fighters. During World War I fighters had a 50 percent advantage in speed, but by the early 1930s most military thinkers estimated that this advantage had been reduced to 10-20 percent. Until the advent of the fast low-wing fighter and of radar, the bomber enjoyed a considerable advantage over the fighter.[48]

Although Felmy's plan was still beyond the capacity of German industry, it did have a decisive effect on the development of prototypes. In July 1932, technical-tactical specifications called for the design of five new warplanes suitable for joint army and navy use, including a heavy bomber with a range of 2,500 km. and a bomb load of 2,400 lbs.[49] Felmy's plan had also followed the thinking in the Army Ordnance Office on the need to expand the aircraft industry's production capability to meet the demands of the mobilization calendar. The Ordnance Office had argued as early as March 1930 that the industry had to have the means as soon as possible to fulfill its commitments to the mobilization plans. Furthermore, it estimated that if mobilization were implemented and hostilities occurred, the air force would lose approximately 50 percent of its existing unit strength monthly. This meant building sizable reserves of aircraft and devising plans for the firms to produce enough airplanes to cover losses beginning the second month of hostilities. No later than the sixth month of hostilities, the firms had to be geared up to produce at least 300 aircraft per month.[50] Felmy's plan largely incorporated the Ordnance Office's estimate of losses and of ready reserves needed, and reiterated its position on industrial production planning. However, in the spring of 1932 the Truppenamt examined the state of the aircraft industry in reference to Felmy's plan and was understandably shocked to find that it could produce only a fraction of the needed war materials.

On April 4, 1932, the Air Inspectorate Office of the Truppenamt submitted a detailed report to the Operations and Organizational Branches on the production facilities of the aircraft industry.[51] It found that among the airframe firms of Junkers, Dornier, Heinkel, Arado, Focke-Wulf, Albatros, and Klemm, only Junkers and Heinkel were able to produce aircraft in series, and then only on a limited scale. The others could produce only custom-made aircraft; their material reserves, manpower, equipment, and space limited these plants to a maximum output of six airplanes per month. Important semifinished assemblies for aircraft did not exist in Germany and had to be imported. The Air Inspectorate Office estimated that by doubling the work force through a second shift, the airframe manufacturers could achieve a maximum output of one hundred single-engined aircraft per month in nine months after the activation of the mobilization plans.

The situation of the individual firms was not much better. At the time of the report the largest aircraft firm, Junkers, had not produced a single model that could meet the military specification of the Defense Ministry.

Its financial position was critical and only an immediate state subsidy, which the Transportation and Defense Ministries were already negotiating, could save the firm. Heinkel, the other firm capable of series production, was solvent, and, as the chief manufacturer for the Defense Ministry in the 1920s, had had considerable experience building military aircraft.[52] At the time of the inspectorate's report, the company had contracts for the construction of seven army He 45 reconnaissance aircraft, five He 38 sea fighters, two multipurpose He 59 planes for the navy, and three long-range reconnaisance planes and two trainers for the German flying schools. Heinkel was not, however, able to manage large series production.

Among the smaller firms, Dornier had contracts for three army aircraft: a four-engined bomber, the Do P; a two-place fighter, the Do 10; and a twin-engined bomber, the Do 11. But heavy unsuccessful expenditures in building and promoting the huge Do X flying boat had forced the firm into difficult financial straits. A previously arranged subsidy of 0.7 million RM for 1932 probably was not adequate. Arado was much more secure financially; it had designed and delivered six Ar 64 and two Ar 65 fighters to the army and had contracts for seven more Ar 64s and ten more Ar 65s for the next fiscal year. The Albatros firm, before its fusion with Focke-Wulf A.G. of Bremen, had been one of the army's major developmental firms. By 1931 Albatros and Focke-Wulf had under development the highly regarded Al 84, a two-seat fighter; the FW 39/40 for the army; and the W 7 for the navy. The fused firm, despite the Defense Ministry's efforts to channel contracts to it, was having difficulty competing with the larger plants. This was particularly disturbing since Focke-Wulf-Albatros, with its large, underused facilities, had an important role in the mobilization calendar. Its major contract for 1932-33 was for the production under license of twelve Ar 64s and He 45s. Klemm G.m.b.H. was primarily a builder of light sport aircraft and relatively unimportant to the Defense Ministry.

The aircraft engine firms of Junkers, Argus, BMW, and Siemens were in even worse condition than the airframe plants. Their financial position was precarious, especially that of Junkers. Despite the recent construction and expansion of many of the engine firms, they were still dependent on foreign designs and raw materials. Their own stockpiles and those of their subcontractors were practically nonexistent. In the unlikely event that they could secure access to the necessary raw materials when mobilization occurred, the Air Inspectorate estimated that in six months at the earliest all four firms working with double shifts could reach a production of 160 engines monthly. Of these, 100 would be used for front-line aircraft and the remainder for trainers and civilian planes.

The situation in the ancillary industries was as bleak. The supplies of aviation fuel were sufficient for only three months of mobilization. Airborne radio equipment could not be ready for issue for at least six months.[53] The bomb-casing manufacturers, despite a shortage of large presses, were able to deliver a sufficient number of casings within a month's time, but the explosive for them would take longer. An ambitious program for the production of bomb casings had been launched in the summer of 1928 calling for a wide variety of splinter, smoke, high-explosive, and incendiary bombs and a variety of fuses,[54] but it was not until some time later, after the transition was made to cast steel bomb casings, that the industry could fulfill its quotas.

At the moment that Felmy's planning study was anticipating a 1,000-aircraft force and the mobilization planners were projecting a monthly production of three hundred aircraft six months after the plan's activation, the aircraft industry was unable to meet their expectations. Employment in the industry slumped in 1932 to 3,800 employees. Casualties among the aircraft firms mounted, and the last hope among the survivors was for a quick and massive fiscal transfusion from the central government.

NAVAL AVIATION BEFORE 1933

The German navy was permitted to keep a few aircraft until 1920 to assist in mine-clearing operations in the North and Baltic Seas. The naval air stations of Norderney in the North Sea and Holtenau near Kiel were maintained until the mine clearing was completed. The only other aviation activity the Versailles Treaty allowed the navy was the operation of some antiaircraft artillery at the large naval base at Königsberg. Since the Reichswehr was denied possession of any antiaircraft artillery, the navy had sole responsibility for its development. Naval experimentation centered on the perfection of existing World War I weapons. The famed 88-mm. antiaircraft gun was also developed under the auspices of the navy. By 1930, when flak units were again introduced into the army, the basic research work of the navy on the 88-, 105-, and 76-mm. guns facilitated the smooth integration of these weapons into the army.[55]

From the closing of the mine-clearing bases in 1920 until the Ruhr crisis of 1923 the navy operated no aircraft, although it was conducting negotiations with the Russians. They offered the use of the airfield at Odessa on the Black Sea which had a good year-round flying climate, was close to the sea, and could therefore be used as a training and testing station for both land and sea aviation. The navy rejected the offer probably more from political resentment than technical reservations. However, it did make limited use of the army's Russian base at Lipetsk.[56]

The navy preferred to train most of its future fliers at home, and the first class of sea cadets entered naval aviation ground school at Stralsund in 1922, followed by a second class in February 1923. During the Ruhr crisis, the government began purchasing aircraft for the navy. With funds collected from leading German industrialists, an order for ten seaplanes of the He 1 type was placed with the Heinkel firm at Warnemünde. These aircraft officially were being constructed for an anonymous South American country. Heinkel built the parts and shipped them to Stockholm, where they were assembled, test flown, disassembled, and recrated for shipment back to Germany. Six World War I aircraft were also purchased for use as transports, trainers, and target-towing planes.[57]

Actual flight training began in the navy in 1924 when a group of former pilots and observers were given a refresher course at a civilian school at Warnemünde. Other flying schools were started the same year under the control of a civilian firm, Severa G.m.b.H., which had its home office in Berlin. Founded with secret navy funds, Severa was to operate ostensibly as a commercial hauler and tow-target mover but in reality became the main trainer of the navy's air arm. Operating out of the former bases at Norderney and Holtenau, the company provided a civilian cover for military training of pilots, observers, technicians, designers, and workers. Severa aircraft, most of which were purchased through Sweden from German-affiliated firms, were also used in reconnaissance and training missions for the navy. By 1928 Severa was spending 1.35 million RM annually.[58]

From 1924 to 1929 the organizational structure of naval aviation grew at a rate parallel to but proportionally smaller than that of the army. Additional air bases at Wangerooge and Wilhelmshaven-Rüstringen were added to the Severa chain. Technical matters were handled in a Development Section (Entwicklungsreferat) in the naval Transport Office under the command of Captain Günther Lohmann. Lohmann was able to purchase for the navy the Caspar Aviation Company at Travemünde, which was converted into a testing station. All but the most obvious military equipment was tested there, the remainder in Russia. The major manufacturers for the navy before 1933 were Heinkel, Dornier, and Junkers. Ernst Heinkel, a designer for Caspar Aviation before he founded his own firm at Warnemünde, developed the He 22 and He 24 trainers, the He 5 and He 9 reconnaissance planes, and the single-place He 38. From 1930 to 1933 he designed the He 51 single-seat fighter, He 60 reconnaissance plane, and the multipurpose He 59, all used extensively in the 1930s.

In 1926 the aviation office of the Naval Command initiated a competition for various types of naval prototypes. Heinkel established its dominance with float aircraft, while Dornier concentrated on flying boats. In 1927 Dornier earned a contract to develop the gigantic twelve-engine flying boat Do X, which was built in Switzerland. On its maiden flight from Bodensee in 1929, the Do X carried 165 persons in its triple-decked fuselage. In January 1931, the huge aircraft successfully flew to the South Atlantic under the command of the famed World War I flier Friedrich Christiansen. Returning to Germany via New York, it created a worldwide sensation. The navy had originally intended the big flying boat as a long-range reconnaissance, mine-layer, and torpedo plane, but its military usefulness proved to be limited. More successful for the navy was the Do Wal series of smaller flying boats evolved from Do X.

Navigational difficulties spurred the development during this period of radio communications by the firms of Lorenz and Telefunken, while the testing base at Travemünde successfully developed, tested, and made troop operational the first radio direction equipment for the navy.[59]

The army and navy aviation programs were only very loosely coordinated until late 1929, when the Defense Ministry ordered closer co-operation in an effort to reduce needless parallel developmental work for the two branches and to maximize the limited funds spent on aviation. Henceforth the navy would continue to develop seaplanes according to its own guidelines, but whenever possible its specifications for new aircraft would be combined with those of the army. Thus the tactical-technical specifications for new aircraft development submitted to industry after 1929 listed three types of aircraft: those specifically for the army, those for the navy, and those to be used jointly.[60] The navy was wary about this arrangement, but profited enormously from its cooperation with the army, especially in the conversion of land aircraft to sea use and in the extensive field testing conducted by the army in Russia. Despite the navy's determination to keep the development of its aviation program under its own control, the decision to combine the air programs of the two services became a harbinger of the future. The prevailing attitude in the Air Inspectorate Office of the Truppenamt was that the navy's desire to remain independent was hurting the whole aviation cause.

How successful was the secret rearmament program during the Weimar Republic? There can be no doubt that the French and British had continual, accurate appraisals of the nature and extent of German aerial rearmament or that the perfunctory manner in which the Allies enforced the treaty restrictions, especially after the Paris Air Agreement of 1926, encouraged the Reich government to subvert the spirit and letter of the aviation restrictions. As with other punitive provisions of the Versailles Treaty, the Germans quickly saw a growing lack of basic agreement between England and France on enforcement in aviation matters and merely capitalized on the differences. By 1929, when the ban on the stockpiling of military aircraft in the Reich was lifted, the German government was already committed to a policy of open defiance of the treaty's provisions. It was not a question of intent, but of timing as to when the last remaining hurdle—that of publicly proclaiming the resumption of aerial rearmament—would be attempted. The depression intervened, and the relatively low priority of open aerial rearmament in relation to other, far more pressing foreign and domestic problems meant that it was deferred for a time. By the time the Nazis took power, the plans were drawn, the equipment was in the hands of some units, and the administrative machinery was in place for massive aerial rearmament. The only thing needed was the pretext and the will to act.

The degree to which the secret rearmament helped the Luftwaffe after 1933 has been the subject of considerable speculation. Albert Kesselring, Erhard Milch, and the authors of the von Rohden documents emphasize that the combination of Allied controls and lack of adequate financial support by the Weimar government had a marked adverse effect on the Luftwaffe.[61] Valuable years of experience in production, field testing, and command operations were lost. Many of the Luftwaffe's shortcomings during the war were attributed to the haste and inexperience of the aircraft industry and the military in attempting to make up for the lost time.

Quite naturally, most Western writers tend to emphasize the beneficial effects of the secret rearmament on the Luftwaffe. F. L. Carsten, Eugene Emme, Hauptmann Hermann, and John Killen consider the preliminary work in the development of aerial capabilities crucial in launching the massive aerial rearmament of the 1930s.[62] More balanced in their views are the German writers Wolfgang Sauer, Karl-Heinz Völker, Richard Suchenwirth, and Walter Hertel. On the question of the value of the secret rearmament, Sauer flatly states, "The answer can be summed up in one sentence, that until 1933 practically nothing was operational that the Versailles Treaty had expressly forbidden."[63] While acknowledging that the biggest failure of secret rearmament was that it encouraged the republic's enemies while not affording Germany comparable additional military protection, Sauer does admit that it prompted rapid rearmament once Hitler openly renounced the treaty provisions. Völker and Suchenwirth, on the other hand, admit the limitations of the secret rearmament but stress the continuity in planning and developing the air force from the Weimar period. Völker in particular attempts to destroy the prevailing myth that

Hermann Göring and the Nazis were the builders of the Luftwaffe from its inception. Hertel, a top administrator in the aviation program, is in substantial agreement that the framework for rapid expansion of the aircraft industry was established in the Weimar period.[64]

The debt the Luftwaffe had to the Weimar period in terms of aircraft development and experimentation is widely acknowledged by most writers, but the debt it owed Weimar for training its leadership is even more striking. Of the estimated 450 flying officers in the 4,000-man officer corps of the Reichswehr in 1933, 97 army and 19 naval officers achieved the rank class of general during World War II. An additional 12 fliers from Lufthansa and the various secret reserves of the Weimar period reached the general rank class.[65] The same could be said for the aircraft designers, industrialists, and aviation administrators: with few exceptions, the builders of the Luftwaffe were the secret rearmers of the Weimar Republic.

NOTES

1. German pilot licenses were rated in the following way:

Number of motors	Persons	Flight Weight	Class
1	1	0-500 kg.	A1
1	1-3	to 1000 kg.	A2
1	1-4	to 2500 kg.	B1
1-2	1-8	to 5000 kg.	B2
unlimited	unlimited	unlimited	C

2. For a detailed account of the entire Reichswehr training program, see Hauptmann a.D. Karl Gundelach, Oberst a.D. Rudolf Koester, and General der Flieger a.D. Werner Kreipe, "Ausbildung in der Fliegertruppe," B/III/1b, KDC/M.

3. Suchenwirth, *Development of the German Air Force*, p. 27; Carsten, "Reichswehr and Red Army," p. 124; Völker, *Luftfahrt in Deutschland*, p. 141.

4. Burkhart Mueller-Hillebrand, *Das Heer 1933-1945: Entwicklung des organisatorischen Aufbaus*, vol. 1, *Das Heer bis zum Kriegsbeginn* (Darmstadt: E. S. Mittler, 1954), p. 17; Suchenwirth, *Development of the German Air Force*, pp. 29-34; Völker, "Luftrüstung in Reichswehr," pp. 543-45; Grundelach et al., "Ausbildung," p. 31.

5. Völker, "Luftrüstung in Reichswehr," pp. 544-45; von Rohden study, NA Microcopy T-971/27/883-84; Grundelach et al., "Ausbildung," p. 31.

6. Speidel, "Reichswehr und Rote Armee," pp. 20-34; Felmy, "Luftfahrt Ausbildung," p. 38.

7. Georg Thomas, *Geschichte der deutschen Wehr- und Rüstungswirtschaft (1918-1943/45)*, ed. Wolfgang Birkenfeld, Schriften des Bundes-Archivs, vol. 14 (Boppard am Rhein: Boldt, 1966), p. 54; Wheeler-Bennett, *Nemesis of Power*, p. 143; Craig, *Politics of the Prussian Army*, p. 407. Both Craig and Wheeler-Bennett use the later designation of Rüstungsamt for this office.

8. Berenice A. Carroll, *Design for Total War: Arms and Economics in the Third Reich* (The Hague: Mouton, 1968), pp. 59-60.

9. General Hans von Seeckt, *Thoughts of a Soldier* (London: E. Benn, 1930), pp. 65-66; Craig, *Politics of the Prussian Army*, pp. 406-7; Wheeler-Bennett, *Nemesis of Power*, pp. 143-48.

10. Thomas, *Geschichte der Rüstungswirtschaft*, pp. 55-59; Carroll, *Design for War*, pp. 66-67; Mueller-Hillebrand, *Das Heer*, p. 34.

11. Carroll, *Design for War*, pp. 67-71.

12. Generalfeldmarschall a.D. Albert Kesselring, *Soldat bis zum letzten Tag* (Bonn: Athenäum, 1953), pp. 22-23, called himself the "Sparkommissars des Reichsheeres"; Suchenwirth, *Development of the German Air Force*, p. 18, referred to him as a "simplification expert" (Vereinfachungskommissar), but it would seem that "efficiency expert" is perhaps more accurate.

13. Völker, *Luftfahrt in Deutschland*, pp. 162-64; Suchenwirth, *Development of the German Air Force*, pp. 17-21.

14. For a detailed discussion of the administrative structure of the air force offices in these years, see Völker, *Luftfahrt in Deutschland*, pp. 161-65, 176-80.

15. DIN stands for Deutsche Industrie Norm (German Industrial Norm). Information on the activities of Fertigungs is from "Die Deutschen Luftwaffenindustrie vor und während des Krieges," NA Microcopy T-971/27/ 377-80, and "Beitrag für eine kriegsgeschichtliche Studie die Beschaffung von Luftwaffengeräten," Lw 103/66, DZ/MGFA.

16. Obersting. Haase-Berton, "Der Aufbau der Luftwaffe-Rüstungsindustrie," dated 24 Februar 1954, Lw 103/39, DZ/MGFA. For the British experience, see Robin Higham, *Armed Forces in Peacetime: Britain, 1914-1940, a Case Study* (Hamden, Conn.: Archon Books, 1962), and for the American see John B. Rae, *Climb to Greatness* (Cambridge, Mass: Harvard University Press, 1968).

17. Walter Hertel, "Die Flugzeugbeschaffung in der Deutschen Luftwaffe," KDC/M, pp. 8-10.

18. Ibid., pp. 10-13; Völker, "Luftrüstung in Reichswehr," pp. 544-45.

19. Suchenwirth, *Development of the German Air Force*, pp. 22-23; Völker, *Luftfahrt in Deutschland*, p. 160; "Kurze Angaben über Geschichte des 4-mot. Bombers von General der Flieger a.D. Wilhelm Wimmer," Lw 103/58, DZ/MGFA.

20. Hertel, "Flugzeugbeschaffung," pp. 13-14; Generalingenieur a.D. Gerbert Huebner, "Der tatsächliche Ablauf der Aufgabenstellung und Auswahl der Flugzeuge für die deutsche Luftwaffe," dated 1956, KDC/M.

21. Hertel, "Flugzeugbeschaffung," pp. 19-20.

22. Ibid., p. 13. Technical data for engines and aircraft are from Kens and Nowarra, *Flugzeuge*.

23. Kens and Nowarra, *Flugzeuge*, pp. 590-91; Gilles, *Flugmotoren*, p. 123.

24. Georg Feuchter, *Der Luftkrieg* (Frankfurt: Athenäum, 1962), p. 107; Generaling. a.D. Huebner, "Die Bomberentwicklung vom 1933-39," Lw 142, DZ/MGFA.

25. Adolf Bäumker, "Zur Geschichte der Luftfahrtforschung," Lw 103/61, DZ/MGFA. W. M. Knight-Patterson [Wtadystaw Wszebôr Kulski], *Germany from Defeat to Conquest* (London: Macmillan, 1945), p. 405, and Georges Castellan, *Le Réarmement clandestin du Reich, 1930-1935* (Paris: Librairie Plon, 1954), p. 146, cite approximately the same figure.

26. Hertel, "Flugzeugbeschaffung," pp. 70-71; Kesselring, *Soldat*, p. 458.

FROM THE PARIS AIR AGREEMENT TO THE THIRD REICH

43

27. Kens and Nowarra, *Flugzeuge*, pp. 581-82.

28. Wi/IF 5.420. Nr.159/25 B z, "Die organisatorische Lage für eine personelle Heeresverstärkung vom Jahre 1931 ab," dated 27.4.25, NA Microcopy T-77/98/822602-22.

29. See Carroll, *Design for War*, pp. 59-60; Mueller-Hillebrand, *Das Heer*, pp. 18-19; Gerhard Meinck, *Hitler und die deutsche Aufrüstung 1933-1937* (Wiesbaden: Franz Stein, 1959), pp. 5-7; NA Microcopy T-971/27/922-29.

30. Truppenamt Nr. 943-27 g.Kdos. "Z" T2 III A, dated 30.6.1927, in DZ/MGFA.

31. Wi/IF 5.126, Jena Br.Nr. 1765/27, Org. "Z" wi/Wi, dated August 15, 1927, NA Microcopy T-77/18/728901-7. The number and type of aircraft were 24 HD 33s, 72 L 70s, 47 D.XIIIs, 47 L 65 IIIs, 37 Dornier Merkurs, and 20 G 23s.

32. Hertel, "Flugzeugbeschaffung," p. 75; Suchenwirth, *Development of the German Air Force*, p. 35; von Rohden study, NA Microcopy T-971/27/925-26.

33. Wheeler-Bennett, *Nemesis of Power*, p. 187, which seems to be based on Knight-Patterson, *Germany from Defeat to Conquest*, p. 405, or Jacques Benoist-Méchin, *Historie de l'armée allemande*, vol. 1 (Paris: A. Michel, 1936), p. 380. A comparison of these figures for aerial rearmament with those of Bäumker, "Luftfahrtforschung," would indicate substantial agreement although Bäumker's are slightly higher.

34. Carroll, *Design for War*, pp. 64-65.

35. Figures from Castellan, *Réarmement clandestin*, pp. 146-47, which are based on the French Second Bureau estimates and usually very accurate.

36. Völker, *Luftfahrt in Deutschland*, p. 220.

37. Carroll, *Design for War*, pp. 57-59, rightly takes exception to the extremists like Erich Eyck, *Geschichte der Weimarer Republik*, vol. 2 (Zurich: E. Rentsch, 1956), p. 69, who asserts that Germany never disarmed, and Meinck *Hitler und Aufrüstung*, p. 4, who says that Germany now and then only slightly overstepped the Versailles Treaty's limitations.

38. Emme, "German Air Power" p. 44, and Schwipps, *Kleine Geschichte*, pp. 88-89.

39. Castellan, *Réarmement clandestin*, pp. 156-57.

40. "Gedanken und Vorschlage zur deutschen Luftfahrtpolitik unter Berücksichtigung der Wehrfragen," Denkschrift des Dir. Sachsenberg (Junkers-Werke) 1929, with marginal comments by Hauptmann Volkmann, 3.3.1929, and Sachsenberg's "Luftkrieg-Friedenszwang," 1928, Lw 103/25, DZ/MGFA. In late 1932, Milch suggested a similar plan to the Reichswehr for the construction for Lufthansa, at a cost of 4 million per year (to be paid for by the War Ministry), of a fleet of Ju 52/3 transports which could quickly be converted into bombers. The Reichswehr rejected the scheme for financial reasons. (Irving, *Milch*, p. 56.)

41. Völker, *Luftfahrt in Deutschland*, p. 183.

42. Aktenvermerk des Reichswehrministers, Berlin, den 3. Dezember 1930, gz. Gr[oerner], KDC/M.

43. For the strength and organization of these squadrons, see Völker, *Luftfahrt in Deutschland*, Anlage 16, pp. 260-61.

44. Protokoll über den am 18.2.1932 vor dem Herrn Amtschef gehaltenen Vortrag über das Arbeitsgebiet der Wa Prw 8, Lw 103/65, DZ/MGFA. Cf. this emphasis on big bombers with the operations plan (T.A. Nr. 500/30 Jn III g.Kdoz. "Z," 12. Nov. 1930, DZ/MGFA) only fifteen months earlier, where

there is no mention of a long-range bomber and the emphasis is on tactical bombers for ground support. On plans for conversion of mail and Lufthansa planes, see Wa Prw 8 Nr. 1829/32 V. geh. Kdos., 9.9.1932, Folder Wi/IF 5.404, NA Microcopy T-77/92/817433-36.

45. In 1 Nr. 1224/31 VII/V P1, den 1.2.1932, DZ/MGFA. For the antiaircraft strength, see Anlage II, Luftschutzkräfte.

46. General Giulio Douhet's best-known and most widely translated book was *Il Dominio dell'aria. Probabili aspetti della guerra futura* (Rome: Ferrari, 1921).

47. In private interviews with Völker (*Luftfahrt in Deutschland*, p. 173), Generals Felmy and Wilhelm Speidel argued the defensive character of the proposed air force. The von Rohden studies are filled with similar assertions.

48. Von Rohden materials, NA Microcopy T-791/27/915-16.

49. NR 1460/32 III geh.Kdos., dated 9.6.1932, Doc. 4376-2994, BA/F.

50. H.Wa.A. Nr 200/30 g.Kdos. "Z" Wa.Wi., dated 17.3.1930, DZ/MGFA.

51. "Die augenblickliche Lage der deutschen Luftfahrtindustrie," In 1 Nr 832/32 In 1 III g.Kdos., dated 31.3.1932, DZ/MGFA.

52. Wilhelm Treue, "Die Einstellung einiger deutscher Gross-industrieller zu Hitlers Aussenpolitik," *Geschichte in Wissenschaft und Unterricht* 17 (1966): 493, observes that German exports to the Soviet Union rose rapidly during the depression until they peaked in 1932 at 626 million marks, or 10.9 percent of the total exports. Most of the exports to the Soviet Union consisted of machine tools, autos, and semiprocessed materials. Treue comments that a number of optical firms and the Heinkel aircraft works were saved from bankruptcy in 1931 by purchases from the Soviet Union.

53. Von Rohden materials, NA Microcopy T-971/27/929-30.

54. For the bomb program, see "Aufstellung eines Bombenprogramm für den Sommer 1928," dated 20.12.1927, L10-4/14, DZ/MGFA.

55. Otto Wilhelm von Renz, "Beitrag zur kriegswissenschaftlichen Arbeit von G.F.M. Kesselring—Flak," p. 3, Lw 103/49, DZ/MGFA; von Rohden materials, NA Microcopy T-971/27/309-22.

56. Völker, *Luftfahrt in Deutschland*, p. 135, cites personal interviews with Generals Felmy and Speidel in 1960 for this information.

57. Erich Raeder, *Mein Leben*, 2 vols. (Tübingen: Fritz Schlichtenmayer, 1957), 2: 92; Schüssler, "Der Kampf gegen Versailles 1919-1945," geheime Dienstschrift Nr. 15, Oberkommando der Kriegsmarine, Berlin, 1937, in *Der Prozess gegen die Hauptkriegsverbrecher vor dem Internationalen Militärgerichtshof*, vol. 34 (Nuremberg: USGPO, 1949), pp. 579-80.

58. Carsten, *Reichswehr and Politics*, p. 287. For further information on Severa, see Theo Osterkamp, *Durch Höhen und Tiefen jagt ein Herz* (Heidelberg: Kurt Vowinckel, 1952), and General a.D. Hans Siburg, "Vorbereitende Massnahmen der Marineleitung auf dem Gebiet des Seeflugwesens in den Jahren 1920-1933," KDC/M.

59. Carsten, *Reichswehr and Politics*, pp. 362-63; Völker, *Luftfahrt in Deutschland*, pp. 157-58.

60. Protokoll über den am 18.2.1932 vor dem Herrn Amtschef, Lw 103/65, DZ/MGFA.

61. Kesselring, *Soldat*, pp. 20-21, 458-59; Bericht von Milch, 28 Juli 1945, document in von Rohden materials, code number (4376-463) BA/F; von Rohden materials, NA Microcopy T-971/26/957-59; "Die technische Luftrüstung und Luftwaffenindustrie Beschaffung-Fertigung," Lw 103/39, DZ/MGFA; and

Georg W. Feuchter, "Geschichte der deutschen Luftwaffe," *Flug-Wehr und Technik*, Nr. 1, Jan. 1949, Lw 108/21, DZ/MGFA.

62. Carsten, "Reichswehr and Red Army," p. 132; Emme, "German Air Power" pp. 96-101; Hermann, *Luftwaffe*, pp. 90-91; Killen, *History of the Luftwaffe*, pp. 50-56; Tantum and Hoffschmidt, *Rise and Fall of the German Air Force*, pp. 1-4; and Castellan, *Réarmement clandestin*, chap. 4.

63. Karl Dietrich Bracher, Wolfgang Sauer, and Gerhard Schulz, *Die national-sozialistische Machtergreifung,* Schriften des Instituts für Politische Wissenschaft, vol. 14 (Cologne: Westdeutscher Verlag, 1960), p. 779.

64. Karl-Heinz Völker, *Die Deutsche Luftwaffe 1933-1939,* Beiträge zur Militär- und Kriegsgeschichte, vol. 8 (Stuttgart: Deutsche Verlag, 1967), pp. 203-5; Völker, *Luftfahrt in Deutschland*, pp. 225-30; Suchenwirth, *Development of the German Air force*, pp. 188-89; Hertel, "Flugzeugbeschaffung," pp. 70-71.

65. Völker, *Luftfahrt in Deutschland*, Anlagen 30-33, pp. 284-88.

CHAPTER 3

The Risk Air Force:
Shield of Rearmament

CONTRARY TO the arrogant boasts of the mythmakers of the Third Reich, the Luftwaffe was not a creation of Hitler's genius or Göring's inspiration. As an independent branch of the armed forces, it was as much a product of the general economic and political conditions in the Reich and the prevailing military thinking as it was of Nazi aspirations. The principle of an independent air arm and the general guidelines for it slowly evolved from the secret rearmers of the Weimar Republic.

The immediate origins of an independent Luftwaffe are evident in the year preceding Hitler's acquisition of power. Lieutenant Colonel Felmy's ambitious planning study of February 1932 for a 1,000-aircraft force by 1938 and the April Air Inspectorate report on the near bankruptcy of the aircraft industry coincided with the Foreign Office's optimistic appraisals of Germany's chances to achieve parity in armaments. During the waning days of the Brüning government, German diplomatic sources reported that incoming French premier Edouard Herriot appeared conciliatory toward an expansion of the German army. The long and arduous diplomatic negotiations between the Reich government and the Western powers seemed to be fruitful.

A shift in the previously intransigent attitude of the French government touched off a wave of military planning in the Reich. Under the catchword "the new Peace Army," the military envisioned an enlarged regular army with a corresponding "Peace Air Force" (Friedensluftwaffe). The Peace Army, to be distinguished from the already planned twenty-one-division mobilization army, was first formally proposed to the Minister of Defense, General Kurt von Schleicher, by Lieutenant General Wilhelm Adam, chief of the Truppenamt, on July 14, 1932.[1] Adam's plan introduced flak batteries into the army by October 1933 and made provisions for training flying personnel in the near future. On July 28, 1932, the Air Inspectorate Office proposed a timetable for the inclusion of flying units: in fiscal 1933-34, training cadres would be formed; in 1934-35, they would be enlarged and group commands established at Berlin, Königsberg, and Nürnberg-Fürth. Each command would have one or two reconnaissance squadrons and a couple of fighter squadrons. Every year thereafter the strength of the units would be increased until 1938, when they would reach the level envisioned by the Felmy study.[2]

The military planners thought it was possible to build a tactical air force, but they hesitated to include heavy bomber formations in the program. General Adam and others deemed bombers of vital importance; but given the sensitivity of the issue for Germany, open inclusion of bomber forces had to wait for appropriate guidelines from the current international disarmament talks. In the meanwhile, Germany could rely on larger formations of reconnaissance aircraft that could double as bombers and on contingency plans for the conversion of civilian transports to bombers.[3]

Even before the Peace Luftwaffe could be built, widespread structural changes had to be made in the organization, training, and operations of the existing air agencies. The scarcity of funds and the expectation of even less in the future required that the diverse agencies dealing with aviation be centralized and their operations streamlined. The complexity of the task is apparent in the administrative sprawl in aviation during the planning period for the Peace Luftwaffe. Within the Defense Ministry, under the direction of the army's Truppenamt, the principal office of Air Inspectorate (In 1) was charged with preparations for the training, tactics, and administration of the air arm. It was to coordinate its work with that of the Operations (T 1), Organization (T 2), and Training (T 4) Departments of the Truppenamt. In addition, in the Defense Office the Inspectorate for Infantry (In 2) was in charge of developing antiaircraft machine guns; the Inspectorate for Artillery (In 4) for antiaircraft artillery and searchlights; the Inspectorate for Communications (In 7) had airborne communications; while the Army Ordnance Office handled all other technical aviation matters. The Transportation Ministry, which supervised civil aviation, was also involved since most of the secret armament funds were funneled through it.[4] The navy had its own somewhat more centralized structure for aviation under the direction of the single office of Air Defense, or Gruppe LS (Luftschutz). In July the Air Inspectorate Office, at the request of the Truppenamt, recommended a thorough centralization of army and navy offices in the areas of supply, administration, weaponry, and research and development within the Defense Ministry.[5] The suggestion was carried one step further in late summer after the planning for the Peace Luftwaffe had begun. Captain Hans Jeschonnek, director of the tactics and training division of the Air Inspectorate, wrote an important memo calling for the concentration of all aviation agencies under the direction of the Reich Defense Ministry.

In his memo, Jeschonnek, the future chief of staff, argued that when the Versailles Treaty denied military aviation to Germany, two options were open. Either Germany could comply strictly with the treaty, thereby losing her technical proficiency and falling from the ranks of major air powers, or she could develop her civilian aviation as a stand-in for her prohibited military aviation. Germany had chosen the latter course. Unfortunately, as civilian aviation developed in the twenties, civilian objectives took precedence over military ones. For example, by the late 1920s only 5 million of the 40 million RM allotted to the Transportation Ministry for aviation was spent on military needs. Jeschonnek attributes this confusion of objectives to pacifistic attitudes and the shortage of money. The Reichswehr contributed to the confusion when after 1924 it allowed the army and the navy to develop separate and competing programs. The results were grotesque. By 1930 there existed in a country with scant resources three largely uncoordinated aviation programs. The solution was obviously to consolidate all aviation under one agency. Jeschonnek suggested that the Reich cabinet withdraw the Air Office from the Ministry of Transportation and place it under the Reich Minister of Defense. If this were not politically feasible, the office could for purposes of concealment be allowed to remain within the Transportation Ministry but under the authority of the Defense Minister.[6]

Jeschonnek's tightly reasoned memo largely ignored, for purposes of argumentation, the strides already made in coordinating the aviation program. It did, however, evoke a sympathetic response from the military and met uniform acclaim from the Truppenamt for its suggestions to centralize the aviation agencies and repossess the Air Office of the Transportation Ministry as a way of stretching the limited defense funds. But the army departments were suspicious of anything that would remove command of its air units. A separate, independent Luftwaffe was emphatically rejected as too imitative of the French Air Force, which had difficulties coordinating with its army and navy. Conditions were different in Germany, where the air force was closely bound to the army and navy, and was considered an integral branch of the service, much like the infantry, artillery, or cavalry. The army was willing to accept a joint army-navy aviation inspectorate under the existing chiefs of staff, but nothing more.[7]

By October 28, 1932, when Jeschonnek's memo, now properly endorsed by his commanding officer, General von Mittelberger of the Air Inspectorate, was discussed in the Truppenamt, opposition to a centralized air office within the Defense Ministry weakened and its establishment was recommended to the Reich cabinet. The new aviation office would combine all civilian and military aspects of aviation, including the division and disposition of funds, the technical development and construction of aircraft, and the military training and preparation for the new Peace Air Force. The Truppenamt envisioned the new office with two major divisions, one for air defense and the other for aviation (Luftschutz and Luftfahrt). In the air defense division there would be a joint army-navy inspectorate to coordinate aviation in their respective spheres. General Adam, chief of the Truppenamt, directed his Organization Department (T 2) to begin discussions with the navy for their approval and the immediate implementation of this project.[8]

The motive behind the change of attitude toward a centralized air office was the lack of money. In the midst of a great depression with the prospects exceedingly dim for new funds, the military realized that the only hope for completion of its plans lay in tapping the funds of the Aviation Office in the Transportation Ministry. The risk that the new office might achieve a degree of autonomy from the military was recognized and accepted. Further support for a centralized air office came on November 11 in a report from General von Mittelberger's office which gloomily surveyed the depressed state of the aircraft industry and concluded that even minimal plans for emergency rearmament could not be completed with the existing shortage of funds.[9]

The last stage of centralization of aviation occurred as a result of the changing political conditions in the Reich. On January 30, 1933, Adolf Hitler was appointed Reich chancellor. On February 3, he appointed Hermann Göring, his ambitious and powerful lieutenant, to head a Reich Commission for Aviation (Reichskommissariat für die Luftfahrt). Göring's appointment removed the last vestige of opposition to centralization within the army and navy. Both service branches knew that Göring would never restrict himself to civil aviation. To protect themselves, they quickly agreed that all developmental work on air equipment should be concentrated within the Army Ordnance Office.[10] To head off the organization of an independent Luftwaffe under Göring's direction and to keep military aviation under the jurisdiction of the Defense Minister, the military agreed to complete reorganization of all aviation matters under a new Air Defense Office (Luftschutzamt). General Werner von Blomberg, the new defense minister, ordered the merger of the army and navy aviation offices on February 8. The directive outlining the responsibilities of the Air Defense Office was signed by Blomberg on February 21 and was to take effect on April 1, 1933.[11] The new office comprised the army In 1 (L) agencies, the Ordnance Office, and air defense sections, as well as the navy agencies under the LS branch. At long last military aviation was centralized, but the arrangement lasted only one month. Under the energetic prodding of Hitler and Göring, on April

27, 1933, Reich President Hindenburg upgraded the Reich Commission
for Aviation to the status of a ministry. The new Reich Aviation Ministry
(Reichsluftfahrtministerium, or RLM) took over the Air Defense Office
on May 15, and the realization of an independent Luftwaffe had begun.[12]
It is ironic that the centralization of aviation agencies, initiated and given
impetus by the desperate shortage of funds, should occur at precisely the
time a deluge of money became available. It is doubly ironic that the
military, which so long and jealously fought for independent army and
navy air units, finally could agree to a united control of aviation, only to
see it slip from their hands. The Nazis had stepped into a ripe situation and
turned it to their advantage.

THE NAZIS AND AVIATION

Hitler's ascension to political power in January 1933 introduced a
new and dynamic note into aerial rearmament. The Nazi movement, a
youthful one, had grown up in the air age. The heroics of the daring fliers
of World War I like Richthofen, Max Immelmann, Osward Boelcke, and
Ernst Udet and the intrepid exploits of aviators of the twenties like Charles
Lindbergh enthralled the imagination of the generation. Even among the
top leaders of the Nazi movement there were a number of fliers, including
Rudolf Hess, first secretary of the party, a former wartime flier and glider
enthusiast, and, of course, Hermann Göring, number two man in the
movement and the famed last commander of Baron von Richthofen's
Jagdgeschwader 1.

Adolf Hitler, too, had shown a lively interest in flying and aviation
technology before 1933. He had first flown in 1927 with Ritter von Greim,
who later became the last commander in chief of the Luftwaffe. Although
Hitler never particularly enjoyed flying, he was keenly aware of its
political advantages and was the first German politician to use an airplane
extensively in his campaigns. In the presidential election campaign of
1932, he rented an airplane from Lufthansa, undoubtedly through the
offices of its managing director, Milch, and in three "Deutschlandflugs"
visited forty-six cities in two weeks in April and later fifty cities in another
two-week tour.[13] Once, twice, sometimes three times a day Hitler's plane
would descend, bringing the Führer to speak to the gathered thousands of
the party's faithful. Hitler beautifully exploited the thrill and adventure of
flying. The picture of the dashing young politician alighting from an
airplane, dressed in a long leather coat and distinct, snug-fitting leather
flying helmet, became commonplace to millions of German newspaper
readers. The artfully contrived image of the simple, brave, common

soldier turned politician flying across the country became one of his trademarks. Appropriately, the opening sequence of Leni Riefenstahl's masterful propaganda film of the Nürnberg party rally of 1934, *The Triumph of the Will*, shows Hitler's plane majestically flying out of the clouds to arrive at the medieval town.[14]

Hitler's influence on and understanding of aviation is difficult to judge. After the war, Göring, Milch, and General Hans von Seidel asserted that he was disinterested and ill-informed, but others, such as Colonel Nicolaus von Below, Lieutenant General Theo Osterkamp, Colonel Werner Baumbach, Luftwaffe Adjutant General Dr. Alexander Kraell, and the aircraft designers Ernst Heinkel and Willy Messerschmitt, attested to Hitler's interest and confidence in aviation as well as his well-known fascination with technology.[15] Most of these judgments are based largely on wartime experiences. Very little is known about his earlier opinions, for aviation is rarely mentioned in his writings or speeches. Milch contends that Hitler relied completely on Göring's advice on aviation matters until the middle of the war, an idea substantiated by most later writers.[16] Hitler did have a keen appreciation of the geopolitical capabilities of the airplane. Through Rudolf Hess, a friend and student of Professor Karl Haushofer, he learned the doctrine that control of the great Eurasian land mass, not control of the sea, was the first aim of high politics. Haushofer taught that the era of dominating the trade routes was gone and the era of dominating the interior production centers had begun. The new continental trade economy based largely on industrialization had outdated the old commercial system in which coastal or peripheral areas controlled the great interior spaces. Besides, the development of the airplane and U-boat meant that the sea lanes would be vulnerable to attack and the great surface fleets useless. They would transform the great surface fleets into scrap iron.

On February 3, 1933, at the first meeting of his military commanders after becoming Chancellor, Hitler espoused the Haushoferian doctrines of expansion. His first political objectives were destroying pacificism and Marxism at home and reeducating the youth to the heroic aims of war and defense of the Fatherland. Only after the young were sufficiently military-minded (*Wehrwillen*) could he proceed to his foreign policy aims of overturning the Versailles Treaty and achieving arms equality. Starting with the basic premise that the reservoir of the race, the German peasant, had to be saved, Hitler rejected a policy of increased industrial exportation as a solution to the economic problems posed by the depression. The amount of exports that could be absorbed abroad was limited, and dependency on export trade would leave Germany dependent on the whims of the world market. The ultimate solution for the German jobless and the peasant was expansion of Germany's Lebensraum. This could come only through conquest, but Hitler needed time to build a powerful war machine. By changing the psychological climate within the Reich, the political leadership would set the stage for an army based on a universal draft. Once the mass army was built, it would be used to conquer the required living areas in the east. Through ruthless Germanization of those areas by resettlement, Germany's economic problems would be solved. The most dangerous time in this process, Hitler thought, was during the rapid build-up of the Wehrmacht. France, in particular, might be tempted to intervene.[17] How he intended to prevent that is not clear, but his writings and talks from 1928 to 1935 reveal this was the gestation period for his foreign policy methods of combining diplomacy and military bluffing.[18]

It was in these years when Hitler was groping for solutions to the foreign policy question that the possibilities of air power were first realized. Lindbergh's dramatic flight, the transoceanic flights of the Do X, and the appearance of the first German translation of General Douhet's writings were only a few of the events that coincided with the emergence of Hermann Göring as second-in-command of the Nazi movement and, of course, as Hitler's chief confidant and all-round expert on aviation and foreign affairs. It was from Göring that Hitler derived the idea of using air power to neutralize his enemies, especially France, during the critical period of rearming.

Göring's rise to prominence in this period was somewhat surprising. The famous World War I flyer, holder of Prussia's highest decoration, the Pour le Mérite (only ten of fifty-seven recipients survived the war), had played an active part in the Nazi movement in the early 1920s. In November 1922, he first met Hitler at a political rally in Munich and quickly was captivated by the Führer. In 1923, Hitler made him commander of the Storm Troops (Sturmabteilung, or SA). Göring was in the front ranks of the abortive march to the Feldherrenhalle on November 9, 1923, and when the Bavarian State Police opened fire he was seriously wounded. He fled first to Innsbruck, Austria, later to Italy, and finally to Sweden, the home of his first wife. This long exile eroded what personal power base he had within the party. Only through the courtesy of the political parties of the right and with the support of the Communists did a general political amnesty allow him to return home in late 1927. Although Göring had little contact with Hitler during his exile, the casual relationship was renewed on his return to Germany. Soon he received Hitler's approval to run as a National Socialist candidate for the Reichstag.[19] On May 20, 1928, he won one of the twelve Nazi seats in the Reichstag, and his parliamentary career began.

Göring's new power derived from his personal loyalty to Hitler and his own abilities. There was an element of truth in his frequent boast that his proudest title was "the truest paladin of our Führer."[20] Hitler assiduously built up Göring to offset the threats from potentially dangerous rivals like the independent Gregor Strasser and the radical Julius Streicher.[21] The shift of Hitler's support to Göring also indicates a basic change in the party's fortunes. The Streichers and Strassers had their place within the Nazi movement when it was an insignificant and notorious crank party of the streets, but once it moved into the drawing rooms of prominence and power it needed a new kind of leadership. Göring and other socially acceptable Nazis such as the grandson of Bismarck, Prince Otto von Bismarck, were to meet that need.

Göring's qualifications for a leadership role were considerable. A bona fide war hero, the affable former fighter pilot had excellent connections with the military, the conservatives, and nobility both within and outside the Reich. During his war days, he was friendly with Prince Philipp of Hesse, who had married Princess Mafalda, daughter of the king of Italy, and his own wife was the Swedish baroness Karin von Fock-Kantzow. Göring moved easily through the social world of Germany. His impressive bearing, remarkable diplomatic skill, and flair for expensive living made him the ideal front man for the party in Berlin. He enhanced his position by constantly acquiring new connections among the German elite, including the rather controversial Crown Prince Friedrich August von Hohenzollern; the vain and ambitious Dr. Hjalmar Schacht, president of the Reichsbank; and the important steel magnate Fritz Thyssen. After the impressive Nazi electoral victories in 1930, even President von Hindenburg invited Göring to his ancestral estate at Neudeck. The contrast between the congenial, popular proprietor of the fashionable apartment in the Badenschestrasse and his sullen, perennial outsider boss, Hitler, worked to the advantage of both men. Göring supplied a humane, respectable image to the movement, while Hitler played the role of the aloof, great man.[22]

Göring, the future commander of the Luftwaffe, had only a peripheral interest in German aviation from 1918 to 1928. In 1927, when he returned to Germany, he brought with him the Swedish patent rights for the Tornblad parachute. With the help of his old friends Bruno Loerzer and Paul (Pilli) Körner, he soon had contacts with most of the fliers and administrators in commercial aviation, including Erhard Milch, a director of the state-owned monopoly, Lufthansa.[23] Milch, who had known Göring during the war, was in position to do a number of favors for him. In what was to be his characteristic blending of politics and profits Göring established himself as a business agent for aircraft companies, including Heinkel and BMW. Once elected to the Reichstag in 1928, he received substantial "consulting fees" from Lufthansa and other firms and repaid his benefactors with his unstinting support for appropriations for aviation. In one furious speech after another, he demanded funding for an industry that would soon have a great patriotic task to accomplish, hinting openly that the Nazis intended to build an air force once they came to power. In 1931, when Göring first introduced Milch to Hitler, the Nazi leaders promised to build up German aviation, including an air force, if Milch would help them. Nevertheless, after the war Milch asserted that Hitler had rented Lufthansa airplanes in the usual way during the 1932 election campaign, contrary to the accusation that he had allowed the Nazis 23,000 rent-free air miles for the campaign.[24]

It was Göring, moreover, who educated Hitler to the potentialities of air power. Göring had no clear idea of strategic air power, for he was not a methodical or profound military thinker. He was, however, an excellent assimilator and promoter. He thought about air power along Douhetian lines, as an independently organized weapon capable of inflicting a decisive blow on an enemy. Air power was a type of third-dimensional extension of Schlieffen's annihilation battle (*Vernichtungsschlacht*), a concept embedded in the Prussian military tradition. Göring and Hitler, with their sharp political sense and intuitive grasp of mass psychology, appreciated its uniqueness for their immediate purposes.

By the time the Nazis assumed power, Hitler and Göring were committed to a massive build-up of civilian aviation under the control of Göring and the establishment of a cabinet-level ministry as a preliminary to further military expansion in aviation. The concept of the air force as a separate branch operating as a second war ministry closely associated with the party was appealing, but Hitler and Göring knew it might offend the sensibilities of the established military services, whose skills were needed for the future enlarged Wehrmacht.[25] The older leadership in both the army and the navy had strong opinions about controlling their own air units and were inordinately suspicious of Göring's ambitions for an independent air force.[26]

Air-minded Young Turks in the Defense Ministry like Jeschonnek and Felmy had also come to the conclusion that Germany needed a unified and separate air arm. Partly from the experiences of World War I, their study of aerial warfare, their official examination of the organizational development of foreign air forces, and their convictions about Germany's needs, they were convinced that the roots of military and civil aviation were one and the same. They advocated that research and development be directed and fostered by one agency with one budget. This was the essence of Jeschonnek's memo, which Colonel Walther Wever, then branch chief of training in the Troop Office, labeled nonsense.[27] It is quite correct that prior to taking power Hitler and Göring had no contact with these aviation advocates from the Reichswehr, but nevertheless they arrived at the same conclusions.

It was not, however, a Reichswehr officer or Göring who supplied Hitler with an answer to his dilemma of checking France during the critical period of German rearmament, but one of Milch's associates, Dr. Robert Knauss. An aviation theorist who had written a number of books under the pseudonym Major Helders, Knauss had been a flight officer in the war and afterward an official in Lufthansa. In 1935 he followed his boss, Milch, into the Luftwaffe, where he became commander of the important Training Wing, or Lehrgeschwader. He eventually rose to the rank of general and headed the Air War Academy at Berlin-Gatow.

In May 1933, Knauss sent a secret memo to Milch outlining his aerial warfare concepts.[28] In part 1 of the memo, he presented a modified Douhetian argument that air power would be the decisive weapon of strategic importance in future wars instead of the auxiliary one it had been in the last war. Future wars would be decided quickly because of the enormous striking power of air weapons and the acute vulnerability of the modern, complex system of living. It was necessary to build a small, highly trained technical army and an air force to fight this kind of war. In part 2, Knauss delineated Germany's predicament of facing a two-front war with France and Poland in the event she tried to rearm. To counter this, he proposed the creation of a large heavy bomber force to shield the Reich until her army and navy could be brought up to strength. The plan was a "risk" strategy à la Tirpitz's pre-1914 plan, but this time the risk fleet would be bombers instead of battleships. Germany's geographical position dictated an "inner line" strategy of mobile forces based on air units which could be massed quickly to strike a decisive blow. Facing Germany were at best only 460 enemy bombers, a force which Germany could surpass in a few years. The cost of the risk fleet would be slight compared to that of more conventional arms. For the same amount of money needed to build two battleships or equip five divisions, roughly 80 million RM, Knauss estimated Germany could build a fleet of 400 bombers. By concentrating defense spending in one decisive area, Germany could achieve a military shield to check the "preventive war" advocated abroad, and permit the time-consuming rearmament of the army and navy at home. Knauss reasoned that no one, not even the Italians, dared build such an air force. This would add to the psychological impact abroad should Germany decide to do it. In parts 3 and 4, Knauss defined the implications of his plans much as Colonel Felmy had in his 1932 report. The proposed size and deployment of the force, use of big bombers, and even suggested order of battle against France and Poland were included.

Knauss's memo was new in the emphasis it placed on the political, diplomatic, and psychological impact that a strategic air force would have. He clearly anticipated much of the deterrent strategy used in game-theory analysis in the nuclear weapons age. Milch noted on the memo that he was in complete agreement and arranged a meeting with Generalmajor Walther Reichenau, chief of the Wehrmachtsamt on June 19, 1933, to discuss the acceleration of the air force build-up along the lines suggested by Knauss.[29]

The regular army leadership had, of course, given considerable attention to the much discussed theory of strategic bombing. As early as 1927, they had framed technical specifications for a long-range, four-engined night bomber and had commissioned the Dornier firm to develop it. But in 1933 the army was unmoved by Knauss's arguments for three reasons: First, the progress on a high-performance heavy bomber had been slow and unpromising. Even with a crash program it would take three years to get the big plane into series production. Second, the concentration on a big bomber would use up most of the existing capacity of the aircraft industry, leaving little or nothing for training and tactical aircraft. Third, the foreign policy aims of the Reich indicated that a big bomber was not necessary, since Hitler had posited France and Poland as potential enemies. Both of these nations could effectively be attacked by short-range, twin-engined bombers.[30] Except for a few young officers in the Air Inspectorate Office, the army believed that the proper role of air power was support of the army, or tactical rather than strategic.

Hitler and Göring, to the contrary, accepted Knauss's risk fleet concept in their own eclectic fashion. They wanted the diplomatic punch of a strategic air force; but bowing to the sober and more conservative advice of their military counselors, who argued for a tactical air force, they accepted a compromise. The risk fleet had to look like a strategic air force abroad while it functioned as a tactical one at home. Much later, on August 1, 1939, Göring acknowledged in a frank speech that the risk fleet was a bold attempt to neutralize France and allow enough time for Germany to rearm. He commented, "At that time we possessed only limited means, but we did have enough to build a risk fleet which could ensure further rearmament and prepare the way for the Führer to proclaim the resumption of the universal draft."[31]

ORGANIZING THE AIR MINISTRY

With the establishment of the Reich Air Ministry on May 1, 1933, Hermann Göring achieved ministerial ranking equal to that of Defense Minister von Blomberg. At the same time, as head of the future air arm, he was to be subordinate to Blomberg. In this unique position Göring found himself in a situation ready-made for his special talents. As the man next in line to Hitler, he had easy access to the Reich Chancellor to promote his own ideas and interests and, of course, those of the air force. This advantage was of inestimable value for the air force, a fact clearly perceived by the other branches of the armed services. The firm support of the Führer and his own great personal authority meant that Göring could go directly to Hitler, bypassing the obstacles of the regular military chain of command.

At first, Göring had a free hand in organizing his ministry. Its simple structure was divided into two parts, military and civilian. The military half was under the Air Command Office (Luftschutzamt, LS or LA) headed by Colonel Eberhardt Bohnstedt. Directly under him was a chief of staff, Frigate Captain Rudolf Wenninger, whose most important duties were directing offices for operations, organization, training, and

TABLE 2

ORGANIZATION OF THE REICH AIR MINISTRY (RLM), SEPTEMBER 1933

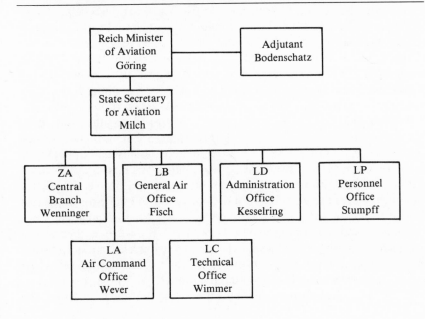

air defense. The civilian half of the ministry was under the state secretary for aviation, Milch, and consisted of the important offices of flying safety, ground organization, aviation technology, sport flying, and air transportation. This administrative structure was a transitional one, lasting from May 15 until August 31, 1933. It provided cover for illicit military aviation activities and allowed time to transfer personnel from military and civilian agencies to staff the ministry. On September 1, the state secretary for aviation assumed responsibilities as the representative for the aviation minister in military as well as civilian matters. The two parts of the ministry were then consolidated into a single administrative structure under the direction of Göring and Milch (see table 2).

The personnel for the new organization were drawn mainly from the Reichswehr, the bureaucracy, and Göring's cronies. Although Göring had considered building the air force from the party as the Italians had done, he gave it up when he realized how few members had the technical competence to run an air force and how bitterly the Reichswehr would oppose the idea. Göring had wanted Admiral Rudolf Lahs, closely associated with the Heinkel firm, as his secretary of state, but he had to accept Milch. Lufthansa's general director had done a number of favors for Göring and Hitler, and his appointment was "payment for services rendered."[32] Quite possibly Franz von Papen and Alfred Hugenberg were behind Milch's appointment. Earlier when von Papen was trying to appoint a cabinet with Hitler as the vice chancellor, Milch had declined a post because he did not wish to leave Lufthansa. In Hitler's cabinet with a new air ministry, Milch could retain his post with Lufthansa while serving as secretary of state.[33] A non-party member at the time with one Jewish parent, Milch had served as an aerial observer in World War I.[34] He had left the service as a captain and served until 1920 in the Prussian flying police force on the Polish frontier. He then organized an airline after securing a concession to fly the Danzig-Warsaw route. In 1923 his airline was bought out by Junkers and he worked for that firm until 1926, when he was selected as one of three directors of the newly formed Lufthansa. A bull of a man with a tremendous vitality and appetite for work, Milch had impressive industry and ability. His mastery of aviation technology, his gifted sense of administration, and his keen nose for scenting the prevailing political winds soon made him the most important director of Lufthansa and offset his personal liabilities of outspokenness, arrogance, and unusual personal sensitivity. He became the perfect complement to his boss, Göring, who despite his inventiveness and short bursts of energetic work was incapable of long and methodical labor. As secretary of aviation, Milch surrounded himself with able subordinates and useful political friends, thereby entrenching himself with Hitler and the Nazi party. At the same time he became the indispensable right-hand man of Göring, even though there was never genuine warmth between the two.[35]

The Reichswehr's contribution to the Air Ministry's personnel was impressive. The regular military was eager to counterbalance the influence of the Nazi party and Milch's civilian advisers. Because of their distrust of the party, the army and navy released to the Air Ministry excellent officers steeped in military tradition. On July 1, 1933, Hans-Jürgen Stumpff, one of the first officers transferred, became Chief of the Personnel Office, where he carefully guided able, trusted officers into the new ministry.[36] Although it was headed by persons like Göring and Milch who had jumped from company-grade officers without experience in field-grade positions, Stumpff was determined to surround them with men of long service in the officer corps of the Reichswehr. Stumpff generally favored older, sometimes retired officers for administrative and command staff positions, thus guaranteeing continuity with the traditional military administration. Nonfliers in key positions were carefully assigned aides who were well versed in flying through years of secret training. Young, brilliant field-grade officers such as Colonels Helmut Felmy, Hugo Sperrle, and Ernst Mueller; Lieutenant Colonels Wilhelm Speidel, Dietrich Volkmann, Fritz Loeb, and Rudolf Wenninger; Majors Paul Deichmann, Josef Kammhuber, Hoffman von Waldau, Hans Jeschonnek, and Herhudt von Rohden; and Captains Hermann Plocker, Josef Schmid, and Andreas Nielsen, most of whom rose to the rank of general in World War II, formed the professional hard core of leaders at the second echelon of command.[37] About two hundred Reichswehr officers, the famous class of generals, were transferred to the new Air Ministry during 1933 and 1934. Later when the real expansion of the Luftwaffe occurred, these Reichswehr officers rose quickly to positions of authority where they remained an elite in the officer corps. The overwhelming majority of the Luftwaffe officers came from elsewhere—the police units (Landespolizei), Lufthansa personnel, World War I reserves, or from among the young career flying officers trained in the 1930s. Only the contribution of the latter—eager, bright, imbued with Nazism—can be compared with that of the Reichswehr officers.[38]

Colonel Stumpff suggested to Göring that commander-in-chief of the army General Kurt von Hammerstein-Equord transfer three top Reichswehr staff officers to the Air Ministry. On September 1, 1933, Colonel Wilhelm Wimmer was named chief of the Technical Office, Colonel Albert Kesselring chief of the Administration Office, and Colonel Walther Wever chief of the Air Command Office. Wever, in particular, was highly regarded. He and Erich von Manstein were considered to be the most outstanding young officers in the Reichswehr, but Stumpff felt that Wever would be more compatible with Göring and Milch.[39] Although he was forty-six when he learned to fly, Wever emerged as a keen air strategist. His acceptance of the developments of modern air technology and his organizational ability made him a natural leader of the new air force. Proud and intensely nationalistic, Wever had no difficulty in identifying with Hitler's aspirations for a remilitarized powerful Germany. Although in 1932 he had labeled Jeschonneck's pleas for an independent air force nonsense, he became its champion by 1934. He wanted a strong, independent air arm spearheaded by a strategic bombing force consisting of heavy "Uralbombers," as he informally called them.[40] Wever's enthusiasm for a strong air force did not distort his views on the need for the careful, gradual build-up of the Luftwaffe. He was too much the exact planner and level-headed thinker to be swept up by flights of fancy.

Wimmer and Kesselring were also methodical, reliable officers. Wimmer had been a flier in World War I; and although he had not served on the General Staff, he was placed in charge of aeronautical developments in the Army Ordnance Office during the Weimar period. He had compiled a distinguished record as a specialist capable of translating general military strategy into exact staff planning and he moved easily into the new office, which was largely involved with a continuation of his previous work. Like Wever, Wimmer was an advocate of the heavy bomber, but only as the capstone of a balanced force of both tactical and strategic aircraft. The bluff, optimistic Kesselring also had an excellent service record. A popular commander with his troops, Kesselring saw himself more as a command than a staff officer and was reluctant to leave the army for the new branch. His sincere interest in the welfare of his subordinates, his love of military life, and his honest and blunt method of operating were peculiarly suited to the early days of the build-up of the Luftwaffe when élan and tempo were needed.[41]

Göring's personnel choices from the bureaucracy were less fortunate. Apart from Milch and his coterie, Göring selected persons on the basis of personal friendship or political orthodoxy. As a result, for every able civil servant like Ministerial Director Wilhelm Fisch, there were many political hacks. Göring's most notable omission was the extremely competent Ministerial Director Ernst Brandenburg of the Transportation Ministry, who had so diligently directed the secret air rearmament during the Weimar period. Brandenburg's strong personality and deep-rooted distrust of Göring and his Nazi followers made him anathema to Göring and Milch.[42] His years of experience in aviation were ignored and his talents unused, as were those of the head of the DVS (Deutsche Verkehrsflieger-Schule, German Aviation School), Carl Bolle, a former fighter pilot and Cambridge scholar who was married to a Jew. After a short service in the Air Ministry, Bolle left for private industry because of differences with Milch.[43] Foremost among the personal friends of Göring in the new ministry were Karl Bodenschatz and Bruno Loerzer. Bodenschatz, the former adjutant of Göring's World War I squadron, became adjutant to the Reich minister of aviation. Bruno Loerzer was named head of German Sport Fliers, Inc. (Deutschen Luftsportverband, or DLV), the new Nazi umbrella organization designed to incorporate all private aviation groups.

To maintain the fiction that Germany did not have an official air force and at the insistence of President Hindenburg, officers transferred from the military and its reserves were discharged but given equivalent rank in the DLV. In the usual efficient and frugal German manner, the DLV uniform was converted into the Luftwaffe uniform merely by changing the insignia with the formal proclamation of the new service branch in March 1935.

In assessing the team that Göring assembled in 1933, Suchenwirth cites three factors that weakened the top-level command structure of the new Luftwaffe: the personal quirks and lack of thorough experience in Göring and Milch; the newness of the organization and conspicuous lack of flying experience among the top leaders (Milch, Kesselring, Wever, and Stumpff learned to fly only after they were assigned to the air force); and the lack of an adequately large, highly trained, and unified General Staff. The century-old training and tradition so typical of the army was completely lacking in the Luftwaffe.[44] Baumbach, Killen, Hauptmann, Rieckhoff, and the von Rohden writers agree. General Andreas Nielsen even speaks of "orgies of dilettantism"; Georg Feuchter calls the Luftwaffe "weakest at the highest level"; and Friedrich Hossbach summarized the army's view by writing, "A firm foundation was lacking in the new structure whose façade was so quickly and threateningly built; the inner solidarity wasn't there."[45]

There is, however, enough evidence to support an opposing argument. While most writers stress Göring's faults, Kesselring pointed out that the Göring of 1933 and 1934 was entirely different from the Göring of 1942 and 1943.[46] He was an energetic, confident, aggressive leader willing and able to impose his will on Hitler and the conservative leaders of the military. It is doubtful that anyone except Göring could have managed the administrative overlapping and rigidity that characterized the aviation world. His thrashing techniques of operating, bullying one moment and cajoling the next, set the necessary pace. His verve and cockiness, brash and disconcerting to the older military, helped offset some of the insecurity of his subordinates. Göring usually gave his underlings considerable latitude in doing their jobs. He inspired them, and they had confidence in him and worked hard for him.[47]

In Milch and Wever, Göring had the ideal subordinates who, in a safe and orderly fashion, could channel his reckless energies and impulses along constructive lines. The same is true of his other chief appointees. Although most of them had little experience in aviation, Wimmer, Kesselring, and Stumpff had great administrative and executive talent. Their enthusiasm, flexibility of mind, and receptiveness to modern technology enabled them to grasp quickly the complexities of modern aviation.

The criticism that the new ministry was too hastily constructed can also be reinterpreted. Statements such as that of General Nielsen—the "establishment of the Luftwaffe had to be undertaken literally from the ground up; the desultory preparations made during the Reichswehr period were hardly worth mentioning"[48]—do not conform with the facts. There was a great deal done in the Reichswehr period, and the continuity in ideas, personnel, and administration from that period to the Nazi one is striking; nor are haste and newness entirely disadvantageous. The compensatory advantages of freshness and originality in the Luftwaffe can be seen when it is compared with the French Air Force, which had been progressive and innovative in the twenties but languished in the thirties.

THE INITIAL REACTION OF THE AIRCRAFT INDUSTRY

The small, financially wobbly aircraft industry followed the events of 1932 and 1933—the consolidation of military aviation and the organization of an Air Ministry—with considerable interest. Their very existence depended on the actions of the new regime. The aircraft designer-owners and the heavy industry owners knew from the speeches of Göring and Hitler that a Nazi government would help the economic upswing by placing a great volume of orders with business. Baron Kurt von Schröder, the spokesman for heavy industry, thought the Nazi economic program would consist of rearmament, extensive highway construction, heavy subsidies for housing and street repairs, large-scale public transportation system improvements, support for synthetic rubber and gas development, and a rapid build-up in the auto and aircraft industries.[49] Because of their difficult economic straits, the aircraft manufacturers were favorably disposed toward the Nazis, but little is known about their direct, immediate contribution to the cause. Certainly they donated nothing comparable to the contribution of steel tycoon Thyssen, who allegedly gave 150,000 RM for Göring and the party in 1930 and 1931.[50] Few aircraft plant owners could afford generosity on that scale for political purposes.

As a group, the aircraft designer-owners were vain, ambitious, intensely jealous of each other, suspicious, and extremely gifted. But the industry's most common characteristic was the individuality of the aircraft producers. Most of them were primarily inventors and designers and only secondarily entrepreneurs. Men like Professor Hugo Junkers, Ernst Heinkel, Dr. Claude Dornier, Hanns Klemm, and Heinrich Focke founded and ran their companies in a highly personal manner with little outside interference.

The aircraft industry leaders can be divided into three groups by their responses to the Nazis in 1933: those who were either not interested in or opposed to rearmament; those in favor of rearmament; and fence-sitters. Opposed to or not interested in rearmament were Junkers, Klemm, and Focke. Hugo Junkers had had a bad experience with the Reichswehr over his Russian plant and with Lufthansa over his airline. The old gentleman was also apparently a sincere pacifist who distrusted the Nazis and their military intentions. Eventually his adamant stand on rearmament and his staunch individualism cost him and his family controlling interest in his plant. The finely woven intrigues spun by the army, Nazis, Air Ministry, and other industrialists drove him out of aviation and into disgrace.[51] Hanns Klemm, the small, excitable Swabian, was primarily interested in sport planes, and his deep Protestant faith made cooperation with the Nazis difficult. Heinrich Focke, who with his close friend, collaborator, and chief pilot, Georg Wulf, had founded the Focke-Wulf Corporation, voluntarily withdrew from active management of the Bremen plant to continue research on his helicopter after Wulf was killed in an airplane crash in 1927. The financial backers of Focke-Wulf, a group of Bremen businessmen led by Dr. Ludwig Roselius, owner of the Kaffee Hag, and Dr. Werner Naumann of the powerful Allegemeine Elektrizität Gesellschaft, were, however, eager to participate in the aerial rearmament of Germany. In 1931, after Dr. Focke founded what would become Focke, Achgelis and Company for the design and production of helicopters, they eased Focke out. He remained on the board of directors in name only until 1933. The Bremen businessmen brought in the energetic Kurt Tank, director of the project bureau of Bavarian Aircraft Works (BFW) of Augsburg as technical director. Tank's views on the future of Focke-Wulf were more compatible with those of the politically astute Bremen group than were Dr. Focke's. Tank had contacts, too, for he knew Messerschmitt and Udet from his BFW days and was probably recommended to the Bremen businessmen by Milch.[52]

Messerschmitt, Adolph Rohrbach, and Heinkel were among the first and most enthusiastic supporters of German aerial rearmament. From his earliest days of Rhön gliding, Willy Messerschmitt had had a passion for speed records and personal triumphs. In the twenties he began designing slim, aerodynamically efficient racing planes which led to his famous line of fighters in the thirties and forties. A friend of Hess and Göring, Messerschmitt virtually owed his existence as an industrialist to the Nazis. In 1931, despite a number of design successes, BFW was bankrupt and Heinkel sought to take it over. It was only the change in political climate and the timely intervention of Theodor Croneiss, long-time friend of Messerschmitt, Alter Kämpfer (Old Party Fighter) and director of the North Bavarian Aviation Transportation Company that managed to keep BFW afloat until April 27, 1933, when a court-ordered settlement was reached allowing a continuation of aircraft production.[53]

The case of Dr. Adolf Rohrbach was somewhat different. He had started with Dornier in the Zeppelin Company. After the war he formed his own company in Berlin with affiliates in England, Japan, and Denmark, and built a number of all-metal flying boats, all of them high-wing cantilever monoplane models with sweeping, graceful lines. Heavily subsidized by the army, Rohrbach's luck ran out in the late twenties. A series of crashes, overly ambitious projects, and his own arrogance brought his downfall. The army cooled to his projects, the subsidies dried up, and the firm collapsed. He tried to organize another company after the Nazis took power but his firm was taken over by the Krupp affiliate Weser. He was never able to regain his prior prominance as a designer, and died shortly before World War II.

No one else in the aircraft industry was as closely linked to the secret rearmament as Ernst Heinkel, an inventor-designer par excellence. A vain, difficult person to work with, he had established a considerable reputation with the Reichswehr in the 1920s for his brilliant versatility. He could and did design literally everything from single-engined trainers to multiengined bombers. His structural designs included wooden planes, steel structures with fabric covering, alloyed structures with diverse coverings, combinations of all these, and, finally, his famous metal stressed-skin construction. With a sharp eye for young talent, he gathered around him such gifted engineers as the brothers Siegfried and Walter Gunter. The Heinkel team was ready to lead Germany to the forefront of aircraft designing in the early thirties. On December 1, 1932, Heinkel's He 70, a superbly contoured, duralumin monocoque fuselage aircraft with elliptical wings, the Heinkel trademark, made its debut. The remarkable four-passenger plane, dubbed the "Blitz," was the fastest commercial plane flying, and it could easily outrun any contemporary European fighter. The "Blitz" was an obvious prototype for future fighters.

Heinkel's amazing technical talents were coupled with his equally remarkable business skill. An aggressive businessman, he saw possibilities everywhere and was quick to capitalize on them. His uncanny instinct for the source and flow of political power allowed maximum latitude for his many talents. This bold, progressive, pioneering aircraft designer was so clever that when the Nazis started rearming, he was in an ideal situation with a foot in each camp. He had worked for the Reichswehr and was trusted by them, while at the same time he knew Göring and Milch and had their confidence.[54]

Edmund Rumpler and Dornier must be classified as fence-sitters. Rumpler was Jewish and unacceptable to the Nazis, although Göring and Udet liked him. But even before the Nazis came to power, this designer of so many successful World War I planes had shifted his attention from aircraft to motor cars. Dornier, on the other hand, remained active in aviation throughout his long life. He had started as an engineer with the Zeppelin Company, where he became the top designer of all-metal flying boats. In 1922 he started his own plant; and although the Versailles Treaty prohibited German production of flying boats, Dornier continued his specialty in his subsidiaries in Italy, Spain, Switzerland, and Japan. He had excellent connections with the Reichswehr, but only tenuous ones with the Nazis. He knew Friedrich Christiansen, a famous World War I pilot, captain of his Do X flying boat, and confidant of Göring. But on the whole, Dornier maintained a reserved, circumspect attitude towards the Nazis until he was sure they were politically entrenched.[55]

Apart from the old-line producers, the Nazi assumption of power with its prospects of large rearmament contracts attracted a new breed of manufacturers to aviation. By April 1933, six new entrants had joined the original eight airframe and six aircraft engine works which had constituted the aircraft industry.[56] The trade organization of German aviation, Reichsverband der Luftfahrtindustrie (Reich Aviation Manufacturers' Association), under the direction of Heinkel's protégé Admiral

Lahs, was singularly unsuccessful in limiting access to the field.[57] The Henschel Aviation Company (Berlin), Siebel (Halle), Blohm and Voss (Hamburg), ATG (Leipzig), Gotha Chassis Works (Gotha), and MIAG Company (Braunschweig) were being formed in early 1933, and their origins indicate the extent and speed of big business participation in aviation. MIAG was the aviation division of the MIAG Combine (Mühlenbau und Industrie-Aktiongesellschaft) under the direction of the pilot and designer Richard Dietrich. Blohm and Voss was the aviation division of the great German shipyard firm. Its first designer was Reinhold Mewes, who helped build the He 59 for Heinkel, but he was shortly lured away to the Fieseler firm. His replacement, Dr. Richard Vogt, had from 1923 to 1932 been a designer in Japan, where he had worked on flying boats. His experience and interest in electric welding techniques and sheet-steel construction coincided with those of the shipyard. The outcome was the production of all-metal flying boats. The Gotha plant was the reactivated World War I firm which had produced the big bombers. In 1933 under Dipl. Ing. A. Kalkert it resumed operations to build airplanes under license and to develop its own designs. The Siebel plant was an offshoot of the Klemm company. In 1933 Klemm received a contract from the Air Ministry to relocate a division of his firm in central Germany. By 1934 land for the plant was purchased in Halle and a hundred workers from the main plant formed a cadre for the new operation. Fritz W. Siebel, Klemm's business representative in Berlin and a close friend of Göring, eventually assumed control over this division, renamed it, and broadened its production program to include the manufacture under license of not only Klemm aircraft but also those of Heinkel, Focke-Wulf, and Dornier.

While the Siebel plant was definitely an inside job, organized by the Air Ministry, Henschel forced his entrance into the aviation field through another door. As early as 1931 the old, distinguished locomotive firm of Henschel and Son had shown interest in purchasing the near-bankrupt Junkers firm. When negotiations got nowhere, Oskar R. Henschel broke them off, and in February 1932 ordered the founding of his own aircraft firm. By March 30, 1933, the Henschel Aircraft Plant was established in Kassel under the direction of Erich Koch. A second plant, the factory of Ambi-Budd Waggon-und Apparatebau A.G. standing empty at Berlin-Johannisthal, was added in July. A third building site at Schönefeld, near Berlin, later to become the main plant, was dedicated with ground-breaking ceremonies on October 15, 1934, and went into production on December 22, 1935. Henschel's intrusion into the aviation field was resented by Milch and the older firms. Complaints that Henschel managed without the proper guidance of the Air Ministry and made personnel raids on other firms—including an unsuccessful attempt to lure Kurt Tank from Focke-Wulf—were heard frequently.[58] (The pool of talented aircraft designers was so small at the time that many moved rapidly up the corporate ladder by hopping nimbly from one company to another in a manner reminiscent of the American aviation industry of the forties and fifties.)

The scent of fast, juicy profits in aviation attracted not only locomotive, shipbuilding, and auto companies, but also some of the giants of the German business world. The ubiquitous Flick concern, which already was feverishly involved in procuring contracts from the Air Ministry for the production of flak, began investigating possibilities in the aircraft industry in early 1933. Flick's Heinrich Koppenberg, technical director and member of the board of Mitteldeutsche Stahlwerke A.G., held conversations with Heinkel, Dornier, and the Junkers people about the possibilities of joint enterprises. Heinkel was cool to the idea, while Dornier was more receptive. Both aircraft designers were skeptical about the establishment of another aircraft plant, feeling that current capacity of the industry could meet Germany's requirements short of a full-scale war. Dornier in particular noted that he ran his own factory without outside direction or control and with little help from the state. He was, however, interested in more government contracts. When Koppenberg suggested a joint enterprise between Dornier and Flick at the old Deutsche Flugzeugwerke plant at Leipzig, Dornier remained noncommittal pending further exploratory meetings to be held in May.[59] Koppenberg organized a series of meetings between the Flick, Vögler, and Thyssen combines and the Air Ministry on converting the newly purchased ATG (Allegemeine Transportmaschinen G.m.b.H.), the former Deutsche Flugzeugwerke, to aircraft production. Koppenberg had purchased ATG for Flick's Mitteldeutsche Stahlwerke early in 1933, but it was not until after Milch appointed him chairman of the board of Junkers that the consortium organized by Flick gained the technical competency it desired.

Milch's role in this matter is open to speculation. In a meeting on October 20, 1933, with sixty to seventy aircraft producers, Milch and Göring outlined the developments in the industry and their plans for rearmament.[60] Shortly thereafter the Reich acquired 51 percent of Junkers (the firm was officially nationalized on April 3, 1935) and Koppenberg was commissioned by Milch to inspect the Junkerswerke to ascertain what could be done to help the insolvent firm. Koppenberg had no experience in the aviation industry, but he had a reputation as an innovator of assembly-line techniques in the steel industry. On December 6, 1933, in the middle of Koppenberg's negative report on the

"handmade aircraft" techniques of Junkers, Milch interrupted and
declared him the new general director of that company at 170,000 RM
per year—a decision not welcomed by members of the Junkers family
and their close associates.[61] Koppenberg, still a member of the
Mitteldeutsche Stahlwerke board, could then license the production of
Junkers planes and parts to the ATG plant. Big business had made its
debut in the aircraft industry.

The intrusion of big business broke wide open the clubbish nature of
the aircraft industry. The trade organization of German aviation,
handmaiden of the old-line producers, was shunted aside and replaced by
the initially quiet but increasingly loud voice of the all-powerful Air
Ministry. As in other industries, rapid expansion of existing plants was
the only defense against the newcomers, but this proved in the long run
to be impossible. In aircraft manufacturing as with other sectors of the
economy, expansion provided a golden opportunity for the Nazis to seize
control.

NOTES

1. Der Chef des Truppenamtes, Nr. 562/32 geh. Kdos. T2, Chef/III, Berlin,
den 14.7.1932, DZ/MGFA.

2. Der Chef des Truppenamtes, Nr. 1845/32 geh. Kdos. In 1, Chef/V, Berlin,
den 28.7.1932, DZ/MGFA.

3. "Organisatorische Grundlagen für die Aufstellung von Luftstreitkräften im
Rahmen des Neuen Friedensheeres," In 1 Nr. 1786/32 geh. Kdos. V, Berlin, den
10.8.1932 and T1 Nr. 6888/32 g.Kdos. T1 III, Berlin, den 13.9.1932,
DZ/MGFA.

4. Völker, *Luftfahrt in Deutschland*, pp. 194-95; Suchenwirth, *Development
of the German Air Force*, pp. 44-46.

5. Vorschlag der In1 am 10.8.1932 zu T 2 Nr. 549/32 geh. Kdos., III B vom 15.
Juli 1932, DZ/MGFA.

6. "Begründung der Notwendigkeit die gesamte deutsche Luftfahrt unter dem
Reichswehrminister zusammenzufassen," Anlage 23 in Völker, *Luftfahrt in
Deutschland*, pp. 273-75.

7. T1 Nr. 756/32 g. Kdos. T 1 II vom 19.10.1932 Vortragsnotizen zur
Denkschrift General von Mittelberger, DZ/MGFA.

8. Der Chef des Truppenamtes Nr. 132/32, g.Kdos. TA Stab, Berlin, den
8.11.1932, DZ/MGFA.

9. In 1 Nr. 2710/32 geh. Kdos. V., Berlin, den 11.11.1932, Stand der
Luftrüstung, Anlage A) Materielle Rüstung, Stand 15.11.1932, B) Personnelle
Rüstung, Stand 15.11.1931, DZ/MGFA.

10. General der Flieger a.D. Hans Siburg, "Vorbereitende Massnahmen der
Marine Leitung auf dem Gebiete des Seeflugwesens in den Jahren 1920-1933,"
A/V/1; Speidel, "Reichswehr und Rote Armee," pp. 20-34; Generalleutnant
Andreas Nielsen, *The German Air Force General Staff*, USAF Historical
Studies, no. 173 (Air University, June 1959), pp. 20-21.

11. Der Reichswehrminister, TA Nr. 109/33 geh. Kdos. T2 III B In 1 (L) V, Berlin, 21. Februar 1933, Anlage 24 and 25 in Völker, *Luftfahrt in Deutschland*, pp. 276-78.

12. Der Reichsverteidigungsminister und Befehlshaber der gesamten Wehrmacht, LA Nr. 617/33 geh. Kdos. L 1 (H) II A, Berlin, den 10.5.1933, DZ/MGFA.

13. Eine Rechtfertigung für die Niederlage und die Fehler der Luftwaffe, von G.F.M. Milch, von Rohden document (4376-2112), BA/F.

14. Konrad Heiden, *Der Fuehrer* (Boston: Houghton Mifflin, 1944), pp. 444-53; Martin Broszat, *Der Staat Hitlers: Grundlegung und Entwicklung seiner inneren Verfassung*, DTV-Weltgeschichte des 20-Jahrhunderts, vol. 9 (Munich: DTV, 1969), pp. 44-45.

15. Suchenwirth, *Development of the German Air Force*, pp. 49-50.

16. Milch, "Eine Rechtfertigung," von Rohden document (4376-2112), BA/F; Raeder, *Mein Leben*, 2:103.

17. "Hitlers erste Bekanntgabe seiner Endziele als Reichskanzler 3.Feb.1933 vor den Befehlshabern des Heeres und der Marine anlässlich eines Besuch bei Gen. d.Inf. Frhr. v. Hammerstein-Equord in dessen Wohnung in Berlin," Lw 106/1, DZ/MGFA; Bracher et al. *Machtergreifung*, p. 719.

18. Gerhard L. Weinberg, ed. *Hitlers zweites Buch* (Stuttgart: Deutsche Verlags-Anstalt, 1961), pp. 81, 149-60; "Brief Hitlers an Oberst von Reichenau vom 4.12.1932," *Vierteljahrshefte für Zeitgeschichte* 7 (1959): 434; Hermann Rauschning, *The Revolution of Nihilism* (New York: Alliance, 1939), pp. 195-97.

19. Richard Suchenwirth, *Command and Leadership in the German Air Force*, USAF Historical Studies, no. 174 (Air University, July 1969), pp. 120-21; Heiden, *Der Fuehrer*, pp. 298-99; Roger Manvell and Heinrich Fraenkel, *Göring* (New York: Simon & Schuster, 1962), pp. 64-65.

20. Hermann Göring, *Aufbau einer Nation* (Berlin: Eher, 1934), p. 53.

21. F. L. Carsten, *The Rise of Fascism* (Berkeley: University of California Press, 1967), pp. 136-40; Heiden, *Der Fuehrer*, pp. 290-99; Joachim C. Fest, *Das Gesicht des Dritten Reiches: Profile einer totalitären Herrschaft* (Munich: R. Piper, 1963), p. 108; Broszat, *Der Staat Hitlers*, pp. 80-81.

22. Fest, *Gesicht des Dritten Reiches*, pp. 106-7; Charles Bewley, *Hermann Göring and the Third Reich* (New York: Devin-Adair, 1962), pp. 76-77; Graf Schwerin von Krosigk, *Es geschah in Deutschland* (Stuttgart: Rainer Wunderlich, 1951), p. 225; Emmy Göring, *An der Seite Meines Mannes* (Göttingen: K. W. Schütz, 1967), pp. 32-33; Manvell and Fraenkel, *Goering*, pp. 68-69.

23. Heiden, *Der Fuehrer*, pp. 298-99; Suchenwirth, *Command and Leadership*, p. 121; Irving, *Milch*, pp. 45-47.

24. Milch, "Eine Rechtfertigung," von Rohden document (4376-2112); Bericht von Milch, 28 Juli 1945, von Rohden document (4376-463), BA/F; Hermann, *Luftwaffe*, pp. 87-99; Irving, *Milch*, pp. 45, 48, 53, 397-98, says Göring received over 1,000 RM per month from Lufthansa.

25. Interviews of Generalleutnant a.D. Bruno Maass, 15.7.1953, M-und Quellen, Lw 101/3, and Major a.D. Helmuth Pohle, 15.4.1956, Lw 103/49, DZ/MGFA; Friedrich Hossbach, *Zwischen Wehrmacht und Hitler, 1934-1938*, (Wolfenbüttel: Wolfenbütteler Verlag, 1949), pp. 114-16.

26. Interview General der Flieger a.D. Hellmuth Felmy, 16 Feb. 1954, D/II/1 KDC/M; Speidel, "Reichswehr und Rote Armee," pp. 40-45; Erich Raeder,

Statement VII, *Nazi Conspiracy and Aggression*, 10 vols. (Nuremberg: USGPO, 1947-49) (henceforth cited as *NCA*), 8:695-97; Rieckhoff, *Trumpf oder Bluff*, p. 33.

27. Interview of Maass, 15.7.1953, M-und Quellen, Lw 101/3, and interview of Major Pohle, 14.4.1956, Lw 104/5, DZ/MGFA.

28. Bernhard Heimann and Joachim Schunke, "Eine geheime Denkschrift zur Luftkriegskonzeption Hitler-Deutschlands vom Mai 1933," *Zeitschrift für Militärgeschichte*, 3 (1964): 72-86; Gerhard Förster, *Totaler Krieg und Blitzkrieg: Die Theorie des Totalen Krieges und des Blitzkrieges in der Militärdoktrin des Faschistischen Deutschlands am Vorabend des Zweiten Weltkrieges* (Berlin: Deutscher Militärverlag, 1967), pp. 150-53.

29. Ibid., pp. 73-74. As usual, Milch later asserted that he originated the risk fleet idea (Irving, *Milch*, pp. 63-64, 67, 403).

30. Völker, *Die deutsche Luftwaffe*, pp. 28-29; General der Flieger a.D. Wimmer, "Geschichte des viermotorigen Bombers," Karlsruhe Document Collection, DZ/MGFA.

31. Von Rohden materials, NA Microcopy T-971/27/905; Nielsen, *German Air Force General Staff*, p. 153. See also the statement of George S. Messersmith, U.S. consul general in Berlin at the time, in *NCA*, 5:25, when he commented that the Nazis decided to concentrate on air power as the "weapon of terror most likely to give Germany a dominant position and the weapon which could be developed the most rapidly and in the shortest time."

32. Ernst Heinkel, *Stürmisches Leben* (Stuttgart: Mundus, 1953), p. 273.

33. Bericht von Milch, 28. Juli 1945, von Rohden document (4376-463) BA/F. Kesselring (Kesselring über GFM Milch, Wiessee 31.1.1955, Lw 103/29, DZ/MGFA) as well as many other officers thought Milch had something on Göring to explain his appointment and continual service to Göring. For Milch's later account, see Irving, *Milch*, pp. 61-62.

34. The Reichsschatzmeister Franx X. Schwarz requested from Hess on February 26, 1934, a backdated party membership for Milch and Bruno Loerzer. Milch received number 123,585, dated May 1, 1929. Loerzer's membership was changed from March 1, 1933, to April 1, 1929. Early party affiliation was highly esteemed by Nazi officials. (Milch File, Berlin Document Center.) Milch's ancestry was the subject of some discussion. He was born in 1893, the son of Anton, a Jewish chief of staff pharmacist in the Imperial Navy, and a Gentile mother. Later his mother swore he was the son of Baron Hermann von Bier with whom she had committed adultery. Erhard Milch's original birth certificate was withdrawn and a new one issued calling him the "adopted son of Anton Milch." See Willi Frischauer, *The Rise and Fall of Hermann Goering* (Boston: Houghton Mifflin, 1951), p. 99; Hermann, *Luftwaffe*, pp. 77, 95; and NA Microcopy T-175/211/2750257. Irving, *Milch*, pp. 72-74, gives a sympathetic but basically the same story.

35. There is unanimity on Milch. Generalleutnant a.D. Uebe, no friend of Milch, remarked, "I don't believe you could have found a better man in all of Germany for the build-up than Milch" (Lw 104/7); Ministerial Director Knipfer called him "ambitious" and a "braggart" but thought he had tremendous ability (Lw 104/3); General von Seidel said Milch had a "sharp understanding" and "quick grasp" and was "loaded with vitality and energy, with a rich background in aviation, including its technology and industry," but added that "he loved intrigue" (Lw 101/3), DZ/MGFA.

36. Rieckhoff, *Trumpf oder Bluff*, pp. 41-43; Hossbach, *Zwischen Wehrmacht und Hitler*, pp. 114-16.

37. Nielsen, *German Air Force General Staff*, pp. 44-45.

38. Ibid., pp. 33-34; NA Microcopy T-971/25/1225-59.

39. Bericht über die Befragung des Generalobersten Stumpff von 22.11.1954, Lw 104/3, DZ/MGFA.

40. For Wever's "Uralbomber," see General a.D. Paul Deichmann, "Die Deutsche Luftwaffe und die viermotorigen Bomber," Lw 103/29, DZ/MGFA; Nielsen, *German Air Force General Staff*, p. 29; Suchenwirth, *Command and Leadership*, pp. 4-6; Rieckhoff, *Trumpf oder Bluff*, pp. 43-44. On Wever, Ministerial Director Willy Frisch called him "the best man" Field Marshal von Blomberg gave up to the Luftwaffe, while Milch compared him in ability to the elder von Moltke.

41. Heinkel, *Stürmisches Leben*, pp. 273-75; Nielsen, *German Air Force General Staff*, pp. 31-32, 42-43.

42. Suchenwirth, *Command and Leadership*, p. 127; Rieckhoff, *Trumpf oder Bluff*, p. 33; Irving, *Milch*, pp. 54, 61, 401.

43. Major a.D. Helmuth Pohle über die DVS 1933, Befragung durch Prof. R. Suchenwirth, 15.4.1956, Lw 103/49, DZ/MGFA.

44. Richard Suchenwirth, *Historical Turning Points in the German Air Force War Effort*, USAF Historical Studies, no. 189 (Air University, June 1959), pp. 1-4.

45. Baumbach, *Life and Death of the Luftwaffe*, pp. 4-6; Killen, *History of the Luftwaffe*, pp. 51-52; Hermann, *Luftwaffe*, pp. 109-10; Rieckhoff, *Trumpf oder Bluff*, pp. 38-40; von Rohden materials, NA Microcopy T-971/27/1225-30; Nielsen, *German Air Force General Staff*, p. 25; Feuchter, *Luftkrieg*, pp. 12-14; Hossbach, *Zwischen Wehrmacht und Hitler*, p. 116.

46. Generalfeldmarschall a.D. Albert Kesselring, *Gedanken zum Zweiten Weltkrieg* (Bonn: Athenäum, 1955), pp. 173-74.

47. Kesselring, *Soldat*, pp. 458-59; Suchenwirth, *Hermann Göring, ein Versuch*, Lw 104/3, p. 13, DZ/MGFA.

48. Nielsen, *German Air Force General Staff*, p. 22.

49. Arthur Schweitzer, "Business Policy in a Dictatorship," *Business History Review* 38 (1964):418-20; Louis Paul Lochner, *Tycoons and Tyrant: German Industry from Hitler to Adenauer* (Chicago: H. Regnery, 1954), pp. 214-15.

50. Lochner, *Tycoons and Tyrant*, p. 96. For information on industry's support of the Nazis, see Wolfgang Wagner, "Die deutschen Flugzeugwerke," Lw 103/41, DZ/MGFA, and Henry Ashby Turner, Jr., "Big Business and the Rise of Hitler," *American Historical Review* 75 (October 1969): 56-70.

51. Hermann, *Luftwaffe*, pp. 92-96; Irving, *Milch*, pp. 68-70, 76-77.

52. Kens and Nowarra, *Flugzeuge*, p. 412; Wagner, "Flugzeugwerke," Lw 103/41, DZ/MGFA; Heinz Conradis, *Nerven, Herz und Rechenschieber; Kurt Tank, Flieger, Forscher, Konstrukteur* (Göttingen: Musterschmidt, 1955), p. 91.

53. Kens and Nowarra, *Flugzeuge*, p. 412; Hermann, *Luftwaffe*, pp. 48-50; Gen. Ing. a.D. Huebner, "Deutsche Flugzeugfabriken vor Neuaufstellung der deutschen Luftwaffe," Lw 103/39, DZ/MGFA; Irving, *Milch*, pp. 68-69.

54. Irving, *Milch*, pp. 77-78; Hermann, *Luftwaffe*, pp. 51-54. Heinkel's character can readily be perceived from his memoirs, *Stürmisches Leben*.

55. Kens and Nowarra, *Flugzeuge*, pp. 137-38; Hermann, *Luftwaffe*, pp. 44-46; Wagner, "Die deutschen Flugzeugwerke," Lw 103/41, DZ/MGFA.

56. The old-line firms were Dornier, BFW, Heinkel, Focke-Wulf, Klemm, Junkers, Arado, and Fieseler in airframes, and Junkers, Argus, Daimler-Benz, BMW, Siemens, and Hirth in engines.

57. "Ueber die Entwicklung der deutschen Luftfahrtindustrie in der Zeit von 1933 bis 1941 insbesondere bei der Firma Junkers," originally written by Dr. Koppenberg, March 6, 1946, with additional comments based on questions by General Deichmann, dated 22.10.1957 and 7.1.1958, Lw 103/28, DZ/MGFA.

58. Koppenberg's Letter to Mitteldeutsche Stahlwerke director Steinbrinck, dated April 20, 1933, NA Microcopy T-83/68/3440499-503; Kens and Nowarra, *Flugzeuge,* p. 312; Heubner, "Deutsche Flugzeugfabriken," Lw 103/39, DZ/MGFA; United States Strategic Bombing Survey (henceforth cited as USSBS) 4d56, Interview No. 10; May 19, 1945, Dr. Karl Frydag and Mr. Heinkel, National Archives.

59. NA Microcopy T-83/68/3440499-503.

60. *Trials of War Criminals before the Nuremberg Military Tribunals under Control Council Law No. 10* (Washington: USGPO, 1951-53), 6: 104-5, Document NI-10114 (henceforth cited as *Minor Trials*); Koppenberg, "Entwicklung Luftfahrtindustrie," Lw 103/28, DZ/MGFA; Irving, *Milch,* pp. 69-70, 76-77.

61. Ibid., "Steno Nr. 3, 10 Jan. 1941, 6 Jahre Junkers, eine Betrachung! 1934-1940," document (4376-2178), BA/F.

CHAPTER 4

Broadening the Base

THE AIRCRAFT INDUSTRY the Nazis inherited from the Weimar Republic was one of the smallest and most insignificant areas of manufacturing. It employed a mere 3,200 men at the nadir of the depression during the third quarter of 1932, and in May 1933, according to the Reich Statistical Office, stood 97th among 279 industrial branches for which there were official statistics. It had a net production of 37.5 million RM, only 0.2 percent of a total German industrial production of 17.3 billion RM. By contrast, in 1936 the aircraft industry stood in 14th place with a net production valued at 527 million RM or 1.6 percent of the total industrial production. Its total production was 15 times greater than in 1933, while that for German industry as a whole had increased 1.9 times in the same period.[1] Even the automobile industry, which was 7 times larger in 1933, was overtaken by the middle of 1936, when the aircraft industry claimed 124,878 employees compared to the automobile industry's 118,148.

More than any other, the aircraft industry was a child of the Nazis. Like its counterparts elsewhere, it was completely dependent on public spending. Despite the pious pleading of the Nazis about maintaining private ownership, the aircraft industry was controlled, directed, and financed by the government to a degree unparalleled by any other major industry. For this reason alone, Nazi business theories had a broader impact on its management than on that of older, established industries. The difficulties of the Nazis in adjusting their economic doctrines to their military and political planning and even their extraordinary problems in mastering modern technology are clearly seen in this area of production. Anomalies were to abound everywhere.

THE 1,000-AIRCRAFT PROGRAM OF 1933

Goring's deputy, State Secretary Erhard Milch, realized in May 1933 that the first task of the new Aviation Ministry was expansion of the industry. Only two plants, Heinkel and Junkers, were capable of even limited series production, and Junkers was beset with financial and managerial problems which were not resolved until the Air Ministry took control of the firm. The annual production of the entire industry was at best several hundred aircraft, three-quarters of which were single-engined sport planes.[2] These limitations, however, did not deter Milch; he vigorously pushed ahead. Using the preliminary studies of Felmy and Jeschonnek as guidelines, he sent a questionnaire to major offices in the ministry asking for reactions to a suggested 1,000-aircraft building program.[3] Then Milch and his associates, in two and half days and nights of continuous labor, designed a production program to the smallest detail—timetables, methods of financing, materials needed, and aircraft types, including 244 front-line military airplanes.[4]

The responses of the ministry's offices were guarded and critical. In general they agreed that the Reich's weaknesses in air power should be corrected as soon as possible through maximum use of available equipment and facilities, but they stressed the need for a systematic program for the build-up. Obviously peeved that they had not been properly consulted, many of the respondents requested closer coordination in the future. Operations Branch (LA-I) proposed a more modest plan for the construction of 225 aircraft by May 1, 1934, and the same number within the following year.[5] Operations doubted that the existing industry possessed the necessary skilled personnel or the required materials to support even this plan, singling out critical weaknesses in engine development and suggesting the purchase of at least one-half the needed fighters from Italy in 1933.

On the basis of the answers, Milch improvised a production plan for 1933 largely designed to tool up the industry for future production. The key operative factor was the ability of the aircraft plants to expand production. Schedules, budgets, and model selections were altered to fit the rapidly developing capacity of the industry. The selection of models was determined entirely by what could be produced. Since the Reich's position necessitated a quickly established air force, the Air Ministry chose to produce three kinds of aircraft: civilian airplanes that could be converted, older military types already developed and tested, and modern military aircraft in the final stages of development that could soon be produced in series. Milch and Göring were willing to build older, inferior models even though much of the first years' production might be scrapped when a new generation of aircraft could be developed.[6]

Milch's plan changed daily. For example, the initial budgetary request from the Technical Office (Development, Testing, and Production) was 87.6 million RM, but this was doubled by the end of July. Colonel Wimmer estimated that 177.3 million RM would be needed in 1933 to produce 804 aircraft, including 234 front-line warplanes, 52 auxiliary bombers (carried on the books as Lufthansa aircraft), 88 trainers, 2 test models, and 480 civilian airplanes. The magnitude of the new program can readily be seen. Developmental costs in the July request were budgeted at 18.9 million RM, up 4.7 million from the original request, while procurement and factory preparation expenses rose from 66.1 million to 150.9 million RM. Wimmer remarked that the new funds would be approved by the end of July 1933, but the exact amount was still uncertain because of the tentative nature of his production projections.[7]

Even though sizable, the defense expenditures were carefully disguised. Of the original 30.0 million RM requested for airframes alone, only 5.4 million appeared in the official public budget, while the remaining 26.6 million was carried on the unemployment work program. Wimmer commented that the additional moneys requested would be recorded in the ratio of 1 to 5. In the developmental program a higher percentage of costs were publicly acknowledged; 10.2 million of the 18.9 million RM for 1933 openly appeared in the public budget.[8]

The military planning which paralleled the 1,000-Aircraft Program progressed rapidly during the summer of 1933. In a meeting on June 19, 1933, Milch and Colonel von Reichenau, representative of the defense minister, approved plans for the construction of a combat air force of 600 planes in 51 squadrons by the fall of 1935.[9] Göring and Blomberg formally approved them on June 27. Even though considerably larger than those drawn up in May by Milch, the plans were deemed inadequate by General Adam of the army High Command. He wanted the number of reconnaissance squadrons increased from twelve to sixteen but was willing to accept the proposed six fighter squadrons provided they were assigned exclusively to field army defense. Home defense would have to be provided by antiaircraft artillery and "Police Fighter" squadrons, a term used to denote black, or illegal, reserves.[10] In addition to the combat aircraft, an equally large number of trainers, communication and transport planes were to be produced. It was clear by late summer that the 1,000-Aircraft Program was too small for current military plans. Incorporating all the changes made during the summer, an interim aircraft production program for 1933-34 and 1934-35 was introduced in September 1933 nearly doubling the old program,[11] which the highest Reich authorities realized would meet neither the strategic and tactical requirements of the military nor Hitler's demands for a risk air force.

The September plan was the last of the constantly changing interim plans based loosely on the capacity of the aircraft industry. The experience gained during the year was of inestimable value to the Air

Ministry, the aircraft plants, and the military. Much was done: the administrative structure of the ministry consolidated, a system of establishing requirements and selecting models designed, a working relationship between industry and government started, and countless construction problems met and solved. In each of these areas, the patterns developed in 1933 dominated German aviation in the years before the war.

In the Air Ministry, Colonel Wimmer, chief of the Technical Office, consolidated all the technical agencies under his direction. His office was structured horizontally so that research and development, under Captain Wolfram Freiherr von Richthofen, was separate from and independent of production under Major Fritz Loeb. The testing and release of new equipment to service units were handled by parallel offices, while the business and fiscal aspects, including price approval, accounting, and auditing, were handled by the Economic Group (Wirtschaftsgruppe) of the Administration Office. The horizontal pattern of administration demanded continual and close coordination between the various offices, a task that proved exceedingly difficult in 1933 and after.

The system of establishing general requirements and selecting equipment was an adaption of the Weimar program. Every branch of the Luftwaffe—operations, training, communications, and weapons inspectorate—submitted to the general staff their specifications for new equipment. These were then worked into general requirements by the General Staff and Göring and relayed to the Planning Group of the Technical Office, under the direction of Guenther Tschersich, which had six sections (Rüstungsreferenten): airframes, engines, airborne instruments and safety equipment, electrical equipment and radios, weapons, and ground service equipment.[12] The Planning Group refined these specifications and submitted them to the aircraft industry for fulfillment. The industry had considerable latitude in designing, programing, gathering raw materials, scheduling, pricing, and testing new equipment as long as the general economy was slack. But once labor, materials, and capital became tighter, the ministry intervened and exercised far more control in overall planning.[13]

The Air Ministry and the industry enjoyed a successful working relationship as a result of the 1,000-Aircraft Program. The ministry's grant of funds and guaranteed bank credits for expansion, the rather obvious courtship of the owners, the general attitude of ministry officials, and the dramatic improvement in the industry's financial condition helped to allay the suspicions of many aircraft manufacturers. The chief characteristic of the ministry's relationship with the industry was benign guidance.

Building on practices in the German business community as a whole in the 1920s, the ministry pushed the process of rationalization in the aircraft industry. The concept of rationalization in its broadest sense meant the application of the scientific method to all aspects of industrial and economic life. It grew out of the experiences of German industry during the latter half of the nineteenth century and the "War Socialism" of 1914-18 and by the 1920s had become an economic faith. Called "the science of industry and economics"—the key to greater national power and prosperity—rationalization permitted the production, distribution, and consumption of goods without all the waste, confusion, and friction that accompanies an unrationalized economy.[14]

Applied specifically to the aircraft industry, rationalization meant the systematic planning, coordination, and integration of the entire industry and included the standardization of work procedures, plans, and parts; coordination of scientific research; patent pooling; and institution of scientific management and uniform methods of financing and accounting. Competition was eliminated and cooperation stressed as a matter of policy. Companies were divided into three basic categories: old-line aircraft firms which were encouraged to carry on developmental work; smaller firms and newcomers which were regarded primarily as producers and allowed only limited developmental work; and newcomers which were exclusively satellite or "shadow-plants" for concerns with strong design departments like Junkers and Messerschmitt and which were strictly whole-assembly or subassembly firms.

Already by 1933 the system of complexes built around one important parent firm, a characteristic feature of the German aircraft industry, was present. An extension of the rationalization principle adopted so generally in the Third Reich, the system of complexes was initiated by Junkers. Its purpose was to utilize fully the few competent engineering and design firms and maximize production in the subcontracting plants. For example, Junkers controlled the manufacturing methods, operations sequences, machining methods, and engineering design; maintained proper quality control; supplied the basic tools and jigs; and even took care of materials and facilities requirements.[15] The Junkers complex became operational with the ABC Program of December 13, 1933, under which the RLM ordered 179 Ju 52/3s to be built by four firms under Junkers's control.[16] Seven separate subassembly divisions were to produce parts and whole sections of the aircraft which were then sent to the main Junkers plant at Dessau for final assembly. One of the aims of the ABC Program was to train the personnel of non-aircraft firms in metal aircraft construction. It marked the first time since World War I that an airplane was built by several subassembly firms and was the forerunner of the great series production of the later 1930s.[17]

For several licensees to line-produce airframes with a complete interchangeability of parts, Junkers needed to solve the assembly tooling problem. The airframe industry was conspicuously different from the aircraft engine industry because it did not make extensive use of machine equipment. The average metal-working plant might have most of the principal machine equipment used for fabrication of parts: hydraulic presses, punch presses, power brakes, metal shapers, shears, routers, stretchers, and a small number of machine tools for forging and casting. However, airframe manufacturing on a line-production basis required elaborate assembly jigs. The many structural parts of an airframe, the ribs, longerons, stiffeners, and skin, required precise tooling and holding fixtures to ensure accuracy in the desired aerodynamic form. Junkers, assisted by Fertigungs G.m.b.H., devised a basic type of assembly jig which became the standard for the Reich Aviation Manufacturers' Association.[18]

Only Dornier did not use this system; they had their own which minimized the use of assembly jigs. Under the Junkers or standard system a set of production jigs was made from a master. Each plant or licensee had a set of production jigs plus a master to keep them in adjustment. The mother plant of a complex maintained a master control jig to check periodically the accuracy of the masters from the licensee's plant. This system was similar to that used by American firms when several plants made the same airplane. Molding fixtures designed by Junkers were frequently of the rotating type which permitted maximum convenience and accessibility for work. The Junkers assembly tooling was entirely of the universal type and rather mobile. The frames, made of heavy steel members, were bolted together and the check points on the jig which determined the shape of the part to be built were bolted to the frame. Universal jigs of this type could be adjusted within limits to permit fairly extensive changes in design. Since they were not set permanently in the floor, they could be moved easily.[19]

The 1,000-Aircraft Program marked the beginning of massive aerial rearmament in Germany. Although only 197 military airplanes were accepted in 1933 by the new Luftwaffe, the basis for mass production was laid.[20] The available plant facilities had been considerably expanded and new plants established or planned. In terms of construction, standardization of equipment, execution of series-production orders, establishment of production aids and subcontracting procedures, and long-range planning, the program was successful. One obvious gauge of its success was the rise in employment. On January 31, 1933, employment in the airframe plants was 2,813; a year later it stood at 11,102. In the aircraft engine plants employment rose from 1,175 to 5,769. The total employment for both increased fourfold from 3,988 to 16,871.[21] Admittedly, many of the aircraft produced in 1933 were inferior, but by the end of the year the industry had twenty-five models under development and its output had risen to a monthly high of 72 aircraft in January 1934, compared to the monthly average of 31 for 1933.

PLANS FOR THE RHINELAND PROGRAM OF 1934 AND 1935

In January 1934, changes in production and planning resulted in the writing of the first comprehensive procurement program for the aircraft industry. The new plan which superseded the interim plan of September 1933 called for the production of 3,715 airplanes during 1934 and 1935,[22] and was nicknamed the Rhineland Program. By July 1934, the usual changes were made to accommodate additional demands made by the Luftwaffe and the Air Ministry's more optimistic assessments of the industry. In its final form, the Rhineland Program increased the number of aircraft to be produced to 4,021 and moved the terminal date up to September 30, 1935. The plan, as outlined in table 3 represented a compromise between the strategic air force advocates and the tactically oriented developers of the Luftwaffe. The large number of bombers (822) compared to the small number of fighters (245) emphasized that the program's primary mission was to create a deterrent force. At the same time, the 1,760 trainers reflected the thinking of those who wanted a cautious, steady build-up of a well-rounded air force.[23] Among the new models to be programed, three were bombers, the Do 17, He 111, and Ju 86; one a reconnaissance plane, the He 70; and one a flying boat, Do 18; but there were no new fighters. The production of a high-performance fighter and a large four-engined bomber were deferred to the next program.

Forecasts of monthly production for the Rhineland Program projected a rise from 72 aircraft in January 1934 to a high of 293 in July 1935, with a monthly average of 164 for 1934 and 265 for 1935. Aircraft engine production was to rise from a monthly average of 106 in January 1934 to a peak of 704 in July 1935.[24] Employment was expected to increase from 16,000 in January 1934 to an estimated 70,000 by mid-summer 1935.

The Rhineland Program was the first attempt by the Air Ministry to coordinate all aspects of the production of aircraft. Hitler, in consultation with his military and civilian advisers, determined the general guidelines for the Luftwaffe in terms of expenditures, size of force, type of equipment, and time terminals. Then the Air Ministry and its Air Command Office, which for all practical purposes was the general staff of the air force (the general staff did not formally come into existence until August 1, 1936), determined the Luftwaffe's general requirements and submitted them to the Air Ministry's planning agencies. These general staff requirements, as they became known after 1936, were usually tactical in nature, specifying, for example, the amount of equipment needed for a desired operational force, or particular kinds of equipment, e.g., a fast bomber with a speed of 215 mph, range of 600 miles, bomb load of one ton, crew of four, and all-weather capability. From 1933 to 1945 about one hundred general staff

TABLE 3

THE RHINELAND PROGRAM, 1 JANUARY 1934-30 SEPTEMBER 1935

Type	Model	Number
COMBAT AIRCRAFT		
Bombers	Do 11	150
	Do 13	222
	Ju 52	450
Fighters	Ar 64	19
	Ar 65	85
	He 51	141
Reconnaissance		
(long-range)	He 45	320
(short-range)	He 46	270
Dive bombers	He 50	51
		Total 1,718
NAVAL AIRCRAFT		
Reconnaissance		
(long-range)	He 60	81
	Do 15 "Wal"	21
Fighters	He 51W	14
	He 38	12
Multipurpose	He 59	21
		Total 149
		Total combat aircraft 1,867
Trainers (all types)		1,760
Liaison		89
Miscellaneous (including new models)		305
		Total 2,154
		Grand Total 4,021

SOURCE: Flugzeugbeschaffungsprogramm vom 1.7.1934, Akte L II 1296, DZ/MGFA.

requirements were given to the planning agencies. To cover these, the Technical Office organized forty-two procurement programs (*Beschaffungsprogramm*), of which four were unnumbered and thirty-eight carried Technical Office numbers from 1 to 21 and from 222 to 228. Major variants of a program were given a letter designation after the number; for example, just before the war, procurement program no. 13 underwent so many changes that the Technical Office issued 13A and 13B programs. Of the original forty-two procurement programs drawn up by the ministry, thirty-six were finally sent to the aircraft firms in the form of industrial production plans (Industrie-Lieferplänen). The procurement program, the basic planning document of the Air Ministry, showed the total production, number of each type of equipment to be produced, individual factory producing it, date of production, and official designation of each airplane and its accessory equipment. The industry production plan that evolved from the procurement plan after a great deal of consultation carried basically the same information but had legally binding contracts attached. From it, the individual firms would begin to plan facilities, hire labor, secure raw materials, and subcontract for parts. The production plan was especially important for the airframe plants because of their particular need to coordinate their own production with that of the engine and accessory firms.[25]

The first fifteen numbered programs had an equivalent military program, the general staff program, used primarily to establish the strength of operational and training units. Once the war started, however, it was no longer feasible to tie military strength plans to production plans. New prototypes were normally carried as special programs within the production program. They were designated *Versuchsmuster* (experimental models) and were budgeted either singly or in small (10-15) preproduction test series called 0-series (*Null-Serie*). Once a plant received a developmental contract for a prototype, it was on its own. Working within the guidelines established by the ministry, the plant had the freedom to follow a line development with little direction from the Technical Office. Large firms could have ten or more development projects underway at the same time. There was very little coordination between competing firms, which meant that an excessive amount of engineering potential was tied up in projects that would not lead to serial production. It did, however, permit the Technical Office to pursue two or three lines of development simultaneously to determine which might prove most successful.

The problem was in determining quickly which line of development should be pushed and which line should be discontinued. If the decision was made prematurely, a developmental line which initially seemed promising might end in a failure, resulting in heavy losses of manpower and materials. If the decision was deferred too long, heavy losses would occur in time and engineering talent. As a general rule, the Technical Office tended before the war to listen to the usually optimistic reports of the development firms and allow projects to run longer than necessary before selecting a line for mass production. In part, the low production before the war was attributed to this lingering in the developmental stage.

A second problem in the development was insufficient consideration of the construction problems and the lack of experience in mass production that might be encountered in serial production of a prototype. Many promising prototypes had disastrous production problems. The same was true of individual firms; some proved to be far more proficient in adjusting to mass production than others, as the Technical Office learned in the Rhineland Program. Junkers, in particular, quickly gained a reputation for simplicity of aircraft design and efficiency in production of large aircraft and in overall plant management.

At best, planning for an aircraft industry was a precarious task. The long lead time in developing aircraft, rapid obsolescence of equipment, and uncertainties that new models would meet the design specifications and requirements for production and operation were ambiguities. Even the best minds of the Third Reich found analyzing the risks involved in aviation planning a fascinating but elusive job strewn with unforseen difficulties.

THE RHINELAND PROGRAM IN OPERATION

Despite intense efforts to rectify it, the low level of production and generally poor performance of aircraft engines was a bottleneck throughout the Rhineland Program.[26] Aircraft engine development had been seriously retarded by the Allied restrictions during the 1920s; and although the Reichswehr had sought to evade them by building an engine industry, the results were marginal. By 1933 the aircraft engine firms still largely relied on models of foreign design because their own developmental projects had not matured. The industry as a whole was not on a par with that of the other major aviation nations. The special problems involved in production were equally perplexing. Like the airframe industry, the engine industry required an emphasis on precision engineering and quality control. More especially, an engine plant is principally a precision machine tool shop, while an airframe plant is primarily a sheet-metal fabrication and assembly shop. The difference is significant: an airframe plant demands far fewer precision machines and a less skilled labor force while its mode of operation is more adaptable to mass production than that of engine plants, with their elaborate equipment consisting of batteries of engine and turret lathes, drill presses, boring mills, and other machine tools, and the highly skilled workers needed for machining and assembly operations which call for extremely close tolerances. In brief, the know-how required in the engine plant is considerably different from that of the airframe factory because of the greater emphasis on machining operations.

As in the airframe industry, a system of rationalization was followed in the engine industry. Selected concerns with design experience were used as the nucleus of the industry with less experienced or new firms used as licensees. Existing plants were expanded and new ones built either under the management of the older, established plants or under the direction of new, invited industrial concerns. Three firms soon dominated the field: Junkers, Daimler-Benz, and BMW. Only Junkers had been active in the 1920s while the other two were prominent in the field of high-performance automobile engines. The Air Ministry soon brought other concerns into the field as licensees under Junkers and Daimler-Benz. By the time the war started, these licensees had some experience with engine manufacturing and the proper machines for mass production. Junkers's licensees were the Mitteldeutsche Motorenwerke (a subsidiary of Auto Union) and Pommersche Motorenbau (a subsidiary of Stöwer), while Daimler-Benz's were Henschel Flugmotorenbau and the Niedersächsische Motorenwerke (a subsidiary of Bussing NAG).

The low level of aircraft engine production during the first half of 1934 jeopardized the Rhineland Program. It was not until the end of January 1934 that the Siemens Jupiter engine to be used in the Do 11 twin-engined bomber and the Ar 64 single-engined fighter was released for serial production. Difficulties with the BMW VI engine also delayed production of the He 45 and He 60. The solution was either to purchase engines abroad, which was tried,[27] or to expand the industry at home. The Air Ministry decided on the latter for four reasons: the chronic foreign exchange situation limited purchases abroad; foreign governments were reluctant to license their best engines for production in Germany for security reasons; Germany needed to develop a domestic aeroengine industry for wartime self-sufficiency; and Germany's own progress, especially with the diesel engine, was beginning to show substantive promise.[28]

The engine firms were quick to point out the advantages of expansion. BMW cited the experience of its plants in Munich and

Eisenach.[29] Working two standard forty-hour shifts, the Munich plant could produce 80 air-cooled and 80 liquid-cooled engines monthly and the Eisenach plant could produce 50 air-cooled ones. Under the mobilization plan, production was to be increased from 210 to 300 engines, primarily by increasing the work week to fifty-four hours. BMW stated that any further increase must come through expansion, especially in air-cooled engines, which, it estimated, required one-third less labor, material, and time than liquid-cooled engines. A new factory producing air-cooled engines could be operational in four months instead of the six required for liquid-cooled engines. A BMW official, in a personal letter to Freiherr von Richthofen, chief of research and development in the Technical Office, informed him that BMW and Siemens could tool up to produce 3,000 engines a year if they received permission from the ministry.[30]

After months of delays and low production, the Air Ministry assembled the engine producers on September 20 and 21, 1934, for a conference covering a wide range of problems. Freiherr von Richthofen stressed the need to expand the industry in the shortest possible time; the entire Rhineland Program depended on it, as extensive foreign purchases were prohibited. Recognizing that the German industry could not hope in one and a half years to overtake the lead that foreign engine companies had held from the previous decade, Richthofen expressed his confidence that by 1936 it would be second to none. Shortages of money, space, trained personnel, and research facilities would be met by a joint effort on the part of the government and the industry. The ultimate payoff would be a sound aeroengine industry which could compete abroad and sustain the rearmament program at home. For the Luftwaffe, success would mean the production of newer and better high-performance engines, lighter in weight, easier and cheaper to manufacture, with greater reliability and longer service. Most important of all, Richthofen wanted the developmental time for engines cut drastically, from five or six to two years.[31]

By comparison, the problems in the airframe industry were less severe than those of the engine industry in 1934: chiefly poor cooperation between mother firms and their licensees; faulty production programing; the low quality of the aircraft produced; and shortages of skilled labor, raw materials, especially metals, and capital for expansion. The difficulties involved with the licensees were especially acute in the production of large airplanes since most of that work was subcontracted. Despite the efforts of the Technical Office and Fertigungs G.m.b.H., many licensees found it difficult to adjust to the concept of the multiple integrated production operations planned by the Air Ministry in such programs as the ABC. The constant changes and the extraordinary high level of engineering precision necessitated close cooperation with the mother firm to a degree unfamiliar to most plants from non-aeronautical fields. Working under the ministry's injunction "Eilig ist heute alles" (speed means everything today), the businesses realized that cooperation was the key to mass production, big contracts, and high profits.[32] To strengthen cooperation, licensees and subcontractors were chosen because of their proximity to the mother firms, which enlarged their facilities at an alarming rate. The results were predictable. The airframe industry became clustered in virtually self-contained units centered around massive mother firms. By the middle of 1934 the ministry complained that the industry was overly concentrated, the complexes too large, especially Junkers, and vulnerable to air attacks. Its solution was dispersal and decentralization.[33]

Faulty production programing also resulted from the lack of cooperation within the industry, the technical changes continually requested by the ministry, and the inexperience of many firms. The problem was not easily attacked. The installation of better equipment and controls to improve the quality of aircraft added considerably to production problems. Each improvement in the form of higher-rated engines, superchargers, remote fire-control systems, electronic equipment, pressurized cabins, additional armament, and leak-proof fuel cells complicated the manufacturing process. Subcontracting became more imperative, although many of the mother firms preferred to retain the most difficult operations such as construction of the fuselage, center wing section, and cockpit, and, of course, final aircraft assembly. Frequently subcontracted constructions were wing ailerons, leading edges, trailing edges, flaps, wings, nacelles, wing panels, elevators, tabulators, rudders, fins, tail units, landing gear, cowling, cowl flaps, complete engine and cowling assemblies, oil and fuel tanks, piping ducts, and fittings. Since it was not always feasible to subcontract to plants located in the vicinity of the mother firm, there was considerable cross-hauling. The increased amount of subcontracting placed a tremendous responsibility for procurement of materials on the airframe plants; the employment of large staffs for ordering, locating vendors, follow-up, engineering liaison, preproduction planning, and scheduling was necessary. The Air Ministry encouraged subcontracting as a means of utilizing existing facilities and idle labor in depressed areas while substantially reducing the need for new housing and community services in areas growing up around the new aircraft plants. Subcontracting also enabled the ministry to establish duplicate sources of major items and achieve extensive dispersal and decentralization of production.

The shortage of skilled workers was met in a variety of ways. In May 1934, the Reich railroads gave some of their young trainees to the aircraft industry.[34] This was a stopgap measure until the plants, with the financial assistance of the Air Ministry, could develop their own training programs. The Junkers training system (*Ausbildungswesen der Junkerswerke*) was the largest and became a model for the entire industry. Separately budgeted and completely independent from the Junkers production programs, the system enrolled 60 apprentices in 1934, 150 in 1935, and 600 in 1936.[35] The year-long course was the first of many different ones organized by Junkers, the most popular of which was a six-week introductory program for new employees. By the end of World War II nearly 70,000 workers had been trained by Junkers.

In 1934 the government founded the Bureau for Industrial Workers (Büro für Industriearbeiter, or BfI) to help ease the labor shortage. In 1936 the agency became the Plenipotentiary for Aviation Industrial Personnel and was placed directly under the Technical Office. Eventually it was completely militarized under the command of the Air Quartermaster. Its purpose was to train apprentices, workers, master workmen, and employees for the aircraft industry; to give military students in the aviation technical schools familiarity training; and to train airport ground personnel. Under its auspices a regular system of training workers by job classification was organized, with a central educational headquarters at Dessau (Lehrmittelzentrale des RLM Ffl). Vocational training courses varying in length from two weeks to four years were organized by the office to ensure a uniformity and excellence of training unheard of in most nations.[36]

The low quality of the aircraft produced was a continual source of friction between the ministry, manufacturers, and military units. The Do 11 bomber and its improved versions, the Do 13 and Do 23, and the Ju 52 were particularly criticized for lack of speed and poor maneuverability. The Do 11 could not be used at night; when loaded it was sluggish and underpowered; its wings vibrated alarmingly; and its landing gear was subject to many malfunctions. The Ju 52 was criticized for its lack of speed and poor defensive armament. By the summer of 1934 the Technical Office realized that all of the models then in production would have to be replaced by a new generation of aircraft under development.[37] The mounting criticism forced Major von Richthofen, director of research and development in the Technical Office, in August 1934 to issue some "Development Guidelines" aimed at the critics of the aviation program. In part they read:

A conditional, useful, operative piece of equipment is better than no equipment at all.

For every purpose operational equipment must be developed in the
shortest possible time even if it is an interim or emergency solution
to a problem.

The finest and most complete piece of equipment whose development
is not finished is next to worthless,

An air force must be ready for operations at all times. Only the equipment on hand will be used in the few hours given to achieve the
desired, vital objectives.[38]

By December 1934, the Technical Office became so disenchanted
with the bombers then being manufactured that there was some
discussion of halting production until new prototypes were ready.[39] Only
two of the new bomber prototypes, the Do 17 and the Ju 86, had flown
by the end of 1934, however, and it would take another year to eighteen
months to complete evaluation and begin production. The Technical
Office had little choice; if the Reich were to have a bomber force, it
would have to be with models in production.

The problem of shortages of some critical raw materials appeared in
1934 and grew in importance. Although Germany could purchase more
raw materials per unit of currency than formerly on the depressed world
market, she found her own exports sharply down, resulting in a decrease
in her foreign exchange. Under the impact of rearmament her foreign
exchange dwindled rapidly and by the summer of 1934 the shortage of
foreign exchange needed to buy raw materials abroad closed or was
threatening to close a number of firms, including the second largest
electrolytic-copper works, the Zinnwerke Wilhelmsburg. The Air
Ministry immediately began to encourage producers to simplify and
standardize their raw material requirements and wherever possible to
reduce the amount and number of kinds needed. The substitution of
common metals for those in short supply was particularly recommended.
By December 1934, the ministry could report some success. Airframe
plants had reduced the number of light metals used from eighteen to nine
and the kinds of steel from twenty to fifteen. The number of heavier
metals not including steel was reduced from seventeen to eight. The use
of alloys was credited for much of this reduction.[40] In general, the
shortage of raw materials, like the shortage in labor, continued to loom
as a threat as long as Germany had a depressed economy and an
inadequate supply of foreign exchange.

FINANCING THE AIRCRAFT INDUSTRY'S EXPANSION

The German government tried many methods of financing the
aircraft industry in the prewar years: loans, grants, subsidies, depre-

ciation allowances, guarantees, and, in a few cases, state ownership.
Starting in 1933, it was obvious that the impetus for rapid expansion
would have to come mainly from the government. German private
capital was reluctant to invest in such risky enterprises and the chance of
outside capital coming into the Reich was negligible. There was some
discussion early in 1933 of the possibility of state ownership of aircraft
firms, but the Nazis, for ideological reasons, rejected this in favor of
maintaining private enterprise in the industry wherever possible. This did
not, however, preclude the Air Ministry's takeover of the Junkers and
Arado firms.[41]

The ministry's first move to coax private funds from the suspicious
business community was a guarantee of protection plus a return of 2
percent annual interest on investments in the aircraft firms. When these
measures failed to attract sufficient private financing, the Ministry had
to seek other methods. An interim investment credit system
(Investitionszwischenkredite) was devised in 1933 to disburse interest-
free loans for the improvement of air travel and expansion of aircraft
plants. Repayment was to start only after completion of the work.
Beginning on a rather modest scale, this system pumped nearly 600
million RM into aviation before the war. The agency designed to handle
these funds was the Luftfahrkontar G.m.b.H., founded in 1934 with a
listed stock funding of 20,000 RM. At first it acted as a trustee of the Air
Ministry funds for the construction of buildings, airfields, and
navigational equipment; for air travel; and for investment in plant
expansion. In October 1938, after the need for disguising its activities
from the world was over, its capital stock was raised to 70 million RM
and it concentrated on aircraft firm expansion. All of its administrative
duties related to ground facilities, along with a capital of 5 million RM,
were given to a separate, daughter firm owned by the Air Ministry, the
Luftfahrtanlagen G.m.b.H.[42] Another daughter firm, the Gesellschaft
für Luftfahrtbedarf G.m.b.H., established in Berlin with a capital of 1
million RM, subsidized the aircraft repair industry, which had been
neglected by the airframe plants, and handled materials produced in
state-owned operations.

In 1940 all these firms were reorganized into a joint-stock bank
called the Bank der Deutschen Luftfahrt A.G., or Aero-Bank, with a
capital of 150 million RM. The house bank of the aviation industry, it
generated investment funds, which other banks were reluctant to do;
spread risks among the aircraft firms; extended long-term credit at low
interest rates; and provided the usual banking services. By 1944 the
Aero-Bank had become a giant, controlling 859.6 million RM of the
1,094.8 million RM of working capital of the fifty-three joint-stock

companies engaged in aircraft production. It had a majority of the stock holdings of fifty-one of the fifty-three companies and owned 90 percent of thirty-two,[43] the largest of which was Junkers with a listing of 260 million RM. As long as the Reich participated in financing private firms, representatives of the Air Ministry, Technical Office, or Finance Ministry sat on their boards of directors. In most cases, however, definite provisions were made to repay the Reich, ensuring the industry's return to private ownership.

General contracts were another common method used to finance the industry, although firms receiving state funds were not eligible for them. Aircraft contracts were modeled after the munitions contracts of the 1920s whereby the Ordnance Office guaranteed costs and 10 percent profit, plus an interest-free loan to cover the cost of the new buildings and equipment required. In return the company retained ownership of the newly constructed buildings, but the machinery belonged to the Reich and was leased to the firm, which agreed to maintain and replace it.[44] Advance payments on contracts were also made, normally a 3 percent architectural honorarium, paid once plans for expansion were drawn and accepted. But the most useful method was the immediate downpayment of from 15 percent for large firms to 30 percent for small firms of the total cost of a production project once the contract was let. Then in regular installments the manufacturer received a percentage of the contract until it was completed. This was of great assistance to most firms, since they did not have to borrow money while waiting for payment and could, in fact, finance needed expansion from ongoing contracts. Depreciation allowances, which averaged 4 but in some instances amounted to 25 percent of the cost of machinery, also provided a cushion for rapid expansion.

The most important form of subsidy was the "cost plus" contract. Until 1939 all aviation developmental work and most of the production series airplanes and engines were manufactured under cost plus contracts based on preliminary prices. The final price was arrived at during or after production by the RLM and the factory. The Technical Office recognized that the manufacturers often padded their bills with excessive labor, materials, and machinery costs, but it was assumed that the overcapacity created by the cost plus contracts would be useful in the event of full mobilization.[45]

Beginning in fiscal year 1936 conditions changed. Shortages of foreign exchange, sharp competition between the armed services for defense funds, and bulging domestic spending by the government dictated the need for greater economy. The monetary pinch affected the aircraft firms in many ways; some became parsimonious, others did not.

As the Luftwaffe edged toward a firm-price policy, used effectively for some time with the auxiliary industries, direct funding of expansion replaced the cost plus contracts. The Luftwaffe's Economic Office eagerly tried to press the firms into line with comparative statistics, hoping to strengthen the industry through sharp criticism and a firm price-fixing policy which would make it more productive and competitive with foreign concerns.[46]

The heavy subsidization of the industry through indirect methods like the cost plus contract was not uniformly accepted within the government. As Milch pointed out to Defense Minister Blomberg in a September 1934 memo, the rapid build-up of the aircraft and other armament industries had simply outstripped available means to finance further expansion. A coordinated program of direct governmental and private funding was needed to funnel the nation's resources into rearmament. Milch and Blomberg agreed that plants should be privately owned and strive for an independent financial status. Ideally they should be subsidized only under exceptional circumstances such as relocation from exposed border areas to the interior or as compensation for contract changes. In his memo Milch anticipated two things: the need for overall direction of the nation's resources into the rearmament program such as was later provided under the Four-Year Plan, and the shift from indirect to direct state funding of the aircraft firms, which began in 1935-36.[47] Neither man—both were orthodox and conservative in their economic thinking—could possibly imagine the eventual magnitude of the state's participation in the aircraft industry. In September 1934, Milch thought in terms of a short-range solution to the problem of financing, while Blomberg considered expansion of aircraft plants similar to that of automobile plants. He thought the state should have a limited role in helping develop the basic capacity of the industry, which could be converted in wartime to military production. Both Milch and Blomberg were obviously thinking about aerial rearmament on a modest and limited scale; neither reckoned with the baronial style of Göring and the ambitious foreign policies of Hitler.

Göring set the tone for the aircraft industry with his sybaritic private spending, matched only by his public extravagances. He gave the illusion that money was no object in building the new air force. Symbolic of this attitude was the colossal Air Ministry building constructed in the Leipzigerstrasse in Berlin and soon filled with an army of squabbling and jealous bureaucrats intent on furthering their own interests. Successfully avoiding every attempt to coordinate spending with and bring it under the control of the Defense Ministry, Göring encouraged the grand and lavish expansion of the aircraft industry. The aircraft plants responded by planning and building on a scale suitable for Göring's taste. By the time the war broke out, they had single-shift capacity more than adequate for the general staff demands. Roomy, clean, well-lit, beautifully laid-out factories which impressed visitors and journalists from abroad became the hallmark of the industry. With a plant capacity and production tooling designed for a scale of operations much greater than actually needed earlier, it had some tremendous advantages when it went to war.[48] In fact, the key to German mobilization planning was the overcapacity of the aircraft industry. Unlike England, which intended to use shadow plants—plants quickly converted to wartime production— Germany planned to use her overcapacity in plants and machines on a single-shift basis in peacetime, converting them to two or three shifts in wartime. Theoretically this overcapacity was also insurance against bomb damage.

Financing was only one consideration in the lavish expansion of the aircraft industry. The selection of new plant sites and construction of factory buildings illustrate the welter of factors involved. The military insisted that new plants should be located in secluded areas well removed from the borders, away from prominent landmarks, reasonably far from urban areas or other possible targets, and widely dispersed. The factory management wanted just the opposite, preferring locations where the economic infrastructure (transportation system, energy sources, and manpower) could easily support the new plant. This meant rural areas were to be avoided in preference to urban ones. Mayors and other local officials, party leaders, and businessmen deluged the Technical Office with requests for new industry, stressing the particular advantages of their own communities. Milch and the Technical Office were sensitive to these pressures and sought in the earlier years to relieve some of the worst effects of the depression and to maximize the political effect of the Nazi program by the judicious placement of new industry. Naturally, there was not enough money to build plants everywhere and compromises were made. Usually the deciding factor was time, and this dictated that plants be located where there was an adequate labor force and the necessary economic infrastructure.[49] An example of this was the Berlin-Brandenburg location of the Arado firm in a sandy, marshy area with no airfield but with all the other necessities readily available in Berlin.

The physical construction of the plants was subject to numerous considerations. The layout was designed to protect the plants from bombing, the Air Ministry restricting the total ground area of individual buildings to about 75,000 square feet, except in some rare cases. A typical plant consisted of several buildings distributed in an irregular fashion with wide spaces between them over thirty or forty acres. The buildings were usually metal; wind-resistant; equipped with air-raid shelters, alarm warning systems, and darkening apparatus; and, when possible, decompartmentalized and supplied with their own energy source. Some were of the hangar type with wide clearances and many were of the monitor-roof type with overhead cranes and monorail systems. All the detailed plans had to be approved by the Technical Office and were to follow the German Labor Front's "Schönheit der Arbeit" (beautification program) regulations. Particular emphasis was placed on making the new factories blend with their topographical and architectural settings. An outstanding example in this respect was the Heinkel plant at Oranienburg.

Three men—Milch, Colonel Wimmer of the Technical Office, and his section chief for production, Major Loeb—deserve credit for planning and executing the expansion of the aircraft industry in the remarkably short time of three years. By 1936 most of the plant expansion had been commissioned and the basic structure of the industry established. The methods of financing, the manner of plant selection, and the quality of plant construction were such that they appreciably raised the cost of aircraft production in the late 1930s, an important factor when Germany tried to export her aircraft. The Economic Office, which monitored profitability within the industry and arranged contractual details between the ministry producers and foreign buyers, was keenly aware of this problem.[50] The many vigorous complaints about high aircraft costs went unheeded until the foreign exchange pinch of 1936, when exporting became desirable, but by that time the industry had become accommodated to the Göring style of living.

RESULTS OF THE FIRST TWO YEARS UNDER THE NAZIS

Measured by any gauge, the first two years' growth of the aircraft industry under the Third Reich was impressive. The fragile child of 1933 had grown lustily. The original total of eight airframe and six engine firms, debt-ridden and near collapse, grew to fifteen airframe and seven engine firms, all booming and financially sound. The five leading airframe and three leading engine firms already were developing into complexes of considerable size, controlling the production of numerous satellites and subcontractors. The accompanying and expected growing pains developed but were endured and much of importance was learned in these years. The Air Ministry production team of Milch, Wimmer, Richthofen, and Loeb functioned smoothly with Göring's military team of Wever, Kesselring, and Stumpff. These were heady days when the adventure and excitement of building a new, powerful Luftwaffe permeated the air. Soldiers, officials, designers, builders, and flyers considered them the happiest days of their lives.[51]

Statistically these builders of the new Luftwaffe had done their work well. Although by December 31, 1934, 1,959 aircraft—approximately 6 percent below the projected total of 2,090—had been released to the flying units,[52] half were trainers and many of the combat aircraft were inferior, obsolescent models suitable only as reserves; yet they did represent a military force of some importance. By March 1935, when Hitler and Göring openly proclaimed the new Luftwaffe, nearly 2,500 aircraft had been delivered and 800 of them were operationally ready.

Employment statistics in the aircraft industry also indicated the rapid growth during these years. In the first two years of Hitler's rule employment jumped from 3,988 to 53,865 (see table 4). The work force in airframe plants was young (68.1 percent between the ages of eighteen and thirty-five), skilled (71.2 percent were listed as skilled workers), and of course highly susceptible to the draft.[53]

TABLE 4

EMPLOYMENT IN THE AIRFRAME AND ENGINE PLANTS, January 1933-January 1934

Date	Airframe Plants	Engine Plants	Total
January 31, 1933	2,813	1,175	3,988
April 30, 1933	4,344	1,611	5,955
July 31, 1933	5,859	2,381	8,340
October 31, 1933	7,491	4,144	11,635
January 31, 1934	11,102	5,769	16,871
April 30, 1934	20,666	8,265	29,931
July 31, 1934	28,378	11,189	39,567
October 31, 1934	29,541	13,553	43,094
January 31, 1935	37,869	15,996	53,865

SOURCE: Gesamter Personalbestand in der Flugzeugzellen und Motorenindustrie, Reichsverbandes der Deutschen Luftfahrtindustrie, Lw 103/6, DZ/MGFA.

The total value of production from the airframe plants rose from 32,422,529 RM in 1933 to 154,271,856 RM in 1934, a nearly fivefold increase, while that of the engine plants jumped from 26,295,897 RM in 1933 to 87,808,782 RM in 1934, a growth of almost 350 percent.[54] The base of the aircraft industry had been laid.

NOTES

1. Statistisches Reichsamt, Abt, VII, *Industrielle Productionsstatistik, A. Die Flugzeugindustrie 1933-36*, NA Microcopy T-177/32/3720917-20.

2. Wood and Dempster, *Narrow Margin*, p. 35.

3. "1000 Flugzeug-Programm," A 2 Nr. 793/33 geh. Kdos. I, 22.5. 1933, Lw 103/65, DZ/MGFA.

4. Von Rohden materials, NA Microcopy T-971/27/379-81: "Die technische Luftrüstung und Luftwaffenindustrie-Beschaffung-Fertigung," Lw 103/39, DZ/MGFA.

5. "1000 Flugzeug-Programm," Lw 103/65, and answers from A 2 dated 26.5.1933, Lw 103/65, DZ/MGFA.

6. Eberhard Schmidt, "Grundlagen und Wandlungen der deutschen Flugzeugindustrie in den Jahren 1933-1945," *Flug-Wehr und Technik* 1 and 2 (January and February 1947), 20-21; "Einflussnahme der Führung auf die Entwicklung der verschiedensten Flugzeugmuster und Ausstattung der Verbände mit Flugzeugen," Anlage bei Deichmann, 23.4.1956, Lw 124, DZ/MGFA.

7. Haushaltsplan-Gesamtprogramm 1933, C Nr. 1400/33 R, den 21.7.1933, von Rohden document (4376-680), BA/F.

8. Ibid. The official budget for the RLM was listed as 78.3 million RM for 1933-34 and 210 million RM for 1934-35, although Milch asserted it was in reality five times higher using the same formula cited here (Irving, *Milch*, p. 407).

9. Reichwehrminister, Luftschatzamt, LA 1273/33, g.Kdos. A/II, den 7.Juli 1933 mit Anlage, "Protokoll der Besprechung Staatssekretär Milch-Oberst von Reichnau am 19.6.1933," DZ/MGFA.

10. Der Chef der Heeresleitung, TA Nr. 588/33 geh. Kdos., T1 II, Berlin, den 13 Juli 1933, DZ/MGFA.

11. Der Reichsminister der Luftfahrt, Flugzeugbeschaffungsprogramm für den 1. und 2. Aufstellungsabschnitt, LC Nr. 1803/33 B., g. Kdos., 22.9.1933, DZ/MGFA.

12. Haase-Berton, "Der Aufbau der Luftwaffe-Rüstungsindustrie," 24.2. 1954, Lw 103/39; "Planung und Auswahl bei der deutschen Luftwaffe zur Einführung gekommenen Flugzeuge," Lw 142, DZ/MGFA.

13. Fliegerstabsingenieur Belter, "Grundsätzliche Betrachtungen zum Beschaffungsgang: Die Planung der Beschaffung von Flugzeugen," 22.3.1956, Lw 103/25, DZ/MGFA.

14. The most complete study of rationalization is Robert A. Brady, *The Rationalization Movement in German Industry* (Berkeley: University of California Press, 1953), pp. 158-65.

15. USSBS, *Aircraft Division Industry Report*, January 1947, pp. 15-17.

16. The four firms were the ATG (Leipzig), Blohm and Voss (Hamburg), Dessauer Waggenfabrik (Dessau) and the Junkers plant (Dessau).

17. "Die Entwicklung von 'Dessau' im Jahre 1934 von Dr. Dr. Ing. Heinrich Koppenberg," January 1935, Lw 103/43, DZ/MGFA.

18. Suchenwirth, *Development of the German Air Force*, p. 120.

19. USSBS, *Aircraft Industry*, pp. 20-21.

20. Figures for 1933 derived from "RLM, LC III, g.Kdos, Laufende monatliche Lieferung an Flugzeugen vom 1.1.34 bis 31.7.35," Lw 103/6, DZ/MGFA, and "Bemerkungen zur Beurteilung der Erzeugung am Kriegsflugzeugen," G.L. 1/111, Nr. 345/39 g.Kdos. 13.Mai 1939, von Rohden document (4376-1914), BA/F. The total accepted by the Luftwaffe in 1933 were 2 army reconnaissance planes (He 45 and He 46); 12 naval reconnaissance planes (Do Wal, He 60, Do 18); 3 army fighters (Ar 64, Ar 65, He 51); 12 navy fighters (He

38, He 51); 15 bombers (Do 11, Do 17, Do 13, He 111, Ju 52, Ju 86); 119 single-engined trainers; 31 multi-engined trainers; and 2 transports. In addition to the military aircraft, about 175 civilian airplanes were also built in 1933, which meant an average of 31 aircraft per month for the aircraft industry.

21. Gesamte Personalbestand in der Flugzeugzellen und Motorindustrie-Reichsverbandes der Deut. Luftfahrtindustrie, Lw 103/6, DZ/MGFA. For similar problems in the British aircraft industry, see M. M. Postan, D. Hay, and J. D. Scott, *Design and Development of Weapons, Studies in Government and Industrial Organization: History of the Second World War* (London: H.M.S.O., 1964), chaps. 4, 7, 8.

22. LA/LC Nr. 200/39 g.Kdos. A II 2A, Flugzeugbeschaffungsprogramm für den 1. und 2. Aufstellungsabschnitt, 19.Jan.1934, Lw 103/69, DZ/MGFA.

23. Wood and Dempster, *Narrow Margin*, pp. 34-35; von Rohden materials, NA Microcopy T-971/27/381-84; "Planung der Flugzeugzellen-Industrie, Vortrag des Herrn Ing. Haase, am 25.7.1934 für die W. O. Luft," von Rohden document (4376-1805), BA/F.

24. RLM, LC III, Monatliche Motorenausbringung vom 1.Jan.1934 bis 31. Juli. 1935, Lw 103/6, DZ/MGFA.

25. Information on production programs in this and ensuing paragraphs taken from Fliegerstabsingenieur Belter, "Grundsätzliche Betrachtungen zum Beschaffungsgang: Die Planung der Beschaffung von Flugzeugen," 22.3.1956, Lw 103/25, DZ/MGFA.

26. Erstes Flugzeugbeschaffungsprogramm, Stand vom 1.3.1934, Akte II L 49, DZ/MGFA.

27. For example, in the 1930s Germany bought from the United States 19 aircraft valued at slightly over one-half million dollars and 569 engines valued at $3.5 million. By far the most active trade year was 1934, when one-third of the engines and 8 aircraft valued at $300,000 were bought; see Wolfred Bauer, "The Shipment of American Strategic Raw Materials to Nazi Germany: A Study in the United States Economic Foreign Policy, 1933-1939" (Ph.D. dissertation, University of Washington, 1964).

28. Freiherr v. Richthofen Notien, "Protokoll zu Besprechung mit den Vertretern der Motorenfirmen vom 20./21/9/1934," von Rohden document (4406-526), BA/F.

29. RLM Folder 239, Letter to Adm. Lahs from BMW director, June 20, 1934, NA Microcopy T-177/21/3706743-50.

30. RLM Folder 239, personal letter from BMW director to Freiherr von Richthofen, October 20, 1934, NA Microcopy T-177/21/3706739-42.

31. Richthofen Notien, von Rohden document (4406-526) BA/F; "Entworf zu dem Vortrag vor der Flugmotoren—Industrie am 20.9.1934 im RLM," Lw 103/65, DZ/MGFA.

32. Reichsverbandes der Deutschen ·Luftfahrt-Industrie, 9.Mai 1934, RLM Folder 225, NA Microcopy T-83/68/3440508-14.

33. "Planung der Flugzeugzellen-Industrie, Vortrag des Herrn Ing. Haase am 25.7.1934 für die W. O. Luft," von Rohden document (4376-1805), BA/F. There is a partial account of this speech in RLM Folder 255, NA Microcopy T-177/29/3717290-96.

34. RLM Folder 225, NA Microcopy T-83/68/34440508-10.

35. Koppenberg, "Die Entwicklung von 'Dessau' im Jahre 1934," Lw 103/43,

DZ/MGFA.

36. "Die Ausbildung in der Luftfahrt-Industrie," von Dr. Ing. E. Krause, 5.3.1957, Lw 103/40, DZ/MGFA.

37. Aktennotiz vom 18.7.1934 betr. Telefongespräch Oberst Sperrle/Geerdts, Akte II L 51/9, DZ/MGFA; Rieckhoff, *Trumpf oder Bluff*, p. 126.

38. Entwicklungsgrundsätze, LC II (Akte H ib) Nr. 4126/34, g.Kdos., Berlin, den 2.8.1934, RLM Folder 247, NA Microcopy T-177/25/3711534-40.

39. Besprechungsprotokolle LC II, LC- Besprechungen (Akte E 1635), 19.12.1934 Besprechung zwischen Kommodore Sprelle, Keller und Amtschef LC über Sachlage Do 11, DZ/MGFA.

40. "Werkstoff- und Rohstofflage 1934, Vortrag Prof. Beck, 5.11.1934," Lw 103/36, DZ/MGFA; Carroll, *Design for War*, p. 100.

41. For financing of the aircraft industry, see "Gedankengänge zu der Frage der Finanzierung der Luftfahrt-Industrie," 14.2.1937, Lw 103/7, DZ/MGFA; "Wege und Formen der Investitionsfinanzierung der deutschen Luftfahrt-Industrie in den Jahren 1933-1945," von Dr. Nowak, 6.7.1956, Lw 103/25, DZ/MGFA; Hertel, "Die Beschaffung," Maxwell Air Force Base; interviews of Ministerialrat Müller, 17.9.1945, von Rohden document (4376-463), BA/F; "Foreign Logistical Organizations and Methods: A Report for the Secretary of the Army," 15 October 1947, Maxwell Air Force Base.

42. "Aufgaben, Entwicklung und Tätigkeit der Bank Deutschen Luftfahrt A. G. Berlin," 18.8.1956, Lw 103/21, DZ/MGFA.

43. Ibid.; Hertel, "Die Beschaffung," p. 194.

44. Karl Nuss, "Einige Aspekts der Zusammenarbeit von Heereswaffenamt und Rüstungskonzernen vor dem zweiten Weltkrieg," *Zeitschrift für Militärgeschichte* 4 (1965): 436-37.

45. Hertel, "Die Beschaffung," p. 197: Obersting. Mix, "Ueber die Geräteentwicklung bei der Luftwaffe," Lw 103/63, DZ/MGFA.

46. On firm price fixing, see Lt. Col. Ploch's memo to Generalmajor Volkmann, LC Nr. 11779/36 III Geh., Berlin, 12.Dez.1936, von Rohden document (4406-588), BA/F.

47. See Milch's memo to Blomberg and his reply Sept. 25, 1934, on NA Microcopy, Folder Wi/IF 5.326, T-77/70/790458-68.

48. USSBS, *Aircraft Industry*, pp. 19-22; Webster and Frankland, *Strategic Air Offensive* p. 276. For the British example of aircraft industry development, see Postan et al., *Design and Development of Weapons*, pp. 150-53.

49. On plant selection, see "Vortrag des Herrn Ing. Haase am 25.7.1934," von Rohden document (4376-1805), BA/F; "Industrieplanung und Industrie-Ausbau," Lw 103/42, DZ/MGFA; Obersting. z. Wv. Haase-Berton, "Der Aufbau der Luftwaffen-Rüstungsindustrie," 24.2.1954, Lw 103/39, DZ/MGFA; "Richtlinen der Luftschutzes für den Aufbau der Luftwaffen-Rüstungsindustrie," Haase-Berton, 26.5.1955, Lw 103/43, DZ/MGFA; Hertel, "Die Beschaffung," pp. 221-230.

50. Interviews of General der Flieger Förster, 20.7.1945; Ministerialrat Müller, 17.9.145 and 3.11.1945; and General Christian, 20.4.1945, von Rohden document (4376-463), BA/F; "Die Finanzierung der deutschen Luftrüstung," von Rohden document (4376-470), BA/F; "Die technische Organisation in der deutschen Luftfahrt," Lw 103/25, DZ/MGFA.

51. For a typical account of these euphoric days, see Kesselring, *Soldat*, pp. 43-45, 458-60.

52. Flugzeugbeschaffungsprogramm vom 1.7.1934, Stand vom Dezember 1934, mit Angaben über die ausgelieferten Flugzeuge, Akte L II, 1296, DZ/MGFA.

53. Figures on the labor force computed from RLM Folder 284, NA Microcopy T-177/31/3720917-25.

54. Ibid., frame 3720922.

CHAPTER 5

Quiet Years of Growth, 1935–36

ON MARCH 10, 1935, in an interview with *London Daily Mail* correspondent Ward Price, Hermann Göring announced to the world the existence of the Luftwaffe.[1] A few days later Hitler introduced conscription and proclaimed his intention of building an army of thirty-six divisions. Both announcements occasioned little surprise among informed observers, since German secret rearmament had been reported in the international press. The worldwide response was anger confined to verbal protests.[2] Exactly one month after the Luftwaffe was proclaimed, its new commander, Göring, resplendent in the uniform of a General der Flieger, married the actress Emmy Sonnemann in a dazzling ceremony that was the social event of the year. Lining Berlin streets to see the wedding procession, thousands shouted "Heil Hitler!" and "Hoch Hermann!" while fighter planes of the newly christened Jagdgeschwader Manfred von Richthofen 2 swept overhead in perfect formation. The newest and most glamorous branch of the German armed services was born in an aura of contrived publicity.

The Luftwaffe of March 1935 was not as formidable as the Nazis would have had outsiders believe. The training of its units had just begun; of 2,500 aircraft only 800 were operationally ready. Although Hitler could boast on March 25 to his English visitors, Sir John Simon, Foreign Secretary, and Sir Anthony Eden, Lord Privy Seal, that the Luftwaffe was already the size of the Royal Air Force, he was counting unarmed trainers as combat aircraft. The willingness of foreigners to accept Hitler's exaggerated claims was surprising.[3]

The aircraft industry was also far more formidable in appearance than in reality. The first two years of Nazi rule laid the foundation for it, but the next years brought momentous changes. After the initial steep rise in production, output plateaued around 5,500 planes per year and remained there until 1939, while the relationship between the Air Ministry and the industry underwent fundamental alterations. The entire aerial rearmament program, previously largely uncoordinated and free-wheeling, was more closely integrated into the total armament plans.

Important personnel changes were also made which shifted the direction and nature of the industry, and in the crucial area of aircraft model selection vital decisions were made that materially affected the outcome of World War II.

In foreign affairs, 1935 and 1936 were years of preparation. After the debacle of his attempted 1934 Austrian coup, Hitler was more circumspect in dealing with foreign countries. The Nazis prepared a tremendous propaganda campaign which brought them victory in the Saar plebiscite, the first of a series of Hitler's diplomatic victories leading to Munich. Germany's growing aerial strength paved the way for these triumphs, while the aircraft industry worked mightily to give substance to the Führer's threats. Each of Hitler's moves had repercussions on the industry: programs were expanded or changed, models added or deleted, and personnel cashiered or promoted at an increasingly bewildering tempo.

PERSONNEL CHANGES, 1935-36

The original team that Göring gathered around him worked smoothly and effectively during the first three years. The adroit placement of competent officers in key positions by Stumpff insulated the Luftwaffe from the pernicious influence of enthusiastic but amateurish Nazis. Beneath Göring, the Luftwaffe was well led by Milch, the capable and energetic secretary of the ministry; Wever, the brilliant theorist and chief of staff; Wimmer, reliable and steady in the Technical Office, and his two chief assistants, Loeb in production and Richthofen in development; Kesselring in administration; Stumpff in personnel; and Fisch in general aviation. The party hacks and personal cronies of Göring had been relegated to prestigious but less important posts where they were isolated from the development of the Luftwaffe. The newest branch of the armed services was a highly technical one that had not attracted the organizational attention of the Nazi party. There was no powerful Nazi party organization like the SA in aviation; the Nazi flying groups were tiny and composed primarily of young enthusiasts. Göring held his position in the party as a powerful individual and not as the leader of any mass party organization, so the Luftwaffe was less subjected to party pressure.

The linchpin in the Luftwaffe leadership team was Wever. He had the proper touch to keep the volatile personalities within the top command operating harmoniously. His calm and steady manner, virtually devoid of personal ambition and egoism, had a moderating influence on the sensitive, ambitious Milch and Göring. His warm and open sympathies with Hitler's aspirations and policies reassured both the party and the military that the closest cooperation could be expected from the Luftwaffe.[4] Neither a politician nor an aviation expert, Wever, the professional soldier, presented no personal threat to either Göring or Milch. He got along well with his two superiors, probably because of his unfailing tact and his preference for working unobtrusively in the background. Milch in particular had an exemplary working relationship with him, respecting him more as an equal than as a subordinate—something that could not be said of Milch's relations with later chiefs of staff.[5]

By early 1936 the triangular relationship between Göring, Milch, and Wever was undergoing considerable strain due to Göring's flagging interest in Luftwaffe matters and Milch's growing ambitions. Göring, with his plethora of offices and outside interests, was growing weary of the demanding duties of running the Luftwaffe. Never the worker or professional soldier who had acquired the broad knowledge and skill necessary for his exalted rank through long years of experience, he found himself in an increasingly untenable position. His undiminished love for the pomp and prestige of his high military office was unmatched by his energies and abilities. In the wings his able and tireless crown prince, Milch, watched for the opportunity to become commander in name, as well as in fact, of the Luftwaffe, while his amiable chief of staff, Wever, enjoyed the quiet confidence of the rank and file of the officers corps that Göring had never had. Göring's relationship with Milch had always been one of convenience for both men. Both had rocketed in the military ranks; Milch had one grade lower than Göring but was promoted as rapidly as his chief. In March 1934, Milch was Generalmajor, a year later Generalleutnant, and on April 20, 1936, General der Flieger. In 1938 when Göring received his field marshal's baton, Milch was promoted to Generaloberst, and in 1940 he too became a field marshal when Göring was elevated to the unique rank of Reichmarchall. As his promotions indicated, Milch's military duties increased while his civilian duties diminished. As early as 1935, he was named deputy to the commander of the Luftwaffe, a position of singular importance. Göring soon found that his relationship of convenience had become one of necessity as Milch shouldered the bulk of Göring's aviational responsibilities.

By 1936 Göring was searching for a method to counterbalance Milch, whose position seemed impregnable since his organizational and managerial abilities were indispensable. No one knew better how to cover his exposed political flank than Milch. He had carefully built up his connections with Hitler and the Nazi party, even appointing a ranking party functionary to a high ministerial rank and employing him on his personal staff to handle political matters.[6] Milch was vulnerable in one respect; he, like Göring, was not a professional soldier, a fact which irked the Luftwaffe command.

Additional stress on Göring, Milch, and Wever was caused by the young officers' lobbying for a Luftwaffe general staff comparable to that of the army. Göring had at first resisted the idea, for the indolent and insecure commander did not relish the thought of an all-powerful general staff that might usurp his prerogatives. Wever was also unenthusiastic but for a different reason. He felt that the incorporation of an elite group that might develop into a separate caste would unduly jeopardize the unity of the Luftwaffe officer corps, which was so heterogeneous that he thought it wiser to allow it to mature before instituting a general staff. By 1935 he began to relent, for in that year plans for the Air War and Air Technical Academies were accepted and the Luftwaffe could soon provide well-trained general staff officers. The next year, despite the persistent opposition of Milch and some of Göring's inner circle of friends, Göring approved the formation of a Luftwaffe general staff. The professional soldiers wanted the chief of the general staff above Milch in command, leaving only one "nonsoldier," Göring, at the top. They assumed that, given Göring's nature, the chief of the general staff would actually function as the commander in chief. But this was not to be. Göring insisted on keeping Milch as his deputy and maintaining a safe balance between his two potentially powerful rivals; he could not sacrifice Milch, even though he was increasingly embittered by Milch's many public appearances which gave the impression that he was running the entire show.[7] Göring was further incensed by Milch's occasional private references to himself as the minister; but he had learned well from Hitler, it was far better to have two rivals at each others' throats than a powerful one at one's own.

The order establishing the Luftwaffe general staff became effective on August 1, 1936, but Wever, who would have been its first chief, was dead. On June 3, in his haste to fly from Dresden to Berlin for the state funeral of General Karl von Litzmann, the World War I hero of Brcezeny, Wever, an inexperienced flier, forgot to release the aileron lock on his Heinkel Blitz. He and his flight engineer were instantly killed on takeoff, and the Luftwaffe lost one of its finest officers. Wever's death triggered a series of personnel changes that intensified the already strained relationships in the high command of the Luftwaffe. Kesselring was appointed Wever's successor and soon found himself embroiled in a feud with Milch. Milch bent every means at his disposal to maintain and even increase his influence over Kesselring, but the tough soldier stubbornly rejected his interference. Kesselring was determined to make the chief of the general staff independent from Milch; and when that proved impossible, he requested on May 30, 1937, that he be either relieved or allowed to resign. Göring complied with his request, appointed him commanding general of the Third Air Administrative Area, and brought in the more pliable Stumpff as chief of staff. However, on June 2, 1937, Göring undercut Milch's position by ordering the Luftwaffe general staff directly responsible to himself, thus placing Milch in a state of limbo as far as military operations were concerned.[8]

The death of Wever also brought a major change in the Technical Office. On June 9, 1936, Ernst Udet was named Wimmer's successor as chief of the Technical Office. A colorful and charming character, Udet could have risen to the highest technical office in German aviation only in an intensely propaganda-oriented regime such as the Third Reich. He had been a flying enthusiast in his early school days and by the age of twenty-one, as an enlistee in World War I, had become the top combat pilot of Imperial Germany. He eventually achieved sixty-two aerial victories, a record second only to that of the legendary Freiherr von Richthofen, the "Red Baron." As the ranking surviving ace of World War I he found himself covered with honors, a world celebrity. Rather than remain in the aviationless German army after the war, he chose a career in business, stunt flying, and acting. In 1921 he organized a small aircraft factory which merged with another owned by the former fighter pilot Erich Scheuermann, later a general in the Luftwaffe's Engineer Corps. Lacking business acumen, a restless free spirit, he left his company in 1926. He became involved in movie making in Greenland and Africa and continued to perform in stunt-flying shows. A gregarious man with a quick sense of humor, an avid hunter, story teller, gifted amateur cartoonist, and incredibly daring pilot, Udet moved easily in the world of international celebrities of the 1920s. He enjoyed immensely *la dolce Vita* even though it caused the collapse of his short-lived marriage to Eleonore "Lo" Zink.[9]

Once the Nazis came to power they drew this national hero into the aviation program, although Udet was not personally sympathetic with Nazism. Göring, who had been Udet's commander during the waning days of the war, and Bruno Loerzer, another Pour le Mérite flier, persuaded Udet to accept the honorary post of vice commander of the German Aviation Association (Deutscher Luftverband). His great reputation, his easy and continual association with the ranking military and political leaders of the Third Reich, and his own growing involvement in dive-bombing techniques drew him inexorably to the Luftwaffe. In June 1935, he entered the air force with the rank of colonel, his appointment arranged by Milch, Wever, and Stumpff. On

February 10, 1936, he succeeded Ritter von Greim as inspector of fighter and dive bomber forces, a position for which he was eminently qualified by his superb sense of flying light aircraft; however, he did not remain long at that post. Hitler tapped him for the Technical Office post, quite erroneously believing him to be not only one of Germany's greatest fliers but also one of the Reich's top technical experts in aviation. Göring had no illusions about Udet's limitations, for he had wanted Udet in the Luftwaffe for his fame rather than his ability. Never friendly with Udet, Göring appointed him at Hitler's insistence. When even Udet expressed his reservations about accepting such an important administrative and technical post, Göring brushed them aside with the comment that "others would be there to do the work." Göring was more candid with Milch and complained that Udet had neither the personal balance and strength nor the technical competence to handle the job, but he had to bow in this matter to the Führer's wishes.[10]

Udet inherited a smoothly running, quietly efficient Technical Office from Wimmer. The early, methodical developmental work had paid off in a new generation of superior aircraft. But many problems were brewing, most of them in production, where Udet had the least competence. Quite early in his tour of duty he lost his production chief, Loeb, who was appointed by Göring to head an important office within the Four-Year Plan. His loss was irreparable, and Udet had to build his own staff from less able subordinates. Perforce he gravitated toward the sympathetic and eager Milch. The relationship between the two was harmonious, but soon competition and inner power struggles caused dissension.[11] The sensitive, warm-hearted Udet found himself surrounded by intrigues and slyly calculated plots designed to prey on his human frailties.

PROGRAMS AND PROBLEMS

The first part of the Rhineland Program was so successful that Milch ordered a larger and more comprehensive production plan on January 1, 1935, raising the annual output from 3,183 aircraft in 1935 to 5,112 in 1936.[12] The new procurement plan extended the terminal date of the Rhineland Program from October 1, 1935 to October 1, 1936. It was divided into three stages, one for each of the years involved, and at its conclusion the Air Ministry would have ordered a total of 9,853 airplanes since 1933. The biggest model change occurred in the bombers; the Do 11 and Do 13 were to be phased out of operational into training units as quickly as possible and replaced by Ju 86s and He 111s. Milch depended particularly on the rapid development and deployment of the Ju 86 to meet the needs of the bomber formations. Most of the other models remained the same, but for the first time a heavy bomber, the Ju 89, was included. Seven of the four-engined heavy bomber prototypes were scheduled.

By October 1935, Milch drew up an additional program (Zusatzprogramm Nr. 1) which called for the production of 1,305 more aircraft, including 270 medium bombers of the Ju 86 and He 111 type, and the construction of 38 emergency flying strips (*Einsatzhäfen*) for use as dispersal bases.[13] This new program and the extension of the Rhineland Program were combined and transmitted to the industry in the form of Production Plan no. 1 (Lieferplan Nr. 1) to run from October 1, 1935, to April 1, 1936.[14] It called for the production of the 9,853 airplanes under the old plan plus the 1,305 on the additional program, for a total of 11,158. The breakdown by type, model, and number can be seen in table 5.[15] Two things are of note: the large number of trainers and the marked accent on bombers. Milch and Wever were still counting on the 1,849 bombers as a shield for further rearmament even though many of them were overage and of limited combat effectiveness.

During 1936 three more production plans were devised by the ministry and sent to the aircraft industry. The continual changes in plans were caused by three factors: countless delays due to the unpredictable nature of aircraft development, constant pressure exerted by Göring to increase aircraft output, and production problems within the industry.

Airplanes scheduled for series production were months or even years late. Meanwhile, units being formed needed to be equipped. The Air Ministry had to compensate for delays in new aircraft by substituting existing models, usually by increasing the monthly rate with the assignment of an additional plant to the job or by extending the time a model was to remain in production. Thus the many developmental and production problems encountered in introducing the new generation of medium bombers, the Ju 86, He 111, and Do 17, were compensated for by continued production of obsolete aircraft like the Do 23 and especially the He 70 and Ju 52 auxiliary bombers. The Air Ministry knew that the older aircraft could be used later as transports and trainers; in fact, the German Transport Command was built more by accident than by design. The Ju 52, a rugged, dependable, and easy-to-fly airplane, was kept in production plans as compensation for delays in introducing other aircraft. As a result, the Luftwaffe soon had over a thousand, which eventually allowed it to organize the Transport Command in the late 1930s. Indeed, a miniature history of the Luftwaffe and its procurement programs can be written on the Ju 52 alone.

TABLE 5

PRODUCTION PLAN NO. 1

Type	Model	Number Ordered	Totals
COMBAT AIRCRAFT (ARMY)			
Reconnaissance			
long-range	He 45, Do 17	524	
short-range	He 46	425	
auxiliary	He 70	52	
Fighters	Ar 64, 65, 68, He 51	970	
Bombers			
medium	Do 11, 23, Ju 86, Do 17,		
	He 111	1,221	
heavy	Ju 89	3	
auxiliary	Ju 52	116	
	He 70	36	
dive	He 123	190	
	He 50, Ju 87	283	
	Total combat aircraft (army)		3,820
COMBAT AIRCRAFT (NAVY)			
Reconnaissance			
long-range	Do Wal, Do 18	76	
short-range	He 60	277	
Fighters	He 38, 51	43	
Multipurpose	He 59	66	
	Total combat aircraft (navy)		462
NONCOMBAT AIRCRAFT			
Trainers			
primary (army)		4,509	
(navy)		85	
intermediate (army)		1,232	
(navy)		115	
advanced		122	
Transports		762	
Miscellaneous		51	
	Total noncombat aircraft		6,876
	GRAND TOTAL ALL AIRCRAFT		11,158

Another aspect of the unpredictability of aircraft development is that the intrinsic value of an airplane can be determined by only near-combat or combat use by regular units. No amount of preliminary testing can do it, and some aircraft were never successful. The Do 11, 13, and 23 were examples; the Ju 86 shortly joined their ranks, and the He 177 and Me 210 were classic cases during the war. Some airplanes had

reputations which they eventually overcame; the Bf 109, first considered
a nasty brute, then a favorite with all units, was in this category. Then
some airplanes, like the Ju 52 and He 111, were from the beginning
considered "good birds." The Air Ministry had to make allowances for
this in their planning.

The constant pressure exerted by Göring to maintain and increase
the output further complicated production planning. He and Hitler were
number conscious, and the technical difficulties in production meant
nothing to them. Statistically measured output was their criterion, but
they were not explicit with their subordinate planners. In the increasingly
rare personal interviews that Milch had with Göring from 1934 on, Milch
found it difficult to judge how fast and for what purpose the Luftwaffe
was being built, important considerations for any effective long-range
planning. Since Milch was not privy to the innermost planning of his
superiors, he and the others in the Air Ministry conformed to the
pressure for greater production in an automatic manner: quantitative
demands brought quantitative responses. Maintaining numerical
production became the prime consideration of the Air Ministry; as
Göring so cynically said, the most important thing was "to impress
Hitler and to enable Hitler, in turn, to impress the world."[16]

Milch and the Technical Office planners were far too astute
industrial managers not to realize that the erratic planning of the higher
leadership had to be smoothed out before being forwarded to the plants.
Their objective was to build the basic capacity of the industry and keep it
working at nearly optimum level. Since it took so long to tool up for
serial production, very often Milch had to juggle the political demands
for increased production and the technical demands of the Luftwaffe for
new equipment with the industrial capacity available. Compromises were
inevitable in the attempt to maintain a steady output from the industry.
The results were often lower production, premature forcing of
prototypes or prolongation of older models, and much shifting and
changing, not to mention the enormous strain on everyone involved.[17]

In March, July, and October of 1936, Production Plans no. 2, 3,
and 4 were issued to the industry. Plan no. 2 increased slightly the total
number of aircraft on order, from 11,158 to 12,309, but it was mainly
concerned with adjustment of models that were having developmental
problems. Plan no. 3 was also an interim one designed to make minor
adjustments,[18] but Plan no. 4 was an ambitious, full-blown program
incorporating many new model changes.[19] It was to run from October 1,
1936, to March 31, 1938, and listed an impossibly high total of eighty
models and variants, including a small number of the new so-called speed
bombers, the Ju 88 and the Bf 162. Some principal aircraft ordered were:

Type	Model	Produced before 10/1/1936	Produced from 10/1/1936 to 3/31/1938	Total Ordered
Reconnaissance				
long-range	Do 17	0	270	270
	He 45	392	80	472
short-range	He 46	416	27	443
Fighters	He 51	504	2	506
	Ar 68	242	272	514
	Ar 64, 65	189	0	189
	Bf 109	0	740	740
	Bf 110	0	104	104
Bombers	Ju 86	33	655	688
	He 111	7	824	831
	Do 17	20	498	518
	Do 23	273	0	273
Dive bombers	Ju 87	0	264	264
Auxiliary bombers and transports	Ju 52	787	317	1,104

The shift from the older models to a new generation can be seen from production figures before and after October 1936. Older models were being phased out in preference to newer models, which meant extensive retooling with a corresponding loss in production.

The speed of expansion in the industry can be appreciated from a Technical Office report of early 1935 which indicated that five firms were involved in major relocation projects, forty-four were engaged in major plant expansion, and eight more were planning one or the other.[20] Another gauge of the speed of expansion was the increase in factory floor space.[21] Floor-space capacity in the airframe industry rose as follows:

May 1, 1933	30,000 square meters
May 1, 1934	120,000 square meters
May 1, 1935	231,000 square meters
May 1, 1936	450,000 square meters
May 1, 1937	720,000 square meters
May 1, 1938	1,001,000 square meters

The Air Ministry paid for almost all this expansion. Heinkel's new Oranienburg plant was typical. In 1935 when the He 111 was ready for series production, the ministry ordered a new plant built to produce it exclusively. Heinkel proved difficult during contract negotiations and the ministry threatened that either he build it or the state would. Eventually General Loeb of the Technical Office worked out a compromise whereby the plant was built with government money under Heinkel's direction. Heinkel received 150,000 RM of the new plant's working capital of 5 million RM in return for the use of his name and for his technical assistance. The contract was signed on November 11, 1935, and called for a 2,000-man plant producing 32 He 111s monthly under normal peacetime conditions. The first spade of dirt was turned on May 4, 1936, and exactly one year later the first plane rolled out of the still incomplete plant. By November 1938, production reached full capacity. The total cost of construction was 51,630,000 RM; 802,480 RM was raised through

TABLE 6

EMPLOYMENT BY FIRMS IN THE AIRCRAFT INDUSTRY, JULY 1935

AIRFRAME FIRMS	
Aero Sport	908
AEG (Allegemeine Elektrizitäts Gesellschaft)	170
ATG (Allegemeine Transportanlagen-Gesellschaft)	3,902
Apparatebau Oscherslaben	1,156
Arado	3,749
Bayerische Flugzeugwerke	2,344
Blohm & Voss	1,496
Bücker	196
Dornier	7,080
Erla	698
Fieseler	1,027
Focke-Wulf	3,174
Gotha	492
Grotrian-Steinweg	105
Heinkel	7,611
Henschel	3,672
Junkers	9,483
Klemm	1,527
MIAG	--
Weser	2,178
Von Kehler & Stellino	138
TOTAL	51,106
AIRCRAFT ENGINE FIRMS	
Argus	1,798
Bayerische Motorenwerke	5,841
Daimler-Benz	1,203
Hirth	7
Junkers	5,435
SAM	3,424
Stoewer	80
TOTAL	17,788

SOURCE: *Wirtschaftsgruppe Luftfahrt-Industrie*, 10.Dez.1935, Lw 103/6, DZ/MGFA.

foreign mortgages and the rest came from investment loans from the Air Ministry.[22]

Employment statistics for 1935 and 1936 indicate the size of as well as the concentration and rapidity of growth in the industry. As table 6 shows, in 1935 only three airframe and two engine firms employed over 5,000 workers. Another five airframe and one engine firm employed between 2,500 and 5,000. The rest were considerably smaller, with the exception of BFW, which, with the impending adoption of its Bf 109, was entering its big stage of expansion. The concentration within the industry—the product of the Nazi policy of preferential treatment of larger concerns—was already pronounced. By the middle of 1936 it was even more evident, for the Reich Statistical Office reported that out of seventy-four firms, the eight largest—five airframe and three engine firms—had payrolls in excess of 10 million RM annually, yet they accounted for 41 percent of the total wages and salaries in the industry. The next largest group of fifteen firms with payrolls between five and 10 million accounted for 33 percent of the total. A third group of twenty-eight firms with payrolls between 1 and 5 million had 23 percent, while the remaining twenty-three firms with payrolls under 1 million claimed only 3 percent of the total wages and salaries paid in the industry.[23] The five largest airframe makers accounted for 39 percent of the airframe production, while the top three engine firms claimed nearly one-half of the total output of engines.

Employment statistics for 1936 indicate the highly skilled but youthful composition of the labor force in the industry (table 7). The preponderance of skilled workers was also reflected in the industry's average annual wage, 2,600 RM, compared to the average wage of 1,700 RM for all industrial workers.[24] The small percentage of females (4.7) and the youthfulness of the male workers suggest that the industry was drawing off the ablest workers in the Reich. Other industries protested that the aircraft industry, with cost plus contracts, was paying higher wages and deliberately overclassifying workers to circumvent the rigid Nazi wage scales frozen at the 1933 depression level. As a result, it was drawing workers from the older industries instead of from the 2.5 million unemployed.[25]

Despite the rapid pace of expansion in the labor force, from 68,894 in July 1935 to 124,878 in mid-1936, the Reich Statistical Office concluded that the productive capacity of the industry had not been reached. Most of the plants were still working on a single shift and the addition of a second and third shift could boost production by two and a half times if suitable labor and materials could be found. That was precisely what the mobilization experts in the Air Ministry were

planning. During the first four years of the Nazi rearmament program
the Air Ministry developed an advantage over competing services by
creating an excess capacity in the physical facilities of the industry. Thus,
when shortages in raw materials and labor developed, particularly in the
construction sector after 1936, the aircraft industry was better off than
other branches working for the Wehrmacht.

Actual production in the aircraft industry in 1935-36 was close to
projections. On April 3, 1935, the Technical Office reported that during
the previous month the production of airplanes (214 versus 201 planned),
engines, auxiliary equipment, and parts surpassed planned quotas for the
first time.[26] Even more amazing, in 1936, despite the introduction of
three production plans, all of which raised quotas somewhat, the
industry still kept pace. In June 1936, for example, the monthly output
of aircraft was 399, compared to the projected quota of 381, while the
cumulative total reached 6,903, compared to the quota of 6,854.[27] By
November 1936, the changeover to new model production was beginning
to take effect and monthly output slipped to 378 versus a projected total
of 409; yet the grand total of 8,778 airplanes produced since 1933 was
still slightly higher than the projected quota of 8,733.[28]

Although production schedules were met during 1935-36, aircraft
developmental problems and increasing shortages, particularly in raw

TABLE 7

Employment in the Aircraft Industry by Age, Skill, and Sex, Mid-1936

Classification	Total Industry		Airframe Plants		Engine Plants	
	Number	%	Number	%	Number	%
Male, managerial	5,730	4.6	4,348	4.7	1,382	4.3
Male, technical employees						
under 35 years old	7,907	6.3	6,318	6.8	1,589	4.9
35-45	2,996	2.4	2,258	2.4	738	2.3
over 45	1,460	1.2	1,055	1.1	405	1.3
Male, skilled workers						
under 35 years old	44,944	36.0	35,525	38.3	9,419	29.4
35-45	10,761	8.6	7,382	8.0	3,379	10.5
over 45	6,980	5.6	4,831	5.2	2,149	6.7
Male, semiskilled workers						
under 35 years old	9,918	7.9	6,869	7.4	3,049	9.5
35-45	3,658	2.9	2,335	2.5	1,323	4.1
over 45	2,332	1.9	1,437	1.5	895	2.8
Male, unskilled and trainees	22,326	17.9	16,436	17.8	5,888	18.4
Female, salaried employees	3,549	2.8	2,430	2.6	1,119	3.5
Female, workers	2,317	1.9	1,582	1.7	735	2.3
Total	124,878	100.0	92,808	100.0	32,070	100.0

SOURCE: *Die Flugzeugindustrie. 1933–1936*, Statistiches Reichsamt, Abteilung VII, Na
Microcopy T-177/32/3720923.

materials, soon interfered. The raw materials shortage, which had been building since 1934, reached a climax in mid-1936 when the conservative forces who sought a slower and more controlled pace of rearmament were routed by the radical proponents of rapid rearmament. Rather than decelerate the pace, Hitler elected to solve the shortage with the Four-Year Plan (conveniently headed by Göring), announced at the fall party congress. The raw material shortage in the aircraft industry was manageable until December 1936, when for the first time the Technical Office had to give new combat aircraft production highest priority because of reduced deliveries of raw goods to the plants.[29]

Just as important during these years was the problem of how to finance aircraft development. The old methods of generating funds had proved inadequate. Steeply rising costs of developing more sophisticated aircraft, uncertainties of final acceptance, and the realization that handsome profits could be made from series production dampened the ardor of many firms. The Technical Office sought to correct this situation. Funds could be accrued in the larger firms from direct experimental and developmental contracts, from licensing fees, and from the imposition of higher charges for new aircraft approved for serial production. In addition, the Technical Office continued to finance highly unusual and costly projects, developmental work with little immediate use which did not interest the firms, and developmental projects started by new firms or new inventors.[30] Although the plant owners, as well as Kesselring, chief of administration, would have preferred across-the-board funding for developmental work under the production programs, the Technical Office argued that it would be too generalized, too difficult to control and account for, and too costly. A compromise was reached so that funds for developmental work were covered under a separate part of the Air Ministry's budget, but a distinction was made between developmental firms and others. Developmental firms were allowed to recover costs of developmental work through higher prices.[31] For all practical considerations, they were removed from the normal cost-accounting standards and allowed to determine their own costs in consultation with the ministry. Although the system was not good, Heinkel thought it was far better than tying funds to production programs under a uniform system of accounting, which would have been disastrous for a firm like his with a great deal of experimental and developmental work but little serial production. Production costs varied widely, depending on fixed costs and size even among firms producing the same model of aircraft. Heinkel argued, for example, that a plant producing thirty airplanes per month could do so at a 30 percent lower unit cost than a smaller plant producing only ten to fifteen of the same aircraft.[32]

In lieu of a more exact method of cost accounting, the Air Ministry resorted to steering the industry. A reshuffling in the ministry in 1935 concentrated research, development, testing, and procurement in the Technical Office, now labeled the LC. The Technical Office began insisting on qualitative improvements in aircraft, especially the replacement of smaller engines with more powerful ones, and the completely unfettered exchange of patent rights within the industry.[33] Despite the best efforts of the Technical Office, however, cooperation between firms remained slight. They preferred working directly with the Technical Office rather than with their competitors. The eighty models and variants in the Production Plan no. 4 were examples of the proliferation of developmental contracts which continued well into 1936, but late in the year the shortage of raw materials dictated drastic curtailment. The ministry ordered plants to reduce the number of and to simplify aircraft and engines under development and to curtail parallel projects wherever possible.[34] The action apparently had little effect, for Technical Office officials reported that some firms were using the developmental contracts to finance surreptitiously their peacetime projects and productive capacity.[35]

The Air Ministry in Nazi Germany had as little success as most other governments in trying to finance the developmental work of the aircraft industry. In spite of the protests of Heinkel and Messerschmitt of how unprofitable developmental contracts were, the ingenuity and alertness shown by the aircraft manufacturers in designing new projects and their obvious relish in beating out their competitors indicate that they were profitable. Not only were they so open-ended that firms found them extraordinarily useful in hiding expenditures that might not otherwise be so easily hidden, but they allowed the firms to maintain large staffs of skilled employees and offered the promise of large production contracts.

MOBILIZATION PLANNING

The rapid expansion of the aircraft industry had not taken place in a vacuum. The army and navy as well as the empire builders in the party and government watched with a mixture of suspicion and envy. Göring consistently maintained and acted on the principle that as Reich aviation minister he stood on an equal cabinet level with General von Blomberg, the Reich war minister, who was his superior officer only when he functioned as commander-in-chief of the Luftwaffe. During the first years of the Third Reich, the War Ministry tried to exert its authority over aerial rearmament, but each time Göring successfully parried the move. In the sensitive area of war mobilization, which demanded the closest coordination between the military services, governmental agencies, and private sectors of the economy, Göring's control over aerial rearmament remained unencumbered. He was helped considerably by the large number of agencies involved in mobilization planning: the recently established Reich Defense Council and the Committee for Reich Defense as well as the Ministries of War, Air, and Economics; the military services; and occasionally other governmental or business organizations as they were needed. As one historian has noted, the Third Reich had constructed "a great, sprawling machinery for war mobilization, without any driver."[36] Hitler was the dispatcher who set the destination, but there was no one at the controls.

The accelerated pace of rearmament made it increasingly apparent that the management of mobilization plans needed to be clarified. Each of the three military services was issuing contracts and organizing more firms into its own program without much overall coordination. German industry, which at first had so much unused capacity, was beginning to feel the pinch by early 1934. The astute Colonel Georg Thomas of the War Ministry realized the complexity of the situation and asked Hitler for the appointment of an "economic dictator" to guide the unco-ordinated mechanism of mobilization planning. After considerable delay and innumerable squabbles, Hitler established the new post on May 21, 1935, and ten days later named Hjalmar Schacht as its head.[37] Much to the irritation of Thomas, the new "plenipotentiary general for war economy," or GBK, as he was known, tried to monopolize the entire mobilization field instead of commanding the economy in the interests of the War Ministry, as Thomas had intended. As was often the case in Nazi Germany, the creation of one more special office had an effect just the opposite of that intended; instead of simplifying a situation, it only admitted another powerful but disruptive voice into the existing confusion.

Within the War Ministry itself, much of the mobilization work was to be done by a new office entitled Wehrwirtschaft und Waffenwesen, under the Wehrmachtamt and headed by Colonel Thomas. With an impressive range of responsibilities but very little authority, the office was to deal with the organization and planning for the defense economy, including the conversion of peacetime industry to war production. It had at its disposal in each military district a "Wehrwirtschaft Inspectorate" which maintained for each of the military services reference statistics on the resources in the district. Attached to each of the inspectorates were the economic officers of the army, navy, and air force, who, despite the pleas for cooperation from the War Ministry, retained their independence and controlled their own mobilization plans at the local level. Hopes for unified control of economic mobilization under the auspices of the War Ministry were dashed.[38] The results were, as Junkers director Koppenberg expressed it, "a battle royal with each of the three services looking after itself and fighting all the others for workers, factories, machines, raw materials and supplies."[39]

Finally, the Luftwaffe mobilization plan that was drawn up was loosely coordinated with the plans for the army and navy to avoid duplication of personnel and services. It dealt with the legal aspects of the transition from peace to war and was a basic planning document for the aircraft industry. The procurement of manpower, raw materials, and transportation; the type and amount of production expected from each firm; and hundreds of other details necessary for war production were included. The mobilization planning began in 1934 under the assumption that by 1938 the industry should be able to supply the Luftwaffe with aircraft to meet anticipated war losses. The general staff estimated that monthly losses would be 50 percent in combat units of fighters, bombers, and dive bombers; 25 percent in reconnaissance units; and 15 percent in noncombat units. To replace losses, the basic wartime capacity of the aircraft industry would be raised from 25 percent of the mobilization figure in 1934 to 50 percent in 1936, 75 percent in 1937, and a full 100 percent of anticipated replacements in 1938.[40] This meant, then, that in October 1935, when actual production in the entire industry was about 270 airplanes monthly, the mobilization plan called for a wartime expansion of production to 1,059 aircraft monthly. By April 1, 1938, the monthly output was to be increased to 1,753.[41]

The plan could be activated by a general Wehrmacht or Luftwaffe mobilization and was keyed to a lengthy period of tension preceding the outbreak of war. It covered three stages of preparedness: ready alert, designed to test the performance of certain units and air services but without informing the public that a mobilization was taking place; general mobilization, with the entire Luftwaffe ready for commitment; and immediate and emergency measures designed to achieve absolute combat readiness just prior to hostilities. For security reasons most units and factories received only the sections of the plan involving them. The plan was amended regularly to keep it current with production programs and the introduction of new equipment.[42]

To meet mobilization requirements, the individual factories had elaborate contingency plans to add one or two more working shifts; hire needed labor; and procure the correct amount of raw materials and complete sets of jigs, blueprints, and technical data for the aircraft they were to produce if different from the models currently in production.

Everything was carefully planned to the smallest detail, including food and housing for the enlarged work force, increases in work space, the new machinery needed, instructional programs for untrained workers, and in some rare cases, the complete relocation of vital plants from exposed frontiers to secure inner areas of the Reich.[43] The mobilization plan became the parameter of the aircraft industry's productive capacity during wartime.

The Luftwaffe attempted a large-scale trial run of their mobilization plan early in 1935. The Ministry issued instructions that all the firms in the plan were to complete their assignments within ten days and then maintain preparations, assigning personnel, equipment, and facilities to their specific mobilization tasks. During the summer Milch, Wimmer, and Loeb decided to use the Arado Flugzeugwerke under construction at Brandenburg for an intensive full-scale test. The plant, scheduled for completion in the fall of 1936, was chosen for its proximity to the capital, which would allow close monitoring by the ministry, its relative geographical isolation, and its models already in production. On the first Sunday of October 1935 the ministry sent the appropriate code numbers to the plant, ordering an activation of its mobilization plan starting at 7:00 a.m. the next day. The duration of the test was not stated, but the Arado mobilization plan called for maximum production by the end of the eighteenth week. Production before the test was 20 aircraft per month, but by the end of the sixth week it had risen to 40. By the end of the twelfth week it stood at 70, and finally, in the eighteenth week, it peaked at 120 aircraft per month. At that time the test was closed. The plant's labor force jumped from 2,000 to 6,000, with much of the increase handled by the Air Ministry. The physical plant size was nearly doubled, increasing from 11,000 to 21,000 square meters. The construction time for the plant was narrowed from one year to four months under test conditions.

The Air Ministry's detailed evaluation of the Arado test indicated the feasibility of the mobilization plan but pointed up weaknesses. First, the supply of materials was inadequate, and plants were ordered to stockpile more. Second, the handling of the expanded work force proved more difficult than expected. Arado's solution for housing was mass barracks, from which the workers were taken by either bus or train to the factory. Workers disliked that arrangement. Recreational and eating facilities were inadequate and new ones had to be provided in the housing areas, while canteens were needed in the factory. The four-week training program for new workers was judged successful. Third, the conversion of the plant to the production of a new model, in this case the all-metal Ju W 34, plus continuation of the production of its own Ar 66, Ar 68, and Ar 96, occasioned numerous problems between Arado and the licensing firm. Arado's limited experience in metal aircraft was particularly troublesome, but the problems were solved by closer cooperation with Junkers and by the introduction of a third work shift to supplement the planned two shifts and to compensate for the shortages of trained personnel and machine tools.[44] Fourth, the test confirmed the Air Ministry's contention that the shortage of machine tools was the chief bottleneck in aircraft production. As Wimmer of the Technical Office pointed out to General Blomberg, who had been encouraging the exportation of airplanes to secure much needed foreign exchange, the need for machine tools should take priority even over the production of export items, since further exports were tied to greater production. Once machine tools were made, exports could easily be produced.[45] Not much progress was made, for as late as November 21, 1936, Milch saw the shortage of machine tools as critical, while he complained that factories producing them had contracts years in advance. The shortage of skilled labor was the chief reason the machine tool requirements for the mobilization plan were not being met.[46]

The buildup of the aircraft industry on the basis of the mobilization plan, the far more detailed control over production programs, and the obvious need for better integration of the Luftwaffe rearmament program with the Wehrmacht's rearmament plan ushered in a new relationship between the Air Ministry and the industry. During the first phase, 1933-35, improvised planning based mainly on the existing capacity of the industry determined the program. Starting in 1935, however, the Air Ministry's increasing domination of every aspect of production became clear. The growing complexity of all areas of the economy involved in the rearmament program imposed the need for greater administrative supervision and control. A commonplace phenomenon of industrialization in the modern world, the bureaucratization of economic production, was occurring in the aircraft industry. One important cause of this phenomenon had technological roots.

AIRCRAFT SELECTION AND TECHNOLOGY

The selection of an airplane for production is a crucial decision which focuses the technological capabilities of an industry, the military theories of a nation, and the political intentions of the head of state. The perception of the military theorist and the precision of the technologist are blended with the astuteness of the political leader. Choosing an aircraft not only focuses divergent strains of thinking, but also severely tests the cooperation, skill, and conscientiousness of the military, governmental, and industrial agencies involved. There is no more important decision in the aviation world.

The German method of selection of aircraft grew out of the older methods used during the Weimar period and perfected during the first years of the Nazi era. Göring jealously guarded his prerogative of the final judgment; but as he became more involved with other areas of governmental rule, the decision making devolved increasingly on Milch, the Technical Office, and the general staff. The general staff was responsible for determining the needed aircraft types on the basis of plans for operations in peacetime and wartime. To handle the job, it set up the Tactical and Technical Requirements (IT) Group. The general staff could also utilize the expert consultation of the individual inspectorates such as the First Inspectorate for reconnaissance, the Second for bombers, and the Third for fighters and dive bombers. The inspectorates were links between the general staff and field units and were responsible for making tactical recommendations to improve the efficiency of air crews in accomplishing their assigned missions. The inspectorates' recommendations could be extremely varied, covering modifications of equipment, new or supplementary equipment needed, and training suggestions. It was imperative that close coordination be maintained between the inspectorates, the Technical Office, and the IT Group in the earliest stages of aircraft design.

Once the general staff collated the recommendations of the IT Group and the inspectorates, they formulated tactical-technical requirements for new equipment which were submitted to the Technical Office in the form of a directive. The Technical Office then worked out the technological aspects of the largely tactical demands of the general staff and passed them on to the aircraft industry in research and developmental contracts. At this point the highly creative and individual genius of the aircraft designer was brought to bear in resolving the technology with the tactical requirements. Competitive designs were submitted to the Technical Office, which approved the more promising ones for mockups. Full-sized wooden or cardboard mockups of the airplane were constructed by firms to permit inspection for special layouts, visibility of crew, and accessibility of vital equipment. Representatives from all levels of command and all concerned agencies took part in these inspections.

After evaluation of the mockups, the Technical Office let contracts for the construction of test models or prototypes, which were extensively tested by the developmental firm and the Reich Aviation Ministry. During the testing, numerous improvements based on test results were made and usually additional prototypes were ordered. With the successful completion of testing, a contract for a 0, or preproduction, series was granted, and these aircraft were field tested by Luftwaffe units, usually those of the Training Division. The field testing determined the model's acceptability for unit use by the Luftwaffe. The final decision was made by Göring, with the concurrence of Milch, the Technical Office, and the general staff, usually after a demonstration of the airplane. Some of the considerations in Göring's decision were the dependency of the aircraft on existing engines and the ease in replacing them with more advanced ones, the time required from the acceptance of an airplane until it could be mass produced, the effects of changes based on new tactical-technical specifications of the general staff, and ease of supply and repair for the new aircraft.[47]

The selection of an airplane for mass production usually took four years. At any point in the chain of decision making an aircraft might fail because of developmental problems, or compromises of major importance might be made. Sometimes, too, unpredictable political events such as the Czech crisis, or even personal spur-of-the-moment decisions by Hitler, Göring, or Udet, might upset the carefully drawn plans. The progress of selection was never a smooth continuum, but the time sequence in the 1930s followed this pattern:

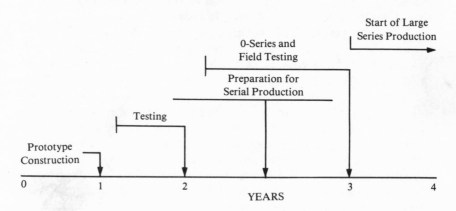

Under the political pressure growing in 1936 there were attempts to compress the time to allow large series production to start promptly at the beginning of the third year. This proved exceedingly difficult, for very often haste in testing resulted in slowdowns in serial production later. Attempts to reduce the 0-series also proved to be ill-advised. The Technical Office found it was necessary to test building procedures, details of construction, and larger engines, and to experiment with other equipment after the initial evaluation. Changes from the prototypes to the 0-series often numbered 5,000 to 20,000, but those from the 0-series to the large series could run as high as 70,000.[48]

To circumvent the many delays, compress the time cycle, and reduce the possibilities of rejection during the selection process, German aircraft planners discovered *Baukastenflugzeuge*, a standardized basic airframe on which more powerful engines and additional heavy equipment could be grafted. The idea was to use one basic type of airframe that could be adapted through modification of equipment to many different missions. This approach led to the principle of commonality, the unification of many types of functions (fighter, bomber, dive bomber) in a single model.[49]

These largely ineffective attempts to speed up aircraft development had some unfortunate results. Successful series were frozen or modified constantly in preference to risking a new line. German planners and designers became unduly cautious in their approach; the sure thing was always the better way. This deflection of much creative talent into redesigning existing types instead of searching for fresh solutions was only intensified by the constant political pressure to produce as much as possible as quickly as possible.

THE BOMBER CONTROVERSY

The selection of bombers for the Luftwaffe in the 1930s illustrates the intertwining of military theorizing, technology, and politics. A strong bomber force had top priority for the offensively oriented Göring staff. The "risk force" idea of Douhet's strategic bombing concept was clearly seen in the productions programs which emphasized bombers. Chief of Staff Wever; the head of the Technical Office, Wimmer; and key operations officers like Deichmann and Felmy were all bomber men who emphasized strategic as well as tactical bombing. Former fighter pilots Göring and Udet, however, and many of the long-line army officers transferred to the Luftwaffe from the Reichswehr were close-support proponents. The selection of bombers reflected these diverse views and the compromises that were made.

During the first production programs the Luftwaffe leaders had no means to fashion the bomber force they wanted. Working under the necessity to create a force as soon as possible, they had no choice but to produce bombers that were already designed or to convert existing civilian aircraft. However, they began planning for new aircraft. The first specifications called for a multipurpose medium bomber with a range of 600 miles, speed of 215 mph, and bomb load of 2,200 lbs. For security and financial reasons, airplanes designed under these specifications had to be suitable for use as transports for the DLH as well as for bombers for the still clandestine Luftwaffe.[50] The military potentiality of the aircraft had top priority, but the civilian aspects were not to be ignored. The widely held contention that these airplanes were progenitors of future bombers with a few civilian features to beguile the aviation community ignores the fact that from the outset they were designed to fulfill both functions without appreciable structural changes. The often repeated charge that they were a perfect example of German duplicity and subterfuge cannot be substantiated, for of the three aircraft accepted under these specifications—the Do 17, Ju 86, and He 111—the Do 17 was designed first as a transport and the other two with their dual role in mind. Nor were the Germans alone in designing bomber-transports; nearly every major aviation nation designed such aircraft in the 1930s.

All three of the twin-engined bomber-transports proved to have serious limitations. The Do 17, first tested by the DLH in early 1935, had exceptional speed, but its slim fuselage limited passenger accommodations in its transport version, making it commercially unprofitable. The Ju 86, designed to be powered by the new Junker Jumo 205 diesel engine, was far more promising as a bomber. The Technical Office had hoped that the engine, although inferior to a comparable gasoline engine in its power-to-weight ratio, would allow construction of a bomber-transport with great range, dependability, and lower operating fuel consumption costs. The initial tests indicated the Ju 86 had excellent flight characteristics, but its narrow landing gear, vertical bomb racks, and, most important, the poor performance of its engines were disappointing. Modifications were made and it was hastily accepted as the standard Luftwaffe bomber, although the problems associated with its engines were not completely solved. The diesel Jumo 205 proved reliable as long as a constant rpm was maintained, but frequent changes in the rpm as in combat situations had a markedly adverse effect on its performance. With extensive modifications, including refitting with new gasoline engines, the Ju 86 commercial version had some success. The third entry, the He 111, at first seemed disappointing to the Technical Office. The original prototypes, equipped with BMW VI engines, performed poorly and were rejected by the Luftwaffe; but in early 1936, when the more powerful Daimler-Benz DB 600A engines became available, the He 111 proved to be the best bomber of the three. It was ordered into production immediately, and the Heinkel firm continually refined and developed the basic design to improve its performance and efficiency and prolong its service life.[51]

In early 1935, on a visit to the Friedrichshafen plant of Dornier, Milch and Wever saw the star pilot of the DLH and former Dornier employee Flugkapitän Robert Untucht demonstrate the speed and performance of the Do 17. Untucht suggested that with some modifications it could be developed into a bomber that would outrun any existing fighter. Intrigued by the idea, and with Dornier's assurance that the aircraft could be in production by March 1936, Milch ordered a military prototype of the Do 17. After extensive testing it was accepted as a long-range reconnaissance-bomber, even though its bomb load was well below the Luftwaffe specification.[52] Meanwhile, the thinking in the RLM was changing. Wimmer and Richthofen led a faction whose arguments for a light, fast, even unarmed bomber culminated in specifications for a speed bomber in 1935.

The result of the search for a standard medium bomber was that Germany had not found one perfect bomber and chose to build three imperfect ones instead. The Do 17 represented one prevalent theory that stressed speed to elude interceptors, the Junker 86 economy and range, and the He 111 defensive armament and bomb load. The limitations of all three were recognized but growing pressure to use the rapidly expanding production capacity of the aircraft industry and the insistence of the military on better bombers dictated producing them. The confusion over the tactical-technical specifications for the medium bomber was typical. The industry never had sufficiently clear guidelines, and the shifting and obvious political decision making in the ministry only aggravated the situation. Eventually the general staff did bring some clarification to the situation by ranking the values it wanted in a medium bomber: (1) bomb load, (2) speed, (3) defensive armament, and (4) range. After the disappointment with the first generation of bombers it was obvious that a newer, high-performance bomber would have to be built as a replacement.[53]

The development of true strategic bomber, a four-engined, long-range aircraft with a large bomb load, had been a major concern of the aviation planners even before 1933. Both Wimmer and Felmy insisted that such a bomber should be included in any future air force, but they viewed it as the culmination of a mature, balanced air force. Rejecting the Douhetian concept of the primacy of the heavy bomber, they realized that the construction of a sizable fleet of strategic bombers could come only at the end of the aerial buildup, after the many staggering technical problems involved were solved. Such an airplane had to be fast, long-range, and able to operate at a high altitude, so new, powerful, highly supercharged engines; pressurized cabins; electronic or visual bombing systems; and long-range navigational and radio equipment would have to be developed. These would need the reliability and serviceability necessary for operational units, and above all, everything had to be combined into a successful aeronautical design. The Reichswehr planners anticipated that such a bomber could be built by the late 1930s as the capstone to a mature air force.

On the day after Hitler took office, the rewritten specifications for a strategic bomber were finally released by the Ordnance Office,[54] but the reorganization of the air offices delayed efforts on the bomber until late 1933. General Wever, the new acting chief of staff, had to be persuaded that the heavy bomber was the decisive weapon in aerial warfare. He was soon won over and indeed became an enthusiastic champion of the "Uralbomber," as he dubbed it. By May 1934, the heavy bomber had first priority in the developmental program, with plans calling for a mockup by the end of June 1934, prototypes by July 1935, preproduction series by the winter of 1937, and large-scale production by 1938.[55] Göring was briefed on these plans in the winter of 1934 and at that time said nothing about the aircraft. However, when he viewed a mockup of the four-engined Ju 89 on a visit to the Junkers plant in early 1935, he became indignant, asserting that he reserved for himself the prerogative of deciding such important matters. He felt that the Technical Office had overstepped its authority in commissioning models of a heavy bomber from Dornier and Junkers. General von Blomberg, war minister, had also seen a mockup of the Dornier model, the Do 19, in 1935, but his reaction was entirely different; he asked when it would be ready. When Colonel Wimmer answered, "About 1939 or 1940," Blomberg thought for a moment, glanced up at the sky, and remarked cryptically, "Das kann richtig sein" ("That is about right").[56]

Work on the two four-engined prototypes progressed slowly; but even before the first three Do 19s and the two Ju 89s were ready for their flight tests late in 1936, the Luftwaffe expressed grave doubts about the project. It was clear that both prototypes, equipped with existing engines of 600 to 700 h.p., were underpowered. But would they be adequate for further development when the more powerful class of 1,000-h.p. engines were ready? Both Major Paul Deichmann of Tactics and Operations and Milch thought so, or at least that is what they reported later.[57] Others in the high command were not as confident of the prototypes' potential, for on April 17, 1936, nearly eight months before their maiden flights, new specifications were issued calling for a bomber with range and speed nearly double those of the prototypes.[58] In his introduction to the guidelines, General Wever stressed that the range, speed, and defensive capability were the most important considerations in a heavy bomber. The existing prototypes could not meet these guidelines; the question is, then, Were they formulated to exclude the prototypes?

The answer can be extrapolated from the progress of the first prototypes in the developmental programs. The decision to halt work on them came in mid-1936 and not on Göring's April 29, 1937, decision. As early as November 21, 1935, the developmental program listed both the Ju 89 and Do 19 for prototypes but without any comment on a preproduction series. Less than two months later, on January 6, 1936, the Ju 89 was listed for three prototypes, with a fourth scheduled as a transport for Lufthansa, and a preproduction series by March of 1938. The Do 19 had about the same dates, but changes in engines were noted and the decision on the preproduction series was not firm.[59] By April, the Ju 89 had one prototype dropped; the third was scheduled for Lufthansa and renumbered Ju 90, and the preproduction series of four was to begin by January 1937. There was still no decision on the preproduction series for the Do 19. On July 20, the Technical Office ordered the Ju 89s refitted with four DB 600C V-1 and V-2 engines of the 1,000-h.p. class, while the number in the preproduction series was increased from four to seven. The program listed three Do 19 prototypes and, for the first time, preproduction series of seven.[60]

By October 27, 1936, the situation had changed drastically. One Do 19 was to be refitted with slightly larger SAM 322B engines, while a second was to have new BMW 132F engines. The first was scheduled for flight in October 1936, delivery to the Luftwaffe test station by February 1937, and completion of testing by September 1937; while the second, with the BMW engines, had slightly later deadlines as did the two Ju 89s. The most important change was that the third Do 19 prototype was temporarily suspended, and the preproduction series of both the Do 19 and the Ju 89 were listed as undetermined and probably not intended.[61]

What happened from July 20 to October 27 to change the mind of the Luftwaffe leadership? The most obvious answer was a major change in key personnel. General Wever's death on June 3 had brought Kesselring to his post, while Wimmer in the Technical Office was replaced by Udet. Apparently these new officers, in consultation with Milch and others, decided that further development of the first generation of heavy bombers was unwarranted, especially in view of the new heavy-bomber guidelines of April 17 personally endorsed by Wever.

Since the first prototypes could not meet the new specifications, the Luftwaffe leadership decided to use them only for testing a more advanced model while concentrating the Luftwaffe's production on smaller bombers. Why commit a disproportionate amount of scarce materials and factory capacity to build a big bomber that would be hopelessly outdated by the time it could be issued to operational units? Why not skip one generation of heavies; develop the new medium, speed, and dive bombers; and then return to a more refined, high-performance heavy bomber? By that time, engine development, bombing systems, and air crew training would have caught up enough that a heavy bomber could be developed and successfully integrated into operational units.

It is plausible that Wever and Wimmer, by the way they fashioned the specifications of April 17, anticipated the decision made later by Kesselring and others. Contrary to the opinions of most historians, the real problem was why there was a delay on the second generation of prototypes. The developmental programs offer an answer. On March 11, 1937, Kesselring requested the conversion of some of the Ju 86s or He 111s to long-range bombers as an interim solution to the problem of a strategic bomber. These two medium bombers were to be altered so that they possessed an extended range of 3,500 km. and could be used for long-range, high altitude bombing and reconnaissance. Kesselring thought the Ju 86 equipped with Jumo 207A engines (diesels equipped with superchargers for high altitude) might work. He hoped that at least one wing each of Ju 86s and He 111s could be successfully converted to meet the Luftwaffe's immediate needs.[62]

A month later, on April 15, the Technical Office's priority list of developmental projects had downgraded the Do 19 and Ju 89 heavy bombers to third priority, along with Heinkel's speed bomber, the He 119; Focke-Wulf's fighters, the FW 159 and FW 259; and the tailless aircraft, the DFS 193 and 194. Given first priority were aircraft such as the Bf 109, Bf 110, Bf 162, Do 17E and F, He 111, Ju 86, Ju 88, and the autogiro FWC 30, most of which were on the verge of acceptance for operational units. In the second category were the Bf 161 high-altitude reconnaissance plane and the He 118 dive bomber.[63] Two weeks later, on April 29, 1937, the very day Göring allegedly stopped the first heavy-bomber prototypes, the Technical Office's developmental program listed two Ju 89s and two Do 19s to be used for testing only. New specifications for a long-range bomber, labeled Bomber A, were under consideration for issuance to the industry. (Two four-engined aircraft, the Ju 90 and FW 200, were still carried on the developmental program as Lufthansa transports.)[64] After that, the notation for the Ju 89 and Do 19 was always the same: "No intention of testing for model production." The new heavy bomber, Bomber A, appeared on the December 22, 1937, developmental program and was scheduled for first flight by June 1938, delivery to the Luftwaffe testing station by October 1938, and complete readiness for production by April 1939.[65] The fate of the first prototypes had been sealed.

The slow development of the big bomber prototypes and the pressing demands of the production program undoubtedly contributed to the decision to cancel the project, but other considerations were equally important. The general staff was preparing an air force for a series of limited continental wars in which the need for a long-range bomber was not pressing.[66] The twin-engined mediums could handle that kind of warfare. Besides, the German aircraft industry could build three medium for every two heavy bombers; and as Göring had often remarked, "The Führer will not ask how big the bombers are, but only how many there are." The choice of building the Luftwaffe a bomber force of twin-engined mediums already developed and in production or gambling on a big bomber still in the developmental stage was in reality no choice at all. Although far from satisfied with the performance of the medium bombers, the general staff also had under consideration the dive bomber and was searching for a speed bomber.

The dive bomber (*Stuka*, or *Sturzkampflugzeug*) was conceived of as an interim solution to the bomber problem and was suitable for a developing air force that did not have yet a strategic bomber. But the concept mushroomed into an exaggerated *Blitzkrieg* idea that eventually warped strategic air warfare. Ernst Udet is usually called the father of dive bombing in Germany, although his actual role was more one of emphasis than initiation. The Reichswehr had experimented with it for years and had the Swedish plant of Junkers build the K 47 dive bomber, which was tested long before Udet was involved with the air force. Tests of the K 47 and the later dive bombers, the He 50 and the Hs 123, were inconclusive in the eyes of the Reichswehr. Udet tipped the scales in their favor. In September 1933, on one of his many trips abroad, he examined a Hawk dive bomber in the Curtiss-Wright plant in Buffalo. He persuaded Göring and Milch to purchase two Hawks for his private use, provided the Technical Office could first test them. The first Hawk crashed at Tempelhof when an elevator jammed, but Udet magnificently displayed the second one at the secret testing station at Rechlin before an audience of air force officials. They were skeptical not only of the aircraft but also of Udet, the civilian "aerial comedian" and *Filmfatzke*. Richthofen of the Research and Development Office, in particular, thought that accurate antiaircraft artillery fire would nullify the advantages of the dive bomber at low altitude. Undeterred by such criticism, Udet persisted in lobbying for the dive bomber even to the point of volunteering to join the air force to promote his cause.[67]

During the winter maneuvers of 1933-34, the army made extensive tests of the feasibility of using bombers in close support of tanks and infantry. Their evaluation of this exercise led to the formulation of tactical-technical specifications for a light and a heavy dive bomber in June 1934.[68] The light dive bomber would be strictly a tactical aircraft doubling as a fighter, while the heavy one would be exclusively a bomber with a two-man crew and much greater bomb load. In the ensuing months the specifications were altered, principally by dropping the requirement of the dual role as a fighter in the light plane and accenting the diving abilities of both aircraft. By October 1934, the stress for the heavy dive bomber was on good diving characteristics (good stability when handled by an average pilot and not diving faster than 360 mph), speed (210 mph at 12,000 ft.), climb rate, and maneuverability. The requirements were slightly different for the light dive bomber.[69] The final specifications for the heavy dive bomber, issued simultaneously in January 1935 to Heinkel, Arado, and Junkers ostensibly for selection on a competitive basis, were in reality closely tailored to the Junkers-designed Ju 87. The previous summer the ministry had authorized the design of three Ju 87 prototypes, which gave the Reich-controlled plant a decided advantage.[70] It was hardly surprising that in the spring of 1936, after a year of testing, the Ju 87 edged out its competitors, the Arado Ar 81, Heinkel He 118, and a last-minute entry, the Hamburger Flugzeugbau (Blohm and Voss) Ha 137.

The dive bombing concept gained many adherents in these years; yet its principal detractor, Richthofen, was always skeptical of the idea (ironically, during World War II he was a stunning practitioner of dive bombing). On June 9, 1936, he sent his superiors a confidential directive for the discontinuation of the Ju 87. The next day, Ernst Udet was named chief of the Technical Office; he immediately rescinded Richthofen's directive and continued the development of the plane.[71]

The Luftwaffe was drawn to dive bombing because of their poor results with horizontal bombing. Germany's medium bombers had relatively low bomb loads and inadequate bombsights. The bomb load of the Do 17 was one 550-lb. bomb, the Ju 86 had three, and the He 111 had four. The Luftwaffe determined from their own experience and that of other countries, primarily the United States, that a minimum bomb load for effective horizontal bombing was four 550-lb. bombs, which only the He 111 could handle. To compound the difficulties, the Goerz-Visier 219 bombsight then in use was effective only with a good deal of practice and in closely limited areas. The more advanced optical sights, the Lotfe 7 and 7D, were not yet available to regular units.[72] Even the very best crews in the Luftwaffe found it difficult to achieve satisfactory results in horizontal bombing under optimum conditions, whereas the dive bomber seemed to promise a high degree of precision. A few dive bombers, it was thought, could place more tonnage on a specific target than many horizontal bombers could, and tests within the Luftwaffe quickly confirmed the theory.

Former fighter pilots Göring and Udet and the youthful new generation of Luftwaffe pilots became enthusiastic champions of the dive bombing technique, for it was daring and accurate and offered a real breakthrough for the Luftwaffe. Another, less dramatic but equally compelling argument for the dive bomber was that it represented a quick and economical solution to the bomber problem. As Eberhard Spetzler rightly pointed out, the Reich "was so limited with regard to raw materials and gasoline that her production capacity and, in turn, her war potential, simply did not permit the construction of sufficient numbers of heavy bomber fleets. She had no choice but to limit herself to medium and light bombers with the highest possible degree of hitting accuracy."[73] This choice was in accord with the Luftwaffe's continental concept of war. A combination of factors led to the acceptance of the dive bombing concept. It was a bridge, an interim solution, to cover the technological deficiencies that had arisen in medium- and heavy-bomber development in the 1930s. A cheap, quick way to achieve maximum bombing punch with a minimum use of resources, the dive bomber was a calculated-risk aircraft designed to serve until a superior heavy bomber or fast medium bomber could be developed. It allowed the ministry to gamble on retooling in 1938-39 for the "wonder bomber" and discontinue the development of the first four-engined prototypes in favor of a much more sophisticated one to be built in the late 1930s. The problem was, however, that as the dive bombing concept became more embedded in the Luftwaffe's thinking, the original purpose became more obscure. Success with dive bombing in Spain further shifted the Luftwaffe's thinking from area to pinpoint bombing. Consequently, the Luftwaffe slipped further and further away from its idea of strategic air warfare.

The last remaining problem in the bomber controversy was the search for a speed bomber. During the winter maneuvers of 1933-34 the air force determined that it needed a heavily armed, close-support warplane equipped with cannons, machine guns, and a small bomb load. It tried to combine these qualities with the medium bombers, but the attempts were unsuccessful. In May 1934, the Technical Office combined some of these requirements into one set of specifications for a multipurpose, high-altitude, long-range reconnaissance aircraft that could fulfill the battle-plane functions. The aircraft was given fourth priority, after the heavy bomber, dive bomber, and medium bomber.[74] In June the specifications for a *Kampfzerstörer* called for a heavily armed airplane with a speed of 240 mph, range of 1,200 miles, and night flying capability.[75] To meet this requirement Focke-Wulf and Henschel developed the FW 57 and the Hs 124, respectively. The Technical Office recognized the difficulty in reconciling the dual assignments as a reconnaissance bomber and as a *Zerstörer* (heavy fighter); throughout 1934 it had increasing misgivings about combining so many functions in one aircraft. By early 1935 it replaced the multipurpose specifications with more specialized demands for three types of aircraft: a long-range, fast reconnaissance-bomber; a heavy fighter; and a *Schnellbomber*, or speed bomber. These new requirements permitted the Do 17 to be accepted for the reconnaissance-bomber, while the heavy fighter evolved from the concept of a battle plane to that of a strategic fighter capable of accompanying bombers deep into enemy territory.[76] Henschel, Arado, and BFW entered competition to meet this specification. The third aircraft was the three-seat *Schnellbomber*, armed with only one defensive machine gun and normal and maximum bomb loads of 1,100 and 1,765 lbs., with a top speed of 310 mph and an excellent climb rate, and capable of flying out of short, rough runways. Focke-Wulf, Henschel, Junkers, and BFW were invited to compete with designs judged by comparative tests. Focke-Wulf declined, but the other three submitted proposals. By February 1936, the specifications were altered slightly to include a range of 1550 miles, but the priority of values was still speed, takeoff and landing characteristics, range, bomb load, and defensive weapons.[77]

How the Luftwaffe fulfilled the speed bomber specifications with the Ju 88 program is germane to the bomber controversy of 1935-36. In concept the speed bomber became enmeshed with the dive bomber and heavy bomber. Although the specifications for it were at that time distinctly separate from those of the other bombers, the differences were blurred by using the speed bomber as a replacement for the others.

FIGHTER SELECTION

The selection of fighters for the Luftwaffe was simpler than that of bombers. The fighter never enjoyed the high priority of the bomber in the prewar years.[78] The search for a new fighter to replace biplanes such as the Ar 68 and He 51 started in late 1933. The Technical Office fashioned a set of specifications which were completed and passed on to the industry in 1934. Four firms were granted contracts for prototypes; Arado had the Ar 80V-1; Focke-Wulf developed the FW 159V-1; Heinkel had the He 112V-1; and BFW entered the Bf 109V-1. All the aircraft were to be monoplanes and use the Junkers Jumo 210 engines, but shortages forced all but the Focke-Wulf firm to substitute the 695-hp British Rolls-Royce Kestrel V engine.

There were still some lingering doubts about the efficacy of the monoplane as opposed to the biplane. Most old-line fighter pilots felt that the key qualities of a fighter were rate of climb, speed, and maneuverability, with emphasis on an extremely short radius of turn.[79] The monoplane was seriously disadvantaged with its high wing loading, greater turning radius, and greater speeds in takeoff and landing, but technological changes in 1933 gave it decisive advantages. Foremost among these was a better understanding of the influence of drag on design. Drag rises rapidly with speed, and as aircraft with more powerful engines approached the 200-mph level, the monoplane with its aerodynamically cleaner design had a tremendous advantage. Two innovations, the variable-pitch propellor and the split flap, which vastly improved performance and control, assured the ultimate victory of the monoplane over the biplane.

Competition for the new German monoplane fighter was keen, although the two leading fighter manufacturers, Heinkel and Arado, had an initial edge. Heinkel's sensational He 70 "Blitz," in particular, with its remarkable aerodynamic design and finishing, seemed the perfect model to be refined into a fighter.[80] The Arado firm had a graceful, beautifully designed, open-cockpit aircraft (only the Bf 109 at first had an enclosed cockpit) which, despite its fine lines and performance, was seriously handicapped by a fixed landing gear and substantially higher airframe weight. Focke-Wulf's entry was a parasol-wing fighter that owed much to the earlier FW 56 "Stösser," a trainer and early dive bomber. The bracing of the wing and clumsy landing gear that retracted into the fuselage eliminated it from the competition.

At BFW the ingenious young designer Willy Messerschmitt and his chief assistant, Walter Rethel, were drafting the surprise of the competition. In 1933 Messerschmitt had designed a light touring plane, the Bf 108 "Taifun," a low-wing cantilever monoplane with an all-metal monocoque, stressed-skin constructed fuselage. It was an extraordinary aircraft with a structural integrity and quality of workmanship which looked as modern and sleek as any sport plane of today. Its handling characteristics, sensitive, quick responses with a margin of reserve, made it a delight to fly. It was a genuine thoroughbred, and Messerschmitt used it as the basis for his new fighter. The design concept of the Bf 109 was simple; Messerschmitt incorporated every successful element of his Bf 108 into the lightest and smallest airframe he could design and then mated it to the most powerful engine available. Messerschmitt's team began work on the plane in the summer of 1934, and in September 1935, the Bf 109 made its maiden flight. Aside from the usual bugs t' at plague every new design, the team was pleased with the fighter. It had all of the simplicity of its predecessor and the brute strength and power of a fighter. Its narrow and weak landing gear made it difficult to handle on the ground, but its flight performance more than compensated.

The competition for the new standard fighter began at Rechlin in October 1935 and continued later at Travemünde. The Ar 80 and Fw 159 were quickly outclassed by the Bf 109 and the He 112. Both aircraft were low-wing monoplanes with retractable landing gear and were powered by Rolls-Royce Kestrel V engines. The He 112 was slightly larger and heavier than the Bf 109 but was remarkably similar in flight performance. Both fighters had a maximum speed of slightly less than 300 mph and were so similar in other respects that the Air Ministry awarded contracts to both firms for ten prototypes for accelerated tests. In the subsequent testing there was little difference in the two: the He 112's superior ground handling characteristics were offset by the Bf 109's advantages in the air. Finally, production factors favored the Bf 109. Messerschmitt had not been a favorite with State Secretary Milch, but his airplane was easier and cheaper to construct than Heinkel's. Messerschmitt had developed a completely new system of fuselage construction, first used on the Bf 108, in which one bulkhead and one section of skin were formed from the same sheet of metal simultaneously. This system was adaptable to mass production with a minimum of skilled labor and cost. Besides, Heinkel was heavily involved with other projects and the ministry feared a contract for a fighter might interfere with mass production of the He 111. Of course, Messerschmitt's close connections with Hess, Göring, and Udet probably also helped, but the choice of Messerschmitt's design over that of Heinkel was a sound one. It even gave balance to the industry by distributing a major contract to another firm. BFW went on to become the prime builder of fighters for the Luftwaffe.[81]

Throughout this period Luftwaffe theorists were working out doctrines of aerial warfare which affected aircraft development. In late 1934 Göring insisted that the Luftwaffe develop a long-range strategic fighter capable of accompanying bombers on long bombing missions. This type of aircraft had to carry large fuel supplies for range but had to possess the speed and maneuverability of a small fighter once in action. In addition to its bomber escort role, the heavy fighter was assigned a secondary mission, that of a long-range interceptor. The time necessary to detect incoming enemy bombers, scramble defensive aircraft, and direct them to the bomber was fifteen to sixteen minutes. A fast spot interceptor like the Bf 109 was needed, but a long-range one of at least three hours' flight duration was necessary to intercept bombers far from their intended targets, pursue them to target, and attack upon their withdrawal. Thus by the summer of 1936 the Luftwaffe had clearly defined the need for at least two basically different kinds of fighters.[82] By December 1936, the tactical-technical specifications for these fighters were approved by the chief of staff and sent to the Technical Office.[83] They called for a fast, lightly armed fighter, presumably the Bf 109, and a long-range fighter, heavily armed with cannons and machine guns. The heavy fighter was to have a speed of 350-370 mph with a flight duration of three hours and an all-weather capability. Its climb rate, service ceiling, and takeoff and landing characteristics were somewhat less than for the single-engined fighter. To meet these requirements, the Technical Office had already issued developmental contracts to Henschel, Arado, and BFW. The Bf 110, designed by Messerschmitt, quickly emerged as the most successful model, and its development was pushed by the Air Ministry. In May 1936, the first prototype was flown, and in October and December two more prototypes followed. In January the Bf 110 V-2 was sent to Rechlin for Luftwaffe tests in which it proved disappointing in maneuverability, but its top speed of 316 mph in level flight was promising enough to continue development. The Bf 110 needed another year of testing and modification, including the usual refitting with different engines, before it was ordered into production. The Luftwaffe had a heavy fighter, but it was unsuccessful in fulfilling its primary mission of escorting bombers.[84]

The development of the heavy fighter owed much to the theorizing of Luftwaffe leaders in 1936. For the first time a handbook, Service Manual 16, establishing guidelines for the strategic and tactical employment of the German air force was written. Although it was prepared by Generalmajor Wilberg, the influence of the first chief of staff, Wever, was quite pronounced.[85] As early as 1926 the aviation branch of the Truppenamt had compiled directives for the strategic deployment of the air force, and soon other sections were written. In 1933 Wilberg was charged with the responsibility of compiling a comprehensive manual for the instruction of all commanders and staff officers. It was a curiously conservative document that described the primary mission of the Luftwaffe as the achievement of air supremacy through the destruction of the enemy's air force, ground organization, and aircraft industry; the destruction of the enemy's war-making potential; and the support of the army and navy in "decision-seeking battles." The last point revealed a noticeable lack of conviction, for the manual observed that the decisive battles might be fought before the effects of strategic bombing could be felt. There is no clear emphasis on strategic bombing; although the Luftwaffe might appreciate strategic bombing, it aimed at a tactical bombing force to support the Blitzkrieg style of war in which the quick destruction of the enemy's armed forces was of paramount concern.

Attack was identified by the manual as the dominant principle. The best defense was to attack the enemy to disable his air force, on the ground if possible, and then to attack and destroy his ground and sea forces once aerial supremacy was established. Only then could the air force destroy the enemy's war-making potential. The emphasis was overwhelmingly on tactical rather than strategic bombing.[86] There were, for example, nineteen paragraphs in the manual devoted to operations against enemy rail and highway facilities, compared to five on strategic bombing. The evidence of Douhet's revolutionary thinking that does appear indicates an awareness but hardly a wholehearted acceptance of strategic bombing.

The manual emphasized the tactical employment of the Luftwaffe because it was intended to supply guidelines for commanders and staff officers and naturally reflected their immediate concerns, but it also subtly depicted the existing state of the Luftwaffe in 1936. The underlying theory reflected the fact that Germany did not have a true strategic bomber and implied the preparation for a limited continental war which would be decided by short, sharp military battles rather than a long drawn-out global struggle which would eventually be decided by the long-term military capabilities of the participants. Moreover, the manual identified the enemies of Germany as her immediate neighbors, not countries like England or even the Soviet Union. Those enemies with air fleets within the range of Germany's medium bombers were vulnerable to surprise assault and could be struck down by a tactical air force. The Luftwaffe was meant to be and was built as an air force for a Blitzkrieg.

Service Manual 16 was intended, not as the unalterable dogma of aerial warfare, but as a convenient summary and guideline, to be revised and modified in the light of subsequent developments in weaponry, further experiences in combat, and new theorizing at home and abroad. But instead of merely summarizing prevailing thought on aerial warfare in 1936, it crystallized the Luftwaffe's principles. New sections were written and inserted, but when it was reissued in 1940, it was still substantially the 1936 version with a fundamentally conservative concept of aerial warfare.

The personnel changes, the selection of aircraft, and the numerous alterations in the production programs during 1935 and 1936 foreshadowed some of the major characteristics of the aviation world of the Third Reich. The prejudicial exercise of political influence in all three areas boded ill for the future, as did the unduly large role played by the aircraft manufacturers in development and production programs. Some of this could have been eliminated had the general staff been more explicit in the formulation of their tactical-technical specifications or had the technical experts in the ministry been more resolute in their judgments and more skilled in their administration. But under the urgent pressure of time and the acute shortage of strong, independent technical experts, particularly in the selection and planning of aircraft, an acceptance of political decision making was conditioned into the Luftwaffe. The instant decisions made by the political leaders, often without sufficient consultation and based largely on the spurious doctrine of the *Führerprinzip*, eroded what little detached and critical thinking had developed in the still very young and malleable Luftwaffe. Particularly unfortunate was the loss in 1936 of the steady hand of Wever, who might well have been able to obviate or at least defer some of the deep personnel splits and prevent the growth of political influence in the air force that occurred after his death.

NOTES

1. "Unterredung Görings mit dem Sonderberichterstatter der *Daily Mail,* Ward Price, von 10.3.1935," A/I/2, KDC/M.

2. For recent accounts of foreign reactions, see, Gerhard L. Weinberg, *The Foreign Policy of Hitler's Germany: Diplomatic Revolution in Europe, 1933-1936* (Chicago: University of Chicago Press, 1970), and Walter Bernhardt, *Die deutsche Aufrüstung, 1934-1939* (Frankfurt: Bernard & Grafe, 1969).

3. Bernhardt, *Aufrüstung*, pp. 49-51.

4. On Wever's sympathies towards National Socialism, see: Freiherr Geyr von Schweppenburg, *Erinnerungen eines Militärattachés London 1933 bis 1937* (Stuttgart: Deutsche Verlags-Anstalt, 1949), pp. 52, 58-59, 166; Nielsen, *German Air Force General Staff*, pp. 126-27. However, I could not verify from documents the comment repeated by Rieckhoff, *Trumpf oder Bluff*, p. 83, that Wever said, "Our officer corps must be National Socialistic or it will not be at all."

5. Nielsen, *German Air Force General Staff*, p. 29. Milch was lavish in his praise of Wever, for he told Suchenwirth in an interview on September 29, 1954 (D/I/2, KDC/M), that Wever possessed not only professional skills "but also great personal qualities. He was the only General Staff Chief since the end of World War I who came close to Moltke. Wever, not Beck!"

6. Nielsen, *German Air Force General Staff*, p. 151; Suchenwirth, *Command and Leadership*, p. 25.

7. Interview of Generaloberst a.D. Bruno Loerzer, 26.Jan.1955, D/II/1, KDC/M; Suchenwirth, *Command and Leadership*, pp. 25-29; Irving, *Milch*, pp. 97-98.

8. On Kesselring's resignation, see his *Soldat*, p. 41; letter from General der Flieger a.D. Hellmuth Felmy to Prof. Suchenwirth, 31.Dez.1954, D/II/1, and Milch interview of Sept. 29, 1954, KDC/M; Irving, *Milch*, pp. 103-4, 412.

9. There is not a satisfactory biography of Udet. Jürgen Thorwald, *Ernst Udet: Ein Fliegerleben* (Berlin: Ullstein, 1954) is a popular account, while Suchenwirth, *Command and Leadership*, chap. 3, "Ernst Udet, Chief of Luftwaffe Supply and Procurement," is restricted to his Luftwaffe role.

10. Irving, *Milch*, pp. 94-95; Milch interview of Sept. 29, 1954, D/II/1, KDC/M; letter from Generalingenieur a.D. Erich Scheurenmann to Suchenwirth, Jan. 10, 1957, D/II/1, KDC/M; "Nach Angaben des Generalleutnants Vorwald am 25.10.1945, von Rohden document (4376-435), BA/F; von Rohden study, NA Microcopy T-971/10/496-98.

11. Interviews of Generalmajor a.D. Dipl. Ing. August Ploch, March 7, 1955, and Col. Max Pendele, Sept. 3, 1955, by Richard Suchenwirth, D/II/1, KDC/M. Freiherr von Hammerstein commented in October 1945 (von Rohden document [4376-473], BA/F), that there was much opposition in the military to the rapid promotions of Milch and Udet, another reason they were bound together.

12. Flugzeugbeschaffungsprogramm, L.A./L.C. Nr.1/35, g.Kdos., 1.1.1935, on NA Microcopy T-177/48/37338956 ff.

13. Zusatzprogramm 1935/36, L.A. Nr. 5400/35 g.Kdos. L.A. 2 A, 24.10.1935, RLM Folder 1621, NA Microcopy T-177/48/3738840-45, /3738846-84; Irving, *Milch*, p. 91.

14. There were a number of variants of this plan; see, for example, RLM Folder 1621, Lieferplan la, on NA Microcopy T-177/48/3738845-55; Gestrecktes Programm 35/36 mit Zusatzprogramm von 24.10.35, frames 3738856-62, and Lieferplan Nr. 1, frames 373886-82.

15. Flugzeugbeschaffungsprogramm L.A./L.C. Nr.1/35, g.Kdos, LA II 2 C von 1.1.35, Zusammenstettung der insgesamt bis 1.4.1937 (einschl. Zusatzprogramm) zu beschaffenden Flugzeuge nach Flugzeugkatergorien, Klassen und Typen, Lw 103/65, DZ/MGFA.

16. Richard Suchenwirth, "Hermann Göring, der Oberbefehlshaber der deutscher Luftwaffe," Lw 104/3, pp. 20-25, 61-65, DZ/MGFA; Interview of Dr. Alexander Kräll, June 24, 1955, KDC/M; Milch interview, July 24, 1945, von Rohden document (4376-463), BA/F.

17. Hertel, "Flugzeugbeschaffung," pp. 287-89.

18. Lieferplan Nr. 2, LCIII 1 Nr. 527/36 la g.Kdos., 21. März 1936, RLM Folder 1621, NA Microcopy T-177/48/3738835-36; Lieferplan Nr. 3, 1.Juli.1936, Lw 103/70, DZ/MGFA.

19. Information extrapolated from the following fragmented accounts: Lieferplan Nr. 4, A-Amt, 1.10.1936, Lw 103/10; Flugzeugbeschaffungen-Programm 1.10.36, Lw 103/70; Lieferplan Nr. 4E, Lw 103/13, DZ/MGFA.

20. Rüstungsfirmen der Luftfahrtindustrie, Anlage I zu LC Nr. L0690/35 III m, RLM Folder 255, NA Microcopy T-177/29/3716561-71.

21. Vortrag des Herrn Amtschef LC am 21.7.1938, RLM Folder 174, NA Microcopy T-177/15/3699740-51.

22. Heinkel, *Stürmisches Leben*, pp. 313-23; RLM Folder 1631, NA Microcopy T-177/49/3740173-218.

23. Statistisches Reichsamt, *Die Flugzeugindustrie 1933-1936*, NA Microcopy T-177/15/32720919-23.

24. Ibid., frame 3720934.

25. *Die Arbeitslosen im Deutschen Reich*, Reichsanstalt für Arbeitsvermittlung und Arbeitslosenversicherung, Berlin-Charlottenburg, n.d., von Rohden document (4406-819), BA/F, lists the following unemployed:

March 31, 1935	2,401,899
April 30, 1935	2,233,255
August 31, 1935	1,706,230
January 31, 1936	2,520,499

For complaints about the aircraft industry's overpaying their workers, see Folders Wi/IF 5.201-3, NA Microcopy T-77/35/747673-81, /747928-35, /748182-87.

26. Bericht über die Besprechung am 3.4.1935, von Rohden document (4406-802), BA/F.

27. Beschaffungsmeldung, Stand vom 30.Juni 1936, LC III, Nr. 366/36 III, 7.Juli 1936, Lw 103/8, DZ/MGFA; Organisationsstab, LA.V. (Monthly Reports on Production, October 1934 to March 1936), Folder E 1143, BA/F.

28. Beschaffungsmeldung, Stand vom Nov. 1936, LC III, Nr. 3611/36 III, 4.Dez.1936, Lw 103/8, DZ/MGFA.

29. L.C. III, Besprechungen, 15.Dez.1936, von Rohden document (4406-635), BA/F.

30. Besprechung über zükünftige Finanzierung der Entwicklung, 30.4.1935, von Rohden document (4406-526), BA/F.

31. Grundsätze für die Bewirtschaftung des Entwicklungstitels, 27.Juni 1935, von Rohden document (4406-818), BA/F.

32. On developmental costs, see Heinkel's memo in RLM Folder 174, NA Microcopy T-177/15/3699772-78.

33. Richthofen Notizen, LC Nr. 425/35 Ig, 14.Jan.1935, von Rohden document (4406-526); Qualitative Verbesserung der Luftrüstung, 17.März 1936, LC II, Nr. 191/36 II g.Kdos., von Rohden document (4406-574), BA/F.

34. Richtlinen für des C-Amt 1936, Aktenvermerk über die Besprechung am 16.November 1936 in Karinhall, Lw 103/50, DZ/MGFA.

35. Richterliche Ueberprüfung des Geschaeftsbereich des Technischen Amtes nach dem Freitod des Generals Udet, corrected copy dated 14.3.1956, Lw 103/25, DZ/MGFA.

36. Carroll, *Design for War*, p. 86.

37. Ibid., pp. 77-91; "Die Luftrüstung im Rahmen der deutschen Gesamt-wehrmacht-Planung 1938-1944," by Greffrath, 10.Mai.1955, Lw 103/25, DZ/MGFA; Gerhard Meinck, "Der Reichsverteidigungsrat," *Wehrwirtschaftliche Rundschau* 8 (1956): 411-22.

38. Carroll, *Design for War*, pp. 112-15; Mueller-Hillebrand, *Das Heer*, pp. 105-7; Emme, "German Air Power," pp. 302-3; Robert John O'Neill, *The German Army and the Nazi Party, 1933-1939* (New York: Heineman, 1966), pp. 156-58; Thomas, *Geschichte der Rüstungswirtschaft*, pp. 62-65.

39. Koppenberg, "Junkers 1933-1941," Lw 103/28, DZ/MGFA.

40. Planung der Flugzeugzellen-Industrie, Vortrag des Herrn Ing. Haase am 25.7.1934 für die W. O. Luft, von Rohden document (4376-1805), BA/F.

41. Nachschubzahlen für Luftfahrtgerät, RLM, LC III, Ing., g.Kdos., ab 1.10.1935 and 1.4.1938, NA Microcopy T-177/48/3738945-46.

42. "Mobilmachungsplan der Luftwaffe," Oberst a.D. Adolph Hörning, 12.5.1956, with additional comments by General Plocher, Lw 101/4, Teil IV, DZ/MGFA; Generalmajor a.D Conrad Seibt, "Mob. Plan," LDv 151, KDC/M.

43. For example, see the two-phase withdrawal plan in Mob./Plan/Rüstung, 25.Juni 1936, RLM Folder 250, NA Microcopy T-177/27/3714165-90.

136

ARMING THE LUFTWAFFE

44. Information on the test run was taken from the folder "Arado Flugzeugwerke Probemobilmachung," Lw 103/42, DZ/MGFA.

45. Letter from Wimmer to General Blomberg, March 16, 1936, NA Microcopy T-177/28/3716452.

46. "Notiz für Vortrag vor Staatssekr.Gen.d.Fl.Milch am 21.11.1936," Milch Collection, vol. 57, Foreign Document Centre, Imperial War Museum, London (henceforth cited as FDC).

47. Information about the selection of aircraft was drawn from "Planung und Auswahl bei der deutschen Luftwaffe zur Einführung gekommenen Flugzeuge," Lw 142, DZ/MGFA; Generalingenieur a.D. Gerbert Heubner, "Der tatsächliche Ablauf der Aufgabenstellung (Planung und Auswahl der Flugzeug für die deutsche Luftwaffe)," KDC/M; "Einflussnahme der Führung auf die Entwicklung der verschiedensten Flugzeugmuster und Ausstattung der Verbände mit Flugzeugen," Anlage Deichmann, 23.4.1956, Lw 124, DZ/MGFA. The British experience was similar; see Robin Higham, "Government, Companies, and National Defense: British Aeronautical Experience, 1918-1945, as the Basis for a Broad Hypothesis," *Business History Review* 39 (1965): 321-47.

48. Vortrag des Leiters LC II Beim Amtschef am 10.10.1936, RLM Folder 174, NA Microcopy T-177/15/3699772-78; von Rohden study, NA Microcopy T-971/26/1156-58.

49. Suchenwirth, *Development of the German Air Force* , p. 143; von Rohden study, NA Microcopy T-971/27/917.

50. "Die Bomberentwicklung von 1933-1939," Gen.Ing.a.D. Huebner, Lw 142, DZ/MGFA.

51. Technical data for these aircraft plus a detailed account of their development can be found in William Green, *War Planes of the Second World War*, vols. 8, 9, 10 (London: Macdonald, 1967-68).

52. "Die Bomberentwicklung," Lw 142; General Wimmer interview, 27.4.1956, Lw 103/55, DZ/MGFA.

53. "Die Bomberentwicklung," Lw 142, DZ/MGFA; Asher Lee, *The German Air Force* (London: Duckworth, 1946), pp. 7-8.

54. "Kurze Angabe über die Geschichte des 4-motorigen Bombers," General der Flieger a.D. Wilhelm Wimmer, 26.April 1956, Lw 103/58, DZ/MGFA.

55. Ergebnis der Besprechung zwischen A-Amt und C-Amt am 11.Mai 1934, Lw 10-4/13, DZ/MGFA.

56. Wimmer, "Geschichte des 4-motorigen Bombers," Lw 103/58, DZ/MGFA.

57. General der Flieger a.D. Paul Deichmann, "Warum verfügte Deutschland im Zweiten Weltkrieg über keinen brauchbaren viermotorigen Bomber?," 1953, C/IV/2cc, KDC/M; letter from General Deichmann to GFM Milch, February 21, 1954; letter from Admiral a.D. Lahs, president of the Reichsverband der deutschen Luftfahrt-industrie, to GFM Milch, dated November 2, 1942, 390/42, KDC/M.

58. Richtlinien für die Entwicklung eines Fernbombers, L.A. Nr. 845/36, g.Kdos., A.I.3, 17.April 1936, von Rohden document (4376-2994), BA/F.

59. Flugzeugentwicklungsprogramm, LC II, Nr. 12591/35, II, geh.Kdos., Stand vom 1.11.35, and LC II, Nr. 13616/35, Stand vom 1.1.36, 6.Jan.1936, NA Microcopy T-177/16/3700870-96.

60. Flugzeugentwicklungsprogramm, LC II, Nr. 870/36, 1 zbV. geh.Kdos., Stand vom 1.7.36, 20.Juli 1936, NA Microcopy T-177/16/3700788-824, and LC

II, Nr. 250/36, 1 zbV. geh. Kdos., Stand vom. 1.4.36, 9.April 1936, NA Microcopy T-177/16/3700825-58.

61. Flugzeugentwicklungsprogramm, LC II Nr. 1380/36, 1 zbV. geh.Kdos., Stand vom 1.10.36, 27.Okt.1936, NA Microcopy T-177/16/3700678-726.

62. Akennotiz, LC II, Nr. 431/37, 1. geh.Kdos., 11.März 1937, NA Microcopy T-177/19/3705144.

63. Dringlichkeitstufe der Flugzeugmuster-Entwicklung, LC II 1, Stand vom 15.3.1937, LC II Nr. 2303/37, geh. 26.April 1937, LW 103/50, DZ/MGFA.

64. Flugzeugentwicklungsprogramm, LC II, Nr. 622/37, 1 zbV. geh. Kdos., Stand vom 1.4.1937, 29.April 1937, NA Microcopy T-177/16/3700614-64.

65. Flugzeugentwicklungsprogramm, LC II, Nr., 1388/37, 1 zbV. geh.Kdos., Stand vom Oktober 1937, 22.Dez.1937, NA Microcopy T-177/16/3700551-98.

66. Kesselring, *Soldat*, pp. 460-61; von Rohden study, NA Microcopy T-971/17/75-76; Baumbach, *Life and Death of the Luftwaffe*, pp. 115-16.

67. Killen, *History of the Luftwaffe*, pp. 60-61; Heinkel, *Stürmisches Leben*, pp. 341-44; Wood and Dempster, *Narrow Margin*, pp. 38-39; Cajus Bekker [pseud.], *The Luftwaffe War Diaries* (New York: Ballantine, 1968), pp. 40-43.

68. Auszug aus der Denkschrift zum Winterkriegsspiel 1933-34, Lw 10-4/13, DZ/MGFA; L.A.Nr. 6093/34, g.Kdos., 31.Juni 1934, von Rohden document (4376-2994), BA/F.

69. L.A.I. Nr 7827/34, g.Kdos. A.I.3, 1.Okt.1934, von Rohden document (4376-2994), BA/F.

70. Green, *War Planes*, 10: 53.

71. Ibid., p. 57; Kens and Nowarra, *Flugzeuge*, pp. 356-57.

72. Generalmajor a.D. Krauss, "Die Ausbildung im Bombenwurf und im Bombenzünderwesen bei den Kampfverbänden (ohne Ju 87-Verbände)," KDC/M; Heinkel, *Stürmisches Leben*, p. 341.

73. Eberhard Spetzler, "Der Weg zur Luftschlacht um England in Kriegsgerechtlicher Bedeutung," *Wehrwissenschaftlicher Rundschau* 6 (1956): 442.

74. Ergebnis der Besprechung zwischen A-Amt und C-Amt am 11.Mai.1934, Lw 10-4/13, DZ/MGFA.

75. Taktische Richtlinien für Rüstungsflugzeug III, L.A.I. 6816/34, 5.6.1934, von Rohden document (4376-2994), BA/F.

76. Ueberlegungen zur Frage des Z.Flugzeuges grosser Reichweite (2100), Ta/LS, 22.1.1935, von Rohden document (4376-2994), BA/F.

77. L.A. 190/36 g.Kdos., A.I.3, vom 1.Feb.1936, von Rohden document (4376-2994), BA/F; Green, *War Planes*, 10: 83-85.

78. Adolf Galland, *Die Ersten und die Letzten: Die Jagdflieger im zweiten Weltkrieg* (Darmstadt: Franz Schneekluth, 1953), pp. 76-81.

79. Ibid., p. 76; von Rohden study, NA Microcopy T-971/26/969-70, reported that the inspector of fighters initially wrote a long tract advising against the monoplane.

80. P. St. John Turner, *Heinkel: An Aircraft Album* (New York: Arco, 1970), pp. 62-68, 85-86.

81. Information on the competition between the fighters was taken from Martin Caidin, *Me 109: Willy Messerschmitt's Peerless Fighter* (New York: Ballantine, 1968); James F. Craig, *The Messerschmitt Bf 109* (New York: Arco, 1968); Turner, *Heinkel*; Green, *War Planes*, vol. 1; Kens and Nowarra, *Flugzeuge*; Heinkel, *Stürmisches Leben*; Bekker, *Luftwaffe War Diaries*;

138 ARMING THE LUFTWAFFE

William Green, *Augsburg Eagle* (Garden City, N.Y.: Doubleday, 1971).

82. "Denkschrift über das unmittelbare Zusammenarbeiten der Jagdverbände mit Auflkärern," Fl.In.3, Nr. 544/36 geh. I, 8.Juli 1936; Denkschrift über Gliederung und Weiterentwicklung der Jagdfliegenwaffe," Fl.In.3 Nr. 636/36, g.Kdos. I, 8.Juli 1936, von Rohden document (4376-742), BA/F.

83. Takt.-techn. Forderungen an das leichte und schwere Jagdflugzeug, L.A. I/Fl.In.3 Nr. 2076/36, g.Kdos., A I, 3z 19.Dez.1936, von Rohden document (4376-2994), BA/F.

84. Green, *War Planes*, 1:165-66; Kens and Nowarra, *Flugzeuge,* pp. 433-34; Galland, *Ersten und Letzten*, pp. 78-79.

85. Reichminister der Luftfahrt und Oberbefehlshaber der Luftwaffe, Generalstab, "Luftkriegführung," L.Dv.Nr. 16, 1936, Lw 106/12, DZ/MGFA; also reproduced in Karl-Heinz Völker, *Dokumente und Dokumentarfotos zur Geschichte der deutschen Luftwaffe*, Beiträge zur Militär- und Kriegs-geschichte, vol. 9 (Stuttgart: Deutsche Verlags-Anstalt, 1968), pp. 466-86.

86. "Die Entwicklung der deutschen Luftstrategie," von Rohden document (4376-447), BA/F; Dr. K. Grundelach, "Die deutsche Auffassung über den Luftkrieg zu Beginn des 2. Weltkrieges," Lw 106/2, DZ/MGFA; Völker, *Die deutsche Luftwaffe*, pp. 198-202; Suchenwirth, *Development of the German Air Force*, pp. 167-71.

CHAPTER 6

The Illusion of Strength

BY THE SUMMER OF 1936, crises abroad and at home were affecting the pace of aerial rearmament. Abroad, Germany's diplomatic and military position was considerably enhanced by the Italian conquest of Ethiopia, the Rhineland occupation in March, and the outbreak of Spanish civil war in July. The feeble groping of the Western democracies for a policy of accommodation toward the Fascist dictators led the German aviation leadership to believe that the first, critical, bluffing phase of their rearmament program was a success. The second phase, the retooling for more advanced models of aircraft, could begin. It brought some dangers, for production would be slowed down for six to nine months while the plants converted to new models. The Air Ministry sought to minimize the risk by overlapping the production of old models with that of new ones. The production of the new aircraft, all of which were designed after 1933, was scheduled to begin in early 1937.

At home a crisis over the nature and direction of the rearmament program bubbled over in 1936. The early coalition of big business, the military, and the Nazis dissolved in an argument over the pace of rearmament. Hitler and Göring, with the support of the chemical, machine tool, auto, and aircraft industries; the military; and the top echelon of the Nazi party, wished not only to continue but to accelerate the rate of rearmament. Schacht, backed by a fragmented business community of banking and agrarian interest groups, most of the steel and coal industry, and the "socialistic" wing of the Nazi party, argued that the pace of rearmament was threatening the stability of the entire economy.[1] He cited the rapid depletion of foreign exchange, the low level of exports, and the deepening shortage of raw materials as ominous signs.

In searching for a way to speed up rearmament and answer the criticism of Schacht's group, Hitler and Göring agreed on the interim solution of developing Germany's synthetics industries to solve the raw materials shortage and save Germany's dwindling foreign exchange reserves. The Nazis were not the first to think of this, for in 1930, Major

Georg Thomas of the Reichswehr had suggested that the construction of synthetic oil, rubber, and fiber plants in central Germany was vital for future mobilization plans. Germany's World War I experiences had indicated the need for the government to protect and encourage the development of the domestic synthetics industries through taxation and tariff and pricing policies.[2] Although the government and most of private industry had shown little interest in Thomas's recommendation, the Nazi party and the chemical industry had supported the idea. Within the party, Wilhelm Keppler, Hitler's special adviser on economic affairs, had established a special office for the improvement of Germany's raw materials situation. In the chemical and heavy industries, I. G. Farben director Heinrich Gattineau, an acquaintance of Hitler and his circle since 1923, promoted the manufacture of synthetics and by 1932 had established close enough connections with Hitler that he was aware of Farben's progress in synthetic gasoline production. When the Nazis took over, I. G. Farben had a considerable investment in this project with no hope of profit unless the state aided them with direct subsidies, guarantees, or price supports.[3]

In September 1933, the new I. G. Farben director, Carl Krauch, sent a memo to the Reichswehr regarding alleviation of the raw materials situation and at a meeting sponsored by the Air Ministry on September 15 suggested that the production of synthetic gasoline could, with a modest investment of 400,000,000 RM, be raised from .5 million tons annually to 1.8 million. On December 14 the first contracts, which became models for the synthetics industries, were signed protecting and encouraging the production of synthetic gasoline. In the fall of 1934 the synthetic textile industry was established when similar contracts were signed with the Braunkohle-Benzin-A.G. (Brabag). At the same time a mineral oil section headed by Krauch was included in the mobilization plan.[4] More ambitious proposals for the development of synthetic materials were stymied by Schacht, who realized their military importance but felt a massive investment in that sector would be uneconomical. As always, he wanted to see plans for the manufacture of synthetics established on a solid and businesslike basis.

By 1935 the situation had changed markedly. A combination of foreign and domestic factors had created a serious trade deficit for the Reich. World prices for raw materials rose sharply from their depression levels while German demands increased rapidly. German exporters were unable to keep pace by expanding their sales abroad to gain the needed foreign exchange. The "bread crisis" of the winter of 1935-36 compounded the problem. German food production declined noticeably, necessitating the expenditure of more foreign exchange to import foodstuffs, particularly fats. The alternative, food rationing, was unacceptable to the Nazi government's pride. Schacht attempted to save foreign exchange by sharply reducing agricultural imports, but that only led to a clash with the agricultural leader, Richard Walter Darré. In mediating the disagreement, Göring sided with Darré and left Schacht the choice of boosting export production or cutting back rearmament, alternatives which Colonel Georg Thomas had foreseen.[5]

While the trade deficit deepened, German leadership was also involved in a dispute over oil policy. German consumption of oil had risen enormously just as its price had reached a level permitting competition from synthetic fuel. Göring and I. G. Farben immediately pressed for an expanded synthetic fuel program, and Göring wanted to appoint a special fuel commissioner to the Air Ministry. Blomberg was reluctant, but Göring pointed out that nearly one-half of the German oil imports came from Rumania and the Soviet Union (36.8 percent and 12.3 percent, respectively). Hitler was impressed with the vulnerability of Germany's oil position. The much discussed (but never applied) League of Nations oil sanctions against Italy only strengthened his determination to free the Reich from outside fuel sources.[6]

In early 1936, a rough industrial survey by the government uncovered three major areas of concern. First, Germany's industrial capacity was overconcentrated in the Ruhr, Saxony, Upper Silesia, and Berlin. By spreading to middle sections of the country, industry could relieve pressure in the overcrowded areas, reduce vulnerability to bombing in time of war, and revive depressed areas such as Mecklenburg, Pomerania, and Hanover. The Hermann Göring-Werke alone was expected to relocate about one-third of the iron and steel industry to this new, safe area. Second, the survey noted the considerable dependency of the Reich on imported raw materials which could be offset by a program of self-sufficiency. Third, it indicated low labor productivity, which could be improved through extensive rationalization of the leading branches of industry, especially those associated with armament production.[7]

The connections between the foreign exchange crisis, the raw materials and oil needs, the food shortage, the failing export program, the rearmament and building boom at home, and the results of the industrial survey were obvious to many, including Schacht. With the support of Blomberg and Hans Kerrl, special minister for economic affairs, Schacht went to Hitler in the summer of 1936 when the foreign exchange deficit hit a high of a half-billion RM to suggest that Göring be placed as a watchdog over currency regulations. Schacht's motives are not entirely clear. Perhaps he hoped that Göring could curtail the unwarranted party expenditures (something Schacht himself could not do) and shield his conservative financial measures against further radical proposals from the party. Schacht was as much concerned about the drift of economic power from the hands of the more respectable, "conservative" elements to the radicals as he was about the tempo of rearmament.[8] Hitler's reaction was not what Schacht had intended or expected. Der Führer not only accepted the kernel of Schacht's proposal to appoint Göring as head of a central control over currency matters, but took the suggestion as an open invitation to plunge the Nazi party further into the economy. The result was the spectacular, highly publicized Four-Year Plan.

THE FOUR-YEAR PLAN AND AERIAL REARMAMENT

The avowed purpose of the Four-Year Plan, introduced in October 1936, was to achieve autarky, to make Germany as self-sufficient as possible while also permitting her to continue the rearmament program. It encouraged the development of industries to produce substitutes for needed raw materials, for example, synthetic oil through the hydrogenation of coal, synthetic rubber (buna), and textiles (cellulose). At the same time, Germany was to tap her low-grade iron deposits in the Salzgitter area. A consortium of the private firms of Krupp, Flick, and Röchling and the state-owned Hermann-Göring-Werke (established especially for this purpose in 1937) was organized to develop the blast furnace capacity to handle the uneconomical, low-grade ores. Nonferrous substitutes for iron were also to be sought, particularly through the use of aluminum and magnesium. Lesser aims of the plan were the development of adequate substitutes for leather and animal fats and the improvement of agricultural production by increasing both the acreage under cultivation and the use of machinery and chemical fertilizers. The German public also had a well-publicized role to play in the "battle for raw materials." The government organized massive scrap-metal collections, encouraged gardening, and urged the substitution of margarine for butter, fish for meat, dark grain for wheat breads, and pork for beef in the diet. To support these goals, agencies (*Überwachungsstellen*) were established to control the import and export of raw materials, stockpile critical raw materials, rationalize industry, and improve German agriculture.

Industrial rationalization was to be achieved by standardizing products, simplifying design and component production to facilitate repairs, increasing labor productivity with better training and more labor-

Stuttgart glider club at the Rhön contest in 1923. (National Archives)

Junkers Ju 47, the first German dive bomber developed for the Swedish air force, 1929. (National Archives)

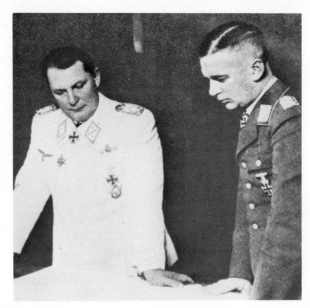

Hermann Göring (left) and his young chief of staff, Hans Jeschonnek, believed that Hitler's fivefold increase in the Luftwaffe could be accomplished after the Munich Conference. (Albert F. Simpson Historical Research Center, Maxwell Air Force Base)

Generalleutnant Walther Wever, the first chief of staff of the Luftwaffe and one of its ablest officers. (Albert F. Simpson Historical Research Center, Maxwell Air Force Base)

Erhard Milch, architect of the aeronautical industrial build-up under the Nazis. (National Archives)

Wolfram Freiherr von Richthofen, cousin of the renowned Baron von Richthofen of World War I, helped to develop new aircraft in the Technical Office and later to test them in the Spanish Civil War. (Albert F. Simpson Historical Research Center, Maxwell Air Force Base)

Ernst Udet, famous World War I ace, became head of the Technical Office in 1936. (Albert F. Simpson Historical Research Center, Maxwell Air Force Base)

Albert Kesselring, one of the best-known Luftwaffe commanders, feuded with Milch when he was chief of staff. (Albert F. Simpson Historical Research Center, Maxwell Air Force Base)

Junkers Ju 52/3m, one of the Luftwaffe's first bombers, later the major transport aircraft. (Air Force Museum)

The Heinkel He 45 was initially designed as a light bomber and reconnaissance aircraft but later was used as a trainer. (Air Force Museum)

In the foreground, a Dornier Do 23, in 1934 one of the first twin-engined bombers
built for the Luftwaffe. In the background, a group of Focke-Wulf Fw 58Bs, used
first as bombers and later as trainers. (National Archives)

The first fighter for the new Luftwaffe was the Heinkel He 51. First used in Spain,
it was soon outclassed by the Bf 109. (Air Force Museum)

The Bf 108, Messerschmitt's sleek sports plane, was the forerunner of his famous fighter. (National Archives)

Heinkel's He 111 transport-bomber evolved into the standard medium bomber of World War II. (U.S. Air Force)

Entrance cone of the Göttingen wind tunnel, 1936. (National Archives)

Junkers Ju 86, one of the first dual-purpose transport-bombers mass produced in the 1930s. (Air Force Museum)

Dornier's Do 17 transport-bomber set many speed records in the mid-1930s. (Air Force Museum)

The fabled Junkers Ju 87 dive bomber. (Air Force Museum)

The Bf 109, the Luftwaffe's standard fighter. (Air Force Museum)

Dornier Do 19, one of the first heavy bomber prototypes built for the Luftwaffe. (U.S. Air Force)

Junkers Ju 89, the other first-generation heavy bomber prototype, which was canceled in 1937. (Air Force Museum)

The Bf 110B twin-engined long-range fighter that never lived up to the Luftwaffe's expectations. (Air Force Museum)

Heinkel He 115. On March 20, 1938, a specially built variation of this aircraft set eight international speed records for float seaplanes. (Air Force Museum)

By 1939 the Henschel Hs 126 was the basic short-range reconnaissance aircraft of the Luftwaffe. (Air Force Museum)

Fuselages of Hs 126s in all-purpose production jigs. (National Archives)

Junkers Ju 88, the Luftwaffe's "wonder bomber." Initially designed as a speed bomber, it was redesigned as a dive bomber before the war. (National Archives)

Heinkel He 177, the second-generation heavy bomber that proved to be a major disappointment. (Air Force Museum)

The Messerschmitt Me 210 was originally designed as a heavy fighter, fast reconnaissance plane, and dive bomber. It was destined to be the Luftwaffe's most dismal failure. (Air Force Museum)

Willy Messerschmitt congratulating Flugkapitän Fritz Wendel after he established a world speed record of 469.225 mph in an Me 209 on April 26, 1939. (U.S. Navy photo)

Focke-Wulf Fw 190, designed in 1938 by Kurt Tank as a successor to the Bf 109. It did not go into mass production until 1941. (National Archives)

saving machines and techniques, reducing the detrimental effects of competition by pooling patent rights, and increasing (indeed compelling) coordination within economic groups. Labor in particular was to be more effectively managed through the establishment of a labor-allocation office with nearly dictatorial powers and the introduction of the work book law, which amounted to a complete census of workers and established control over them.

While industry in general profited from these measures, the most important concomitant benefit was that Germany was able to continue the pace of rearmament by strengthening her strategic position. Moreover, economic planners were given more latitude in preparing the Reich for a war economy and even greater governmental control was exercised over labor, investment, and taxation. With the introduction of the Four-Year Plan, the German economy moved from a "heated rearmament boom" to a virtual wartime economy.

The full implications and ramifications of this massive intrusion of government into the economy were unclear, although Hitler hoped to save 600 million RM of foreign exchange by investing 3 billion over the next four years in the synthetic products industries alone. He expected that by 1939 100 percent of the oil, 50 percent of the rubber, 30 percent of the textile, 33 percent of the animal fats, and 50 percent of the iron ore requirements for the mobilization plan would be met by the Four-Year Plan.[9] Evidence that the program was to prepare Germany for military expansion can be read clearly from a memo of Hitler's written in August 1936.[10] It was completely consistent with his earlier writings in *Mein Kampf*, his address to the army shortly after seizing power in 1933, and the views he later expressed openly at the Hossbach Conference. He held that the ultimate key to Germany's economic problems was geographic expansion, not development of the ersatz industries or an increase in exports. The Wehrmacht and the economy must be ready in four years to support the acquisition of new territories.[11] Hitler quite explicitly rejected any delays in rearmament due to economic or fiscal considerations.

The Four-Year Plan has been cited as a major turning point in the Nazis' relationship with private business. The uneasy tripod of industry, army, and party gave way. The Nazis dominated first business, and then shortly thereafter the army. Large corporations like I. G. Farben melded with official agencies and became quasi-public entities.

Much of this was anticipated in the aircraft industry where a similar pattern had developed in 1933. Although most of the aircraft firms were technically in private ownership, they were controlled, directed, and "owned" by the state. The division between state and private functions became indistinguishable. Air Ministry officials sat on boards of directors and helped plan and finance every expansion and every contract which they, as ministry officials, had to approve. Officers of private firms moved easily from business to government and back again. Indeed, many individuals became half functionary of the state and half private entrepreneur.[12] The aviation economic group operated after 1933 as a quasi-public agency, and its relationship to the Air Ministry was comparable to that of the rest of German industry under the Four-Year Plan. Many of the Air Ministry staff moved into the Four-Year Plan Office, including Colonel Fritz Loeb, the former chief of production in the Technical Office, who became chief planner for the industrial projects to be carried out under the Four-Year Plan.[13]

Along with the chemical industry, the aircraft industry and the Luftwaffe were the chief beneficiaries of the Four-Year Plan and its allocation of labor; raw materials, notably steel, aluminum, and synthetic oil; and money. One of the first actions of Göring's new labor-allocation office (Arbeiteinsatz) was to establish a system of priorities to funnel the needed labor into the aircraft factories.[14] More important, however, was the preferential treatment the Luftwaffe and the aircraft industry received in the allocation of raw materials and money. Although the plan was not organized soon enough to prevent widespread reductions in the aerial rearmament program due to shortages in raw materials in late 1936 and 1937, Göring was able to prevent cuts as deep as those in the army and navy programs. Indeed, the other military services complained bitterly that Göring used his economic powers to achieve a privileged position for his air force. Blomberg in particular felt that Göring's new position as head of the Four-Year Plan threatened the unified direction of the Wehrmacht.[15]

The first substantial raw materials pinch experienced by the aircraft industry occurred in early 1937 when Göring was informed that his plans for aerial rearmament could not be met unless the industry was given priority over the other military services. Shortages of aluminum, iron, and steel were cited, especially of construction steel, which forced the industry to defer the purchase of capital equipment such as cranes, milling machines, and presses, and to rely on more hand-labor techniques.[16]

The roots of the iron and steel problem lay in the low capacity of that industry and the poorly coordinated allocation system. In 1937, after the Four-Year Plan's low-grade iron ore program had started, the German iron and steel industry used 29,143,127 metric tons of iron ore, of which 20,620,876 metric tons, or 70.7 percent, was imported. In terms of the iron content of the ore, the foreign ore's percentage was even higher (76.7 percent). About 45 percent of the imported ore came from Sweden and 27 percent from Alsace-Lorraine; these ores had a much higher iron content (60 percent in the case of the Swedish) than the domestic ore, which averaged 30.66 percent. The industry produced a total of 19,848,924 metric tons of crude steel in 1937. Although plans had been drawn up to expand steel production, the major result of the ambitious Four-Year Program in iron and steel was to reduce Germany's dependency on ore imports without substantially increasing the output.[17]

The creation of an effective overall steel-allocation system proved equally baffling to the German leadership. Instead of devising a system of priorities for allocating raw materials, labor, and money and establishing a unified economic command, Hitler preferred that each group fight for its share. The results were chaotic. Throughout the summer of 1937 the steel shortage deepened and some layoffs occurred.[18] From May through September the aircraft industry ordered 99,800 tons but received only 35,000. By July, Wehrmacht officials were advised that there was no chance of receiving more steel than they had in 1936, and despite the founding of the Hermann Göring-Werke there was little expectation of raising the steel quotas in the foreseeable future. The aircraft industry in particular was warned that no new projects were to be initiated unless the steel necessary for their completion was on hand.[19] The shortage became so severe the Wehrmacht found in 1937 that with steel production running close to 1.8 million tons per month, it could get only 300,000 tons instead of its requested 750,000 tons per month.[20] Finally, Milch reported on October 30, 1937, that engine development and construction were gravely affected and that the overall Luftwaffe production plans would have to be reduced by 25 percent in aircraft, 66 percent in plant construction and expansion, 75 percent in the flak program, and 100 percent in the civil defense program.[21] By January 1, 1938, the Luftwaffe alone estimated it was 117,000 metric tons in arrears.

The situation in aluminum was somewhat better. Production had been increased fivefold since 1933 and stood at 100,000 metric tons annually. Germany produced 27 percent of the world's total and stood second only to the United States. Most of the ore for aluminum came from bauxite, which was readily obtainable in Hungary and Yugoslavia and—just as important—could be paid for by barter for German goods instead of by scarce foreign exchange. The Air Ministry was planning to increase the existing production capacity to 140,000 to 150,000 tons and to double production by constructing three new plants. The domestic mining of bauxite was also to be rapidly developed, although results of previous attempts had been disappointing. The Wehrmacht estimated that by 1940 it would need 288,000 tons annually to meet the mobilization plan requirements. To cover the immediate gap, it planned to restrict the use of aluminum and to stockpile reserves of bauxite. By the end of 1937 about 200,000 tons had been stockpiled.[22]

The development of a synthetic oil industry had been one of the earliest and most persistent concerns of the Air Ministry. Germany depended on imported aircraft fuel, and she needed an immediate supply to cover her needs in the event of mobilization. Moreover, she lacked experience with the new fuels just being introduced in high-performance aircraft engines. Rather boldly the Germans decided to develop suitable synthetic fuels and to stockpile as much fuel as necessary for mobilization. Stockpiling was given top priority, and in September 1934, the first of three large depots in Derben, Nienburg, and Stassfurt were begun. With no costs spared, the Derben operation was ready for use by mid-May 1935. The depots were to be underground if possible, well concealed, and removed from built-up areas, and were to contain elaborate temperature controls and have a capacity each of 75,000 cubic meters of gasoline and 10,000 cubic meters of lubricants. They were to have an expansion capacity to 100,000 cubic meters of gasoline and 18,000 cubic meters of lubricants. By 1942 six more depots were constructed, boosting the total capacity to 810,000 cubic meters.

Each of the fuel depots was to have loading facilities to handle 30 railroad cars of 20 cubic meters' volume per hour. Before 1934, most of the German aviation fuel was of a non-tetraethel lead type, but thereafter the need for high-octane fuels necessitated special storage and mixing facilities at the depots and specially built tank cars for the tetraethel lead additives, which were extremely volatile and sensitive to moisture. A survey of the 30,000 available railroad cars in Germany indicated that because of age, lack of safety, or prior use, only 1,500 could be used to transport fuels (aircraft fuel absorbed the foreign substances in old tank cars and deposited them as carbon in the engines after combustion). As a result, in 1935 the general staff ordered the first 350 specially built, all welded, intricately ventilated railroad tank cars. By 1941, 5,200 such cars had been built and another 3,800 were on order.[23]

The stockpiling of fuel had served only the immediate needs of the Reich and did not relieve her great dependency on outside producers; in 1933, for example, Germany consumed about 3.8 million tons, of which 3.0 million came from outside. She had to develop synthetic fuel. By 1933, I. G. Farben had close contacts with the Air Ministry, especially Göring and Milch. The firm even appointed a liaison official to ensure close cooperation with the ministry. In December 1933, Milch signed a preliminary agreement with Farben to help defray costs of developing synthetic fuel,[24] and by the end of March special offices for aircraft fuel had been organized within the Technical Office. Synthetic fuel at first offered little hope since Farben could produce gasoline suitable only for use in automobiles. By the end of 1934, however, the firm had developed a synthetic gas for aircraft which, with the use of additives, reached an octane rating of 87-89, allowing its use in the new high-performance engines. On July 3, 1935, Farben informed the ministry that with 1,380,000 RM it could, within nine months, be in a position to produce 300,000 tons of synthetic fuel annually. The higher cost of synthetic fuel (in August 1936, the ministry bought synthetic fuel from the Leuna plant for 185.30 RM per ton, compared to 124.25 RM for Rumanian and 98.52 RM for California fuel) and its poorer quality made the ministry hesitate. Doubts about the quality were removed in the spring of 1936 when the Technical Office, after extensive testing, approved the use of the newer Leuna II fuel, later designated A4 or B4, for Luftwaffe use. On June 10, 1936, the ministry signed an agreement with the Ammoniakwerk Merseburg G.m.b.H. to develop facilities at Leuna to produce up to 200,000 tons of aviation fuel yearly, the cost of the plant to be covered by the Reich.[25]

The synthetic aviation fuels reached the required octane rating only with the additive tetraethel lead, which was supplied by the American patent holder, the Ethyl Gasoline Corporation, a subsidiary of Standard Oil of New Jersey. I. G. Farben's close business associations with Standard Oil were used by the Air Ministry to open negotiations for a license to produce the additive in Germany. Cognizant of its importance to the Luftwaffe, the American government applied pressure to delay negotiations for the licensing agreement. Even before approval was given, however, Ethel-G.m.b.H., a new corporation owned jointly by Ethyl Gasoline and Ammoniakwerk Merseburg, was organized to begin construction of a plant at Gapel near Berlin with a capacity of 1,200 tons yearly. Since the additive was used in small amounts, this was enough to cover the normal Luftwaffe requirements. A second plant was started in 1938 at Nachterstedt-Frose by Magdeburg, and like the first one, it was built at the expense of the Reich. Finally, in 1939, I. G. Farben received permission to produce the additive in Germany and the Air Ministry breathed a sigh of relief. The first steps toward self-sufficiency in aviation fuel had been taken. Curiously, the ministry and I. G. Farben did not press the development of the super aviation fuel Issoktan, which was rated at 100 octane. The Americans and somewhat later the British, began equipping their forces with engines that could use it, but the Germans were far slower. Although Farben had a complex process of producing the fuel from coal or coke, neither the firm nor the ministry seemed eager to encourage its widespread use. As a result, the Luftwaffe entered the war using fuels that were not of the quality of those of their Western opponents.[26]

By 1936, with the rearmament and increased use of automobiles, the Reich's consumption of oil grew to 5 million tons, of which only 1.78 million tons, or 34 percent, was covered by domestic production. The Four-Year Plan called for an increase by the end of 1937 to 3.8 million tons, which would cover 80 percent of the lubricants, 39 percent of the heating oil, 68 percent of the diesel fuel, and 84 percent of the gasoline requirements of the Reich. Instead, actual production reached only 2.34 million metric tons by 1938, and Germany still had to import about 60 percent of her fuel. By 1942, 5.8 billion RM were invested in the oil sector, far and away the most important and costly part of the program.[27] I. G. Farben and the Four-Year Plan became virtually synonymous as 20 percent of the top ninety-eight leaders of the program and two-thirds of the total investment were concentrated in the "verstaatlichten [nationalized] I. G. Farben," as Albert Speer later jokingly referred to it. The appointment of Farben's director, Krauch, as the plenipotentiary for production of synthetic materials on August 22, 1938, clinched the firm's dominant position in the program. The entire problem of fuel acquisition and research within the Air Ministry was transferred to the Four-Year Plan office in July of 1939. By the time Germany went to war, she had stockpiled 500,000 tons of primarily synthetic aviation fuel, but she was far from being self-sufficient.[28] Nearly 60 percent of her oil still had to be imported, and only the capture of large quantities of oil, lower troop requirements than anticipated, and imported Soviet oil kept her from suffering a critical deficiency during the first two years of the war.

The effect of the Four-Year Plan on aerial rearmament was generally advantageous, but by no means completely so. Göring's enhanced economic power enabled him to mitigate the worst effects of the raw materials and foreign exchange shortages on the aviation program, but it drew him further away from his primary duties of running the Reich's aviation world. Moreover, the Four-Year Plan's successes in rearmament and autarky were, in fact, limited. The basis of the synthetic products industry was laid, but this accomplishment appeared more important, especially to outsiders, than it was. It seemed that Hitler had achieved a degree of independence in raw materials which allowed him more flexibility in foreign policy. In reality, the plan glossed over the basic shortages of raw materials, skilled labor, and industrial products like gasoline and steel which affected aircraft model selection and production programs. At the same time, it vastly increased the power of the state to intervene in the economy while dividing all industry between winners and losers. Although the aircraft and chemical industries benefited, they felt the effects of the superbureaucracy of the Four-Year Plan.

PRODUCTION PROGRAMS FROM JANUARY 1937 TO THE MUNICH CRISIS (SEPTEMBER 1938)

The production programs for the aircraft industry from January 1937 until the Munich crisis of September 1938 suffered a series of convulsive jolts caused by raw materials and budgetary difficulties, the phasing of new aircraft models into mass production, and the erratic demands of the German leadership. Plans prior to 1937 called for the manufacture between 1933 and April 1, 1937, of a total of 11,158 airplanes, including 4,282 combat aircraft, 6,063 trainers of all types, 762 transports, and 50 miscellaneous planes.[29] As early as March 7, 1936, Hitler approved the phasing in of new models and by August 31, 1936, the RLM estimated that the necessary changes could be made at an additional cost of 2.6 billion RM over the currently approved budget.[30] Following literally Göring's maxim, "It is stupid to rack one's brain because of a few million marks," the RLM continued to overspend its budget, much to the displeasure of Finance Minister Lutz Schwerin von Krosigk and Reichsbank president Schacht. Production Plan no. 4, to be effective from October 1, 1936, to March 31, 1938, anticipated the mass production of the newly developed models, the Bf 109, Bf 110, Ju 86, He 111, Do 17, and Ju 87, and required nineteen firms to convert within a few months.[31] By November the RLM updated the Mobilization Plan; the new models were to be in production effective April 1, 1937, in spite of financial difficulties.

At a conference on December 2, 1936, Göring reiterated Hitler's intention to accelerate the rearmament program, noting the worldwide concern over German rearmament and military intervention in Spain. While he acknowledged the desirability of maintaining peace until 1941, he felt it was necessary for the Reich to rearm quickly. Therefore, he ordered that starting January 1, 1937, all aircraft plants were to run at mobilization pace with more emphasis on spending for military hardware and supplies than for factory and airfield expansion, airfield installations, and barracks.[32]

The problem of systematically reequipping the Luftwaffe with new models had received the close attention of the general staff and the RLM. By mid-1936 the developmental program had progressed to a point where there were two or three new models in nearly every category and reasonable projections could be made for the next three years (table 8).

TABLE 8

MODEL CHANGES IN PRINCIPAL LAND COMBAT AIRCRAFT

	1933-34	1934-35	1935-36	1936-37	1937-38	1938-39
Bombers						
Medium	Do 11, Ju 52	Do 11, Do 23, Ju 52,	Do 23, Ju 52	He 111, Ju 86, Do 17	He 111, Ju 86, Do 17	He 111, Ju 86, Do 17
Heavy					Do 19, Ju 89	Do 19, Ju 89
Heavy dive				He 50, Ju 87, He 118	Ar 81, Ju 87, He 118	Ar 81, Ju 87, He 118
Speed						Bf 162, Ju 88, Hs 124, He 119
Fighters						
Front	Ar 64, Ar 65	Ar 65	Ar 65, He 51	He 51, Ar 68	Ar 68, Fw 159	Fw 159
Light dive				Hs 123	Hs 123	?
Battle						
Pursuit				Bf 109	Bf 109, He 112	Bf 109, Fw 187[1]
Heavy					Bf 110, Hs 124, Fw 57	Bf 110, Hs 124, Fw 57
Reconnaissance planes						
Short-range	He 46	He 46	He 46	He 45, He 46	He 45[2], Hs 126	He 45[2], Hs 126
Long-range	He 45	He 45	He 45	He 70, Do 17	Do 17, Bf 161	Bf 161, new[3]
Liaison					Fi 156, Fw 105, Bf 163	Fi 156, Fw 105,

SOURCE: Planung für Landflugzeuge, Document E 1143, BA/F.

[1] New two-engined pursuit aircraft.

[2] Second series with improved 30-liter engine.

[3] New three-seat model with two or more engines.

Despite Göring's braggadocio, RLM officials knew that the lack of money and raw materials would necessitate reductions in development and production. At a meeting on December 16, the RLM Technical Office decided to discontinue further work on the Ar 81, Ha 137, He 245, Bf 161, He 112, FW 159, Hs 124, He 116, and Ar 95 and sharply reduce the number of different engine mountings they were trying on various models. The cutback in production models was discussed a week later: it was thought desirable to have fewer models, especially of older aircraft, in production. Given the loss of time and materials that reduction would entail, a quick switchover to new models was planned in order to maintain full employment and keep valuable production facilities from lying idle.[33]

On January 11, 1937, Göring announced new changes—with a concomitant budgetary overrun—in Production Plan no. 4 to modernize the Luftwaffe's aircraft. The biggest differences were an increase from 758 to 1,400 Bf 109s, from 270 to 444 Do 17Fs, and smaller increases in other combat models, with reductions in trainers and transports.[34] On the twenty-first, Udet's Technical Office made a number of far-reaching developmental decisions in line with Göring's new programs. With the exception of Heinkel, Junkers, and BFW, firms were to have no further major projects in the immediate future so they could concentrate on their production commitments. Junkers and Heinkel were to focus their developmental work on bombers, with which they had a particular advantage, and BFW was to stress fighters.[35] The Technical Office was particularly concerned that the defects in the Ju 87 and Bf 109 just coming off the assembly lines be worked out as fast as possible. The Ju 87 needed a larger engine to improve its climb rate and a method of preventing an oil film from covering the cockpit when the aircraft dived, while the Bf 109 needed a stronger landing gear and minor technical changes.[36]

In February and March the Technical Office worked out the details to conform to Göring's new goals. As was typical, instead of making extensive alterations in the current Production Plan no. 4, the office scrapped it and issued the new Production Plan no. 5, effective from April 1, 1937 to October 1, 1938.[37] It called for total cumulative aircraft production of 18,620, with 10, 677 built by April 1, 1937, and 7,943 in the eighteen months the plan was to run. The average monthly production of 441.2 aircraft was somewhat lower than the actual prevailing average of 483.8 because of anticipated difficulties in introducing new models.[38] Some principle aircraft ordered were:

Type	Model	Produced before March 31, 1937	Produced from April 1, 1937, to Sept. 30, 1938	Total
Reconnaissance Planes				
long-range	Do 17	28	371	399
short-range	Hs 126	——	101	101
Fighters	Bf 109	22	1,307	1,329
	Bf 110	——	160	160
Bombers	Do 17	104	423	527
	He 111	33	804	837
	Ju 86	202	390	592
Dive Bombers	Ju 87	——	348	348
	Hs 123	111	124	135
Transports	Ju 52	839	153	992

A comparison of Production Plan no. 4 with no. 5 reveals some interesting changes. While no. 4 anticipated a total cumulative production of 11,158 aircraft by April 1, no. 5, using actual figures, begins with a total of 10,677, or 481 less. More important, no. 4 called for a total production of 18,000 by March 31, 1938, while no. 5 estimated that 18,620 would be reached only by September 30, 1938. Meanwhile, the developmental program blossomed. Using a more refined method of accounting, Production Plan no. 5 included 241 separate line contracts for development, compared to 80 in Production Plan no. 4. Among the developmental line contracts were 113 for multi-engine bombers and transports, including two heavy four-engined bombers and two four-engined transports; 79 for fighters; and 49 for reconnaissance planes and miscellaneous items.[39] It is clear that the Technical Office anticipated cuts in funds and raw materials: Plan no. 5 was deliberately designed to scale down monthly production and stretch it out a few extra months while it boosted the conversion to new models and increased the number of developmental contracts to cushion the industry from sharp cutbacks.

By the end of April 1937, the bubble of optimism in the RLM burst. The hope that their powerful protector Göring would be able to shield them against shortages proved ill-placed. Cutbacks were ordered; the first major program that felt the ax was the Ju 86E-1, a medium bomber with Jumo 205 diesel engines. The plane, which had been hurried into series production, proved to be a disappointment. Results from field testing confirmed that the engines were unreliable, the aircraft was slow, and the landing gear was too narrow, causing landing difficulties in crosswinds; in general, the plane had little to recommend it.[40] On April 29, Milch ordered the program curtailed, and on May 5, Udet brought in a detailed report. The Ju 86 had an 8-month building time (3 months for cutting, forming, and subassembly; 2.5 months for fuselage construction; 1 month for engine and final assembly; and 1.5 months for testing and acceptance); and if production were immediately stopped, 162 aircraft in various stages of completion would have to be scrapped and 2,100 workers released at a cost of 10.3 million RM. Even if the raw materials difficulties could be solved, the ATG assembly plant of the Ju 86 at Leipzig would take eight or nine months to convert to production of He 111s. Udet proposed a better solution: of the 162 aircraft, 89 would be completed for the Luftwaffe, 50 equipped with the BMW 132F engines; 10-20 more exported; and the rest scrapped. Later in the year, another 250 Ju 86s already in service could be rebuilt with the BMW 132F engines. Milch agreed.[41] Shortly thereafter, all offices of the RLM were ordered to investigate ways of reducing their other programs.

By the end of May the Technical Office was discussing the need for more peacetime work to stabilize the aircraft industry and maintain its mobilization capacity. The limiting consideration was no longer factory capacity but the amount of money and raw materials at hand. The Technical Office decided to stop new construction, including that of needed repair plants, even though it meant that part of the mobilization plan could not be fulfilled.[42] In early June the office reported new construction at only 10 percent of the planned level and ordered prolonged use by the Luftwaffe of some aircraft engines to save 65.5 million RM. It also altered the production program by extending the delivery date for some aircraft and reducing purchases, and estimated that another 81.58 million RM could be saved by eliminating 4 Hs 126s, 59 He 111s, 17 Do 17Ms, 7 Do 17Ps, 22 Ju 87s, 103 FW 58s, 121 Bf 109s, 17 Bf 108s, 19 Bf 110s, and 60 Ju 86s from the construction program.[43] These cutbacks would reduce the industry's work force of 109,750 by 11,500: 5,000 in the airframe and 6,500 in the engine firms. Another 2,800 would probably be laid off in the auxiliary industries.[44] On June 5, Göring endorsed these measures, designed to save 0.55 billion RM in construction costs, and approved a total budget for the Technical Office of 3.7 billion. While insisting that the reductions should not adversely affect procurement of the newest combat aircraft but be made in training aircraft and industrial expansion, he nevertheless alluded to the possibility of further cuts the next year.[45]

In June a production plan was issued calling for a drop in production during the last quarter of 1937 and the first two quarters of 1938, with an upswing to begin in the third quarter. The terminal date was again extended six months, meaning that the Technical Office estimated that a grand total of 22,200 aircraft would have been produced

March 31, 1939. For the first time since the Nazis took power, the RLM
planned for an interruption in the steady increase in production in the
aircraft industry.[46]

The RLM convened a conference of the industry in July and
presented its grim prognostication for the immediate future in as favorable a light as possible. After reviewing the rapid build-up of the industry, both Milch and Udet centered their remarks on the need for greater
efficiency to obtain more for the funds available. Despite steady
increases in its budget, the RLM found that the cost of aircraft rose even
more rapidly. Acknowledging that the per unit cost of airplanes
depended on the amount of preparation required, length of production
series, and a number of technical changes made, the ministry still felt that
costs had risen alarmingly. The newly planned reductions could help the
industry become more cost conscious while lightening the load on the
taxpayer. Udet, in particular, felt that too many peculiarly German
secondary costs were being computed in the production costs of the German aircraft, which were more expensive than comparable airplanes on
the world market. Nazi social programs such as the *"Schönheit der
Arbeit"* (work beautification), housing, labor training, and civil defense
measures, and the necessity of building up capital formation in the
capital-poor industry all conspired to drive costs up. Most of these
expenses were now behind the industry; this was the time to decrease
costs and become competitive.

The companies responded that the tempo of the build-up had been
too rapid. Everything had had to be done at once—labor hired and
trained, equipment bought, factories built or relocated—all accomplished while the ministry was continually changing its mind. Company
after company cited instances of higher costs due to the ministry's
vacillation. Focke-Wulf lost 30,000 hours of engineering time on changes
of one airplane, the FW 58, which eventually was produced in a series of
only sixty. AGO spent 800,000 RM converting their assembly line, only
to be asked to produce sixty aircraft. Heinkel and Junkers complained
that unclear directives, constant changes in model development, and the
slow pace of engine development drove their costs up, while Henschel
and BMW attributed excessive costs to inadequate control over
subcontracting and parts. All agreed that the RLM had to reduce the
number of changes demanded, freeze models, run longer series, and
more adequately control parts and subassembly production. The RLM
was also accused of being too demanding in requiring so many different
model types be produced in the same factory and too lax in its standardization program; for example, Heinkel, Focke-Wulf, Fieseler, Junkers,
and AGO each had five models in production at that time. As for parts

standardization, "Is it really necessary to have eleven kinds of sunken rivets and scores of different kinds of screws and bolts to build one airplane?" asked the Henschel delegate. What started as a somber warning to the industry by the RLM erupted into a thorough ventilation of the industry's grievances against the RLM.

Three days after the conference, the RLM sent a sweeping directive calling for the normalization of procedures, exchangeability of parts, and simplification of models within the program. There were too many aircraft for the same purpose, complained the TA. There were two standard fighters, the Ar 68 and the Bf 109, but some units still had older equipment such as the Ar 65 and He 51. Still worse, the Ar 68 had twelve variants using four different engines and three different types of radios! The situation was just as bad in the bomber squadrons. The TA ordered a reduction in the number of models and types of equipment and the introduction of new ones only where they were clearly superior to the old. At the same time, producers were to pay more attention to the interchangeability of parts, while subcontractors and license producers were to subscribe to the exact standards of the designing firm. Changes were to be reduced to the absolute minimum.[47]

After considering the industry's criticisms, in early September the RLM completed Production Plan no. 6, to run from September 1937 to March 1939. It concentrated on fewer models with longer serial productions. The key planes were 434 Do 17P long-range reconnaissance bombers; 1,535 Bf 109 fighters, of which 924 were to be the new E series; 520 Bf 110s, mostly C series; 1,202 He 111s, with 952Es and Hs; 885 late-model Do 17Es and Ms; and 499 Ju 87Bs. The total cumulative production was still listed at 22,200 by March 31, 1939.

The acute fiscal and raw materials crisis continued to impair the program as the RLM tried to throttle back production during the last quarter of 1937. On the national level the crisis brought the downfall of Schacht, who had had a running fight with the Nazis over the rearmament program. Schacht's argument that rearmament had to be cut along with some of the less important programs in the Four-Year Plan was firmly rejected by Hitler; and the stiff, unyielding conservative was finally replaced as economics minister in the fall of 1937 by the more pliable Walter Funk. By January 11, 1938, Finance Minister Schwerin von Krosigk, who agreed with Schacht on the need to reduce rearmaments, reported to the RLM that the Reich's financial situation was "extraordinarily desperate." Newly levied taxes were expected to yield an additional 2 billion RM in 1938, making a total of 16 billion available from taxes and customs revenues, but this was far short of the nation's expenditures. The upper limits of credit for rearmament had been reached, in Schwerin von Krosigk's opinion. Further defense spending would touch off an inflationary cycle which, in spite of controls, could not be handled. As far as the RLM was concerned, the finance minister estimated that only 4.5 billion RM per year for the next two years could be placed at its disposal.[48]

On January 18, 1938, the RLM tried to work out the broad outlines of its budget for 1938-39. Its planned budget for 1937 of 5.4 billion RM had been successfully reduced by sharp cutbacks. Current statistics indicated the budget was running at about a 4.4 billion rate. The initial preliminary requests for 1938 were estimated at 6.1 billion, which meant they would have to be pared by 1.6 billion to reach the suggested 4.5 billion limit.[49] Hardest hit was the Technical Office, whose procurement budget was to be cut, resulting in what Udet predicted would be "an exceptionally sharp decline in the employment of the industry."[50] Cutbacks were also particularly severe in the two step child divisions of the industry, aircraft repairs and spare parts. By 1937, the Luftwaffe had forty-nine different aircraft models in service, but the twenty-six repair plants worked on an average of ten different models, making rational planning and specialization impossible. There were 916 planes in the repair plants, with an average repair time of 3.6 months by June of 1938, compared to 789 aircraft with a stay of 3.3 months a year before.[51] Nor was the situation much better in the spare parts division, where frequent changes made by the ministry and the pressure in the industry to complete whole aircraft while ignoring parts production were pinpointed by the chief of Luftwaffe supplies as major weaknesses during the Austrian and Czech crises.[52]

The Austrian crisis of March 1938 had no immediate effect on RLM planning. In line with budget limitations the RLM worked out a new Production Plan no. 7, to run through 1938 and the first half of 1939. The accent was again on combat planes, with a total of 8,205 aircraft to be produced in the eighteen-month period for a monthly average of 455.8. The new program listed the cumulative total of aircraft produced from 1933 to June 30, 1939, as 22,681, compared to the 22,200 planned under Production Plan no. 6 for March 31.[53] On the basis of its production plan forecasts, the Technical Office notified the Luftwaffe general staff in May 1938 that by the end of fiscal year 1939-40 the entire Luftwaffe should be reequipped with new models. Furthermore, the industry would have each model, with the exception of the Ju 87, in production in at least two separate plants. Barring any decrease in the labor force, the industry should be producing 45-50 percent of its intended Mobilization Plan output, with about 80 percent of its workers engaged in the production of bombers and fighters. At the same time, the

Technical Office planned to cut down the number of mobilization plan models to one per category. In the bomber category, for example, the He 111 and Do 17 would be carried until April 1939, when the Ju 88 would be phased in. Then by October 1939 the He 111 and Do 17 would be phased out, leaving the Ju 88 as the single mobilization plan bomber. The Technical Office estimated that by the end of fiscal 1939-40 the general staff could count on 2,133 Bf 109Es and 915 Bf 110Cs for fighters; 1,560 He 111Hs and Ps, 941 Do 17Zs (reconnaissance bombers), and 1,060 Ju 88s, or a total of 3,561 bombers, with 973 Ju 87B dive bombers; 786 Hs 126 short-range reconnaissance planes; and 2,048 transports. The total strength, discounting losses, of the Luftwaffe would be 9,098.[54]

These projections anticipated the major decision to mass produce the Ju 88 as the standard bomber for the early 1940s. Clearly the growing international crisis demanded freezing models and mass producing them. The earlier hesitation about overspending was also gone as Göring presented the Oberkommando der Wehmacht (OKW, armed forced general staff) a huge bill of materials, men, and money needed to complete the rearmament program for the Luftwaffe. Among other things, he wanted 677,681 tons of steel and iron, 28,500 tons of copper, 90,400 tons of bauxite (all of which had previously been requested); an additional 98,000 workers, including 23,000 skilled and 75,000 construction laborers; plus 2.185 billion RM for industrial expansion and production preparations.[55] The seizure of Austria had temporarily eased the crisis in foreign exchange while adding considerably to Germany's industrial capacity. This development, combined with the growing Czech crisis, eliminated any inhibitions that Göring might have had about restricting spending. As the Wehrmacht began to mobilize, Göring's Technical Office disbanded their previous plans and placed further demands on the aircraft industry, including a ten-hour work day in June.

On July 8, 1938, Göring gathered the key figures from the industry at Karinhall for a major conference. The situation had changed dramatically since their conference a year earlier. In a speech filled with war prophecies, Göring pointed out that although the European states did not want war, they might be forced into it; Germany had to be prepared. Everything would depend on winning, and all the petty problems bothering the industry would be irrelevant. Should anyone balk, Göring was prepared "to take away the shirker's property and life with one stroke of a pen." Once Germany won the war, she would be the leading power in the world; the world markets would belong to her, and she would be rich. But first, Göring said, "You have to take some risks and put up your stakes." Of more immediate concern, he wanted the industry to conserve labor and raw materials while concentrating on the

mass production of fewer models in larger series. He especially wanted
the manufacturers to stop bickering and apply themselves to the task of
organizing their factories for war mobilization. Problems such as
securing enough workers, including women, working out licensing
arrangements, and stocking raw materials and equipment had to be
solved now. Further, Göring wanted the developmental firms to continue
their programs, especially in the areas of rocket engines, high-altitude
aircraft and engines, and long-range bombers.[56]

Three days after the Karinhall conference, the Luftwaffe
commander for the southern district was ordered to commence
preparations for operations "Case Green" (Fall Grün), the attack on
Czechoslovakia. A month later, on August 12, Hitler requested urgently
a top-secret survey of the disposition of the Wehrmacht and its
mobilization plans as of the first of October. The production of flak,
munitions, bombs, and aircraft armament was alarmingly low—ranging
from nothing to as little as 50 percent of mobilization plan levels. In
aircraft production the Technical Office estimated that the total for
September would be 493, compared to the mobilization plan quota of
1,179. The industry would need from four to thirteen months, depending
on the aircraft model, to reach its full mobilization level.[57]

By the middle of August the RLM had issued Production Plan no. 8,
which projected a program for two years beginning April 1938. In
keeping with Göring's dictum to "freeze models and mass produce," the
new plan called for the production of 2,739 Bf 109Es, 1,005 Bf 110Cs,
962 Ju 88s, 1,185 He 111Hs, 913 Do 17Zs, and 1,092 Ju 87Bs.[58] Such an
ambitious program could be fulfilled only if all the deferred expansion
projects were revived and the raw materials shortage alleviated, but the
evidence from the summer of 1938 indicates that there were still
bottlenecks. By October 7, 1938, the RLM estimated its steel shortages at
366,000 tons, most of which was for factory expansion. After the
ten-hour day was ordered in June, aircraft production crept up to the
500-per-month level, but further increases depended on industrial
expansion and more skilled labor. Money was no longer a limiting factor
apparently, for by November the Technical Office budget alone was 5.3
billion RM, or nearly .8 billion over the January estimate for the entire
Luftwaffe,[59] while overall spending for the Wehrmacht increased from
the planned 11 billion to over 14 billion. By the time of the Munich crisis,
September 1938, the RLM had reversed the flow of the industry,
reinstituted expansion, and accelerated production. Given the inertia in
any large industry, it was not until May 1939 that actual aircraft
production reached the level it had been at in March 1937.

In summary, the low level of production in the aircraft industry
from January 1937 to the Munich crisis was certainly due in part to the

budgetary and raw materials shortages, factors that were outside its realm of effective control. Yet the masters of the Third Reich were unable to do two important things: fashion a system of priorities, and design a comprehensive program to control and disburse their limited economic resources. During a twenty-two-month period the RLM had in effect five major production plans (nos. 4, 5, 6, 7, and 8), the major intent of which was to introduce aircraft model changes while scaling down total production. The amount of absolute production loss can be gauged from table 9. Hertel asserts that had the original production plans been followed, 6,226 aircraft would have been produced in 1937, but a cut of a billion RM in 1937-38 so hindered production that Germany lost nearly a year regaining its momentum in rearming. He further posits that if the normal expansion in the air industry had occurred, production in 1939 would have reached the 1941 average of 1,200 aircraft a month.[60]

RESEARCH AND DEVELOPMENT

The three principal areas of concern for German research and development in 1937 and 1938 were engines, the second generation of combat aircraft, and standardization and improvement of production procedures. All were interrelated, but engine development seemed crucial. By the end of 1936 the first generation of engines of German

TABLE 9

GERMAN AIRCRAFT PRODUCTION, 1931-39[1]

USSBS Estimate				Hertel's Estimate		
Year	Combat	Others	Total	Year	Total	Increase or decrease from previous year
1931	0	13	13	1931	——	——
1932	0	36	36	1932	——	——
1933	0	368	368	1933	——	——
1934	840	1,128	1,968	1934	1,817	——
1935	1,823	1,360	3,183	1935	3,307	+ 1,490
1936	1,530	2,582	5,112	1936	5,248	+ 1,941
1937	2,651	2,955	5,606	1937	5,749	+ 501
1938	3,350	1,885	5,235	1938	5,316	- 433
1939	4,733	3,562	8,295	1939	7,582	+ 2,266

SOURCE: USSBS, Overall Report (European War), September 30, 1945, p. 11; Walter Hertel, "Die Flugzeugbeschaffung in der Deutschen Luftwaffe," No. 170 Studiengruppe Geschichte des Luftkrieges, p. 289, Maxwell Air Force Base.

[1] Hertel's figures apparently do not include aircraft produced in Bohemia-Moravia but do include those from Austria, while USSBS figures include aircraft from all of these areas. All figures for 1939 include aircraft produced up to September 1.

design had been developed and factory assembly lines were being prepared for their mass production. Aircraft designers had anticipated these new engines, designing their models well in advance of the available power plants. Although there were numerous delays and considerable amounts of engineering time involved in matching the models to new engines, it was assumed these new models were to be produced on a large scale. On November 16, 1936, the Technical Office reported to Göring that it was prepared to begin the massive conversion to new engines. In the 30-liter class (1,000 h.p. and above) the Luftwaffe had the liquid-cooled DB 600 and Junkers Jumo 211 series, and in the 20-liter class (700 h.p.) the liquid-cooled Jumo 210 and BMW 116, the air-cooled BMW 132, BMW 139, SAM (Bramo) 322 and 323, and the Junkers liquid-cooled diesel Jumo 205. Aside from some easily repaired overheating problems in the 30-liter liquid-cooled engines, all were nearly ready for production. To increase the volume of production and ease supply problems in the military units, Göring wanted only one type of even these new engines produced, with no parallel manufacturing of the same type and class. At the same time, he ordered the simplification and reduction in number of aircraft models to be produced. Among fighters the previous categories of pursuit, front, battle, and heavy fighter were dropped for the simpler classifications of light and heavy fighters. Thus the decision was made to mass produce only the Bf 109 and Bf 110 as the standard light and heavy fighters of the Luftwaffe.[61]

By February 1937, Göring reported to his unit commanders that because of delays both standard fighters would be produced first in series with 20-liter engines and later with the more powerful 30-liter engines. He bragged that if the Bf 109 with its 20-liter engine had performed as well as the French Morane 405 with its 36-liter engine in a recent Paris air show, and maintained that when equipped with a new 30-liter engine it would be far superior. In engine production, Göring reported that only the Jumo 210 liquid-cooled engine in the 20-liter class was to be mass produced, although 30-liter engines and air-cooled ones in both classes would continue to be developed. In aircraft types, he announced that the Hs 126 had been selected as the new army reconnaissance plane and the Ju 87 as the chief dive bomber.[62]

The Technical Office had shown a belated interest in the air-cooled engine for combat planes, mirroring the prevailing opinion in many aviation circles that the large, frontal air-cooled engine would offer too much air resistance compared to the more streamlined liquid-cooled engine. Engineering in the mid-thirties, especially the NACA-designed cowling, had overcome this disadvantage, and by 1936 the Germans were pressing for the adaptation of air-cooled engines to combat aircraft. In

February 1936, Junkers notified Udet that according to its tests, the Curtiss-Wright 30-liter Cyclone engine was more efficient than the German 27-liter BMW 132 (itself patterned after another U.S. engine, the Pratt-Whitney Hornet), delivering 1,100 h.p. versus 850 for the BMW 132. Junkers thought that although the Cyclone was probably at the end of its developmental pattern, Udet should secure manufacturing rights to it; however, the double-row engine like the English Bristol Hercules appeared to have more potential for further development. On March 1, 1937, Udet requested information from the Curtiss-Wright Corporation about building the Cyclone in Germany. Unfortunately, explained Udet, the foreign exchange difficulty precluded cash payment, but he was willing to offer the Jumo 205 diesel engine in exchange. He was also interested in any double-row air-cooled engine Curtiss-Wright had under development. The company was not receptive to Udet's offer, so he turned to Italian and English firms for engines to allow BMW time to develop their own. By the end of 1937 Udet decided that the BMW engines showed sufficient promise to dismiss further negotiations with foreign firms.[63]

Meanwhile, the Luftwaffe, discouraged by the slow pace of development of air-cooled engines, committed itself to building a combat force, principally of fighter and bomber formations, with aircraft having liquid-cooled engines. However, trainers, transports, and a few combat airplanes were to be equipped with air-cooled engines.

The planning for engine conversion proceeded rapidly in the first half of 1937, but soon decisions in regard to engines were affecting model designs and troop requirements. By April 1937, the Technical Office estimated that its engine-conversion program for 1938 and 1939 would depend on some key aircraft selections. In the bomber division, the Ju 86 was expected to be refitted with the air-cooled BMW 132 engine in early spring 1938, but Milch and Udet's decision in the same month to reduce that program sharply meant further changes. The TA drew up an interim program under which construction of the Ju 86 with diesel Jumo 205 engines was halted, but some three hundred of these aircraft would instead be rebuilt in 1938 with air-cooled engines. More perplexing, however, was the choice of medium bombers. In line with Göring's wishes to reduce the number of model types, the TA reckoned that it had four possible combinations: (1) the He 111 with the DB 601 or Jumo 211 liquid-cooled engine and the Do 17M with the air-cooled Bramo 323 engine, (2) the He 111 and either the Ju 88 with the Jumo 211 engine or Bf 162 with the DB 600A engine, (3) a combination of the Do 17 with either the Ju 88 or Bf 162, and (4) the Ju 88 and the Bf 162. The bomber choice affected fighter engine production because the TA projected the conversion of both the Bf 109 and the Bf 110 from the smaller Jumo 210 engine to the DB 601, production of which just could not be stretched to cover all these aircraft.[64]

As a result, the combination of the He 111 and the Bf 162, a bomber program based entirely on DB 600A and 601 engines, was eliminated. The combination of the Do 17 with either the Ju 88 or the Bf 162 was ruled out because of poor results with the Do 17. The Ju 88 and Bf 162 combination seemed far too risky, since both were still under development. The choice narrowed down to combination 1 or 2. Characteristically, the TA attempted to merge these alternatives by keeping both the Do 17 and the He 111 in production while converting the He 111 to Jumo 211 engines and planning for the Ju 88 later. The solution had the advantage of maximizing production by keeping some balance between aircraft with air-cooled engines and those with liquid-cooled engines, while the conversion of the He 111 to Jumo 211 engines would free production capacity for the intended conversions of the fighters to DB 601 engines. In 1937, then, the emphasis would be on producing small series of new fighters with the smaller 20-liter engines while gearing up production of the larger DB 601 engines for 1938 and producing both the He 111 and Do 17 in mass series. Then, in 1938, the big series of Bf 109s and Bf 110s with 30-liter engines would begin; and the standard bomber, the He 111 with the Jumo 211 engine, would remain in production, with the Do 17M gradually being phased out in favor of the new Ju 88. By 1939 the Reich could produce mass series of fighters with DB 601 engines and a bomber force of He 111s and presumably the Ju 88 with the Jumo 211 engine. This meant, of course, that the Ju 88 program was to be delayed until 1939 and the Do 17 and He 111 would remain in production longer than originally planned while the fighter force was built up. The converted Ju 86 would be additional insurance in the bomber force, while the production of the Do 17 would allow a reduction in the number of He 111s so that some of the Jumo 211 engines could be used in the newer Ju 87B dive bomber. These changes assumed that the key models would survive testing and there would not be significant differences between test models.

The implementation of this plan is illustrated in cases of the heavy fighter and the speed bomber. The TA was working under 1935 general staff specifications which called for a fighter with a range of 1,000 km. The Messerschmitt-designed Bf 110 with the Jumo 210 engine met this requirement but lacked speed, so the TA felt it unwise to mass produce it. When the TA ordered the substitution of the more powerful DB 601 engine, the results were disappointing. Although the speed of the airplane improved, it was still below the performance of a single-engined fighter, and the fuel consumption was so high that the range was nearly halved. The TA was reluctant to mass produce the aircraft and the number fluctuated with each new production plan but gradually edged up to 500 planes. Under plan no. 7, for example, the number of Bf 110s was reduced, but during the crisis of 1938, the TA reversed itself and decided to produce between 900 and 1,000. In September 1938, Göring ordered the development of a heavy fighter with a range to cover England (2,500 km., or 1,552 miles) and a 500-kg. bomb capacity—specifications close to those of the dive bomber. Messerschmitt undertook to design a new model, the Me 210, while Junkers adapted its Ju 88. Both turned out to be compromise aircraft with functions of dive bombers and long-range fighters. By early 1939 the poor performance of the Ju 88 as a dive bomber brought into question the validity of the concept of dual-purpose aircraft. The Me 210 had shown remarkable progress, having much better diving characteristics than the Ju 88, so the program was enlarged and the plane became the backup dive bomber for the Ju 88. The results were tragic. Instead of being ready by 1939, the Me 210 was delayed nearly two years and then proved to be a colossal failure. Hundreds were built before it was recognized as unsuitable for combat because of its poor handling characteristics, instability, and tendency to spin. The entire program had to be scrapped, with enormous losses of time, material, and money. No wonder Göring lamented in 1942 that on his tombstone should be etched "He would have lived longer had the Me 210 not been built."[65]

The Ju 88, the so-called high-speed bomber, or "wonder bomber," was the classic example of the intermeshing of engine development and design and production factors. The story of the Ju 88 started in 1935 when the general staff issued specifications for a high-speed bomber. In February 1936, when these specifications were reaffirmed, the bomber was to have a three-man crew, range of 2,500 km., speed of 310 mph, bomb load of 1,100 lbs., and one defensive machine gun behind and above. Within ten months Junkers had designed the Ju 88 and Messerschmitt the Me 162 to meet the specifications. Both aircraft underwent extensive testing in the summer of 1937 and the Me 162 emerged as 1 percent better in performance but had the reputation at the Rechlin test center as the "Reich's Repair Bomber."[66] The more reliable Ju 88, designed by a special German-American team of Ernst Zindel, A. Gassner, and W. H. Evers, combined the solid Junkers construction with the elegant lines of American models.

Although both firms' entries met the general staff requirements, the RLM decided to maintain its current production of medium bombers rather than switch to a new aircraft. Political and monetary factors were also considered, for Hitler needed a modern bomber force to impress Europe, while the RLM wanted to save money by using the full capacity of the industry. Rather than placing the aircraft in limbo until it could gradually be phased into production, the RLM continued its development along slightly different lines. The ministry and the general staff had been disturbed by the poor results with horizontal bombing of the Training Wing under its brilliant commander, Jeschonnek—results which combat in Spain confirmed. Horizontal bombing required a superbly trained crew and a bomb capacity of two tons. The general staff, however, wanted a long-range two-engined aircraft; but since the load and range dilemma of this type of aircraft could not be resolved, they decided a fresh approach was necessary. Slant bombing techniques, would be used, so the requirement was added that the high-speed bomber be able to slant bomb at a 20- to 30-degree angle with a 45-degree capability for training purposes. The crew was increased in size from three to four and placed together to increase its efficiency.[67]

Apparently in December 1937 Udet's Technical Office chose the Ju 88 for the high-speed bomber. Production factors, including BFW's heavy contractual commitments to new fighters, the phasing out of the Junkers Ju 86 program, and the size and experience of the Junkers firm, as well as the merits of the aircraft itself dictated Udet's decision. At about the same time the Technical Office planned to drop the Do 17, but when this was inadvertently reported to Dornier, he persuaded Udet to keep it in production, further delaying the Ju 88 program. Early in 1938 the Ju 88 was programmed into production with an initial small series of 35 in November, but by May 1938 the Technical Office forecast a long series of 1,030. The TA was assuming that the Ju 88 would be the standard bomber replacement for the He 111, but as Udet's actions with Dornier indicated, the need for continuous bomber production was uppermost in his mind.

Meanwhile, military theorists were rapidly turning from slant bombing to dive bombing as the most accurate method of getting the maximum tonnage on a target. When this was mentioned to the Junkers engineers, they expressed the opinion that the Ju 88 could be modified into a dive bomber, so with that the general staff ordered Junkers to modify the Ju 88. A special test group for the Ju 88 was set up at Rechlin by Hellmuth Pohle. At the time, the Luftwaffe planned to produce only a small series of Ju 88 dive bombers as a prelude to mass production. Junkers made the many changes necessary, including installation of dive brakes and other control surfaces, a stronger fuselage, new engines, and higher wing loading. The aircraft's contour remained small but it was radically different. The weight of the plane grew from six tons eventually to twelve to thirteen. Bigger engines were needed for compensation but that did not help; her speed and range dropped sharply. The Ju 88 emerged as an aircraft of average performance that could be used as a dive bomber but performed well enough that Pohle and Jeschonnek declared the tests successful.[68] By the summer of 1938 Göring was convinced that he had a solution to the bomber problem. He considered the Ju 88 a *Wunderbomber*, a twin-engined, long-range high-speed bomber that could deliver its deadly package with an accurate dive. A combination of the Czech crisis, the enthusiasm for the dive bomber in his young air force, the recent publication of Camille Rougeron's *L'Aviation de bombardement*, which stressed the concept of the high-speed bomber, Göring's natural desire to believe in a wonder bomber, and his childish love of astounding the world made him decide the Ju 88 was the bomber of the future. The voices of the critics who referred to it as a "flying barn door" or the "old 1935 Ju 88 dusted off again" were drowned out by a chorus of partisan supporters.

The RLM, general staff, and industry were swept up onto the bandwagon. Udet told Heinkel that the He 111 would be the last horizontal bomber Germany would build, while in the summer meeting of the industry, Göring asserted that he finally had the bomber he needed. In the midst of the Munich crisis Göring named Junkers general director Heinrich Koppenberg, a protégé of Milch, special plenipotentiary for the Ju 88 program, with sweeping power to appropriate men, materials, and factories for the production of the *Wunderbomber*. On September 30, when Göring sent official notice to Koppenberg authorizing him to begin the program, he ended with the words, "Now I am giving you the start, go and build me in the shortest possible time a powerful bomber fleet of Ju 88s!"[69]

In retrospect, responsibility for the Ju 88 program rested with Jeschonnek, Udet, and Göring. Despite his later disclaimer, Milch was also an advocate of a small twin-engined bomber for mass production. His often repeated remark that Junkers could build bombers but not fighters, while Messerschmitt could build only fighters, and his close personal contacts with the Junkers firm indicated that he was more pleased with the program than he later admitted. The contract was, after all, the biggest issued to the aircraft industry before World War II—a much sought prize and the source of bitter feuding among the major firms. In these circumstances, the one man closest to the industry, Milch, certainly played a significant role.[70]

The He 177 heavy bomber was another key developmental project undertaken in this period. As Chapter 5 indicates, Göring formally discontinued work on the first heavy bomber prototypes on April 29,

1937. General Paul Deichmann reported after the war that when he became chief of the general staff's Tactics and Operations in early 1937, he requested a four-engined bomber. He informed Milch that progress reports from abroad and from RLM engineers indicated the superiority of the heavy bomber in range, speed, altitude, and bomb load to the smaller bomber. Milch argued that the reports exaggerated the advantages of the heavy bomber; moreover, the industrial capacity was not sufficient to build a heavy bomber because of the impending Ju 88 program. When Deichmann answered that the industrialists thought differently, Milch replied they did not know all the facts since the full Ju 88 program had yet to be announced.

Thus, although the Ju 88 was only on the verge of being tested at Rechlin and it was not until December 1937 that Udet chose it over the Bf 162, many months earlier Milch had talked about a Ju 88 program that would exclude production of a large bomber, according to Deichmann. He may have been confused about the dates, but Deichmann related that when Jeschonnek replaced him as chief of operations in the fall of 1937, he tried to convince his successor of the value of the four-engined bomber. Jeschonnek, however, opposed his view, stressing the advantages of the smaller dive bomber. Deichmann's account was substantiated by Rechlin engineers, Hermann Franke and Gottfried Reidenbach. Milch, on the other hand, claims not to have known of this conversation and, in fact, heard about the scrapping of the Ju 89 and Dornier 19 projects only accidentally when Freiherr Karl-August von Gablenz, head of Lufthansa, called him to request the use of these aircraft for the airline.[71] The postwar accounts, which date the scrapping of the heavy bomber projects to early 1937, ignore the fact that there was probably a consensus in the Luftwaffe to discontinue or delay the production of a heavy bomber. Given the circumstances of the budget cutbacks, raw materials shortage, poor results with level bombing, slow engine development, limited production facilities, new medium bomber production, and strategy of a limited European war, the decision is easily supported.

The Luftwaffe's real failure to achieve an operational heavy bomber before the war lay in not vigorously pressing the development of the next generation of heavies. After the spring decisions to use the Ju 86 and He 111 as an interim solution and to drop the Ju 89 and Do 19, the Technical Office did not have another four-engined bomber on its developmental program until December 1937, when Bomber A was officially listed. Unofficially, the Technical Office assigned a developmental study project to Heinkel in the summer of 1937. The firm's chief of development, Dip. Ing. Heinrich Hertel, and his team of designers, headed by

Siegfried Günter, proposed the revolutionary He P 1041, which owed much to two previous Heinkel models, the He 116 four-engined transport and the He 119 tandem-engine speed bomber. The most interesting aspect of the design, which later proved the most dismal, was the coupling of two power plants in one nacelle, driving one propeller. This unusual arrangement was devised to solve the problem of underpowered engines which plagued bomber development in the thirties. The coupling of two DB 601 engines obviated the need to wait for the development of sufficiently larger engines. It had the structural advantage of reducing frontal drag, improving the speed and maneuverability of the aircraft.

In late spring of 1938 the Technical Office accepted Heinkel's proposal and assigned it type number He 177 on the assumption that production could be attained within two years. It had questioned whether contracts with other firms for bids might be useful but apparently decided that, for the sake of industrial balance, only Heinkel should be given the contract. The other major developmental firms were deeply involved in perfecting their current production models, whereas Heinkel was between models at the moment. The firm had just missed the big fighter contract with its He 112, and it was assumed that its He 111 contract would expire soon, when Ju 88 was phased in.[72]

About the same time, the general staff was beginning to reconsider its specifications for a heavy bomber. The distinct possibility of a war with England meant that the navy would need a long-range reconnaissance-bomber to operate with its U-boat fleet and as a marine raider. However, the poor results of high-altitude bombing, especially at sea, made it imperative that such a bomber be strong enough structurally to perform 60-degree diving attacks rather than the medium-angle dives called for by the original Technical Office specifications.[73]

The requirement for the He 177 to dive bomb, which came in the midst of its development, caused the undoing of the model. To withstand the stress imposed by diving, the aircraft had to undergo major structural changes. Its gross weight grew rapidly and its performance dropped alarmingly. The specifications for dive bombing violated the entire original premise of the design. The tandem-engine arrangement had been devised to enable the plan to meet the requirements of a top speed of 600 km./h., cruising speed of 500 km./h., and range of 3,600 km. with a two-ton bomb load and 6,000 km. with a one-ton load.[74] Every aircraft is in a sense a compromise, an equation in which certain characteristics are achieved at the expense of others, but when the Luftwaffe imposed the dive-bombing requirement on the He 177, the equation could never be properly balanced. The integrity of the original design had been so abused that it was virtually impossible to correct again.

The He 177 proved to be a bitter disappointment. The tandem-engine arrangement was unreliable and dangerously prone to overheating and fires. Despite prodigious efforts by Heinkel's firm and the Technical Office, the aircraft suffered innumerable delays, accidents, and failures. In some ways it was one of the most technologically advanced and original planes designed in this period; it could have been the big bomber Wever had dreamed of. But its failure and that of the Me 210, with the limited success of the Ju 88, did not detract from the successes of the development program during these years. In technical innovation, the German aircraft industry continued to be amazingly versatile and productive. In 1937 the general staff requested such diverse items as wing and fuselage heating and deicing systems, dive brakes with automatic pullouts, variable-pitch propellers, contact altimeter for bombing releasing, and reflector sights for bombing. These requests were quickly fulfilled, but the needs of following years proved more difficult. The general staff wanted a radio-direction navigation system, a high-altitude engine, and radar, none of which were perfected by the outbreak of World War II. Further, the new short-range reconnaissance planes designed in this period, the twin-engined FW 189 and the single-engined asymmetrical BV 141, fell far short of the expectations of the Luftwaffe.[75]

TESTING THE LUFTWAFFE IN COMBAT

During the first years of the secret build-up of the Luftwaffe the RLM exerted great effort to camouflage the strength of the industry and military units. Starting in 1935 with the official announcement of rearmament, this policy of masking the Luftwaffe was slowly dropped in favor of one that deliberately magnified German aerial strength. The policy of promoting "Mehr Schein als Sein" (more appearance than substance), gathered momentum as the aircraft industry began producing first-rate combat aircraft. Despite Göring's truculent words, it was not until 1936 that the new products of the industry were prominently displayed. At international air shows like those at Paris and Zürich, on important holidays, at official Nazi party rallies, and in the 1936 Olympics, the new Luftwaffe showed its wares. The astounding performance of the Do 17 "Flying Pencil," Bf 109, Ju 88, and Heinkel 111 were soon the talk of the aviation world. The obvious proficiency of Lufthansa with its fleet of smart, fast post carriers added credence to the Luftwaffe's new image. Although during the Rhineland occupation the air force had to resort to the elaborate hoax of repainting the few squadrons of airplanes involved and flying them from one airfield to another, it was only a few months later, with the outbreak of the Spanish Civil War, that the Luftwaffe furnished clear signs of its growing strength. Starting with the 1936 Olympics, a steady stream of prominent foreign visitors, including Charles Lindbergh, Italian Air Marshal Italo Balbo, RAF Vice Air Marshal Christoph Courtney, and, later, the chief of the French Air Force, General Joseph Vuillemin, were invited to view the prodigy of the Third Reich. German officials, especially Udet and Milch, were also sent abroad to help advertise German air power. With all the consummate craft of a Dr. Goebbels, the RLM propagandized the new aerial power of the Reich. Nothing was left to chance; special editions of aviation magazines, beautifully choreographed air shows, and elaborately staged visits attested to the Nazi claims of being a first-rate air power.

The effect that advertising the Luftwaffe had on foreign observers and governments has received much attention.[76] In general, the Luftwaffe's strength was exaggerated precisely as Hitler and Göring intended. Aerial blackmailing of Germany's neighbors became an important ingredient in Hitler's diplomatic negotiations which led to his brilliant series of triumphs; the policy of appeasement was founded partially on the fear of the Luftwaffe. The reverse of this effort—the effects of the advertised Luftwaffe on internal German policy, especially within the RLM—has been less studied. The warm words of praise from visiting foreigners and the impressive collection of flying records, which became almost a mania by 1938 in the Heinkel and Messerschmitt firms, reassured the German designers and RLM officials that German aviation had surpassed its competition. However, as they knew, the real test of military aircraft was combat; from the Italian campaign in Ethiopia and, above all, from their own experience in Spain the Germans sought evidence that their aircraft were superior.

The Italian experience especially drew the attention of German aviation circles. Deserved or not, the Italians had a reputation in the 1920s and early 1930s as a major air power. It was based largely on the record-breaking performances of carefully designed, hand-built racing planes; a large but antiquated air force; and a clever press campaign which exaggerated the Italian striking power. The invasion of Ethiopia confirmed German opinions. Working against an enemy that did not have an air force, the Italian Air Force proved to be crude but effective. The use of strafing and long-range bombing to demoralize and destroy the enemy illustrated the potential of the weapon better than its immediate power. The Italian experience underlined the effectiveness of an air transport arm; indeed, in a country devoid of railroads, it was crucial. The technical lessons derived from the Italian campaign were the need for heavier-caliber machine guns and cannon in aircraft and the desirability of simple operating equipment for troops in the field.[77] The Germans were not impressed with the Italian tendency to scatter their bomber crews or their lack of interest in wide-view, fully glazed noses, but they judged that the Italians led them in air-cooled engines, airborne machine guns, and gun turrets.

In Spain the Germans had their first opportunity to test their equipment in combat. On July 18, 1936, a Ju 52 Lufthansa liner under the command of Flight Captain Henke was commandeered in Las Palmas to fly Generals Orgay and Francisco Franco to Tetuán. On the twenty-fifth the same crew and airplane flew Johannes Bernhardt, a German merchant; Adolf Langenheim, the German consul at Tetuán; and Nationalist Captain Francisco Arranz to meet with Hitler in Bayreuth, where he was attending a festival. After brief consultation with Göring, Hitler approved their request for German military assistance. A force of 20 Ju 52s to be flown by Lufthansa personnel and Luftwaffe volunteers was dispatched to Spain. To protect these aircraft, 6 He 51 fighters and 20 20-mm. flak guns were shipped by sea. Within days the Luftwaffe set up Sonderstab W under General Wilberg to control the operation. The first Ju 52s were flow to Spain on July 27 and were immediately pressed into action airlifting Nationalist troops from Morocco to Spain. By October 11, 1936, the Germans had transported a total of 13,523 men and 594,438 lbs. of war materials to the Spanish mainland. When the Loyalist cruiser *Jamie I* tried to interrupt the airlift by firing on the Ju 52s, 2 of them were quickly refitted as bombers and on August 13 made a successful attack on the cruiser, forcing her to retire. Meanwhile, the 6 He 51s arrived in Cádiz, where a German advisory team of six pilots and six mechanics reassembled them within two days. Lieutenant Colonel Eberhardt, the commander, was under orders to teach the Spanish how to fly the planes, but when a student crashed on the first day and two more were lost on the first combat mission, the Germans were given permission to fly the fighters into combat.[78] The advisers had become participants.

German military intervention in Spain grew rapidly. By November the German forces, renamed the Condor Legion, numbered 4,500 men and consisted of the following aerial units (the German designations are given in parentheses): a command staff (S/88); one bomber wing with three squadrons of Ju 52s (K/88); one wing of three squadrons of He 51 fighters (J/88); a reconnaissance squadron of 12 He 70s (A/88) with four heavy flak batteries of 88-mm. guns; and two 20-mm. light batteries (F/88) with a communications detachment (Ln/88). Weather, hospital, and supply support detachments made the legion self-contained and mobile. The Germans soon found that their overaged equipment was inferior to the best of their opponents. The Ju 52/3 was unsuitable as a bomber because it was slow and too heavy; lacked maneuverability; and had slight power reserves, poor climbing characteristics, inadequate communications, and a dispersed, poorly coordinated crew. The He 51 was equal to other biplanes but markedly inferior to the Russian-built Rata monoplane. Since the Luftwaffe was eager to evaluate its equipment in Spain, a special combat reporting team was set up with orders to send reports directly to Berlin for analysis and evaluation. The importance of this operation was underlined in January 1937, when Colonel Freiherr von Richthofen, former head of development in the Technical Office (who found it difficult to work with Udet and was eager for combat) was sent to Spain as General Major Sperrle's chief of staff.[79]

In 1937 the Germans began reequipping the Condor Legion with their latest models, including the Bf 109, He 111, and Do 17. A limited number of Ju 87s, Ju 86Ds, Hs 123s, Hs 126s, and the new-model Bf 109Es were also sent for brief testing. The newer aircraft quickly proved their value. The Bf 109 dominated the air over Spain, sweeping away the new models of Soviet I-15s and I-16s, while the He 111 and Ju 87 conducted wide-ranging raids against Loyalist positions. By the fall of 1938, when the legion reached its peak strength of 40 He 111s, 3 Ju 87s, 45 Bf 109s, 5 Do 17s, 4 He 45s, 8 He 59s, and eight batteries of heavy and light flak, it was able, along with the other Nationalist air units (146 Spanish aircraft and 134 Italian), to establish supremacy for General Franco and pave the way for his ultimate victory.

While the Germans evaluated their equipment in Spain, they also learned how to employ tactical air power. In fighter tactics they changed from the tight wing-to-wing "V" to Werner Mölders's more flexible, loose-pair *Rotte* and two *Rotten* or *Schworm* style (a finger four grouping). The Italian preference for tight support of bomber formations was also abandoned for the loose-sweep method.[80] The bombing tactics were the classic tactical ones of close ground support and interdiction. German bombers were "highly mobile artillery" used to attack enemy strong points, formations, transportation, and communications. The emphasis was on developing a pattern of harmonious cooperation between air units and the army. Colonel Richthofen devised the technique of sending forward air controllers to the battleground to direct air strikes. The Germans learned the importance of detailed maps; quick, positive target identification; and excellent ground-to-air and air-to-air radio communication in close support work in Spain and later perfected these techniques in the French campaign of 1940.[81]

However, they were less successful with interdictory bombing. The Germans found that high-level precision bombing was difficult at best and virtually impossible against heavily defended or pinpoint targets; dive bombing offered a greater chance of success. On the other hand, results with the use of low-level attackers against enemy flak, troops, and especially rail stock were good. Strategic bombing was seldom used in Spain, despite the widely publicized attacks' on cities such as Madrid, Guernica, and Alicante. Daylight bombing was possible only with heavy fighter escort, while night bombing was inaccurate and, at the same time, very demanding in training, navigation, and mission execution. The importance at night of weather forecasting, communications, and new bombing techniques, such as the use of pathfinder aircraft and incendiaries and bombing on lights and gun flashes, were underlined. Attacks on naval vessels were rare and generally ineffective in Spain, but the Germans sensed their limitations in this area. Torpedo attacks and dive bombing offered the best results. The need for greater unit mobility confirmed Italian experiences in Ethiopia, and by 1939 every squadron was assigned two Ju 52s for transport and use as radio or direction finding stations. The ability of units to be deployed rapidly depended largely on their air transport system, and the Germans found that their old Ju 52s and, if necessary, their medium bombers could be used to great advantage.[82]

The impact of the German experience in Spain on aircraft development, production programming and general aviation theorizing was as profound as the tactical lessons. The general staff's concept of the offensive and defensive roles of fighters was confirmed: the fighter was the chief weapon against enemy bombers and the best defense for one's own bomber formations. The short range of the Bf 109 hastened the search for a long-range escort fighter; the result was greater emphasis on production of the Bf 110 and the development of the Me 210. The surprising resistance of bombers to flak and fighter damage stressed the need for heavier and better-grouped weapons in fighters. The Oerlikon 20-mm. cannon was successfully tested in the He 112 and was installed in the production models of the new Bf 109s, along with new and better radios. But the Luftwaffe decided against substituting the He 112 for its slower basic fighter, the Bf 109. "We will win the war with the 80 kilometer slower Bf 109," Technical Office engineer Lucht told Heinkel.[83]

The overall production plans of the RLM were changed, however, as the ratio between fighters and bombers was reduced from 1:3 to 1:2, effective with Udet's production plans after January 1937. Less important for the Luftwaffe was the obvious need for drop tanks to increase the range of the Bf 109.[84] The older He 51, which performed poorly as an air supremacy fighter, was converted to an "assault fighter" to attack enemy flak and troop formations. It was so successful in Spain that the army general staff in December 1937 requested a new assault fighter for close support of infantry and tank units. The plane needed to have a long loiter time over targets and to be slow enough to attack small targets accurately but still to have adequate range, speed, and armament. It required defensive armor against flak and movable machine guns with plenty of ammunitions, should carry some light bombs, be capable of flying in all kinds of weather, and have a good air-to-ground communications system. The Luftwaffe set up a special experimental command (VK/88) in Spain on January 15, 1937, and tested the Ju 87, Hs 123, Bf 109, and He 112 for these specifications. All the planes were inadequate, but the Ju 87 was the best even though it needed a larger engine to improve its flight characteristics. On the basis of the test results, the Luftwaffe reorganized some of its intended dive-bomber wings into assault wings. Five were trained in the summer of 1938 and by November, four of them were reequipped with Ju 87s and the fifth with He 51s. At the same time, the Luftwaffe developed an armored version of the FW 189 as an assault fighter. During 1939 the general staff changed its mind again and converted four assault wings back to dive-bomber or training wings.[85] In concept, the assault fighter fell between the strictly close-support aircraft and the tactical bomber. In World War II fighter-bombers handled this role until specially designed airplanes such as the Hs 129 were introduced into units in 1943.

In bomber development, the Spanish war reinforced German military thinking on the efficacy of the fast medium bomber and the dive bomber. Once the fast and heavily armed He 111 appeared, the Germans used this type of bomber for long-range attacks without fighter escort. The success of fast medium bombers working against lightly defended short-range targets vindicated the prevailing German view. The evaluation did not question the concept of the medium bomber but rather called for a bigger, improved version. The Technical Office wanted it to have an increase in range of from three to five hours' flying time, heavier bomb load of at least two tons, better visibility provided by a fully glazed nose, more defensive machine guns, improved radios, stronger landing gears, a strengthened fuselage, and larger engines to handle the new weight and improve the flight performance. In short, they were calling for a "super" medium bomber, and the Ju 88 *Wunderbomber* was it.

The Spanish experience with tactical air power tended to obscure the need for strategic bombing and led the Germans to the erroneous idea that a fast multipurpose bomber could be both tactical and strategic. More than anything else, the Spanish war welded the Luftwaffe to a tactical concept of operations. The successes of the Condor Legion precluded the evolution of a more independent, strategic type of air force, with results seen everywhere in the production and development programs. The heavy bomber was downgraded in early 1937, then redesigned to dive in 1938, while the *Wunderbomber* project was revived and refurbished to fulfill the general staff's requirements. The lessons of the war were interpreted to reaffirm the desires of the general staff and RLM: Germany needed a tactical air force suitable for limited continental wars.[86]

Overall, German intervention in Spain accelerated the pace of rearmament by removing doubts about the combat effectiveness of the principal warplanes and allowing the Germans to begin mass production. It also encouraged the Reich leadership to speed up the introduction of new models as rapidly as possible even though reductions in total output and a vast increase in expenditures would result. The Spanish experience, coupled with the Austrian and Czech crises of 1938, removed the last vestiges of resistance in the more conservative camp that argued for a slowdown in rearmament. In the spring of 1938 the situation in the RLM and the aircraft industry suddenly cleared. The major decisions were made, the models to be mass produced were selected, and further expansion of the industry was planned. Now the race for production began and Germany had the advantage.

NOTES

1. For a general discussion of the division within the business community, see Ingeborg Esenwein-Rothe, *Die Wirtschaftsverbände von 1933 bis 1945* (Berlin: Duncker & Humblot, 1965), pp. 54-55, 85-89; Schweitzer, "Business Policy in a Dictatorship," pp. 419-28; Meinck, *Hitler und Aufrüstung*, pp. 158-62; Carroll, *Design for War*, pp. 114-20; Amos E. Simpson, "The Struggle for Control of the German Economy, 1936-1937," *Journal of Modern History* 31 (1959): 37-45; Tim Mason, "Der Primat der Politik—Politik und Wirtschaft im Nationalsozialismus," *Das Argument* 41 (1966): 473-94; Eberhard Czichon, "Der Primat der Industrie in Kartell der nationalsozialistischen Macht," *Das Argument* 47 (1968): 168-92; Tim Mason's reply in the same issue, pp. 193-203, "Primat der Industrie? Eine Erwiderung," and Dietrich Eichholtz and Kurt Gossweiler, "Noch einmal: Politik und Wirtschaft 1933-1945," same issue, 210-27.

2. Dieter Petzina, *Autarkiepolitik im Dritten Reich: Der Nationalsozialistische Vierjahresplan*, Schriftenreihe der Vierteljahrshefte für Zeitgeschichte, 16 (Stuttgart: Deutsche Verlag-Anstalt, 1968), pp. 25-27.

3. Petzina, *Vierjahresplan*, pp. 27-28; Broszat, *Der Staat Hitlers*, pp. 224-25; Wolfgang Birkenfeld, *Der synthetische Treibstoff, 1933-1945* (Göttingen: Musterschmidt, 1964), pp. 18-20; Dietrich Eichholtz, *Geschichte der deutschen*

Kriegswirtschaft, 1939-1945, vol. 1, *1939-1941* (Berlin: Akademie Verlag, 1969), pp. 39-42.

4. Petzina, *Vierjahresplan,* pp. 27-28; Taylor, *Sword and Swastika,* p. 97; Bracher et al., *Machtergreifung,* pp. 818-20.

5. Meinck, *Hitler und Aufrüstung,* pp. 161-62; Carroll, *Design for War,* pp. 114-16; Petzina, *Vierjahresplan,* pp. 31-35; Schweitzer, "Business Policy in a Dictatorship," pp. 423-27; Abschrift, Nr. 118/35, g.Kdos. W., 18.2.1935, Folder Wi/IF 5.383, NA Microcopy T-77/86/809971-82.

6. Petzina, *Vierjahresplan,* p. 39; Arthur Schweitzer, "Der ursprüngliche Vierjahresplan," *Jahrbücher für Nationalökonomie und Statistik* 168 (1957): 348-52.

7. Rolf Wagenfuhr, *Rise and Fall of the German War Economy, 1939-1945,* USSBS, 40 b 21, pp. 3-4.

8. Schweitzer, "Business Policy in a Dictatorship," pp. 427-28; Carroll, *Design for War,* pp. 119-21.

9. Carroll, *Design for War,* pp. 120-21; Petzina, *Vierjahresplan,* p. 45.

10. Wilhelm Treue, "Hitlers Denkschrift zum Vierjahresplan 1936," *Vierteljahreshefte für Zeitgeschichte* 3 (1955): 204-5.

11. Petzina, *Vierjahresplan,* pp. 49-50; Meinck, *Hitler und Aufrüstung,* pp. 163-67; Carroll, *Design for War,* pp. 120-22; Eichholtz, *Kriegswirtschaft,* pp. 36-38.

12. On the fusion of corporate and state function, see Petzina, *Vierjahresplan,* pp. 122 ff.; Arthur Schweitzer, "Business Power under the Nazi Regime," *Zeitschrift für Nationalökonomie,* October 1960; Broszat, *Staat Hitlers,* pp. 228-30, 370-75; Dieter Petzina, "I. G. Farben und Nationalsozialistische Autarkiepolitik," *Tradition* 5 (1968): 250-54. On the general phenomenon in the armament industry, see the writings of John Kenneth Galbraith, especially his *New Industrial State* (Boston: Houghton Mifflin, 1967) and "The Big Defense Firms Are Really Public Firms and Should Be Nationalized," *New York Times,* November 16, 1969. Marxists like Kuczynski, Eichholtz, and Czichon would argue the opposite, that there always was a fusion between the state and the ruling class since the state was an instrument of the class.

13. Carroll, *Design for War,* pp. 130-32.

14. Schweitzer, "Der ursprüngliche Vierjahresplan," pp. 386-87; Folder Wi/IF 5.201-3, NA Microcopy T-77/35/747673-81, /747928-35, /748182-87.

15. Petzina, *Vierjahresplan,* p. 134; Meinck, *Hitler und Aufrüstung,* pp. 163-67; Carroll, *Design for War,* pp. 120-21; Eichholtz, *Kriegswirtschaft,* pp. 43-45; Mueller-Hillebrand, *Das Heer,* pp. 36-37, 106-12; *NCA,* 7:342; Taylor, *Sword and Swastika,* pp. 123-24; von Rohden study, NA Microcopy T-971/27/390-92; Thomas, *Geschichte der Rüstungswirtschaft,* pp. 65-67; although Milch disagreed with this, "Eine Rechtfertigung für die Niederlage und die Fehler der Luftwaffe," von G.F.M. Milch, von Rohden document (4376-2112), BA/F.

16. Besprechung LC III, 22.Jan.1937, von Rohden document (4406-802), BA/F.

17. USSBS, Overall Economic Effects Division, Report 134, Special Paper No. 3, "The Effects of Strategic Bombing upon the Operations of the Hermann Goering Works during World War II," prepared by A. A. Figen and John H. Reese, pp. 38-40; Petzina, *Vierjahresplan,* pp. 85-87, 107.

18. Von Rohden study, NA Microcopy T-971/27/384-86; Der Generalluft-

176 ARMING THE LUFTWAFFE

zeugmeister, GL Z II, Nr. 3398/20.Juli 1939; Der Roh- und Werkstoffe Programm, von Rohden document (4376-169), BA/F.
19. Besprechung LC III, 24.Mai 1937; 1.Juli 1937; 23.Juli 1937, von Rohden document (4406-802), BA/F.
20. Mueller-Hillebrand, *Das Heer*, pp. 37-38.
21. Von Rohden study, NA Microcopy T-971-27/386; General der Flieger a.D. Felmy, "Die Führung der Deutschen Luftwaffe im Kriege," Studiengruppe Geschichte des Luftkrieges, Karlsruhe, Lw 21/1, DZ/MGFA.
22. Petzina, *Vierjahresplan*, pp. 87-89; USSBS, Light Metal Industry, Report No. 20, pp. 9-12. RWM 23/5, Sofortmassnahmen im Mob-Fall auf Grund der heutigen Versorgungslage auf dem Rohstoffgebieten, NA Microcopy T-971/109 /611513-16.
23. Flugbetriebsstoff-Versorgung der Deutschen Luftwaffe 1934 bis 1945, Lw 105, DZ/MGFA.
24. Irving, *Milch*, p. 79; Czichon, "Primat der Industrie," pp. 176-79. The most complete account is Birkenfeld, *Der synthetische Treibstoff*, chap. 4.
25. RLM Folder 239, NA Microcopy T-177/21/3706759-68; Völker, *Dokumente zur Geschichte*, No. 172 Aktenvermerk des Technischen Amtes im RLM zum Stand der Entwicklung synthetischer Treibstoff, 24.2.1935, pp. 412-13; Birkenfeld, *Der synthetische Treibstoff*, pp. 66-70.
26. *Minor Trials*, 7:1189-94; Flugbetreibstoff-Versorgung, Lw 105, DZ/MGFA; Birkenfeld, *Der synthetische Treibstoff*, pp. 63-74; S. D. Heron, *The Development of Aviation Fuels* (Cambridge, Mass.: Harvard University Press, 1950).
27. Dr. Rudolf Eicke, "Rohstoffversorgung und Aufbaufinanzierung," 21.Juni 1938, NA Microcopy T-77/234/975191-221; Petzina, *Vierjahresplan*, pp. 83-85, 99, 128.
28. A.D.I. (K) Report No. 399/1945 in USSBS work materials 4 d47; Petzina, *Vierjahresplan*, pp. 99, 107-9.
29. Teil 1c Zusammenstellung der ingesamt bis 1.4.37 (einschl. Zusatzprogramm) Flugzeugbeschaffungsprogramm, LA/LC Nr. 1/35 g.Kdos. LA II, 2C von 1.1.35 (Neudruck von 1.1.1936), BA R1 2/v. 200, BA/F.
30. *NCA*, 3:472, Document PS 1301.
31. RLM Folder 268, NA Microcopy T-177/31/3719695-96.
32. *Trial of the Major War Criminals before the International Militarv Tribunal*, 42 vols. (Nuremberg: USGPO, 1947-49) (henceforth cited as *IMT*), 9:44; *NCA*, 9:199-200, Document PS 33474-USA 580.
33. Besprechung über Kürzung des Beschaffungsprogramms am 16.12.36, LC II Nr. 1800/36 g.Kdos., E 2618; Besprechung LC III, von Rohden document (4406-802), BA/F.
34. Ibid.; Aktenvermerk über die Besprechung am 11.Jan. 1937, Lw 103/70, DZ/MGFA.
35. Niederschrift über Besprechung betr. Flugzeugentwicklungsprogramm bei LC II Ch am 21.1.1937, Folder 233, NA Microcopy T-177/19/3705170-79.
36. Technischer Erfahrungsbericht an Fluggerät UK/88 in der Zeit vom 1.12.36 bis 15.1.37, RLM Folder 233, NA Microcopy T-177/19/3704930-46.
37. Beschaffungs-Programm LA gemäss Lieferplan Nr. 5 (21.2.1937), LC III, 1 a. g.Kdos., 23 März 1937, E 2618 BA/F; Flugzeugbeschaffunge-Programm (LC) vom 1.4.1937, LC III (1 a) L.P. Nr. 5 vom 1.4.1937, Lw 103/4 and Lw 103/71, DZ/MGFA.

38. Average for actual production computed from LC III, Beschaffungsmeldung Jan. 1937, Juni 1937, Lw 103/3, DZ/MGFA.

39. Flugzeugentwicklungsprogramm (Stand vom 1.4.1937) LC II Nr. 622/37, 1 zbv. geh. Kdos., 29.April 1937, RL 3/v, 147, BA/F.

40. Typical of the adverse reports on the Ju 86 was the "Technischer Bericht vom 10.5.1937," Folder 233 RLM, NA Microcopy T-177/19/3705006.

41. Notizin für den Vortrag vor dem Staatssekretär über Abbrechen der Fertigung der Ju 86 und des Jumo 205, Lw 103/55, DZ/MGFA; Irving, *Milch*, p. 411; Besprechungen, 3.Mai 1937, NA Microcopy T-177/19/3705075-78.

42. LC III Besprechung am 22.Mai 1937, 24.Mai 1937, von Rohden document (4406-802), BA/F.

43. Übersicht über die Einsparung im Haushaltsjahr 1937 durch Kürzung des Lieferprogramm Nr. 5, Zu LC III, Nr. 1190/37 MB st. g.Kdos., 1 Juni 1937, E 2618, BA/F; Aktenvermerk über Verminderung des Flugzeugbeschaffungsprogramms 1937, LC III, 1 a, 1206/37, Lw 103/10, DZ/MGFA.

44. Freiwerdende Belegschaft durch verkürztes Programm (1937), LC III 1, 3.Juni 1937, Lw 103/10, DZ/MGFA; Freiwerdende Arbeitskräften infolge Kürzung des Haushaltsvorsanschlagen für 1937 (Stand am 5.6.1937), E 2618, BA/F.

45. Aktenvermerk über die Besprechungen am 5.6.1937, Lw 103/65, DZ/MGFA.

46. Flugzeugbeschaffungsprogramm LA, LC III 1 (a), g.Kdos. (1. Entwurf vom 21.6.37), von Rohden document (4376-2767), and Lw 103/10, DZ/MGFA; Hertel, "Die Beschaffung," pp. 75-79.

47. Bericht über die Besprechung mit Vertretern der Flugzeugindustrie am 13.Juli 1937, E 1171; Le Az 67 LE I, 3 Nr. 3325/37 g.Kdos., von Rohden document (4376-1696), BA/F.

48. On Schacht's running battle, see *NCA*, 7:342-43, 380-88. On the finance minister's report, see Vortragsnotiz, von Rohden document (4376-2879), BA/F.

49. Haushalt 1938; Sitzung der Haushaltskommission, 18.Jan.1938, LD Nr. 9036/39 g.Kdos. V, von Rohden document (4376-2879), Folder 241, BA/F.

50. LC III Besprechung, 4.Feb.1938, von Rohden document (4406-802), BA/F.

51. Hertel's remark ("Flugzeugbeschaffung," p. 236) that the repairs industry was not included in Mobilization Plan is in error; see "Stand der Flugzeugreparaturindustrie 30.7.38," LC 7 Az. 66, p. 10/Nr. 143/38, g.Kdos. (IV), 3.Aug.38, RLM Folder 174, NA Microcopy T-177/15/3699711-38 for a list of the industries and their mobilization plans.

52. Erfahrungsbericht über die Aufstellung der Luftwaffenverbände im Jahre 1938, Nr. 3365/38 g.Kdos., 3.Nov.1938, Lw 105/DZ/MGFA.

53. C-Amt Flugzeugbeschaffungsprogramm Nr. 7, vom 1.4.38, LC 7/v. Nr. 6/38 a.g.Kdos. 17.Mai 1938, von Rohden document (4406-594), BA/F, along with its earlier proposals and variants, Lw 103/4, Lw 103/72, Lw 103/113, DZ/MGFA.

54. Beschaffungsprogramm 1939-40; Anlage 1 Staffelerrechnung 30.Mai 1938, Lw 103/10, DZ/MGFA; Staffelerrechnung 19.Mai 1938, von Rohden document (4376-2767), RL 3/ v. 135, BA/F.

55. Der R.d.L. u. Ob.d.L. (LC 2 II, Nr. 319/ 5.39) g.Kdos., 30.Mai 1939, Lw 103/5, DZ/MGFA.

56. *NCA*, 8:221-36, Document R 140.

57. Der R.d.L. und Ob.d.L. (TA) LC Adj. Nr. 540/38. 8 g.Kdos. 12.Aug.1938, Betr: Zusammenstellung für den Führer, Lw 103/14, DZ/MGFA.

58. Flugzeugbeschaffung-Programm LPr. Nr. 8 vom 15.8.1938, Nr. 183/38 g.Kdos., Lw 103/13; Lw 103/72; Lw 103/4, DZ/MGFA.

59. Beschaffungmeldengen für Juni, Juli, August, September 1938, von Rohden document (4376-2747), BA/F; Lw 103/14, DZ/MGFA; Technisches Amt. LC 6 Az. 58.9.10 Nr. 347/39, g.Kdos., 2.Nov.1938, Betr; Stand den Kassenmittel, RLM Folder 241, BA/F; *NCA*, 7:474-78.

60. Hertel, "Die Beschaffung," pp. 78-79, and the von Rohden study agreed that Germany lost about one year's production.

61. Richtlinen für das C-Amt 1936, Aktenvermerk über die Besprechung am 16. November 1936 im Karinhall, Lw 103/50, DZ/MGFA.

62. Vortrag, gehalten bei der Kommandeurbesprechung am 15. Februar 1937, Milch Collection, vol. 57, FDC.

63. Correspondence between Udet, Curtiss-Wright, and Junkers in von Rohden document (4376-3266) BA/F; director Popp's letter to Udet, September 5, 1938, Milch Collection, vol. 54, FDC; Entwicklung der Ju 88, Ju 188, Ju 288, von Rohden document (4376-463), BA/F.

64. LCIII, Nr. 752/37, g.Kdos. III, Ing. 4.1937, Betr: Vorbereitung der Flugzeug- und Motorenmuster für das Friedensprogramm 1938-39 unter Berück-sichtigung des Mob.-Programms ab 1.4.1938, Lw 103/65, DZ/MGFA.

65. Min.A. Nr. 597/38 g.Kdos., 20.9.1938, Lw 103/50, DZ/MGFA; von Rohden study, NA Microcopy T-971/26/966-69, T-971/27/40-46.

66. Letter from Hübner to Pohle, 5.5.1956, Lw 142, DZ/MGFA; Niederschrift über die Aufsichtsratssitzung der Bayer. Flugzeugwerke A.G., vom 11.Juli 1938 im Verwaltungsgebaude der BFW A.G. Augsburg, von Rohden document (4376-3490), BA/F. Specifications for the *Schnellbomber*, LA 190/36 g.Kdos. AI, 3 vom 1.Feb.1936, von Rohden document (4376-2994), BA/F. See above, Chap. 6, on how the specifications evolved.

67. On the poor bombing results, see L.In. 8 B Nr. 84/38, g.Kdos., 5.2.1938, von Rohden document (4376-742), BA/F; von Rohden study, NA Microcopy T-971/27/63-69, T-971/26/963-65; Suchenwirth, *Udet*, pp. 30-31; Zur Einführung des Flugzeugmuster Ju 88 in die deutsche Luftwaffe, Zusammen-gestellt am 1.Oktober 1955 durch die Luftwaffenstudiengruppe Karlsruhe, Lw 103/55, DZ/MGFA.

68. Die Entwicklung der Sturzkampffahigkeit des deutschen Bombenflug-zeuges Ju 88, Lw 103/55, DZ/MGFA; General Ing. a.D. Marguard, "Die Stuka-Idee hat der deutschen Luftwaffe den Untergang gebracht," Lw 142, DZ/MGFA; Suchenwirth, *Turning Points*, pp. 36-37.

69. Irving, *Milch*, p. 118; Heinkel, *Stürmisches Leben*, p. 406.

70. For Milch's account, see Irving, *Milch*, pp. 117-18; for others, see General Ing. a.D. Hermann Francke's comments of January 14, 1956, Lw 103/48, Lw 142, and General Deichmann's statement, Lw 103/56, DZ/MGFA; Heinkel, *Stürmisches Leben*, pp. 413-15.

71. "Bericht des Generals d.Flieger a.D. Paul Deichmann über den Bau viermotorigen Bomber," statement made 1953, corrected on September 30, 1955, Lw 103/56, and "Die deutsche Luftwaffe und der viermotorige Bomber," 26.2.1957, Lw 103/29; Dipl. Ing. Hermann Francke, statement made on January 14, 1956, Lw 103/48; Dipl. Ing. Reidenbach, statement made October 1, 1955, Lw 103/56, all in the DZ/MGFA. For Milch's account, see Irving, *Milch*, pp.

102, 411-12.

72. Bericht über eine Befragung des Majors a.D. Pohle über die Entstehungsgeschichte der He 177, dated 18.4.1956, Lw 103/56, DZ/MGFA.

73. L. In. 8, B Nr. 84/38, g.Kdos., 5.2.1938, von Rohden document (4376-742), BA/F; Green, *Warplanes*, 9:143-45.

74. Kens and Nowarra, *Flugzeuge*, p. 292.

75. Von Rohden study, NA Microcopy T-971/26/963-66.

76. Two of the more recent works are Bernhardt, *Aufrüstung*, which, despite its title, is an account of the Western powers' estimations of German rearmament, and John Edwin Wood, "The Luftwaffe as a Factor in British Policy, 1935-1939" (Ph.D. dissertation, Tulane University, 1965).

77. Feuchter, *Luftkrieg*, pp. 41-43; RLM Folder 1397, NA Microcopy T-177/41/3732072-161, has a series of reports on Italian aviation; Ernst Heinkel's impressions were given to Milch in a cover letter to Colonel von Merkatz's report on the German inspection of Italian aviation, Milch Collection, vol. 57, FDC.

78. Han-Wilhelm Deichmann, "Deutsche Freiwillige und Legion Condor im Spanischen Burgerkrieg 1936-1939," Lw 107/1, and General Schweickhard, "Unternehmen Feuerzauber," Lw 107/10, DZ/MGFA.

79. "Erinnerungen aus dem spanischer Burgerkrieg," von Gen. Oberst a.D. Jaenecke, 2.April 1956, Lw 107/1, DZ/MGFA; General a.D. Grabmann, "Die Erfahrung beim Einsatz deutschen Flieger- und Flakverbände in Spanien," Lw 107/3, DZ/MGFA.

80. Killen, *History of the Luftwaffe*, pp. 70-71; Galland, "The Birth, Life and Death of the German Air Force," USSBS, 4d 14, A.D.I. (K) Report No. 373/1935, pp. 6-7.

81. General der Flieger a.D. Paul Deichmann, *German Air Force Operations in Support of the Army* (U.S. Historical Study No. 163, June 1962), pp. 34-38, 55-57, 130-31; Hans Henning Frh. von Beust, Beitrage zur Studie, "Die deutsche Luftwaffe im spanischen Krieg (Legion Condor)," 19.9.1955, Lw 107/1, DZ/MGFA.

82. General Volkmann, "Kurzer Erfahrungsbericht über den Einsatz der Legion Condor in Spanien in der Zeit vom 1.11.37-31.10.38.," Dez. 1938, Lw 107/3; Grabmann, "Einsatz Flieger- und Flakverbände," Lw 107/3; Oberst a.D. Beust, "Erfahrungen und Lehren beim Feldzug in Spanien in Rahmen der Legion Condor," Lw 107/1, DZ/MGFA.

83. Heinkel, *Stürmisches Leben*, p. 394.

84. Galland, "Life and Death of GAF," USSBS; Grabmann, "Einsatz Flieger- und Flakverbände," Lw 107/3, DZ/MGFA.

85. Generalstab des Heeres, Nr. 406/37 g.Kdos. 8 Abt., 27.Dez.1937, von Rohden document (4376-2994), BA/F; Obersting. German Cornelius und Major Bruecker, "Studie zum Schlachtfliegereinsatz," 1.12.1944, 8 Abt. Lw 107/12, DZ/MGFA.

86. GFM a.D. Albert Kesselring, "Die deutsche Luftwaffe," *Bilanz des Zweiten Weltkrieges: Erkenntnisse und Verpflichtungen für die Zukunft* (Oldenburg: Gerhard Stalling, 1953), p. 148; interview with Kurt Tank, USSBS, 4d42, pp. 1-2; Beust, Beitrag zur Studie, pp. 125-26, 150-51, Lw 107/1, and his "Erfahrungen der Legion Condor," Lw 107/1, DZ/MGFA; Suchenwirth, *Turning Points*, pp. 79-80.

CHAPTER 7

Profile of the
Aircraft Industry in 1938

THE LEADERS of the Third Reich planned to build up the aircraft industry quickly so that their air power could act as a shield for the rearmament program. The risk fleet strategy was based on the assumption that a powerful bomber force would intimidate Germany's neighbors sufficiently to allow her time to rearm. It was so successful that after 1935 Hitler was able not only to protect his rearmament program but also to use his Luftwaffe to blackmail Europe. The step from a protective risk fleet to a political *Druckmittel*, or pressure, was a short one, especially since the writers and journalists of the 1930s had created a veritable cult around the terrors of future air wars. Air power theorists such as Giulio Douhet, Alexander de Seversky, Camille Rougeron, and Billy Mitchell supplied the substance for science fiction, movie and radio script, and even comic books writers. Responsible public officials reiterated these common views, for it was British Prime Minister Stanley Baldwin who coined a slogan for the decade, "The bomber always gets through."

In 1933, German planners had estimated that the aircraft industry could be largely constructed by 1938. They had assumed certain advantages: aerial rearmament had top priority; it had started more quickly than the army's or navy's rearmament; the large unused machine tool capacity of depression-struck Germany lay waiting to be tapped; airframe construction was relatively simple; and, of course, Göring was a powerful patron. Starting with the eight airframe and five engine factories, the industry was to be systematically expanded and, for defensive purposes, dispersed through the central section of the Reich well away from borders. In the west, a boundary from Bremen through Kassel to Friedrichshafen, and in the east from Stettin to Breslau marked the area in which the airframe and engine plants would be located. Only repair plants would lie outside this protected area and the Ruhr.[1] Plants were to be built on a lavish scale with considerable overcapacity. Under the mobilization plan, it was expected that the firms would move from a single eight-hour work shift to two shifts of eight to ten hours, thus doubling their productive capacity. All plants were to have at least a 25 percent capacity over their mobilization plan requirements. Shadow factories like those constructed in England were not a part of the German program. Instead, the Germans counted on unused capacity and at least one backup plant that could produce the same equipment as each major plant.[2]

By 1938, in addition to the numerous individual firms that were established or enlarged, the RLM had backup plants for all of the larger airframe works. For example Junkers had its main plant in Dessau, an assembly plant at Halberstadt, and backup plants in Aschersleben, Leopoldshall, and Schönebeck, while Heinkel had two major assembly plants at Rostock and Oranienburg. Dornier, with a home plant in Friedrichshafen, had a north complex at Wismar, backup plant at Lübeck, and a south complex at Oberpfaffenhofen and München-Neu-aubing. Henschel's main plant was in Berlin-Schönefeld, with backup plants at Johannisthal and Wildau, while the ATG of Leipzig-Mockau also had plants at Leipzig-Eutritysch and Grosstschocher.

The engine industry also had a system of backup plants by 1938: BMW plants at München-Allach and Eisenach; Junkers plants at Köthen and Madgeburg; Daimler-Benz plants at Genshagen, near Berlin, and Marienfeld; and Brandenburgische Motorenwerke plants at Berlin-Spandau and Barsdorf. The smaller firms of Hirth had backup plants in Waltersdorf and Stuttgart-Zuffenhausen. The Daimler-Benz plant at Stuttgart-Untertürkheim and Junkers plant at Dessau remained primarily developmental with production lines moved elsewhere.[3]

As early as February 1934, the RLM had begun detailing a master plan for the industry in 1938 which included the desired strength of operational air units, mobilization plan production requirements, and the expected capacity of the industry. Starting with a staff study which projected a need by October 1, 1938, for a monthly wartime production of 1,170 combat aircraft, Milch's proposals for the expansion of the industry culminated in his master plan of November 1, 1935.[4] Milch anticipated a 100 percent increase in the work force of the industry as it moved from a peacetime single shift to a mobilization double shift, with an expected 250 percent increase in overall production. Milch estimated that by 1938 the operational combat units of the Luftwaffe would include 258 squadrons for a total of 2,370 planes. The mobilization plan was designed to expand the capacity of the industry to cover the requirements of the Luftwaffe completely once it engaged in war. The Luftwaffe estimated its monthly losses at 50 percent of its bombers, dive bombers, and fighters, and 25 percent of its reconnaissance planes, or about 1,165 aircraft.[5] In addition, Milch projected that 673 aircraft would be needed monthly to cover the expected loss in training units, which would number 6,298 aircraft by 1938. He planned, then, for a total production of 1,838 aircraft per month, under mobilization, assuming that the technical preparatory work would have been done and that the necessary materials, labor, and space would be readily available. He assumed also that once the plants shifted to their mobilization plan production, there would be a sharp drop in the number of man-hours per aircraft type. For planning purposes, 18,000 man-hours was assumed for the manufacture of a twin-engined bomber and 4,500 for a single-engined fighter under the mobilization plan.

Milch projected an overall strength for the Luftwaffe in 1938 at 11,732 aircraft, with 2,370 combat planes and 6,298 trainers, for a total of 8,668 in service units (74 percent) and a reserve of 3,064 (26 percent). By a series of complex sliding formulae he computed variations in mobilization plan requirements to take account of changes in factors like estimated losses in wartime, and, more important, the introduction of new types of aircraft into combat units in peacetime. Using a strength of 11,732 aircraft as a constant and estimating four years of serviceability per aircraft type in peacetime, Milch's plan anticipated that when the Luftwaffe was at full strength, industrial production could be throttled back to a lower level which would easily resupply Luftwaffe units with new models.

The theory of this constant air force was faulty and misguiding. If the permanent strength of 11,732 were reached and aircraft were replaced every four years, the industry would need an annual production of about 3,000 planes, or 250 per month. But this extremely low level of production could not sustain the industrial capacity believed needed for the mobilization plan. The classic problem of rearmament—to what use are a large armaments industry and weapons inventory put once they are built?—remained largely unanswered in Milch's master plan. Of course Hitler's answer was to use them. Certainly many in the aircraft industry saw Hitler's intentions, but it seems that Milch's plan was designed to disguise them and to placate those critics of rearmament who anticipated stabilization and a reduction in the general level of rearmament.

DESCRIPTION OF THE AIRCRAFT INDUSTRY IN 1938

The actual buildup of the industry conformed generally to Milch's master plan of 1935. The sharp reductions in 1937 and 1938 caused by shortages of materials and money precluded the possibility that factory expansion would be completed by April 1938, but actual employment at that date—119,200—was over Milch's projected figure of 113,000. As table 10 indicates, employment rose rapidly until 1937, when it leveled off until the second half of 1938. Production figures showed a similar leveling off during 1937 and the first quarter of 1938, with a marked upturn during the second quarter of 1938. Monthly production during the first quarter of 1938 averaged 317.2 aircraft, compared with a second-quarter average of 402. In absolute numbers, monthly production increased from 275 aircraft in January 1938 to 498 in June 1938.[6]

Employment statistics indicate that the RLM succeeded in dispersing the airframe industry throughout central Germany while maintaining a reasonable balance between the firms. Junkers, Dornier, and Heinkel were still the largest airframe firms, followed by Arado, BFW, Focke-Wulf, Henschel, and Weser. Table 11 shows the balance within the airframe industry, but does not indicate clearly the extent of its dispersal, since employment figures are not broken down by individual plants. The differences between the three types of firms—developmental, serial production with limited developmental programs, and licensed serial builders—were not great, but the magnitude of the Ju 88 program is evident in the number of workers—77,716, or 53 percent of the total airframe labor force—involved in it.

The aircraft engine industry tended to be far more concentrated than the airframe industry, with Junkers, Daimler-Benz, and BMW dominating the field. The firms can conveniently be divided into four groups on the basis of the type of engines they built: Group I, air-cooled in-line engines; Group II, air-cooled radial engines; Group III, Junkers engines; and Group IV, Daimler-Benz engines. A comparison of tables 6, 11, and 12 indicates that a few minor firms dropped out of production while the major firms continued to consolidate. Within the aircraft engine industry the predominance of the Junkers and Daimler-Benz complexes, which employed 48.1 percent of the total labor force in 1938 compared with 39.2 percent in September 1935, illustrates the rapidity of concentration. The heavy expenditures of capital necessary for engine development reduced sharply the opportunities for smaller firms to enter production on a limited basis, as could be done in the airframe industry.

A comparison between the airframe and aircraft engine industries reveals other significant differences besides the size of the work force and the marked concentration within the engine industry. The average factory floor space per worker was 23.3 square meters in the engine plants, compared to 19.9 square meters in the airframe firms. The greater space requirements per worker and the far more costly machine tools necessary for engine manufacturing was reflected in the higher book

Table 10

EMPLOYMENT IN THE AIRCRAFT INDUSTRY, APRIL 1, 1933–OCTOBER 1, 1938

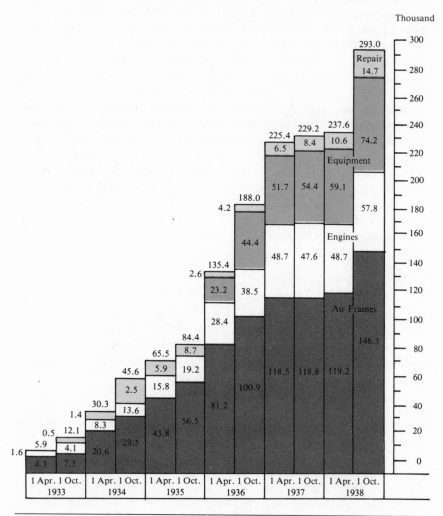

SOURCE: Luftfahrtindustrie-Statistik, LC 1 Nr. 14/39 II B. g. Kdos., 16. Januar 1939, NA Microcopy T-177/15/3700016.

value per worker in the engine industry, although that figure decreased steadily from a high of 8,905 RM in 1933 to 7,527 RM in 1936 and 6,624 in 1938. The book value per worker in the airframe industry, however, increased from a low of 2,004 RM in 1933 to 2,517 RM in 1936 and 3,538 RM in 1938. The differences between the three types of firms within the airframe industry are also striking. The high book value for serial production firms with limited developmental programs confirmed the contention of the RLM that these limited developmental programs were luxuries the Reich could be spared. The variations between individual firms can be seen in table 13; some were obviously able to function on a more economical basis than others. Newer plants argued that they had to expend more capital for the latest equipment and for workers' social

TABLE 11

EMPLOYMENT BY FIRMS IN THE AIRFRAME INDUSTRY, OCTOBER 1, 1938

Firm	Type[1]	Employment	Percentage of Industry	Percent Increase since January 1, 1938
AGO	LD	3,468	2.4	13
Arado, Brandenburg[2]	D	10,081	6.9	32
Arado, Warnemünde	LB	4,009	2.7	50
ATG[2]	LB	6,356	4.3	17
BFW	D	9,257	6.3	35
Blohm & Voss	D	5,272	3.6	36
Bücker	LD	968	0.7	13
Dornier-North[2]	LB	4,969	3.4	15
Dornier-South[2]	D	10,375	7.1	25
Erla	LB	4,310	2.9	10
Fieseler	D	5,548	3.8	30
Focke-Wulf	D	8,428	5.8	7.5
Gotha	LD	3,315	2.3	26
Heinkel-Oranienburg[2]	LB	7,360	5.0	38
Heinkel-Rostock	D	10,937	7.5	17
Henschel[2]	LD	8,851	6.0	17
Junkers[2]	D	25,855	17.7	28
Klemm	LD	754	0.5	18
MIAG	LB	2,848	2.0	28
Siebel[2]	LD	3,869	2.6	39
Weser	LD	9,433	6.5	30
TOTAL		146,263	100.0	(average) 25
Total for Ju 88 Program		77,716	53.0	

SOURCE: Luftfahrtindustrie-Statistik, LC 1 Nr. 14/39 II B g.Kdos., 16.Januar 1939, NA Microcopy T-177/15/3700015-21.

[1] The firms are coded as follows: D = developmental firm; LD = serial production firms with limited developmental programs; LB = licensed serial production firms.

[2] Firms involved in the Junkers 88 program.

programs than did older plants, while the RLM countered that the end cost per unit of production reflected these marked differences and that, if possible, firms should be forced into line with the industry's norms.[7]

In the engine industry the variations between individual plants were as marked as in the airframe industry. Newer plants tended to have higher book values than the older ones and licensed producers higher

TABLE 12

EMPLOYMENT BY FIRMS IN THE AIRCRAFT ENGINE INDUSTRY, OCTOBER 1, 1938

Firm	Type[1]	Employed	Percentage of Industry	Percent Increase since Jan. 1, 1938
GROUP I (air-cooled in-line engines)				
Argus	D	3,007	5.2	31
Hirth-Zuffenhausen	D	486	0.8⎫	42
Hirth-Waltersdorf	LB	285	0.5⎬ 1.3	42
Total, Group I		3,778	6.5	34
GROUP II (air-cooled radial engines)				
BMW-Munich	D	6,194	10.7⎫	17
BMW-Eisenach	LB	1,782	3.1⎬ 13.8	36
Bramo-Spandau	D	6,174	10.7⎫	35
Bramo-Barsdorf	LB	966	1.7⎬ 12.4	
Humboldt-Deutz	LB	1,746	3.0	28
Total, Group II		16,862	29.2	27
GROUP III (Junkers engines)				
Junkers-Dessau	D	7,570	13.1⎫	13
Junkers-Köthen	LB	4,538	7.9⎬ 31.5	20
Junkers-Magdeburg	LB	6,052	10.5⎭	39
Mitteldeutsche Motorenwerke	LB	4,245	7.4	78
Pommersche Motorenbau	LB	900	1.6	35
Total, Group III		23,305	40.5	30
GROUP IV (Daimler-Benz engines)				
DB-Stuttgart	D	939	1.6⎫	39
DB-Marienfelde	LB	2,436	4.2⎬ 16.6	6
DB-Genshagen	LB	6,262	10.8⎭	13
Henschel	LB	2,439	4.2	53
Niedersächsiche Motorenwerke	LB	1,728	3.0	36
Total, Group IV		13,804	23.8	18
GRAND TOTAL		57,749	100.0	(average) 27

SOURCE: Luftfahrtindustrie-Statistik, LC 1 Nr. 14/39 II B g.Kdos., 16.Januar 1939, NA Microcopy T-177/15/3700015-21.

The firms are coded as follows: D = developmental firms; LB = licensed serial production firms.

than the developmental firms. The percentage of the labor force involved in development does not give an accurate picture of the relative size of those departments. For example, although Daimler-Benz at Stuttgart had

TABLE 13

COMPOSITION OF LABOR FORCE, BOOK VALUE AND
SPACE PER WORKER IN AIRFRAME INDUSTRY, 1938

Firm	Type	Composition of Labor Force by Percentage				Av. Book Value per Worker (RM)	Av. Space per Worker (squ. m.)
		Salaried Employees	Prod. Workers				
			Serial Production	Develop. Work	Other[1]		
AGO	LD	20	40	6	34	3,915	20.4
Arado, Brandenburg	D	22	39	12	27	3,276	22.3
Arado, Warnemünde	LB	15	56	——	29	3,853	32.0
ATG	LB	16	54	——	30	3,126	18.2
BFW	D	23	41	2	34	3,584	14.2
Blohm & Voss	D	15	56	6	23	7,478	15.2
Bücker	LD	20	47	2	31	4,461	22.5
Dornier, North	LB	10	62	——	28	1,924	12.7
Dornier, South	D	15	53	6	26	2,282	15.6
Erla	LB	15	59	——	26	2,260	17.3
Fieseler	D	17	50	5	28	3,738	19.5
Focke-Wulf	D	27	39	14	20	2,461	12.1
Gotha	LD	18	66	1	15	3,594	32.3
Heinkel, Oranienburg	LB	15	55	——	30	3,572	13.0
Heinkel, Rostock	D	24	43	7	26	2,057	12.4
Henschel	LD	19	46	2	33	3,010	19.7
Junkers	D	19	47	7	27	3,396	11.1
Klemm	LD	22	34	4	40	512	19.7
MIAG[2]	LB	13	64	——	21	3,353	19.1
Siebel	LD	19	50	5	26	2,499	24.9
Weser[2]	LD	17	42	5	26	3,263	13.2
AVERAGES							
D (Developmental firms)		20	46	7	27	2,867	15.3
LD (Serial firms with limited develop.)		18	46	4	32	4,060	20.2
LB (Licensed serial builders)		14	57	——	29	3,624	20.8
Industry average		19	48	5	28	3,538	19.9

SOURCE: Luftfahrtindustrie-Statistik, LC 1 Nr. 14-39 II B g.Kdos., 16.Januar 1939, NA Microcopy T-177/15/3700018; Die Deutsche Luftfahrtindustrie, 15.August 1938, NA Microcopy T-177/15/3699835-43.

[1]Included trainees and maintainance and aircraft repair shop workers.
[2]Slight errors in the original document.

47 percent of its labor force involved in development, it had only 441 workers, while the 10 percent for Junkers-Dessau represented 757 employees (computed by multiplying employment figures from table 12 by the percentages from table 14).

The situation in the aircraft repair industry was somewhat different. The industy had started on a small scale in 1934 under the assumption that there should be at least one repair plant in each *Luftkreis* (aviation

TABLE 14
DISTRIBUTION OF LABOR FORCE, BOOK VALUE AND SPACE PER
WORKER IN AIRCRAFT ENGINE INDUSTRY, 1938

Firm	Type	Distribution of Labor Force by Percentage					Av. Book Value per Worker (RM)	Av. Space per Worker (squ. m.)
			Prod. Workers					
		Salaried employees	Serial Production	Develop. Work	Repairs	Others[1]		
Argus	D	24	31	9	3	33	5,171	18.1
BMW, Munich	D	27	42	17	2	12	5,035	20.5
BMW, Eisenach	LB	16	43	——	6	35	7,226	34.7
Bramo, Spandau	D	21	32	12	1	34	4,028	7.9
Bramo, Barsdorf	LB	18	22	——	25	35	11,711	19.8
DB, Stuttgart	D	22	14	47	7	10	6,296	26.2
DB, Marienfelde	LB	13	55	——	——	32	3,332	9.7
DB, Genshagen	LB	13	50	——	2	35	8,263	16.2
Henschel	LB	12	51	——	——	37	10,926	34.7
Hirth, Zuffenhausen	D	42	12	17	4	25	2,133	63.9
Hirth, Waltersdorf	LB	17	56	——	7	20	8,448	8.9
Humboldt, Deutz	LB	15	36	4	8	37	6,830	17.8
Junkers, Dessau	D	25	35	10	1	29	4,058	14.1
Junkers, Köthen	LB	12	50	——	——	38	6,278	16.4
Junkers, Magdeburg	LB	12	59	——	——	29	6,570	13.8
Mitteldeutsche Motorenwerke	LB	14	55	——	4	27	7,808	22.3
Niedersächsische Motorenwerke	LB	13	49	——	3	35	9,398	28.7
Pommersche Motorenbau	LB	13	39	——	6	42	6,903	44.6
AVERAGES								
D (Developmental firms)		23	33	13	2	29	4,454	25.1
LB (Licensed builders)		13	48	——	3	36	7,808	22.3
Industry average		17	43	——	2	32	6,624	23.3

SOURCE: Luftfahrtindustrie-Statistik, LC 1 Nr. 14-39 II B g.Kdos., 16.Januar 1939, NA Microcopy T-177/15/3700018; Die Deutsche Luftfahrtindustrie, 15. August 1938, NA Microcopy T-177/15/3699835-43.

[1] Includes nonproduction workers such as maintainance workers and trainees.

administrative district). Gradually the RLM distinguished three types of repair plants: those like Peschke and Basser that had the cell organization for aircraft work before 1933; middle-sized airframe plants with repair divisions, such as Junkers and Focke-Wulf; and new firms organized especially for repairs.[8] Table 15 gives the breakdown for the industry. The grand total of 13,192 does not agree with the total listed in table 10, although they both came from the same report, because table 10 includes workers from the airframe and aircraft engine firms that had minor repair divisions but, for purposes of accounting, were not considered part of the repair industry.

The monthly production projected under the mobilization plan by the RLM was 1,838 planes, but the actual mobilization plan effective April 1, 1938, called for only 1,377. Unlike earlier plans, it sharply reduced the number of models to one or two per type of aircraft. For

TABLE 15

EMPLOYMENT IN AIRCRAFT REPAIR INDUSTRY, OCTOBER 1, 1938

Firm	No. Employed	Percent of Industry	Percent Increase since January 1, 1938
Bachmann	1,200	9.1	25
Badisch-Pfälzische FRW	56	0.4	150
Basser	247	1.9	25
Bayerische Waggon und Flugzeugwerke	757	5.7	50
FRW Braunschweig	337	2.5	15
Brinker Eisenwerk	817	6.2	70
Deutsche Lufthansa (5 plants)	1,624	12.3	8
Espenlaub	139	1.1	30
Focke-Wulf, Johannisthal	815	6.2	15
Friedrich	102	0.8	100
Gerner	482	3.6	150
Hansen	625	4.7	60
Industriewerk Heiligenbeil	678	5.1	90
Jacobs	798	6.1	60
Junkers, Breslau	1,054	8.0	230
Junkers, Leipzig	1,394	10.5	120
Klemm	154	1.2	-
Land-und-See Leichbau	763	5.8	150
FRW Nordenham	248	1.9	new
Peschke	287	2.2	45
FRW Saarpfalz	457	3.5	125
Schwade	158	1.2	60
TOTAL	13,192	100.0	(average) 60

SOURCE: Luftfahrtindustrie-Statistik, LC 1 Nr. 14/39 II B g.Kdos., 16.Januar 1939, NA Microcopy T-177/15/3700015-21.

comparison, the last column of table 16 lists the actual production of some of these aircraft during June 1938.

The degree to which the mobilization plan was intermeshed with actual production in the individual firms is revealed in an extant plan for 1937-38. When these figures were compiled, in April 1937, employment in the airframe industry was 118,500, compared to the 146,263 for October 1938, as cited in the preceding tables, while the engine industry had 47,710 workers, compared to the later figure of 57,749. The mobilization plan called for an increase in employment in the airframe firms from 118,500 to 180,925 and a concentration of production on fewer models. The engine industry was to have a smaller proportional increase in employment, from 47,710 to 68,510, but a similar emphasis on fewer engines and greater output.[9]

As late as April 1937, most airframe plants were producing from two to six different models designed by as many firms, which necessitated an enormous amount of consultation between the design and the licensed plants. This problem was alleviated somewhat when the number of models to be produced was reduced. The major explanation

TABLE 16

MONTHLY AIRCRAFT PRODUCTION: MOBILIZATION PLAN, APRIL 1, 1938,
AND ACTUAL PRODUCTION JUNE 1938

Type	Model	Mobilization Plan Requirements			Produced in June 1938
		Front	Training	Total	
Reconnaissance					
(long-range)	Do 17P, Z	60	25	85	12
(short-range)	Hs 126	85	25	110	13
Bombers	He 111	177	12	189	64
	Do 17M, Z	87	6	93	2
Dive bombers	Ju 87	52	8	60	23
Fighters (light)	Bf 109	240	15	255	112
(heavy)	Bf 110	70	10	80	0
Reconnaissance (navy)					
(long-range)	Do 18	10	2	12	
(short-range)	He 114	19	16	35	
Multipurpose (navy)	He 115	18	2	20	
Trainers, liaison craft,					
transports, and others		32	406	438	
TOTAL		850	527	1,377	498

SOURCE: Monatliche Flugzeug-Nachschubzahlen im Mobfall, ab 1.4.1938, LC III Ing., g. Kdos., von Rohden document (4376-2767), Lw 103/72; Beschaffungsmeldung, Stand 30.Juni 1938, LC III/1, 3806/38, am 9.Juli 1938, Lw 103/14, DZ/MGFA.

for this apparent irrational distribution of work among such conscious rationalizers as the Germans lay in the striving of the RLM to maintain full employment in the face of many alterations in the production programs. With the sharp cutbacks and model changeovers, the RLM decided that retaining a large number of models with limited series production would make work for the industry and cushion it from widespread layoffs. Eighteen months later the situation was completely reversed as half of the industry began gearing up for the big Ju 88 program. Within the aircraft engine industry there were fewer problems since most companies produced the same type of engines from one or two designing firms. Nor were the dangers of cutbacks as severe, since the industry lagged behind the airframe industry in production and development and, during the period of cutbacks, was beginning to mass produce its own newly developed engines.

PROFITS AND PRICES

The aircraft industry, like most others, profited enormously under Nazi rule. Nazi ordinances for the control of labor in January 1934 and the reorganization of plant management a month later instituted a patriarchal system in factories reminiscent of the early days of capitalism. Factory owners were now, according to the *Führerprinzip,* leaders of the factories and the employees were followers. The owner had power limited only by the state trustee of labor. Unions, already swept away, were replaced by the German Labor Front, which operated more as a disciplinary and social organization than as a union. This authoritarian legal structure within the factories, combined with the terror apparatus of the policy and the propaganda of the regime, robbed the workers of their organizations and will to resist. Labor-management disputes were no longer a problem, as they had been in the Weimar period. State-regulated wages were deliberately set at their lowest point during the depression and frozen there. In addition to taming labor, the Nazis offered a variety of inducements to favored concerns: cheap loans; handsome tax provisions, including refunds; rebates; depreciation allowances; price and market guarantees; chances to profit from "arianization"; and, later, booty from captured lands.[10] All profits swelled, but few could compare with those in the aircraft industry.

That miniscule industry of 1933 which grew into one of the largest in the Reich by 1938 owed everything to the regime. Few were so closely identified with the central government as was it. There had been some talk in the RLM in 1933 about nationalizing the aircraft industry, but that was firmly rejected by the Nazi party. Private ownership was to be protected, for, as Hitler said, "We National Socialists see in private ownership a higher stage of development. Bolshevism destroys not only private ownership but private initiative too. It goes against the aristocratic principles of nature."[11] Or as the chief economic editor of the *Völkischer Beobachter* wrote, "The ownership of the economy through the Volk is not a material, but rather a spiritual and idealized fact."[12] The Nazi government would interfere in the economy only when private owners were unable or unwilling to do its bidding.

In the aircraft industry there were only two cases of nationalization—the Arado and Junkers firms—and one case of arianization, or the Germanization of Jewish firms, as it was called. The arianization case dealt with the Jewish owner of the Argus Motoren Gesellschaft of Berlin, Dr. Moritz Strauss. Although he was removed from the company, through the intervention of Göring and Koppenberg it remained under private control.[13] The Arado case was more a question of personality conflicts and poor management. The firm had been a part of the Stinnes empire in the early 1920s, but with its collapse in 1924, Herr Lübbe took control. He had hoped to work with Heinkel, but when the designer proved difficult Lübbe had to provide his own existence. With a working capital of 50,000 RM and a labor force of 58, the plant produced sport planes and motor boats and did repair work. The capital was raised to 150,000 RM in 1929, just before the depression hit the firm. In 1933, the nearly bankrupt business received its first large contract for 360 trainers and acquired through the RLM its Brandenberg site. During that same year the RLM grew dissatisfied with the firm and forced Lübbe out by converting its 1.5 million RM of loans into capital stock and naming a new board of directors. By 1938 the company was thriving, with a working capital of 30,000,000 RM, two main plants, and 14,000 employees. As was typical in the Nazi period, the board of directors was hand-picked by the RLM and consisted of five members from the government, including four from the RLM, and four from private business. Arado's corporate balance sheet for 1937 showed assets of 129,287,634.70 RM and profits of 2,062,932.09 RM, which rose in 1938 to 140,585,926.77 RM and 2,072,521.94 RM, respectively. In 1939 the assets were 165,128,884.85 RM and profits 7,255,787.61 RM.[14]

The Junkers nationalization was more renowned and illustrated the ruthlessness of the Third Reich in handling recalcitrant private firms. Junkers was the largest and best-known aircraft firm in Germany and Professor Junkers, the seventy-three-year-old owner, an internationally respected pioneer in aviation; but the old man was unacceptable to the Nazis. An ardent democrat and pacifist, he was thought to be associated with numerous leftist, Jewish, and liberal causes. Junkers's involvement in the 1920s with the Reichswehr's secret rearmament in Russia and his battle with Lufthansa had led to Reichstag investigations and much unfavorable publicity. Milch in particular had many reasons to distrust him since Milch was considered a renegade by the Junkers group after he left them to become a director of Lufthansa.[15] In March 1933, Göring and Milch wanted to place Junkers's patents and factories at the disposal of the Reich for its new aerial rearmament program. Milch insisted that Junkers release his firm's patents and remove himself from its operations before the RLM would grant the contracts it desperately needed to survive the depression. The old man proved stubborn; he retreated to his home in Bavaria and prepared to fight the RLM. Milch consented to allow him to continue his experimental work but reiterated that the plants and patents were needed by the Reich. He thought Junkers ungrateful, for had the firm not received government subsidies and contracts from the state-owned Lufthansa, it would not have survived. In October 1933 the RLM sent an ultimatum to Junkers: either he sell a majority of the stock in his two firms to the Reich, or he would be banned from his plants. He was further threatened with a renewal of the investigation of financial irregularities in his dealings with the Reichswehr in the Soviet Union as well as of his treasonous activities of leaking secrets about rearmament to Socialist Reichstag deputies and newspapermen.

Party authorities in Dessau had Junkers returned to Dessau from his home in Bayrisch Zell under police supervision. Again he was threatened with court action, and Kesselring, chief of the Administrative Office of the RLM, ordered the public investigation resumed. Under this massive pressure the old man capitulated. He sold controlling interest in the firm to the Reich at the end of October and resigned his directorships on November 24. He was ordered back to his Bavarian home, where he remained under house arrest, and was forbidden to have contact with anyone from Junkers firms, including his own son Klaus. The arrest was lifted in February 1934, when Junkers promised to sell his remaining interest in the firms, but the ban on his contact with the firm remained in effect. He continued to delay final settlement and the RLM issued another ultimatum in August. Finally, further harassment was halted on Hitler's personal order, and the sick man was allowed to die in peace. On April 3, 1935, the Junkers firm was nationalized, becoming virtually the house firm of the RLM, under the direction of Heinrich Koppenberg, personally groomed as Junkers's successor by Milch.[16]

The Junkers concern, the model for the aircraft industry, was developed into the largest, most influential, and best-managed firm in the Reich. Managerial reforms, building techniques, assembly-line production, contracting of subassembling, the complex system, social and recreational programs for workers, and training programs for new workers were inaugurated by the firm and then extended to the rest of the industry. Junkers's sales and profits were also the highest in the industry, sales rising from 52 million RM in 1933 to 670 million RM in 1940, for a total of nearly 2 billion in the seven-year period; the working capital increasing to 280 million RM. Employment grew from 2,200 in October 1933 to 25,855 in the airframe division and 18,160 in the engine division by October 1938.[17]

Junkers's great size and obvious influence with the RLM occasioned much bitterness and jealousy among the other aircraft firms. Messerschmitt and Heinkel in particular felt that the massive Ju 88 program was a cleverly rigged ploy arranged by the Junkers people to maintain their predominance in the industry.[18] The abrasive personality of Koppenberg, who was named special plenipotentiary for the Ju 88 program, did not help. Critics, including Freiherr von Richthofen, asserted that through his executive power, Koppenberg ruthlessly commandeered engineers and specialists from other firms, handicapping their developmental programs. In particular, many Dornier engineers were transferred to the Ju 88 program, seriously retarding Dornier projects.[19] It was also well known that Koppenberg bragged in an unguarded moment that his Ju 88 program had destroyed the competing Do 217 and would destroy the He 177.[20]

Junkers was also resented for paying top wages in the industry. By 1938, when labor was as much a limiting factor as materials, the ability to pay high wages with guaranteed overtime meant growth, contracts, and profits. Junkers's average hourly rate of .88 RM was well above the .81 RM average for all industrial workers and the much lower averages in nonindustrial sectors. Moreover, Junkers's wage earners and salaried employees earned considerably more than most German workers because of overtime. While the average monthly gross earnings in 1939 were 121.68 RM for all industrial wage earners and 231 RM for salaried employees, the comparable Junkers figures were as follows:

Monthly Gross Earnings in RM	Wage Earners by percent	Salaried Employees by percent
0-140	25.7	16.3
141-180	24.0	11.4
181-220	29.4	8.5
221-260	16.7	13.6
261-300	3.8	15.6
over 300	0.4	34.6[21]

In addition to high wages, aircraft industry employees received other important benefits. Housing, in particular, was a key inducement, for many of the new airframe plants were not located in metropolitan areas. The RLM took an active interest in supplying housing and ordered an ambitious apartment-building program for its workers. Financial arrangements were to be made locally, but the RLM guaranteed loans or supplied the money if it were not available. For example, in 1935 7,000 apartments were built under the program at a cost of 47.5 million RM, of which only 8.87 million RM was directly loaned to plants by the RLM; the remainder was raised locally. From 1936 to 1938 nearly 8,000 apartments were built yearly for aircraft workers, but even that was not enough.[22] By the end of 1938 the shortage of housing for workers was so critical that the RLM concluded that expansion of the aircraft industry could take place only where labor was already available.[23] In housing as in other areas, the Junkers program served as a model for the rest of the industry.[24]

Even though Junkers was the largest and best-managed firm, the success story of BFW, or the Messerschmitt Company, as it later became, illustrates the huge fortunes made, in the face of strong opposition, with talent and connections. Messerschmitt had founded a firm in 1923 and incorporated two years later to build transport and sport planes. In 1927 the firm signed a working agreement with BFW of Augsburg, an outgrowth of the Udet Air Company jointly owned by the Reich, the state of Bavaria, and the banking house of Merck-Fink of Munich. Under this agreement Messerschmitt handled development and BFW production. In 1928 Messerschmitt and his associates, principally the Bamberg tobacco man Michel Raulino, bought out BFW and established a company with a working capital of 400,000 RM. Although the firm went bankrupt during the depression, it was saved by its astute Greek business manager, Rakan Kokothaki, and Lufthansa lawyer Otto Merkel, who arranged a settlement with its creditors. To do this, the Carlos Z. Thompsen Banking Company of Hamburg, trustee of the Raulino estate, was brought in to help stabilize the firm. It purchased 12½ percent of the stock and nominated Fritz Seiler as chairman of the board.[25]

Meanwhile, the Nazis had come to power and Messerschmitt's long-time associate and former chairman of the board, Theodor Croneiss, a powerful leader in the SA, began to explore the possibilities of RLM contracts. Messerschmitt knew Hitler, Hess and Göring, but his strained association with Milch hampered his securing contracts. A feud between the two had resulted in the late 1920s when Milch ordered six Messerschmitt Me 20s and three crashed because of design failures. Milch had refused to order more planes from the designer, but after he became state secretary of aviation he was pressured to rescue the firm. On June 8, 1933, Croneiss and Seiler held private talks with Milch and suggested a number of measures to save the firm, ending with the request that Milch give it another chance. According to Milch, he brushed aside these overtures with the comment that although Messerschmitt was one of the most capable and intelligent designers in the world, he had many character faults. He was not only egoistic and insensitive (he had refused to view the victims of his own aircraft failures), but also ungrateful and untrustworthy. Milch would condescend to grant contracts to Messerschmitt only if the firm posted a surety bond of 2 million RM against the crash of a Messerschmitt aircraft due to construction mistakes. Milch's proposal was accepted—much to his surprise, according to his own account.[26]

Messerschmitt asserts, however, that starting in 1933, the firm's working capital was increased to 4 million RM, of which 3 million came from the RLM as a loan. According to the terms, the profits from RLM contracts were to be applied to the principle; and as payments were made, the firm redeemed the stock pledged as collateral. Within three years the loan was paid off. Other, similar generous arrangements followed, such as a 1938 loan of 780,000 RM from the RLM for the construction of a new research and developmental laboratory to be used for the Bf 209 and Me 210 projects,[27] and later in the same year an 8 million RM consolidation loan. Both were to be repaid from profits from ongoing contracts; the firm did not have to risk or invest a single mark of its own. Consequently, it was able to build up its capitalization while it expanded enormously. Official profits, which were carefully monitored by the government, were kept at a modest level, since most of them were used to redeem RLM loans, a process of plowing back profits into the firm through capital investment. By 1938 the capitalization of the firm was 4 million RM, with all but the original 400,000 coming from the RLM in the form of loans and profits. Its staggering growth is reflected in the USSBS estimate that from the original 400,000 RM undertaking, the Messerschmitt combine grew to a point where, just prior to its collapse in 1945, its depreciated assets and all investments totaled 106,001,000 RM.[28] Growth of that magnitude in twelve years, even during a world war, must constitute a record in the annals of modern German business history.

Ownership of the BFW indicated the rising fortunes of the gifted designer Messerschmitt. In 1936 he formed a limited-partnership company to handle his licensing agreements and patents when his Bf 109 was accepted as the Luftwaffe's standard fighter. On April 5, 1938, he signed a contract with BFW naming him head of the firm and chief director. The aircraft and firm were to be renamed Messerschmitt. In exchange for these privileges and a cash settlement, Messerschmitt was to combine his patents and licenses with those of BFW, the Messerschmitt Company becoming the largest stockholder of BFW. On February 19, 1942, the ownership of the firm's 4 million shares of stock were listed as:

Professor Willy Messerschmitt	154,000 shares
Firm Messerschmitt & Co.	2,506,000 shares
Baroness Lilly von Michel-Raulino	798,000 shares
Frau Marion von Doderer	36,000 shares
Baroness Marie von Thüngen	6,000 shares
Bankhaus Carlo Z. Thompsen	500,000 shares[29]

Messerschmitt's many good ideas, his personal charm, and his artistic personality soon helped him become a favorite of Hitler. The Nazi leader considered him a genius who could accomplish the impossible. Göring, Hess and Udet were similarly impressed with the young designer from Augsburg, and soon his firm had more than enough developmental contracts. While the older firms like Dornier, Junkers, and Heinkel worked on two or three models for half a year with 1,000 engineers, Messerschmitt had four or five models under development with a staff a quarter as large.[30] The company spread itself much too thin and as a result had difficulty completing projects and meeting deadlines. Like many creative persons, Messerschmitt tended to become bored with the routine engineering work required by a project once the grand design was completed. His restless, creative mind continually sought other, more challenging diversions and as a result much of what he did was unfinished. Foremost a designer and an artist, Messerschmitt was ill-suited to be general manager of a large firm. He lacked the personal, compulsive attention to detail and the bureaucratic organizational virtues of patience and orderliness so necessary in managing a large, sprawling industrial firm.[31]

In many ways Messerschmitt was the opposite of Milch. His prima donna status with Hitler and Göring irked Milch, and some of Messerschmitt's associates exacerbated the relationship between the two. The SA flying group leader and one of the directors of Messerschmitt, Theodor Croneiss, intrigued against Milch. Openly envious of his position as second man in the RLM, Croneiss tried to destroy Milch by denouncing him as a half-Jew in October 1933. Milch was forced to endure the painful scandal about his supposed illegitimate birth before Göring threatened Croneiss with incarceration in a concentration camp. It was also Croneiss who told Göring about the Ernst Röhm putsch of

1934. Apparently Croneiss had been slated to be the new air minister under Röhm but at the last minute changed sides and informed on him. After the bloody purge Croneiss was rewarded with a command in the SS and a position as aviation expert on Hess's party staff. Messerschmitt sought to fire Croneiss from the board of the firm for his unsavory actions but Seiler defended him.[32] Seiler acted as a balm between the firm and Milch. A reserve air force officer who had annual active duty in the Technical Office, he was everyone's friend. The office notes of Technical Office directors Richthofen and Ploch indicate that Seiler was a frequent conferee in the RLM. His connections with the Hamburg banking world, Messerschmitt, and the RLM were useful in gaining contracts. Although Milch liked Seiler, the feud between the state secretary and Messerschmitt continued unabated, much to the detriment of the entire industry.

Messerschmitt's relations with other members of the aviation establishment were, at times, equally as bad. During the 1938 summer conference with Göring at Karinhall, he openly quarreled with the president of the Reich Aviation Manufacturers' Association, Admiral Lahs. When Lahs apparently made a slur about the Bf 109's being surpassed in performance by the He 100, Messerschmitt had replied that Lahs was poorly informed and prejudiced since he was a member of the board of directors of Heinkel. Messerschmitt later sought permission from his own board of directors to seek an official apology or withdraw from the association, and again Seiler was able to soothe the ruffled feathers of the fiery designer.[33]

The Reich Aviation Manufacturers' Association (Reichsverband der Deutschen Luftfahrt-Industrie) represented the industry on common problems. It collected statistics, helped regulate patent rights, handled export problems, and generally acted as a liaison between the firms and the RLM. As in all German industry, membership in the trade organization was made compulsory after 1934. Normally a firm doing more than 50 percent of its business in the aviation field was automatically included in the association, although there were attempts by the older firms to limit entry.[34] They felt that their power would be diluted by newer firms whose major business activity might be outside the aviation field. By 1938 the association was divided into four divisions: airframe production, engine construction, ancillary equipment production, and lighter-than-air construction. The airframe division listed twenty-four firms as regular members within a subdivision of airframe producers, sixteen in the airframe repairs division, and six in the glider division. The engine construction division had twelve firms in engine construction and two in engine repairs. The ancillary equipment division included forty-two firms, chiefly manufacturers of propellers, airborne instruments, parachutes, and optical works, and engineering firms. The lighter-than-air construction division listed only two firms.[35]

The association was a quasi-public institution operating under the direction of the RLM. All pretense of its private nature was dropped on February 1, 1939, when it was officially placed under the control of Udet of the RLM. Although Lahs argued to Göring in 1942 that the association promoted cooperation within the industry and achieved the objectives of the *Vaterland* without damaging the private business interests of the firms, the facts spoke otherwise.[36] The annual RLM summer conferences were bitter affairs where the vanity, egoism, and naked business interests of the designers and their firms were scarcely concealed by common courtesy. Charges and countercharges were volleyed as each blamed the others or the RLM for shortcomings and errors. Göring and Milch, who conducted these meetings, were prone to what the historian Carl Jacob Burckhardt called "uninhibited outbursts." The association quickly lost its trade group functions and became merely a clearinghouse for information and technical help. What little cohesiveness it possessed was soon lost in the scramble for contracts, favors, and influence. The egoism of the firms precluded any real cooperation within the industry or united resistance to the wishes of the RLM. Historians who explain Nazi actions as the response to a careful plot on the part of businessmen need look elsewhere than to the aircraft firms.[37] They were far too busy caring for their immediate interests and had little time to worry about the ultimate aims of the regime. Leaderless, divided, jealous, they were no match for the Nazis. Firms usually tried to resist the RLM to protect some small margin of advantage. They surreptitiously attempted to continue pet projects, including production of sport and commercial models that might have a potential in the future civilian market; and they later tried to resist the flow of expansion money, which they feared would lead to either nationalization or overexpansion, a handicap after the armament boom. In these respects, the aircraft firms often had the backing of influential party leaders like Gauleiters—district Nazi party leaders—who realized that the economic well-being of their domain depended on sound business. Colonel Richthofen and Günther Tschersich of the TA, in particular, felt that the industry was overbuilt, but the firms were fearful about rejecting funds that were pressed on them for expansion lest they, too, like Arado and Junkers, be nationalized.[38]

A major device for controlling the expansion of the industry and, at the same time, increasing its efficiency would have been to establish a fixed-price policy. In a normal market situation the price mechanism funnels the flow of investment and regulates the productivity within an industry. The German aircraft industry, which preferred to use a monitoring system, had no such fixed-price policy until 1939. Although the RLM tried valiantly to control profits at between 6 and 10 percent, the firms found it easy to circumvent these regulations. The many changes in production programs, the need for expansion capital, the bewildering variety of developmental costs, and, after the seizure of Austria and Bohemia-Moravia, the race to incorporate foreign firms into their complexes made it easy for them to disguise their profits.

The initial pricing policy of the RLM in 1933 was based on the need for quick delivery of equipment and rapid expansion of the industry. The cost plus contracts, under which the costs of development and expansion, preparations for serial production, length of series, delays and changes in production, normal running expenses, and, finally, profits were computed into the unit price, admirably fulfilled the needs of the RLM. The individual firms literally negotiated their own contracts with the administrative division of the RLM (later called the LF Amt), which set down generous and loosely defined guidelines. The Technical Office specified the models to be produced and arranged for the raw materials and labor, while the LF Amt handled all the business arrangements. The LF Amt was headed by a ministerial director and had three subdivisions: LF 1 was concerned with all financial matters, including the letting of contracts and control of Reich investments in the industry; LF 2 checked prices; LF 3 handled general matters of economic interest such as licensing, patents, and banking. At first unit prices for airplanes were not fixed definitely at the time a contract was issued. A preliminary price was given, with the final price arrived at later, usually after production of a series.[39] With the development of long-range production plans in 1935, the LF Amt sought new, tighter methods of pricing and payment. Under the original system, payment generally started with the signing of a contract and acquisition of materials, and then, on the basis of the preliminary price, the RLM would pay the firm a percentage of the estimated cost at regular intervals. Payments were prorated to the length of the production plan until all but 10 percent of the total preliminary price was paid. With the completion of production, the final price was determined and final payment made. Usually this price turned out to be considerably more than the preliminary one because of unexpected costs. The aircraft firms found the system exceedingly profitable.

By 1936 this system of pricing was under heavy criticism. The foreign exchange crisis and increasing competition for funds between various agencies of the government meant that the Luftwaffe had to fight for money. Charges of extravagant spending forced the RLM to reappraise its pricing policy. Subcontracted work, including most of the airborne ancillary equipment, was placed under a fixed-price system, but efforts to bring the airframe and engine manufacturers under a similar system failed because there were too many variables to be considered in each firm's price. In December 1936, Lieutenant Colonel Ploch, Loeb's successor as chief of production in the Technical Office, proposed to eliminate the cost plus contracts. Noting that since fiscal year 1936, the Luftwaffe had been under great pressure to make its funds go as far as possible, he argued that cost plus contracts encouraged padding and should therefore be replaced by fixed-cost contracts to reduce prices paid for aircraft and make firms more cost conscious. The immediate effect might be demoralizing for the extravagant firms, but overall such a policy would lead to sounder management, better relationships within the industry, and less criticism from other agencies. To make his fixed-price policy acceptable to the manufacturers, Ploch devised an ingenious plan by which the Reich would write off 15 percent, or 75 million RM, of the 500 million RM that it had invested in the airframe and engine industries. In return the firms would shift to the fixed-price policy beginning with the fiscal year 1937-38. Ploch estimated that in 1937-38 about one billion RM would be spent in the industry and a 7-8 percent reduction in prices through the fixed-price policy could be assumed. The 7½ percent of one billion RM or approximately 75 million RM that would be saved under the fixed-price policy equaled the amount the Reich was willing to write off from its investments. Thus the firms would be eased through the initial period when there would be acute difficulties over establishing prices. Ploch also wanted developmental contracts placed under this fixed-price policy, although he recognized that it was virtually impossible to hold firms to it since they were usually unable to determine their costs beforehand.[40]

Ploch's suggestions were debated in the RLM but for many reasons rejected. As the RLM administrative office pointed out in early 1937, high profits within the industry were vital to maintaining the initiative of the private firms. In the interests of the Reich's security, these firms should be allowed to exceed 10 percent profits. Moreover, their further expansion with these profits should be continued, since the government professed not to want to increase its own participation in the industry. The real problem seemed to be not how to establish fixed prices, but how to maintain the desired expansion of the industry by means of a price policy.[41]

Despite the RLM's reservations, the government continued to increase its direct participation in the industry, although its actions were somewhat masked by the channeling of funds through quasi-private

banks organized especially for aviation. Throughout 1938 the RLM
inched toward a fixed-price policy. On June 3, 1938, Technical Office
director Udet received special authority from Göring to supervise and
control the budgets for the next two fiscal years.[42] Over the strenuous
objections of the firms, he pushed through a fixed-price policy as Ploch
had recommended. Starting in January 1939, all prices were carefully
reviewed by the RLM to enforce some degree of consistency between
firms manufacturing the same products. By November 1939, charges
totaling 2,714,813,000 RM had been checked and the RLM estimated
that 258,341,000 RM, or approximately 10 percent, was saved, the
largest amount—116-549,000 RM—in engine construction. Some typical
price reductions forced on the aircraft industry were:

Type of Equipment	Price, 1937	Price, 1938	Price, 1939
He 111H	377,200	247,800	195,500
Bf 109E	——	101,600	73,900
Bf 110B	——	284,000	189,200
DB 601	55,655	40,500	34,800
Jumo 211	77,903	48,600	38,000
FW 58	118,700	88,000	67,800[43]

During the first quarter of 1939 the RLM requested detailed reports from
firms on their contracts and production costs. From these the RLM
hoped to establish a fixed price for aircraft produced by developmental
and by licensed firms. The price of similar airframes varied widely from
plant to plant, depending on preparation costs and length of series. For
example, the cost of a Bf 110C airframe built by the developmental firm,
BFW, dropped from an initial small-series cost of 198,495.55 RM to
193,200.00 RM, while the same airframe built by the MIAG plant cost
200,000 RM. In the Gotha Waggonfabrik, however, the cost for a Bf
110C dropped to only 135,000 RM by the third series.[44] The price for a Bf
109E airframe varied from the home firm's 68,988.67 RM to 73,300 RM
(developmental and series preparation costs not included) to Arado's
101,600 RM per unit for the first short series of 42 and 78,000 for the
next series of 398. The cost of a He 111H airframe varied from Arado's
high of 377,200 RM for the first 11 produced to 232,600 RM for the next
196, while the same airframe at the Heinkel-Oranienburg plant cost
268,800 RM for the first series and 230,000 RM for the second. As is
typical in all production series, the cost per unit dropped sharply the
longer the series ran. For example, the Junkers report on the Ju 88
airframe listed the following prices by series:

First	7 units	555,000 RM per unit (0 series)
Second	28 units	321,500 RM per unit

Third	50 units	200,000 RM per unit
Fourth	100 units	185,000 RM per unit
Fifth	286 units	170,000 RM per unit[45]

On the basis of the information gathered from the firms in early 1939, the RLM established a fixed price for comparable airframes, with some degree of variation allowed. It also drew up for foreign buyers a price list (table 17), somewhat higher than that of the RLM, which included complete aircraft with engines and standard equipment.

Although the RLM attempted with its price-fixing policy to bring some order to a chaotic situation, there was far too much money at stake

TABLE 17
EXPORT PRICES OF SOME COMMON AIRFRAMES AND AIRCRAFT, 1939

AIRFRAMES

Model	Producing Firm	Former Price	100 Units	100-200 Units	200-500 Units
Hs 126	Henschel	90	91	87	85
He 111P	Heinkel	250	207	206	205
Ju 88	Junkers	220	170	169	167
Ju 88	Henschel	200	195	183	180
Ju 88	Arado	200	180	175	170
Ju 88	Heinkel	200	200	188	185
Bf 109E	BFW	70	74	72	70
Bf 109E	Arado	90	90	90	85
Bf 109E	Erla	80	96	90	85
Bf 110C	BFW	200		150	140
Bf 110C	Focke-Wulf	300	170	155	140
Ju 87 B	Weser	90	90	89	88
Ju 52	Junkers	118	118	118	118
Ju 52	ATG	150	150	146	135

FULLY EQUIPPED AIRCRAFT

Model	Engine	Up to 50 Units	50-100 Units	100-200 Units	200-500 Units
Hs 126	31	147	137	132	128
He 111P	96	409	352	338	328
Ju 88	98	359	340	325	305
Bf 109E	47	162.4	148	135	130
Bf 110C	94	390	320	308	290
Ju 87B	49	164.45	156	148	140
Ju 52	51	214	207	202	200

SOURCE: Preisliste-Gutig Für 1940, L. C. 1, Az. 58 a 10 L. C. 1 II c, Nr. 13/1.39 g. Kdos (zu Grunde gelegt Beschäftigungsgrad des Werk für 1938), von Rohden doc. (4376-2197) BA/F.

in the awarding of contracts for either the Technical Office or LFI to control the political jockeying. The Third Reich's experience indicates that a dictatorial regime had as much difficulty handling this aspect of its defense spending as had England and the United States. Aircraft firms, with superior knowledge of their own operations, enjoyed a decided advantage in their negotiations with government agencies like the RLM. Whether the governmental agencies had second-choice personnel compared to industry, or whether the decision-making personnel were primarily military men who were too frequently rotated in their jobs, the profit and pricing policies of the Third Reich before the outbreak of war were distinct failures.[46]

EXPORTS AND GERMAN AVIATION

Exportation of German aviation equipment was a minor consideration of the industry and the RLM until after 1936, when the basic expansion had occurred. In 1930 Germany exported 20 million RM worth of aviation goods but in 1933 less than 4 million. During the depression years, the industry supplied mostly spare parts and some new aircraft taken for trade-ins from regular customers such as the Polish and Finnish airlines. The biggest export deal of the period was arranged in 1934 when Junkers contracted to build a factory in China to produce Junker aircraft and engines. The agreement was to run ten years, with the Chinese supplying 3 million Chinese silver dollars as working capital and Junkers the technical knowhow and aircraft. The plant was to have an eventual capacity of four single-engined and one multiengined aircraft per month. Junkers was also interested in establishing an airline with Junkers supplying the aircraft and technical knowledge and the Chinese the money. Both endeavors received the approval of the Reich Finance and Transportation Ministries, but the RLM was less enthusiastic.[47]

The export market was never a concern of the RLM; its policy was to allow German firms to service their older customers but to discourage an active search for new ones, especially when every ounce of energy was needed for its own rearmament. Göring particularly looked at exports more as a means to extend German influence than as a mutually beneficial economic exchange. Although Udet and Milch were more sympathetic to the firms' desire for exports, their first consideration was the Reich's armament program. Next in importance came the need for preserving German aviation secrets. When these two requirements were fulfilled, firms could export their products.

Gradually after 1936 this policy was altered. The acute need for foreign exchange, the desire for international prestige, and the growing search for additional markets after the rearmament boom compelled the industry to develop its export potential. With Milch's approval, Colonel Wimmer's Technical Office was given the authority to handle all requests for sales abroad.[48] The first series of comprehensive regulations covering the export of aviation materials were issued on June 8, 1936, and at the same time a special export organization under Admiral Lahs of the Reichsverband was created to handle the details. Lahs's ostensibly civilian group, however, was placed directly under the control of the RLM, where all final decisions were to be made. Wimmer stipulated that the export group should aim at increasing exports while protecting the Reich's interest and establishing contacts with other foreign aviation industries. It was to decide which German firms could submit requests to sell abroad, but the RLM would select the equipment to be exported, prices to be asked, terms of shipment and sales, and information to be released to foreign buyers. In short, Lahs's group was a cover for the RLM. Wimmer also placed very tight security restrictions on foreign visitations of German plants. And except to Germany's closest allies, he prohibited the export of most of the newly developed products, including fuel-injection motors, superchargers, incendiary bombs, self-sealing gas tanks, rockets, electric horizontal stabilizers, all new 20- and 30-liter engines, dive bombers of any kind, and all modern twin-engined bombers.[49]

German firms found particularly irksome the currency restrictions and the RLM policy of pricing German equipment 15-20 percent over their own domestic prices. Udet soon became a firm backer of exports, arguing that they were extremely important in four areas: advertising German aerial superiority; encouraging foreign exchange; providing training for firms and making them more cost-conscious; and developing future markets for the industry. Unfortunately, he said, German exports were handicapped by too many restrictions, including the insistence on full payment in foreign exchange from nonbarter lands. German aircraft were also too expensive, probably because of the uneconomical, large-scale construction for mobilization, air-raid defense, and social programs, which raised prices; the finer German workmanship; and the lack of cost-consciousness exhibited by many firms. Regardless of the difficulties, Udet felt it was incumbent on the industry to develop the European market, since most of the non-European market was dominated by American firms.[50]

The Technical Office's restrictive guidelines on exporting did not, however, prevent the major firms from moving quickly into new sales areas. By 1936 Junkers and Heinkel, previously at loggerheads with the RLM about exports, led all the others in foreign sales. Hungary alone took nearly half the total sales of 16.6 million RM, followed by Sweden,

Yugoslavia, Portugal, Bulgaria, and China. German firms found a lively market in Europe for warplanes, especially single-engined fighters. The market for sport and commercial aircraft was much tighter and more competitive, but German quality and workmanship were beginning to make inroads. At first the German firms found that the Reich's stringent insistence on foreign exchange and prohibition of long-term credit made it difficult to sell abroad, but they soon learned that the various barter techniques designed by Schacht were nearly as effective as the usual long-term loan arrangements granted by foreign aircraft plants. The fiscal policies did, however, tend to restrict German firms to close markets that accepted Schacht's barter system. The exporters soon realized that prompt and early delivery dates were very important in securing contracts, as was the first sale. Once a country bought equipment, it depended on Germany, and follow-up sales were easier. One alarming factor in 1936 was the frequency of requests by foreign customers for non-German engines for German airframes. The Reichsverband correctly commented in an annual report that airframe producers were not insisting on the use of German engines and that the German taxpayer had to pay the profit on that kind of contract since progress in airframe development was the result of the rearmament program.[51]

Once Udet took command of the Technical Office the aircraft producers found it easier to argue the merits of exporting. The cutbacks in the Luftwaffe program in 1937 especially underlined the importance of foreign sales. The export market could stabilize the RLM program by providing work and experience for German firms while they maintained their mobilization plan potential.

In 1937 German exports of aircraft and spare parts rose to 54.45 million RM, only 4.64 percent of the total 1,326,000,000 RM spent in the industry, but enough to make Germany the prime exporter of aircraft. An additional 7.13 million RM worth of bombs and 28.61 million RM worth of flak were also exported in the same year. The flak exports represented 6.15 percent of the total value produced. Complete aircraft exported that year included 151 warplanes worth 34.13 million RM, 278 trainers and sport planes worth 3.184 million, and 46 transports valued at 6.175 million RM. Among the principal warplanes sold were 48 Ju 86s, 24 He 111s, 19 He 46s, 15 He 70s, 12 FW 58s, 12 Hs 123s, 6 Do 17s, 3 Ju 52s, and 2 Ju 87s. Some of the best customers of the Reich were:

Country	RM for Aircraft and Parts	RM for Flak and Bombs
Hungary	15,765,000	3,983,077 (bombs)
Turkey	9,263,000	1,193,800 (flak and bombs)
Japan	6,534,000	381,000 (flak)

Sweden	2,363,000	91,000 (flak)
Austria	2,352,000	——
Rumania	1,908,000	659,000 (flak)
South Africa	2,549,000	——
Spain	1,602,000	122,000 (flak)
Argentina	1,737,000	1,700,500 (flak)
Yugoslavia	1,242,000	——
Holland	1,061,000	——

Udet had modified Wimmer's guidelines considerably, allowing the export of most newer models of bombers and fighters. As Udet pointed out, the competition was so intense that only first-class equipment could be sold in many areas. Usually the current models being used to equip Luftwaffe units were prohibited, but some exceptions were made for politically reliable countries like Hungary, Yugoslavia, and Turkey.

Individual firms were allowed to export aircraft provided they did not use raw materials requested from the RLM or become lax with their defense contracts. Special raw materials permits were issued for export aircraft, but even then the RLM had the option of buying the planes. By 1938 some of the best sellers were aircraft that the Luftwaffe had showed little interest in, such as the He 112 fighter, holder of a world record, and two models of four-engined aircraft, the Ju 90 and FW 200. In January, Udet granted approval, for example, for the export of 50 He 112s, 11 Ju 90s, and 20 FW 200s.[52] Japan in particular was interested in the FW 200 as a long-range bomber. An agreement was reached with Focke-Wulf to build a military bomber version with a range of 5,000 kilometers, cruise speed of 300 and top speed of 400 km./h. and a bomb load of 1,000 kg. The Japanese wanted Wasp engines for it, but Focke-Wulf recommended the BMW 132 or an improved version. Delivery of the bomber was scheduled for mid-1940.[53]

By 1938, despite the accelerated armament program and the threatening international situation, Udet and the firms still insisted on increased exportation. Udet noted the worldwide increase in the exporting of aircraft and the excellent position Germany had; besides, exports yielded a rich harvest in propaganda. Germany's position might change radically if exports were not pressed. She had rearmed so swiftly that she was now able to capitalize on the situation before England, France, the the United States completed their rearming. It was well known, argued Udet, that through profits and write-offs American and English firms would soon be in a position to cut their prices drastically. Although German prices were high and tended to remain so, if German firms could establish their predominance, they might compete by stressing other sales considerations such as the quality of the aircraft, early and prompt delivery, and advantageous buying terms. First, however, the RLM should abandon all restrictions on sales of the latest equipment, since the military security of the Reich would be protected by the rapid aging of military equipment, and delivery would always be one to one and one-half years after the Luftwaffe received similar equipment.[54]

Ernst Heinkel summarized industry opinion on exporting similarly, observing that his own firm had lost much business because of delayed approvals by the RLM or because the ministry banned the latest equipment. He cited the case of the Yugoslavian government, which wanted his He 112, the plane in which Udet had set a world record of 635 km./h. The RLM would approve only an export model with a Jumo 210G engine, which allowed a top speed of 475 km./h. As a result, the firm lost the contract to the British. The same story was repeated in Switzerland, where Heinkel lost out to the French, and in Hungary, where he was bested by the Italians. In another deal for 70 He 111s for Japan, the RLM halted delivery after the first 10, and the Japanese turned to Italy, where Mussolini personally intervened in their behalf. The contract, worth 80-100 million RM, was lost. Heinkel's message was clear: foreigners would not buy higher-priced German airplanes that were inferior in performance to their competitors'.[55]

The arguments had some effect; the RLM granted tentative approval for the sale of 60 new Bf 109s and 240 Do 17s to Yugoslavia in January 1939, and agreed to an exchange of aircraft and information with Italy in June. Göring personally arranged with General Giuseppe del Valle of Italy to trade 4 He 111Hs or Ps, 4 Bf 109Es, and 4 Ju 87Bs for 4 Savoia 79s, 4 Fiat 50s, and 4 Breda 88s.[56] Although the regulations prohibiting the exportation of modern equipment were relaxed in 1939, however, Udet stiffened control over foreign observations in German aircraft plants. From February to June 15, 1939, all visitations were blocked except for purchasing commissions and one visit of the prominent American scientist George W. Lewis from NACA. Although Lewis's tour was supposed to be open, it actually was carefully manipulated to keep him from seeing the most sensitive projects in the German research institutes he was to visit. On another occasion, Udet rather curtly refused a Japanese delegation permission to visit Ju 88, Bf 110, or Hs 129 factories because Japan had refused permission for a German air attaché to visit Japanese plants.[57]

The total volume of German aviation exports from 1933 to 1938 was not great compared to the total of all German exports, but it represented an area of growth and an important source of foreign exchange. As table 18 indicates, most of the increase in aviation exports occurred after 1936.

The widely held belief that Göring and the German aircraft industry were selling obsolete and inferior aircraft abroad at lower prices and underselling other countries' aviation industries cannot be substantiated by the German documents. The RLM was at first unduly cautious about military security. This policy soon gave way to the more realistic one of selling the best, but technological progress was so rapid in the late 1930s that aircraft purchased one year were obsolete on their delivery the next. Naturally, the RLM was reluctant to see potentially unfriendly powers purchase modern equipment, especially since it could use the total production of the industry. On a number of occasions it did exercise its prerogative of buying aircraft intended for export, but its continual warnings about spending too much energy on export business indicates the intention of the firms to keep their position in the world market. After the war a number of RLM officials stated that firms like Junkers, Heinkel, and Messerschmitt invested an inordinate amount of money, engineering time, and space maintaining their export trade potential, to the detriment of the Reich's armament program.[58]

RESEARCH AND DEVELOPMENT

Research and development in aviation was divided and fragmented. When the RLM was first organized in 1933, a sharp distinction was made between the two areas. In the Technical Office (C Amt) were four principal divisions: Research, C 1; Development, C 2; Production, C 3; and Budget, C 4. In 1938, when the Technical Office was again reorganized, Research remained a separate office, LC 5, while Development was divided according to item: airframes, engines, and weapons. Adolf Bäumker, coordinator of RLM research, remained head of the division until the

TABLE 18

GERMAN AVIATION AND FLAK EXPORTS, 1933-38
(in millions of RM)

Year	Aircraft	Bombs	Flak	Aviation Total	All German Export Total
1933	3.82			3.82	4,900.0
1934	6.47			6.47	4,200.0
1935	3.90			3.90	4,300.0
1936	16.60			16.60	4,800.0
1937	43.45[1]	7.13	28.61	79.19	5,900.0
1938	94.49	0.98	26.64	122.11	5,600.0

SOURCE: Bericht uber den Export von Luftfahrt-und Flakgerät, 27.Feb. 1939, RLM Folder 285, NA Microcopy T-177/32/3721218-41.

[1] This total does not agree with the total of 54.45 mentioned in the text because the earlier report included some equipment sold to China that was awaiting final payment. When the payment did not come, the amount was deducted from the report for the next year.

collapse of the Reich, ensuring a degree of continuity not normally found in the Third Reich.

Bäumker was the son of a university professor, and although trained as a civil servant, he understood and appreciated the importance of science. He was an officer in World War I and later served in the Transportation Ministry, where he was involved with civil aviation. In 1933 he moved to the RLM to head the research division. He found that aviation research was being conducted by four uncoordinated groups of institutes: the prestigious Kaiser-Wilhelm Institute, which concentrated on pure research; Reich or state institutes; university institutes; and private industrial institutes. Utilizing his understanding of the inner workings of government, he attempted to coordinate and centralize these institutes under the direction of the RLM and with Göring's support founded in 1933 the Association for Aviation Research (Vereinigung für Luftfahrtforschung). The association, renamed the Lilienthal Society for Aviation Research (Lilienthal-Gesellschaft für Luftfahrtforschung) in 1936, included the industrial firms and most of the state and university institutes.

Pure research was uncoordinated until 1936, when the German Academy for Aviation Research was founded with 60 regular and 100 corresponding members. Its work was theoretical and was largely ignored by Udet, who was more interested in practical research, and Milch, who disliked its director.[59] Göring, however, supported the group and often intervened in its behalf to obtain money and materials. Other important institutes for pure or applied research were the Technical Academy for the Luftwaffe, Berlin-Gatow (Technische Akademie der Luftwaffe, or TAL), which was funded by the War, Air, and Education Ministries and functioned as a German equivalent to the National Bureau of Standards; the Central Institute for Aviation Research at Adlersdorf; the famed Aerodynamic Research Institute at Göttingen; and the Hermann Göring Institute at Braunschweig. In 1937 these last three were combined with nine smaller institutes into the centralized German Research Institute for Aviation (Deutsche Versuchsanstalt für Luftfahrt, or DVL), which was budgeted and controlled directly under Bäumker's office. By 1938 Bäumker had largely succeded in bringing the aviation research centers under his direction.

The research institutes of the Luftwaffe were beautifully constructed and lavishly equipped and staffed. Employing from 200 to 3,000, but usually small, they were the basic unit of the German research program. The director of the institute controlled it personally, received instructions from the RLM and exercising the prerogative of originating projects himself. The staff of the institutes received many emoluments, including excellent salaries, good housing, titles from technical universities, and freedom from minor annoyances such as time clocks, strict accountability, and cramped working quarters. The facilities were far superior to those of the army or navy.

The attitude of the government toward the institutes was, in the words of Colonel Leslie E. Simon, then director of the U. S. Ballistic Research Laboratories at the Aberdeen Proving Ground, "willing but not intelligent."[60] Bäumker asserted that he had a warm personal relationship with Göring and Hitler and that both were eager to support most of the proposed research projects, but the von Rohden study argues the contrary and indicates that research suffered accordingly.[61] Bäumker's contention is supported, however, by the amount of government subsidies for research, which grew rapidly after 1933, as the following figures show:

1933	4,333,000	RM
1934	13,131,500	RM
1935	17,550,000	RM
1936	38,312,500	RM
1937	46,100,000	RM
1938	49,400,000	RM
1939	63,231,000	RM
TOTAL	232,058,000	RM[62]

The total of 232 million RM compares favorably to the total of 22.9 million RM spent on aviation research during the preceding seven years of the Weimar Republic, indicating the generosity of the Nazis. However, budget director Fritz Mueller estimated that research accounted for only 2 percent of the total spent in aviation.

The RLM entrenched itself as the sole arbiter of aviation research projects. Unlike the army, it took a strong hand in directing the advancement of fundamental knowledge, loosening the corporate grasp on trade secrets and raising the level of integrity in the whole field. But the RLM failed to coordinate research with development. The Technical Office under Udet's direction never took the research division into its confidence, with the result that there were many duplications of effort and poor communications between military units, development offices in the RLM, factories, and the research institutes. As Simon concluded, "Scientific effort was prostituted on one hand and undirected on the other to the point of being random. The frugal Germans thought that they were fabulously rich in science and squandered a priceless asset."[63]

Research in electronics was particularly slighted in the prewar period; the result was costly delays and military defeats later. In precisely this area, where the prestige and competence of the industrial firms were the greatest, the RLM seemed most hesitant and unsure of itself. Later, in trying to explain it, the argument was used that the government did not have comparable technical competence to balance the influence of the firms. Too often the RLM had military officers making decisions which were beyond their level of competence; engineers and technicians were looked down upon by the officers of the old school, or officers were so unfamiliar with the technical intricacies that they were intimidated by the firms' representatives. Government officials were often critized as being inferior to those in industry. Bright people supposedly were drawn into private industry, where their services were more generously rewarded.[64]

Other reasons for the slim research results in this period support the opposite viewpoint. Göring, after the war, thought that although the private firms usually had better men, they tended to become complacent; they became so accustomed to relying on government-sponsored research that they lost their initiative.[65] Regardless, the necessary unity of scientific and military knowledge in the RLM or the top leadership of the Luftwaffe was missing because of the speed of the aviation build-up, the type of personnel involved, and rate of developments in the scientific world.

Starting in the late 1930s, a level of modern technology and science was reached which demanded large-scale reorganization of resources. As the great cooperative scientific successes of World War II—the atomic bomb, radar, and missiles—proved, the age of privately sponsored and conducted research was rapidly drawing to a close. The future belonged to the massive governmental-corporate-university research projects. The RLM did not see this before World War II, for it had not a single major scientific project in this period.

In the more limited area of aviation development and design, the Germans showed as much originality, progress, and achievement as any comparable country. Design and development are essentially engineering processes in which drawings, tolerances, mechanics, and strengths of materials are blended with production designs for assembly-line needs, economic choices of materials, adaptation of machines, and hundreds of other practical matters. Once aircraft leave the drawing boards of the design engineers, they undergo a long process of refinement in which their basic design is enhanced by incessant testing and production. Omissions and deficiencies are discovered, corrections made, and models perfected. Long, tedious work is needed until a model is ready for use, and the process is, of necessity, never ended. In this area, the traditional German virtues of pride in work, love of execution of detail, and desire for precision and completeness were displayed to their best advantage.

German aviation development before the war was characterized paradoxically by its diffusion and its concentration. After the first generation of superior warplanes—the Bf 109, He 111, Do 17, and Ju 87—the Technical Office had great difficulty in controlling the breadth of development. Far too often, the firms were allowed to produce everything from trainers to big bombers, with a resulting division of attention and losses of precious manpower, space, and time. The Heinkel firm, for example, had only one model, the He 111, produced in a large series. Meanwhile, it had models such as the He 74, He 112, He 114, He 115, He 116, He 118, He 119, He 176, He 178, and He 100, which were produced either in prototype or in limited, small series.[66] Production of even the large-series models was often hindered by the introduction of many variations which did not appreciably improve the planes but did cause long delays. Conversely, once the RLM and the firms had a successful model, they became ultracautious in perfecting the old one rather than attempting a breakthrough with a new line. Two examples of this were the Bf 109 and the He 111. The Bf 109 airframe was fitted with a variety of engines ranging from the early 730 h.p. to the World War II 1,800 h.p. All attempts to increase the power plant resulted in greater fuel consumption and lower flight time. As additional equipment—armor, radios, more weapons—was piled into the airframe, the designers had to compensate for the weight and reduced range by adding internal and external fuel tanks, which increased the weight further and lowered the range, ceiling, and performance. The basic airframe was stretched to its limits. In the case of the He 111, the aircraft grew from the 17,600-lb. 1936 version with two DB 600 engines of 882 h.p. each, speed of 240 mph, bomb load of 2,200 lbs., and range of 300-360 miles, to the 35,200-lbs. 1944 He 111P model with two Jumo 213E engines of 1725 h.p. each, speed of 300 mph, bomb load of 4,400 lbs., but a range about the same as that of the earlier plane. To make these improvements took the Heinkel firm four million hours of designing time.[67]

Other factors that limited German development were shortages of wind tunnels and engineers. Before the war the aircraft firms provided their own low-yield wind tunnels; only one powerful tunnel, at Göttingen, was placed at the convenience of the industry. It was invariably overloaded, which meant that there were long waiting periods for its use. Not until after the outbreak of war did the government construct supersonic tunnels like the one built at Kochel and the one started at Ötzal.[68] The lack of engineers and technicians was even more debilitating. A report in August 1938 listed only 20,797 engineers in the entire aircraft industry and the Luftwaffe. Their distribution can be seen in table 19. The report estimated that by the end of 1938 the industry would need an additional 1,060 diploma engineers, 2,605 technical school engineers, and 1,680 technicians, but that only 3,505 students were enrolled in their last few semesters in all the technical programs throughout the Reich. If these were to go in the usual proportion to the other industries—steel, chemical, and mining—the aircraft industry would receive yearly only 60 diploma engineers and 90 technical school engineers. The RLM had a limited program for assisting students in aeronautical fields. In 1938 and 1939 it was budgeted at 200,000 RM and furnished grants to a number of schools, but most of the funds went in the form of 642 stipends averaging 390 RM per semester to students in the late stages of their studies. In 1938 a mere 129 of these stipend holders finished and 104 of them were employed in the aircraft industry.[69] The number of aeronautical engineers had increased tremendously since the late 1920s, when the average was one engineer per semester per technical university, but the Third Reich found it more difficult to produce engineers than aircraft. The shortage of engineers handicapped the development program at every level. RLM officials recognized belatedly that they had been living on research fat accumulated over many years; it was now time to inaugurate crash programs to train students in technical fields and to emphasize pure research.[70]

It is at the final stage of a developmental program—testing—that all of the research, design, and developmental work blends with the military requirements. The closest cooperation between scientist, designer, planner, industrialist, and officer are necessary to bring the long work to proper fruition. The German testing program was under the control of the

TABLE 19

DISTRIBUTION OF ENGINEERS IN THE AIRCRAFT INDUSTRY, JUNE 1938

(number and percent)

	Diploma Engineers[1]	Technical School Engineers[2]	Technicians[3]	Total
Industry	1,537	8,431	5,358	15,326
	10%	55%	35%	100%
Research	696	488	109	1,293
	54%	38%	8%	100%
RLM	727	1,115	243	2,085
	35%	53%	12%	100%
Transportation	62	124	107	293
	21%	42%	37%	100%
Luftwaffe	500	1,000	300	1,800
	28%	55%	17%	100%
TOTAL	3,522	11,158	6,117	20,797
	17%	54%	29%	100%

SOURCE: Deutsche Versuchsanstalt für Luftfahrt e.V., "Ingenieur-bedarf in der deutschen Luftfahrt," 1.August 1938, von Rohden document (4376-1108), BA/F.

[1]Graduates of university programs (Diplom Ingenieur).

[2]Completed technical or professional school programs (Fachschule Ingenieur).

[3]Completed high school type of training program (Techniker).

Technical Office, but key military officers such as the chief of the general staff, chief of troop technics, chief of technical equipment, and inspector for flying safety were immediately involved. The actual testing of aviation equipment was done at the two major test centers, Rechlin and Travemünde, where the Technical Office had the best of its flying technical personnel like Lieutenant Colonel von Massenbach, the director of Rechlin. The famous Training Wing, a crack composite wing of the best fliers in the Luftwaffe, tested new equipment under simulated combat conditions.

The testing program functioned quite well before the war despite the usual teething problems. Close cooperation between the various firms and the military was gradually built up, but the results of the testing were too often not adequately distributed to other interested firms. Although both the testing officials and the firms had a genuine interest in improving products, however, the firms' interests were not always the same as those of the government. Often the choice of equipment was influenced by factors other than technical performance—by production, business, and political considerations.[71] The frequent changes of personnel, the lack of an outstanding designer on the testing staff (at one time Udet and Milch had suggested Tank of Focke-Wulf for such a position), and the growing arrogance and disinterest of top officials like Göring, Milch, and Udet hampered the testing program. Moreover, the authority of the testing personnel was undercut by the frequently unclear directives from the general staff and unit commanders. In an effort to help the firms and improve the testing program, Göring established in February 1938 a special Luftwaffe Inspectorate for Flying Safety and Equipment. Its chief concern was flight safety, for there had been a rapid increase in accidents, but it was also charged with providing technical assistance based on the testing program to plants and subcontractors in hopes of speeding production and avoiding costly mistakes.[72] One of the inspectorate's first suggestions was for the formation of "rings" of manufacturers of similar products, a proposal from which stemmed the "rings" system used so successfully in World War II.

In summary, the research and development program in aviation lacked intelligent guidance. There was no single body or council to formulate clearly the characteristics of desired research and development and to supervise their execution. Neither the general staff nor the RLM had an agency that could bring together the many strands necessary for an orderly progression of development, guide research into areas calculated to bring swift technical accomplishment, and channel research into the appropriate areas of weapon development. Apart from the Luftwaffe, there was no other Reich agency that managed basic research and development on a national scale. Only Göring's Four-Year Plan Office had the political muscle and economic sinew to accomplish such a large task, but it was soon bogged down in short-range objectives and related primarily to the chemical industry. Without proper vision and the necessary supervised coordination, the German research and development program in aviation proved versatile, capable, and potentially great in small things, but diffused and underutilized in the pursuit of larger objectives.

NOTES

1. Hertel, "Flugzeugbeschaffung," p. 4.
2. Ibid., p. 14; General der Flieger a.D. Helmut Felmy, "Die Führung der Deutschen Luftwaffe im Kriege," Studiengruppe Geschichte des Luftkrieges Karlsruhe, Lw 21/1, pp. 169-70, BA/F.
3. Hertel, "Flugzeugbeschaffung," pp. 8-11.
4. Industrie-Rüstungsgrundlagen 1938 (J.R.G.38), 1.November 1935, LC Nr. 12858/35, III, Ing. geh.Kdos., BA o.s. 86, BA/F.
5. There was a lively debate in all military circles about anticipated losses in the next war. The Germans planned for 50 percent, which was based on English and American planning plus their own experiences in World War I, where losses ran 30 percent. The Spanish Civil War was an exception, since only 10 percent a month was typical. For a discussion of German planning, see "Aus dem Handbuch der neuzeitlichen Wehrwissenschaften," III, Teil 2, von Rohden document (4376-463), BA/F; and Hertel, "Flugzeugbeschaffung," pp. 56-57. For British planning, see Higham, *Armed Forces in Peacetime*, pp. 183-90.
6. Beschaffungsmeldungen, Januar bis Juni 1938, von Rohden document (4406-594), BA RL 3/v.440, BA/F.
7. All figures taken from "Die Deutsche Luftfahrtindustrie," 15.August 1938, NA Microcopy T-177/15/3699802-43.
8. Stand der Flugzeugreparaturindustrie 30.7.1938, LC 7 Az. 66 p. 10/Nr. 143/38 g.Kdos. (IV), 3.Aug.1938, RLM Folder 174, NA Microcopy T-177/15/3699711-38.
9. Vorgesehene Leistungen der Flugzeugzellen-Werke und Flugmotoren-werke in Beschaffungsjahr 1937/38, LC III, Ing., 26.4.1937, g.Kdos., Lw 103/39 and Lw 103/4, DZ/MGFA.
10. Eberhard Aleff, Walter Tormin, Friedrich Zipfel, *Das Dritte Reich*, (Bremen: Verlag für Literatur und Zeitgeschehen, 1970), pp. 40-41, 117-18.
11. Ibid., p. 130.
12. Fritz Nonnenbruch, *Dynamische Wirtschaft* (Munich: Eher, 1936), p. 10.
13. Kesselring, *Soldat*, pp. 36-37; Koppenberg, "Junkers 1933-1941," Lw 103/28, DZ/MGFA.
14. Die Arado-Flugwerke, Lw 103/42, DZ/MGFA; Arado papers, von Rohden document (4370-2410), BA/F; Bericht der Deutschen Revisions-und-Treuhand-Aktien-gesellschaft Berlin über Arado Flugzeugwerke, 1937, RLM Folder 1679/1, NA Microcopy T-177/50/3741572-603.
15. Hermann, *Luftwaffe*, pp. 76-78, 89-95; Irving, *Milch*, pp. 40, 50-51, 68.
16. Details of the Junkers case taken from Irving, *Milch*, pp. 76-77, 405-6;

Koppenberg, "Junkers 1933-1941," Lw 103/28, DZ/MGFA; Curt Riess, "Die Junkers Tragödie," *Münchener Illustrierte*, July-August 1955.

17. "Die Entwicklung von 'Dessau' im Jahre 1934," von Dr. Dr.Ing. Heinrich Koppenberg, Januar 1935, Lw 103/43, DZ/MGFA. Production for Junkers was 41 in 1933, 238 in 1934, 433 in 1935, 356 in 1936, 529 in 1937, 684 in 1938, and 922 in 1939, National Aerospace Museum, Washington, D.C., Folder Ju/Mis/Mi/5, Roll 2095, Frame 00306.

18. Heinkel, *Stürmisches Leben*, pp. 413-15; Hertel, "Flugzeugbeschaffung," p. 128, DZ/MGFA.

19. Richterliche Überprufung des Geschäftsbereichs des Technischen Amtes nach dem Freitod des Generals Udet (corrected copy dated March 14, 1956), Lw 103/25, DZ/MGFA.

20. Heinkel, *Stürmisches Leben*, pp. 414-15; Bericht über eine Befragung des Majors, a.D. Pohle über die Entstehungsgeschichte der He 177, 18.4.1956, Lw 103/56, DZ/MGFA.

21. For Junkers, see Haputfinanzverwaltung Statistik, 12.März 1942, Speer Collection, FDC, Nr. 4875/450; for German averages, Aleff et al., *Dritte Reich*, p. 118. For the effects on other firms, see folders Wi/IF 5. 201-3, NA Microcopy T-77/35/747673-81, /747928-35, /748182-87.

22. RLM Folder 269, NA Microcopy T-177/31/3720142-53.

23. Aktenvermerk 26.Nov.1938, Besprechung Fl. Haupt-Stabing. Hertel/Dipl. Ing. Deutschmann, RLM Folder 174, NA Microcopy T-177/15/3699704-5, and Stand der wirtschaftlicher Lage, 1.Okt.1938, frames 3699781-93.

24. For information on the Junkers housing program and other personnel and social programs, see the monthly and quarterly reports of the firm in RLM Folder 1706/1-10, NA Microcopy T-177/50/3742424-716.

25. Irving, *Milch*, p. 68; interview of Professor William Messerschmitt, May 11, 1945, USSBS, 4d42, pp. 1-2; William Green, *Augsburg Eagle* (Garden City, N.Y.: Doubleday, 1971), pp. 9-11; Roger Allan Williams, "The Development of Luftwaffe Aircraft in the Nazi Era" (Ph.D. dissertation, University of Minnesota, 1971), p. 26.

26. Irving, *Milch*, pp. 68-69.

27. Aufsichtratsbesprechung von 29.Juni 1938 im Verwaltungsgebäude der BFW-A.G., Augsburg, von Rohden document (4370-3490), p. 2, BA/F.

28. Protokoll der Hauptversammlung von 19.Dez.1938, BFW A.G., von Rohden document (4370-3490), p. 2, BA/F; USSBS, Air Frame Plant Report No. 6, Messerschmitt A.G., Augsburg, p. 7.

29. Niederschrift über eine ordentliche Hauptversammlung 18.Feb.1941, Messerschmitt A.G., von Rohden document (4370-3490), p. 6, BA/F.

30. Comments of Ing. Emmert over Messerschmitt, von Rohden document (4376-463), BA/F.

31. Speer interview, No. 11, May 31, 1945, USSBS, 4d49, pp. 8-9.

32. Irving, *Milch*, pp. 72-74, 83-84, 407.

33. Niederschrift über die Aufsichtratssitzung der Bayer. Flugzeugwerke A.G., vom 11.Juli 1938 im Verwaltungsgebäude der BFW A.G. Augsburg, von Rohden document (4370-3490), BA/F.

34. For a general discussion, see Esenwein-Rothe, *Wirtschaftsverbände*, and especially on the aircraft industry, Hertel, "Flugzeugbeschaffung," pp. 156-60.

35. Mitgliederliste des Reichsverband der Deutschen Luftfahrt-Industrie, den 28.März 1938, NA Microcopy T-177/15/3699925-34.

36. Brief an Milch, Der Leiter der Wirtschaftsgruppe Luftfahrt-Industrie, 2.Nov. 1942, file RLM; Handakte, Generalfeldmarschall Milch, RL/84, vol. 53, Milch Collection, FDC.

37. Mason, "Primat der Politik," pp. 482-88; Czichon, "Primat der Industrie," pp. 178-85; Eichholtz, "Noch einmal," pp. 222-23.

38. Schmidt, "Grundlagen und Wandlungen," pp. 49-51; Das technische Amt der deutschen Luftwaffe, Generalstabsrichters Frhr. von Hammerstein, 3.9.55, Lw 103/25, DZ/MGFA; Wege und Formen der Investitionsfinanzierung der deutschen Luftfahrt-Industrie in den Jahren 1933-1945, Lw 103/25, DZ/MGFA.

39. Obersting.a.D. Dipl. Ing. Mix, "Über die Geräteentwicklung bei der Luftwaffe," Lw 103/63; "Die technische Organisation in der deutschen Luftfahrt," Lw 103/25, DZ/MGFA.

40. An den Chef des Verwaltungsamtes Heern Generalmajor Volkmann, LC Nr. 11779/36, III geh., Berlin 12.Dez.1936, von Rohden document (4406-588), BA/F.

41. Gedankengänge zu der Frage der Finanzierung der Luftfahrt-Industrie, 14.2.1937, Lw 103/7, DZ/MGFA; Endgültige Fassung der Richtlinien über Preisbildung und Finanzierung, LD I, 1B, Nr. 13266/37, 10.März 1937, von Rohden document (4406-588), BA/F.

42. Die Finanzierung der deutschen Luftrüstung, von Rohden document (4376-470), BA/F. For similar problems in the British aircraft industry, see Higham, "Government, Companies, and National Defense," pp. 323-47.

43. Ergebnis der Preisprüfung von 1.Jan. bis 30.Sept. 1939, LF Nr. 702771/39 geh., 3.Nov., 1939, von Rohden document (4376-1696), BA/F.

44. Auftrags-Bestandsmeldungen: MIAG, 13.April 1939; Gotha Waggon-fabrik 15.4.1939; Messerschmitt A.G. 26.6.1939 on RL 3/v. 112,113, BA/F.

45. Auftragsbestandsmeldung am 31.3.1939 für Zellen im Serienbau, 13.April 1939, Junkers, LC 2 Nr. 1655/39 geh., a.S. RLM 631, RL 3/v. 115, BA/F. Information on the other airframe plants taken from RL 3/v. 113, 114, 115.

46. Schmidt, "Grundlagen und Wandlungen," pp. 21-23; Das technische Amt der deutschen Luftwaffe, Lw 103/25, DZ/MGFA; Denkschrift zur Wehrwirt-schaftordnung und Wehrwirtschaftorganisation, 5.Nov.1938, LC 2 Nr. 4441/38, g.Kdos. Milch Collection, vol. 57, FDC; Hertel, "Flugzeugbeschaffung," pp. 163, 198-200; General d. Flieger Forster, 20.7.1945, von Rohden document (4376-463), BA/F; Felmy, "Führung der Luftwaffe," pp. 203-4, Lw 21/1, DZ/MGFA.

47. On the Junkers plant in China, see the letter from the German embassy dated 2.Jan.1935, OKW/10944 Folder, NA Microcopy T-77/92/5655954-66, and Koppenberg, "Die Entwicklung von Dessau," Lw 103/45, DZ/MGFA.

48. LC Nr. 113, 067/35 IV, 1, 10.Jan.1936; LC/LA Nr. 2372/36, 7.April 1936, von Rohden document (4406-717), BA/F; also Colonel Wimmer's correspondence with General Blomberg, March 16, 1936, on the possibilities of increasing aviation exports, NA Microcopy T-177/28/3716452.

49. Ausführungsbestimmungen für den Export und die Freigabe von Luftfahrtgerät, LC Nr. 1699/36, g.Kdos., IV, 8.Juni 1936, NA Microcopy T-177/15/3699908-23.

50. Bericht über den Export von Luftfahrt- und Flakgerät, 10.Jan.1938, LC IV, Nr. 5/38 g.Kdos., von Rohden document (4406-818), BA/F.

51. Reichsgruppe Luftfahrtindustrie, "Jahresbericht 1936," 2.März 1937, Folder Wi/IF 5.458, NA Microcopy T-77/106/832638-76.

52. Ibid.; see also the Abschrift, LC IV, 77/38, geh.Kdos., 20.Jan.1938.

53. Correspondence of Focke-Wulf plant, von Rohden document (4376-1749), BA/F.

54. Der deutsche Luftfahrtexport, no date, broken file, Lw 103/5, DZ/MGFA.

55. Dr. Ernst Heinkel, "Gedanken zur Exportfrage," 15.Aug.1938, Milch Collection, vol. 54, FDC.

56. On the Yugoslavian contract, see correspondence from the German military attaché in Belgrade, January 26, 1939, on General Simovic's request, von Rohden document (4376-478), BA/F; on the Italian exchange, see Studiengruppe Luftwaffe, Lw 101/3, Teil 2, Italia und Deutschland, DZ/MGFA.

57. On visitation rights, see von Rohden document (4376-2549), particularly Udet's letter to Admiral Lahs, 22.Feb.1939, Az. 8 d 10 GL B.f.S./A, Nr. 615/39, geh.; arrangements for Dr. Lewis, 31.Mai 1939, Az. 8 d 10/Nr. 104292/19/II geh.; and letters on Japanese delegation, LF 1Nr. 2218/38 geh., BA/F.

58. Schmidt, "Grundlagen und Wandlungen," p. 50; Richterliche Überprüf-ung des Geschäfteberichs des Technischen Amtes nach dem Freitod des Generals Udet, Lw 103/25, DZ/MGFA; RLM Folder 259, NA Microcopy T-177/30/3718-298-310; "Der Luftkrieg," von Rohden document (4376-366), BA/F.

59. Von Rohden study, NA Microcopy T-971/27/112-14; "Zusammenfassung der deutschen Forschungsstätten, NA Microcopy T-71/135/639096-100.

60. Leslie E. Simon, *German Research in World War II: An Analysis of the Conduct of Research* (New York: John Wiley, 1947), pp. 12, 56.

61. Von Rohden study, NA Microcopy T-971/27/109-14. Ministerialrat Müller commented that the poor personal relationship was a reason for the slim research results from 1936 to 1940; von Rohden document (4376-463), BA/F.

62. Bäumker, "Zur Geschichte der Luftfahrtforschung," Lw 103/61, DZ/MGFA; Ministerialrat Müller, von Rohden document (4376-463), BA/F.

63. Simon, *German Research*, pp. 96-97, 197-98.

64. Ibid., pp. 93, 200; von Rohden study, NA Microcopy T-971/27/114-20; Gerbert Hübner, "Wehrmacht und Technik," Lw 103/21, DZ/MGFA; Eberhard Schmidt, "Entwicklung und Versuch in der deutschen Flugindustrie," *Flug-Wehr und Technik*, März 1947, pp. 79-82; Robert Schlaiffer, *Development of Aircraft Engines* (Boston: Harvard University Press, 1950), pp. 25-37.

65. Göring Interview, 14 June 1945, USSBS, 4d42, pp. 8-9.

66. Von Rohden study, NA Microcopy T-971/26/1160. Heinkel defended his firm in a letter to Colonel Greffrath (who wrote the section in the von Rohden study) dated July 18, 1952, Lw 103/39, DZ/MGFA. For a similar British experience, see Robin Higham, "Quantity vs. Quality: The Impact of Changing Demand on the British Aircraft Industry, 1900-1960," *Business History Review* 42 (1968): 443-66.

67. Information of the Bf 109 taken from von Rohden study, NA Microcopy T-971/27/8-15; on the He 111, see Heinkel, *Stürmisches Leben*, p. 310.

68. Simon, *German Research*, pp. 131-32, 136-55; Rudolf Lusar, *Die deutschen Waffen und Geheimwaffen des 2.Weltkrieges und ihre Weiterentwick-lung* (Munich: J. F. Lehmanns, 1959), pp. 248-50; Schmidt, "Entwicklung und Versuch," pp. 79-80.

69. RLM Folder 1354/1, NA Microcopy T-177/41/3731915-56, has a list of stipend holders and grants for 1938-39.

70. Über die Notwendigkeit einer Neugestaltung der Wissenschaftlichen Forschung in Deutschland, Berlin, 6.April 1940, Lw 103/61; Fl. Obersting. a.D. Johannes von Riedmann, "Die fliegertechnische Ausbildung," Lw 103/44, DZ/MGFA.

71. Simon, *German Research*, p. 200; Hübner, "Wehrmacht und Technik," Lw 103/21; Felmy, "Führung der Luftwaffe," Lw 21/1, pp. 187-88, DZ/MGFA; Conradis, *Kurt Tank*, pp. 310-11.

72. RLM Folder 174, NA Microcopy T-177/15/3699763-68.

CHAPTER 8

On to War: From Munich to
the Attack on Poland

BEGINNING WITH the famous Hossbach conference on November 5, 1937, when Hitler clearly outlined his plans for aggression in eastern and central Europe, the rush to war was evident.[1] He methodically moved against those who opposed his decision to risk war. In November 1937, Schacht was removed as economics minister. In February 1938, the Blomberg scandal broke, allowing Hitler to remove the field marshal, dissolve the War Ministry, and replace it with the newly formed OKW under General Wilhelm Keitel. General Werner von Fritsch, the logical successor to Blomberg, was pushed aside because of a trumped-up charge of homosexuality, and General von Brauchitsch was given command of the army. Within a short time, sixteen generals were retired and forty-four transferred. In the Foreign Ministry, the conservative Konstantin von Neurath was replaced by the Führer's favorite, Joachim von Ribbentrop, and a number of old-line ambassadors were recalled. By the time of the Czech crisis, Hitler had succeeded in removing most of those leaders who did not fully support his dangerous plans.

The changes in the RLM were not as great or as widely publicized as in the other ministries. Göring, always eager for new offices and titles, had taken an active part in the plots against Blomberg and Fritsch, for he hoped to replace Blomberg as commander of the Wehrmacht. Hitler dismissed that possibility, allegedly with the statement that Göring was too lazy to be commander. More likely, Hitler wanted to extend his own authority over the Wehrmacht.[2] Elsewhere in the RLM, the major changes were more subtle. The relatively young and enthusiastic pro-Nazi Luftwaffe had no old-line soldiers to purge, but important struggles took place. The chief power plays were directed against Milch, whose position was gradually undermined by a combination of factors. The newly formed general staff of the Luftwaffe had removed much of his influence from military decision making, while Göring elevated Udet in the Technical Office to a status nearly equal to Milch's. The outcome was a series of administrative changes which isolated Milch, brought Udet and Jeschonnek to prominence, and dangerously split the RLM.

The changes within the aircraft industry were also pronounced. The years of hesitation and delays occasioned by fluctuating production programs, shortages of funds, and irresolute leadership seemed to be over. Starting in the spring of 1938, the RLM began moving toward a high-geared production program. Although the leadership of the industry was erratic, it was clear about objectives—maximum production as soon as possible. From the launching of the massive Ju 88 program in the fall of 1938 until the first bomb dropped on Poland a year later, the RLM rushed the industry to war.

HITLER'S FIVEFOLD EXPANSION PROGRAM

On October 14, 1938, scarcely two weeks after the Munich conference, Göring announced Hitler's gigantic new armament program, which would dwarf all previous programs. Ambitious plans were made for the navy, and the army was to have improved offensive weapons, including new artillery and tanks. Large increases in the manufacture of fuel, explosives, and flak and in military construction were projected, but the greatest increase was reserved for the Luftwaffe. It was to be "immediately enlarged fivefold," and was given top priority.[3] Implicit in the program was an awareness of the possibility of a two-front war. Emphasis was placed on the construction of air bases to support operations against England and the development of long-range bombers and fighter-escorts capable of striking the island kingdom. The RLM began preliminary feasibility studies on war against England and completion of the new armament program.

In military strategy, the emphasis was on offensive power. Göring told Milch on October 24 that the first strike of the Luftwaffe in war had to be made with all available units, including training units. Moreover, they must be fully mobile to follow up their first strike, capable of moving quickly not only their aircraft but their entire ground-support detachments from one base to another. Surprise, mobility, and power were the keys to a Blitzkrieg, and the Luftwaffe had to be ready. Two days later at a conference at Karinhall, the Luftwaffe's specific needs for war against England were discussed. Armor-piercing bombs of at least 2,200 lbs. would be required for use against heavy warships, and Jeschonnek of the general staff thought a force of at least 500 long-range bombers of the He 177 type would be needed by 1942.[4]

The Technical Office's response was guarded and pessimistic. For example, it did not think the He 177 would be ready for unit deployment until late 1942 since it was just in the testing and developmental stage, although the rest of the aircraft types could theoretically be produced under the proper circumstances. However, more skilled labor in the aircraft industry; more construction workers for expansion; more machine tools, building materials, money, and foreign exchange were essential. The Technical Office thought the fivefold program possible in theory but in practice impossible, especially should key aircraft such as the He 177, Me 210, or Ju 88 experience difficulties in development. It recommended that the general staff work out a more realistic program.[5]

The Technical Office offered its first draft of Hitler's new program at a conference on October 26. The aircraft industry would have to produce about 45,700 aircraft by the spring of 1942 to give the Luftwaffe a force of 10,300 in operational units and 8,200 in ready reserves. The fuel supply for such a force would require importing 85 percent of the existing world production of aviation fuel.[6] The entire program would cost an estimated 60 billion RM (almost the same amount spent from 1933 to 1939 for all military preparations), and the office doubted that it could be fulfilled.

By November 15, the Technical Office had worked up a second draft of a new Production Plan no. 9. It called for the construction by March 31, 1942, of 4,331 Bf 109s; 3,320 Bf 110s and Me 210s; 2,002 Ju 87s; 703 He 177s (production to start in December 1940); 7,327 Ju 88s; 900 Do 17s; and 2,000 He 111s.[7] This would be an enormous achievement, thought the Technical Office. Yet despite the skepticism of the Technical Office and the known difficulties—shortages of labor, money, foreign exchange, factory capacity, and materials—Göring accepted Hitler's program at face value. On the eighteenth, he told the Reich Defense Council that he planned to triple the level of armaments even if it meant nationalizing some of Germany's industry, and threatened to use his powers ruthlessly to accomplish the Führer's goals.[8] On November 21, questionnaires were sent to the aircraft plants to determine their needs for fulfillment of the program.

Meanwhile, all divisions of the Technical Office and the General Staff of the Luftwaffe were making their own assessments. Colonel Joseph Kammhuber, chief of the Organization Division, proposed a more realistic "*Notprogramm*," or emergency program, which called for about one-third the production of Hitler's. Both General Stumpff, chief of staff, and Milch considered it a more feasible interim program until the RLM could work out the difficulties of Hitler's program. When Milch presented it to a full conference of the RLM and Luftwaffe, everyone seemed in agreement; Hitler's program was impossible to fulfill. Just as Milch was to go to Göring with Kammhuber's plan, however, Jeschonnek stood up and said, "I am opposed! Gentlemen, in

my view it is our duty to support the Führer and not work against him."
He alone thought Hitler's program could, or at least should, be fulfilled.
Milch took the young officer with him to Göring and soon returned to
the conference with the terse remark, "Gentlemen, the Field Marshal has
decided that the Führer's program can be carried out."[9]

By December 6 the Technical Office had received the answers to its
questionnaires from the aircraft industry. The amount of expansion
needed was astonishing: by January 1942 the industry would require
230,000 more workers, about 2.2 billion RM for expansion costs, and
372 million RM for machine tools, approximately 124.8 million RM of
which would have to be in foreign exchange for purchases abroad. In the
area of explosives alone, the Technical Office estimated it would have to
build six new plants for fuses, eight for torpedoes and mines, and six for
bombs.[10] Combining the figures from the industry with its own
estimates, the Technical Office prepared a detailed report for Göring.
There would be a sharp reduction in number and simplification of
aircraft models with emphasis on mass producing newer ones. Udet
figured the industry could build about 43,100 aircraft by April 1, 1942,
with about 31,300 of these after January 1, 1939. The general staff had
wanted 45,700 aircraft, including at least 12,000 bombers, but Udet's
estimate called for only 10,900, of which 7,700 would be the newer Ju
88s and He 177s. The number of fighters was the same, 4,300, but the
number of twin-engined fighters in Udet's plan was about 300 less than
the 3,500 wanted by the general staff. The other large differences
between the Technical Office and general staff specifications were in the
number of advanced trainers (6,400 vs. 7,000) and transports (2,400 vs.
4,000).[11]

Udet called for an increase in monthly production of airframes from
500 in 1938 to 950 to 1,000 in 1941. Engine production was to rise from a
monthly average of 950 in 1938 to a peak of 2,000 for the last quarter of
1941. By 1942 the airframe industry would reach roughly 65 percent of its
mobilization plan capacity, but to do this would require the expansion of
a number of firms. In addition, the industry would need one new plant
the size of the Arado firm (19,000 employees) for the construction of
transports, and the aircraft firms in Czechoslovakia would have to be
licensed to produce trainers and transports. The engine industry needed
expansion of older firms plus two new plants for the DB 601 and the As
410 engines. It would then be at about 60 percent of its intended
mobilization plan capacity. The repairs industry, to be increased
fivefold, would probably require nationalization of many of the private
firms, while the aerial bombs industry would literally have to be built
from scratch.

With Udet's figures, Göring and Milch presented their case before the combined military services' staffs on December 13. The needs of the RLM in raw materials and money was staggering. The Four-Year Plan had projected an increase in aviation fuel production from the current 38,000 cubic meters monthly to 300,000, but the mobilization plan required 1.1 million cubic meters for the first month of operations, tapering off to 320,000 by the eleventh month. The RLM estimated it would need 10.3 million cubic meters of storage tank space, or about 6.6 million more than it had available, which would necessitate the expansion of the existing five storage depots and construction of fourteen new ones varying in size from 300,000 to 500,000 cubic meters. To transport the fuel, the Luftwaffe would need 9,000 railroad cars; only 1,500 were then on hand and 500 more on order. The cost of fuel purchases abroad would total about half a billion RM annually by 1941. In terms of labor, the fivefold program would take about 45 percent of all industrial and construction industry reserves by 1940. In addition, the RLM called for monthly production increases as follows:

	1938	1941
Iron and steel	100,000 tons	290,000 tons
Aluminum	4,800 tons	8,900 tons
Copper	6,000 tons	18,200 tons
Cement	120,000 tons	480,000 tons
Wood	100,000 cu. m.	450,000 cu. m.
Explosives for aerial arms	1,000 tons	23,000 tons

The production of flak guns, also handled by the RLM, was projected as follows:

Type	Monthly Average, 1938	Desired Monthly Average, 1942	Total Wanted
20-mm. flak	400	682	30,000
37-mm. flak	50	100	5,000
88-mm. flak	20	155	8,200
105-mm. flak	20	152	2,000
128-mm. flak	developed and first 100 in serial production		

The response of the other military services was hardly encouraging. Each had its own building program to consider and therefore refused to grant the Luftwaffe priority in raw materials or labor. The result was one of the typical bureaucratic answers in the Third Reich: the Wehrmacht leadership agreed to subscribe to the Führer's program but not to grant the means necessary for its fulfillment. Göring and the RLM, now in the habit of accepting unrealistic demands, made plans and issued orders for the new program as if it were feasible. It is doubtful that Göring ever understood how impossibly high the demands for it were, and it is even more doubtful that he so informed Hitler. Given Göring's love of exaggeration and his unwillingness to offend the Führer, Hitler may well have believed that Göring was indeed fulfilling his fivefold program for the Luftwaffe.[12]

During December 1938 and January 1939, the RLM worked out the details for Production Plan no. 10, which varied somewhat in quality but not in quantity from plan no. 9. The delays in the He 177 and Ju 88 were already felt, and the RLM extended the production of Do 17s and He 111s to cover the gaps in the newer models.[13] By February 10, the Technical Office had to report that the general staff goal of equipping each fighter squadron with 18 planes and the rest of the squadrons with 12 could not be achieved except with older models like the Do 17P, Bf 109C and D, and He 111. The general staff's objective of 50 percent reserves for all units could not be reached until April 1940. The Technical Office estimated that by 1940 the older-model fighters could be phased out in favor of the Bf 109E and older dive bombers for the Ju 87B. In the bomber category, the older He 111, Ju 86, and Do 17 would be phased out in favor of the Ju 88, He 111H, P, and B, and the newer Do 17Z.[14]

By the end of February even these estimates were revised downward as the first drafts of a new Production Plan no. 11 took shape. The General Staff's version took cognizance of the delays but still listed production of 3,918 new bombers, including 938 Ju 88s, 653 He 111Ps, and 900 Do 17Zs, by June 1940. The key bomber, the Ju 88, was not scheduled for production until October 1939; but once production started, it was to accelerate quickly. Some other changes were the inclusion of the newer Bf 109Fs and Me 210s.[15] During the next month the Technical Office worked out two preliminary drafts of the program and a final draft for the industry. The new Production Plan no. 11 was a far more realistic projection of what the industry could accomplish by April 1942 than the previous ones. For example, it called for 7,748 bombers instead of 10,900 and 4,419 He 177s and Ju 88s (with only 199 of the former) rather than 7,700. The number of twin-engined fighters was reduced from 3,200 to 1,978, with only 646 of these the new Me 210. The principal aircraft ordered under Production Plan no. 11, to run from April 1, 1939, to April 1, 1942, were as follows:

Model	Total Wanted	Delivered by April 1, 1939	Delivered after April 1, 1939
Hs 126	689	218	471
Ha 141A	261	——	261
Do 17P	330	269	61
Ju88F	157	——	157
Ju 88 Series I	2,802	——	2,802
Ju 88 Series II	1,261	——	1,261
He 177	199	——	199
He 111H	1,322	204	1,118
He 111P	849	258	591
He 111D	30	20	10
Do 17Z	913	88	825
Do 17U	15	1	14
Bf 109E-1	1,107	183	924
Bf 109E-3	1,702	325	1,377
Bf 109F	1,072	——	1,072
Bf 110C	1,332	8	1,324
Me 210	646	——	646
Ju 87B	964	187	777
Ju 52	2,260	453	1,807
FW 189	1,587	——	1,587[16]

By April 1939, even this revised program was in jeopardy. The Technical Office reported on the twelfth that shortages and changes in aircraft and equipment meant Production Plan no. 11 could not be completed on schedule. Bombs and explosives in particular were lagging; only 40 percent of the quota would be met.[17] Nevertheless, Göring ordered an acceleration in the program, for he thought Hitler might not wait to strike Poland. Each passing month brought new reports of shortages. In early May, Milch warned Göring that plan no. 11 was in serious danger because of a lack of iron, steel, and other metals. He thought aircraft production might have to be cut by 30 or 40 percent.[18] The same day Jeschonnek, chief of staff, notified Luftwaffe commanders that about half the units could not be brought up to full strength because of reduced production,[19] and a few days later the quartermaster general warned that sharp reductions in supplies of aircraft, fuel, and munitions were to be expected.[20]

The monthly reports from the industry confirmed these dire prognostications. A report of May 15 indicated that by sacrificing everything to maintain production, the schedule for aircraft and engines was being met. But shortages in nonferrous metals continued to worsen. The shortage of aluminum, which had been running about 1,800 tons monthly during the previous six months, was now up to 2,358 tons, and that of copper rose from 322 to 451 tons. Comparable shortages were noted in tin, zinc, cadmium, and nickel. The lack of these nonferrous metals was felt most severely in the bomb, fuse, and airborne instrument industries, especially in radio production. Aircraft fuel shortages persisted, and the Luftwaffe had only an estimated 2.8-month supply in reserve.[21] The shortage of skilled labor was also acute; Udet noted that expansion of the aircraft industry was being curtailed by the lack of labor everywhere except in the Saarland and recently seized areas of Bohemia-Moravia and Austria.

By the beginning of the summer of 1939, the Technical Office reported that the airframe industry was still keeping pace but that engines and auxiliary equipment were falling from 3 to 37 percent behind. The flak program was particularly hard hit by shortages in high-grade bar steel and optical equipment, both of which were in heavy demand by the army and navy. The Luftwaffe secured new quotas for raw materials in June, but they were still not sufficient to meet the demands of Production Plan no. 11. For example, the Luftwaffe wanted 139,350 tons of iron and steel monthly but got only 102,760 tons, or 74 percent. It received only 45 percent of its desired quota of wood, 43.5 percent of cement, 37.5 percent of copper, 43.8 percent of zinc. 73 percent of aluminum, and 31.5 percent of nickel. To fulfill plan no. 11 the Technical Office estimated that it would need supplemental allotments of 225,300 tons of bar steel, 34,184 tons of copper, 28,110 tons of aluminum, 11,910 tons of tin, 1,150,400 tons of cement, and 764,200 cubic meters of wood. In addition, about 53 million RM in foreign exchange would be required to purchase many of these raw materials from abroad.[22]

Despite Udet's earlier assurances that he would keep the Technical Office's annual budget around 3.6 billion RM, it seemed to grow faster than the shortages. By May 23, it was running at 4.33 billion RM, with only 70 million for research and 182 million for development; the rest was for production. By July, when Hitler, Göring, and the Luftwaffe general staff began to press the flak program, Udet's office was estimating that their budget might reach 5.4 billion RM.[23] Ironically, that figure was virtually the same as the 5.356 billion first projected for the fivefold program in November 1938. After cuts and changes, the Technical Office had spent about as much as it could, leading Colonel Richthofen and other observers to conclude that the industry simply was saturated and could not absorb much more regardless of how much money the government wanted to spend.[24]

The flak program, which had lagged badly, finally received the attention it deserved when the threat of war grew in the summer. The quartermaster general of the Luftwaffe insisted in June that unless shortages of steel, labor, and money were immediately alleviated, the air force would be short 50 batteries of 88-mm. guns, fifty of 20-mm. guns, and about 30 of searchlights by April 1940. On July 25, Göring and Milch ordered a sharp increase in production, especially of the heavier guns. The Technical Office asserted, however, that the flak program could be pushed through only if Hitler personally granted it a higher priority than the Navy's building program. By August 3, Göring had secured Hitler's permission to raise the production of heavy flak guns (88-mm. and 105-mm.) immediately to 150 per month with corresponding increases in ammunitions. At the same time Hitler wanted the developmental programs for the 128-mm. and 150-mm. guns speeded up.[25]

Meanwhile, the aircraft program was running into unexpected trouble. Production schedules were being met, but the slow development of the Ju 88 indicated that a "bomber gap" would occur in 1940 as the He 111s and Do 17s were being phased out in favor of the Ju 88. Although Koppenberg had been given special plenipotentiary powers for the Ju 88 program and seven major firms were assigned to it at the time of the Munich crisis, the aircraft still was not ready for production. On July 22 Udet reported to Göring that the Ju 88 would be delayed three months by technical difficulties, but full assembly-line production could begin within nine months. He reassured Göring that under the new Production Plan no. 12, then taking shape, 2,357 Ju 88s would be delivered by April 1941, and Göring would have 5,000 by April 1943. The major difficulty was that the Ju 88 had undergone nearly 250,000 change orders since its first flight. After a quick inspection trip to the Junkers plant, Göring decided that not enough was being done on the program, but the Junkers people convinced him that the delays would soon be over and that 300 Ju 88s could be produced per month, with 50 in parts.

On August 5, Göring ordered Udet, Milch and Jeschonnek to a special meeting to discuss a "concentrated production program" for the aircraft industry. Aboard Göring's yacht, the *Karin II*, leaders of the Luftwaffe heard their commander order top priority for the He 177, Ju 88, Me 210, and Bf 109 warplanes, with all others sharply reduced in number or stricken. Göring did not want this to interfere with further developmental plans but insisted on greater simplification of production and more attention to multipurpose utilization of the same type of aircraft, or commonality, as it was later called. He proposed the following quotas: a total of 800 He 177s by April 1, 1943, with a monthly production of 50 thereafter; 3,000 Me 210s by the same date with 30 per month thereafter; and 2,460 Ju 88 by April 1, 1941, with a monthly output of 300 thereafter. Cutbacks were to be made in the Ju 87, He 115, Hs 126, and Ju 52 (1,400 to be built by April 1, 1942, and then only 15 per month thereafter). Stricken from the new program were the Ju 90, Fi 104, FW 189, Hs 129, BV 141, Ar 197, and Ar 199. Göring wanted a bomber force of 32 wings of 4,330 aircraft with 670, or 15 percent reserves by April 1, 1941. It would include 2,460 Ju 88s, 1,180 He 111Hs, 640 He 111Ps, and 720 Do 17Zs. If the industry were able to produce more Ju 88s, then Göring wanted to restrict the Do 17Zs and He 111Ps in favor of the He 111Hs and the *Wunderbomber*.[26] His "concentrated program" was a calculated gamble which heavily comitted the Luftwaffe to four models, of which two—the He 177 heavy bomber and the Me 210 long-range fighter and ersatz dive bomber—were not successful. There were not more than a dozen He 177s in operational status by April 1943; and after 352 Me 210s were completed, the aircraft was scrapped, although some of its parts were used in the Me 410.

Göring's new requirements were returned to the Technical Office, where they were worked into a new production plan. In July, Udet's office had prepared Production Plan no. 12 to replace no. 11. It had the same terminal date of April 1, 1942, but had about 80 percent of the earlier production goals. The reduction had been blamed on shortages and delays, but now all that had to be changed. The increases in Ju 88s, He 177s, and Me 210s were hastily incorporated into Production Plan no. 13, but the events of August 1939 quickly turned that plan to scrap. By the time Germany went to war in September 1939, still another production plan, no. 14, was under advisement, but like Plans no. 12 and 13, it was never issued. In short, from the time of the Munich crisis to the outbreak of the war, there were three production plans, nos. 9, 10, and 11, that were partially completed and three more, nos. 12, 13, and 14 drawn up but never issued. When war started, Production Plan no. 11 was still in effect for the aircraft industry.[27]

The production reports from the industry for July indicated shortages in iron, steel, aluminum, and magnesium, but those in nonferrous metals had been eased somewhat by purchases abroad. In general, production in the airframe plants continued on schedule, with only the Bf 110Cs in arrears, while the engine industry was behind from 5 percent with the Jumo 211A engine to 27 percent with the Jumo 211B/D. Production of bombs, flak, flak ammunition, fuses, and personal flying equipment lagged more seriously, from 25 to 65 percent; and the

Technical Office estimated that after a maximum effort to increase aircraft fuel supplies, the Reich still had only enough for 3.9 months in the event of full mobilization.[28]

During the last turbulent days of August 1939, the Technical Office's planning changed literally every day. On August 16 the office estimated that under mobilization, the aircraft industry would have to build 1,137 planes a month by March 1, 1940. Two weeks later their planning called for a monthly production of 1,144 aircraft (including 300 Ju 88s), with an objective of 1,553 aircraft by the summer of 1941. Of those, 1,138 would be combat aircraft—principally Ju 88s (330), He 177s (100), Bf 109s (210), and Me 210s (190)—and 275 would be trainers.[29] When, however, the general staff asked for a detailed monthly projection of combat aircraft production for the ten months starting September 1, the Technical Office offered the following estimate (cumulative totals in parentheses).

Aircraft Type	Sept. 1939	Dec. 1939	March 1940	June 1940
Hs 126/Fw 189	35 (383)	47 (500)	83 (713)	105 (1,018)
Ju 88 (recon.)	——	17 (33)	36 (122)	55 (267)
Ju 88 (bomber)	——	48 (66)	165 (446)	205 (1,016)
He 111H	60 (540)	74 (750)	75 (975)	75 (1,125)
Bf 109E	120 (1,080)	125 (1,445)	142 (1,855)	157 (2,315)
Bf 110C	40 (115)	51 (246)	84 (469)	120 (794)
Ju 87B	55 (485)	60 (655)	65 (850)	15 (930)
He 111P	38 (446)	40 (562)	50 (707)	50 (857)[30]

For comparison, actual production for August 1939 was 427 combat aircraft: 30 Hs 126s, 8 Do 17Ps, 64 Bf 109E-1s, 45 Bf 109E-3s, 10 Bf 110Bs, 25 Bf 110Cs, 90 He 111Hs, 40 He 111Ps and Ds, 60 Do 17Zs, and 55 Ju 87Bs.[31]

Even these figures did not please Göring. A day before the war broke out, he notified State Secretary Körner of the Four-Year Plan Office that Hitler had personally approved raising Ju 88 production to 300 per month as soon as possible and giving it third highest priority behind the munitions program and the crash program for explosives and gunpowder. So on September 12, Udet temporarily ordered a sharp reduction in all developmental projects, including four-engined bombers and transports like the FW 200, He 179 (a version of the He 177 with four separate engines), Ju 90, and BV 222 in favor of a concentrated effort on the Bf 109, He 177, Me 210, and Ju 88.[32] Germany was committed to fight with these aircraft. By the time she went to war, the aircraft industry was maintaining its schedule under Production Plan no. 11, turning out about 700 airplanes a month (the USSBS estimated a 691.2 monthly production for 1939), a sharp rise over the average monthly production of 436.2 for 1938 and 467.1 for 1937.[33]

Although most of this increase can be attributed to expansion inside the Reich, the Germans obtained some limited but highly timely help from the conquest of Austria and half of Czechoslovakia. Austria had no aircraft industry of its own, but the country of 6.7 million, with 321,000 unemployed at the time of seizure, offered many possibilities. The major firms quickly surveyed Austria for companies to seize and for new plant sites. Messerschmitt, in particular, built a large assembly plant at Wiener-Neustadt during the war. Of more immediate importance, however, were the raw materials and industrial capacity Austria added to the German economy. Primarily a raw materials producer, Austria had assets that complemented those of Germany. The annual production of 1.8 million tons of iron ore, the large coal deposits which could be used to produce synthetic gas, and the untapped potential for electrical energy were extremely useful in overcoming shortages affecting the aircraft industry. Electrical energy, which is used so abundantly in the production of aluminum, was running short in Germany, but Austria's huge hydroelectric potential offered a means of expanding aluminum production. Austria's estimated 230 million RM in foreign exchange reserves and additional 75 million in unminted gold and clearing accounts arrived in time to save the rearmament program. By comparison, Germany's foreign exchange reserves were only 90 million RM at that time, so the Austrian seizure allowed the Reich to purchase abroad many of the raw materials and machines it had lacked since 1937.[34]

The situation in Czechoslovakia was somewhat different. The Czechs had a sizable armament industry—150,000 workers, including the world-renowned Skoda Works. The Czech aircraft industry was small but as well developed as the rest of the armament industry, with a monthly capacity of 60 aircraft and 150 engines and a work force of 10,500. The Czechs were producing a number of aircraft of their own design as well as some foreign models, including a few late French ones. The industry could be used immediately by the RLM. Shortly after the Munich Conference, the Czech Finance Ministry opened talks with the RLM on the possibility of keeping the plants in operation. The Czechs were prepared to supply credit to maintain operations until the Germans could integrate them into their own program. Staff engineer Diederichs of the RLM, who had been sent to survey the industry, recommended continuing its current production until German contracts could be issued. The Czech aircraft were to be used as trainers, glider tugs, and transports.[35]

After the seizure of Bohemia-Moravia, however, Göring blocked out the area for exploitation, showing favor to the aircraft plants. Acting under his authority as head of the Four-Year Plan, he wanted the area under his personal control and incorporated into the Greater Reich more smoothly than Austria and the Sudentenland had been. It was absolutely necessary that Czech industry not be unduly disturbed; a wholesale scramble by German firms to buy foreign or domestic Czech interests had to be prevented. Göring ordered that purchases over half a million RM for land or businesses must have his personal approval. All arianization was also to be approved by him. Wages and prices were to remain frozen and the whole economy carefully exploited for the Reich.[36] The Czech bank's 25 million pounds sterling and 3,421.3 million kronen in foreign exchange were earmarked by Göring for Wehrmacht purchases.[37]

With Göring clearing the way, the RLM and the aircraft industry had by the end of March 1939 let contracts totaling 400 million RM to the Czech firms of Aero, Avia, Bata, Böhmische-Mährische Flugzeugwerke, Letov, Mrasz, Poldihütte, Skoda, Tschechomorawska, and Walter. These plants were to produce the Fi 156, DFS 230, and Fw 189 airplanes; the As 10c and DB 601/605 engines; and spare parts. A year later the Technical Office estimated that there were 5,634 Czech workers in the airframe industry in Bohemia-Moravia and another 1,523 in the engine industry working full-time on German contracts.[38] The scramble among the large German aircraft firms to control the Czech plants unleashed bitter strife within the industry.

REORGANIZING THE RLM

From 1937 until the outbreak of war the Air Ministry and the Luftwaffe underwent a series of reorganizations based as much on the changes in personnel as on the growing size and maturity of the RLM and the Luftwaffe. Until the death of Wever, his staff operated like a personal staff to Göring and Milch, much as the OKW did under Hitler. But the professional officers' attitude began to change as the Luftwaffe general staff was formed in 1936 under General Kesselring. He thought the chief of staff should be more independent and play a role similar to that of the chief of staff in the old Imperial Army, the highest military adviser to the commander. Göring and Milch, both nonmilitary men with a subconscious distrust of the "red trousers," felt threatened by this new arrangement. Göring was eventually won over; Milch was not. His bitter opposition led to Kesselring's resignation as chief of staff and the reorganization of the RLM on June 1, 1937. Under this new plan Milch's authority over the chief of staff in military matters was sharply reduced, and General Stumpff, the new chief of staff, was made coequal with Milch. A few weeks later Göring cut Milch's authority even further when he allowed the heads of the Technical and Personnel Offices to report directly to him, bypassing Milch. Milch never accepted this arrangement and worked constantly to undermine it. As a result, cooperation between the military and the civilians began to falter. After the war Milch insisted that was the beginning of the downfall of the Luftwaffe.[39] The tight line of control in the RLM was broken.

When Göring seemed to organize Milch out of military affairs, the personal relationship between the two also became estranged. Milch, suspicious and sensitive, felt that he had lost Göring's confidence and magnified every new incident as part of a deliberate plot to destroy him. By the end of the year, their relationship was so strained that in a tense interview at Karinhall, Milch asked Göring either to restore his former authority or allow him to resign and return to Lufthansa. Göring scornfully refused, telling Milch that only a higher authority, either Hitler or himself, could tell him when and how he could quit. Furthermore, Göring warned him not to feign sickness, although suicide was allowed.[40]

On January 18, 1938, shortly after the Karinhall interview, Göring ordered another reorganization of the RLM. Effective February 2, the division chiefs were to report directly to him without going through Milch. Milch remained Göring's personal representative, but the chain of command through Milch was broken. At the same time, the Technical Office was reorganized from its simple vertical structure of four sections, C I, Research; C II, Development; C III, Production; and C IV, Budget, to a horizontal one of thirteen sections. Milch, who felt that Udet and Göring had changed the Technical Office without proper consultation, argued that the division of the office into many sections hindered coordination with the RLM and Luftwaffe and weakened Udet's administrative control.

In late 1936, when Udet prepared Production Plan no. 4 in direct consultation with Göring, bypassing Milch, the secretary had felt slighted. Relationships between Milch and Udet worsened through 1937 as Udet's aircraft won military victories in the Spanish Civil War and Udet, the popular war hero, began to enjoy obviously the acclaim that went with his difficult but glamorous job. The final break occurred with the reorganization of the Technical Office in 1938 when Udet was guaranteed virtual independence from Milch except for those rare times when Milch functioned as temporary head of the RLM during Göring's absences. The final insult and, in Milch's eyes, the clinching proof of the plot to outmaneuver him was the appointment of another enemy,

Lieutenant Colonel Hans Jeschonnek, as chief of the Planning Staff under General Stumpff.[41]

Göring had hoped that the reorganizations might eliminate the differences between Milch and his coworkers, but instead they only exacerbated them, although he had a somewhat better relationship with General Stumpff than with the others. After Kesselring resigned in May 1937, Goring discussed the situation with Field Marshal Blomberg, and a number of possible replacements outside the Luftwaffe were mentioned. General Halder was apparently considered; but when he was offered the position, he refused as he had in 1936 after Wever's death. Blomberg accepted Halder's decision, commenting that he could not order any officer into the difficult spot of working with Milch.[42] After Halder and others outside the RLM rejected the post, Göring's choice devolved on the congenial RLM chief of personnel, General Stumpff. It was clear from the beginning, however, that Stumpff's appointment was an interim one until Göring could appoint someone more favorable to himself and to the old guard in the RLM. Stumpff's personality and his obvious limitations—he made no pretense of wanting the post or even being an aviation strategist—did not offer a threat to Milch. The power struggle over the relationship between the secretary of aviation and the chief of staff was left in abeyance during Stumpff's tour of duty. Meanwhile the triumphs in Austria and Czechoslovakia were obscuring the rapid strides Hitler was making in purging and dominating the Wehrmacht, Foreign Office, and economy.

In early 1939, the last sweeping reorganization of the RLM before the war occurred. On February 1, Göring named Colonel Jeschonnek as Stumpff's successor as chief of staff and Udet as head of the new, powerful office of Generalluftzeugmeister (chief of Luftwaffe Procurement and Supply). Udet was now head not only of the Technical Office but also a conglomerate of other offices related to the supply and production of all aircraft and equipment for the Luftwaffe, with a total of twenty-six separate divisions reporting directly to him. Holding vast budgetary and administrative power, he was to determine in secret consultation with Göring the aircraft for the Luftwaffe. Göring must have had some misgivings, for a few weeks later he said to Jeschonnek in the presence of General Beppo Schmid, "What are we going to do with Udet? He just isn't doing the job!" When Jeschonnek suggested that four or five top-notch general staff officers be assigned to Udet's staff, Udet rejected them personally.[43]

Milch's position in this new arrangement was ambiguous. He was named inspector general of the Luftwaffe and representative of the commander-in-chief, and as such was the superior of all except Göring.

It appeared that his many offices were being consolidated and that he had won back his earlier position of authority. Actually, however, Milch was being boxed in by Göring. Military matters were handled by the chief of staff and production matters by Udet. Milch suspected that Göring was setting him up as a scapegoat in the event things did not turn out well.[44]

Jeschonnek's relationship with Milch was unfortunate, for Jeschonnek was the *Wunderkind* of the Luftwaffe. Born in 1899, he had attended cadet school and saw limited action during World War I as an infantry officer and after 1917 as a flier, recording two kills with the 10th Fighter Squadron. After the war he served with the border patrol and then secured a regular commission in the Reichswehr. During the 1920s he was assigned as a staff officer to Kurt Student's Inspectorate for Weapons and Equipment, a position that allowed him to travel widely at home and abroad inspecting equipment. In 1928 he finished general staff school, where he ranked top in his class, according to the director, General von Brauchitsch. He then served under Colonel Felmy in the important Air Inspectorate in the War Ministry. When the RLM was formed, he moved to the new ministry to become Milch's adjutant (Milch had known him since World War I).

After 1933, Jeschonnek's rise was spectacular. A captain in 1932, he rose to major in 1935, lieutenant colonel in 1937, colonel in 1938, general major in 1939, general in 1940, and colonel general on March 1, 1942, becoming the youngest colonel general in the Wehrmacht. His duty posts were just as impressive. He was made bomb squadron commander in March 1934, commander of the crack Training Wing III in Greifswald in October 1936, chief of the Luftwaffe Planning Staff in February 1938, and chief of the general staff on February 1, 1939, at the age of thirty-nine. (By comparison, the great Helmuth Moltke was fifty-eight when he became chief of staff; Alfred Graf von Schlieffen and the younger Moltke were both fifty-eight when they were appointed to that position; Hindenburg was sixty-nine; and during World War II, Franz Halder, Kurt Zeitzler, and Heinz Guderian were fifty-four, forty-seven, and fifty-six, respectively. The Luftwaffe chiefs had been younger, however; Wever was forty-six, Kesselring and Stumpff, forty-eight; and later in the war Günther Korter and Karl Koller were forty-five and forty-seven, respectively.)

The burden was heavy for such a young man, but all who knew Jeschonnek recognized his talent. The epitome of the classic Prussian staff officer, he was exact in appearance and thought, correct, formal, intelligent, and "unshakably loyal to Hitler."[45] His support for Hitler's fivefold program in late 1938 when only he and Göring backed it was typical. Critics of Jeschonnek argued that he backed Hitler only to better himself, since he was promoted shortly thereafter to chief of staff, but that ignores the fact that he had the attitude Göring and Hitler thrived on. "We don't know the word impossible," was more than a cliché for the Nazis; it was an article of faith.

Something of a loner, Jeschonnek was sarcastic, aloof (he was painfully shy), and tremendously ambitious and hard-working. He seemed out of place in the blustering Luftwaffe of Göring and Milch, and his meteoric rise to power was certain to cause resentment in the RLM. Milch in particular soon found much to criticize in the young man. An open break occurred when, in his zeal to press low-level attacks as commander of the Training Wing, Jeschonnek foolishly advised the pilots to "touch the tops of the waves" with their propellers. Three crews were lost during the exercise, and Milch threatened to court-martial Jeschonnek. Finally he was dissuaded from his threat, and because of an excellent career record Jeschonnek received only a verbal reprimand. Jeschonnek never forgot it, and he and Milch became bitter enemies. After the war, Milch called Jeschonnek "an inexperienced officer, especially in the technical matters," a "poor pilot," "pathologically ambitious" (Er war Krankhaft ehrgeizig. Er musste immer die Stelle Nr.1 haben.), and "narrow in outlook" and interests.[46]

Jeschonnek typified the young, aggressive, activist image that the Luftwaffe had with the Nazi leadership. By no means a protégé of the party, he was first and foremost a soldier who combined the best of the military tradition with the highest aspirations of the party. He had worked energetically and devotedly for the ideals of the new state. Naturally, Göring would feel more comfortable working with him than with an older officer raised in the Imperial Army and Reichswehr traditions. No matter that the new chief of staff had a running feud with Milch or trouble getting along with Udet and others. It was more important that, as Göring had commented earlier, "Der Kerl Charakter besitzt" (He had character).

Milch's relationship with Udet was just as strained. As Udet assumed more power and authority, Milch began to seek out his faults. When Udet's developmental and production programs for the Ju 88, He 177, and Me 210 ran into trouble, Milch was quick to criticize. Their earlier friendly competition turned into a bitter, fierce power struggle that ended only with Udet's tragic suicide in 1941. In 1938, when Udet had seen Milch's growing animosity, he tried to defend himself by allying with others. He was particularly delighted when Koppenberg was given full powers over the troublesome Ju 88 program.[47] A strong personality and adept at bureaucratic in-fighting, Koppenberg was seen as a counterbalance to his former protégé, Milch, especially since he was a well-known production man. Udet's other choice of allies, the designers Messerschmitt and Heinkel, was less fortunate. When their designs failed to materialize on time, he was blamed and charged with playing favorites.

That the organization of the RLM should deteriorate so badly was largely the responsiblity of Göring. After the Luftwaffe was firmly established, Göring's control became increasingly lethargic and erratic. He intervened on large issues but relegated the day-to-day operation of the Luftwaffe to others. He seemed more concerned with problems of foreign policy and internal politics. As a result, there was a power vacuum into which both Milch and the chiefs of staff tried to move. Göring knew that Milch and, later, Jeschonnek aspired to be his successor. In this situation, Milch was more vulnerable. His nonmilitary career in industry, his insolent manner, and his penchant for rash judgments were thoroughly disliked by the career military. Admiral Erich Raeder, in particular, was outspoken about Milch. Jeschonnek evoked envy but he belonged to the group; he had served his time in grade and he looked and acted like a proper officer. The career soldiers felt much more comfortable with such a person than with the talented, industrious, but brash Milch. They wanted to erode Milch's power and make sure that once Göring stepped out, the command of the Luftwaffe would return to the professionals, where it belonged. At every opportunity Göring heard how well Milch liked to play the role of de facto commander of the Luftwaffe or how capable Milch was. It was acutely embarrassing when Hitler would say to Göring, "Milch will handle it; that is what he is good at."[48]

Göring tried to steer a middle course between the various factions in the Luftwaffe and RLM. He feared and distrusted but needed Milch. Milch had strong party connections and enjoyed the trust of Hitler, whom he flattered often by clothing his suggestions in homilies taken from Der Führer's favorite wild west writer, Karl May.[49] He was also an exceedingly useful counterbalance to the professional soldiers. Udet's relationship with Göring was different. The famed World War I ace was, at first, flippant and lighthearted in his approach to "Der Eiserne" (the iron man), as Göring so loved to be called. And Göring sought to use Udet as leverage against Milch and the soldiers; he was especially aware of Hitler's high esteem for Udet. Although he realized quickly that Udet was over his head as chief of the Technical Office, he broadened Udet's powers in 1939 when he appointed him Luftzeugmeister. Göring apparently felt it politically advantageous to build up Udet, perhaps thinking that Udet would be a figurehead while the real work would be done by his chief assistants, Tschersich, Lucht, and Ploch. Besides, the military side of the Technical Office's work would be ably handled by Jeschonnek; his deputy quartermaster, Major Hans Georg von Seidel; and Jeschonnek's general staff officer for industrial affairs, Major Walter Storp. Even the appointment of Koppenberg was probably insurance against Udet's shortcomings.

The Luftwaffe leadership that Göring had gathered around him in February 1939 was a curious group. As Telford Taylor remarked, "The odor of amateurishness pervaded the entire establishment."[50] The officer corps was a collection of youngsters, reservists, and former army men who had not had the time to develop the traditions and professionalism of the old army. The officers in the middle-level staff and command positions were particularly lacking in the homogeneity and maturity of view that comes only with long years of service. At the top level, the faults of the Luftwaffe were most acutely evident. Göring, Milch, Udet, and Jeschonnek were four extremely sensitive, intelligent, ambitious, egocentric persons who found cooperation with others difficult. None of them had the experience necessary for high-command problems. In particular, they all lacked the understanding of the interdependence of military tactics and technology that is so crucial in aerial warfare.

By ignoring the personalities of his top staff, Göring decreased their effectiveness, especially that of Milch, who possessed the abilities necessary for solving the problems of the German aircraft industry. Milch labored in a shadow from 1937 to 1941, a time when his talents could have augmented those of Udet and Jeschonnek. Göring, however, was neither a soldier nor a "Techniker," but a gifted politician whose verve and braggadocio were just the right touch for 1933 but resented and out of place by 1939. Prone to sloth and love of luxury, incapable of sustained work, given to snap judgments based on his facile intelligence, and addicted to flattery, Göring was an easy mark for those who knew how to use him. He made a shambles of orderly administration, and his gift for inspiring others to work hard deserted him when Germany entered war.

Milch was an able, ruthless administrator, but he lacked the military expertise that his post demanded. His suspicious nature and constant feuding with every would-be rival made him exceedingly difficult to work with. Although he understood the industrial side of aircraft production, he was unimaginative and conservative in research and development. A shrewd percentage player, he preferred the calculated risk to the bold gamble. A master practitioner and lover of intrigue, Milch covered his steps more carefully than the others. He was easily the best bureaucratic in-fighter of all. By the time of the February 1939 reorganization of the

RLM, Milch was temporarily eclipsed by Udet and Jeschonnek, but he was by no means defeated; he would wait his turn.

Udet's increase in power could not disguise his limitations. He tried to match the changing and often vague wishes of the general staff to the needs of the aircraft industry; he demanded constant changes in production programs which profited the industry enormously; but he rarely had enough time for the directors. His impossibly large and sprawling conglomerate of offices fell to fighting among themselves, and as a result, key projects such as the He 177 soon bogged down for lack of overall direction. The influence of the RLM in the everyday operations of the industry did not decrease, however; to the contrary, it sharply increased. The technical and business directors of the airframe plants were constantly forced to consult with the corresponding division of the Technical Office, but instead of seeing one or two officials, they had to deal with nine or ten. Coordination between the Technical Office, industry, and military, even more demanding as weapons became more sophisticated, broke down.[51] Only the Ju 88 program had any overall coordination, but here the abrasive personality of Koppenberg was felt. The firms thought he was much too conscious of Junkers's dominant position in the industry to give fair and impartial treatment. As Udet's assistant, Gen. Ing. Gottfried Reidenbach commented after the war, "The case of Koppenberg showed in a shocking manner how much dilettantism, coercion, and improvisation became a pattern with us and how little people like Koppenberg learned from it."[52]

AIR POWER IS TRUMP

The Munich Conference has often been cited as the greatest triumph of the Luftwaffe. Hitler's adroit manipulation of the threat of aerial warfare helped Germany achieve its stunning diplomatic victory over England and France. The distinguished American air historian Eugene Emme called it a vindication of the Douhetian strategy of the Luftwaffe, noting ironically that the Luftwaffe was hardly a strategic air force.[53] Another historian, Edward Mead Earle wrote, "The Luftwaffe, especially, was intended to be a means of terrorization and perhaps more than any other single weapon at Hitler's command was responsible for the Munich capitulation of Britain and France."[54] Major George Fielding Eliot put it more bluntly in 1939, "It is blackmail which rules Europe today, and nothing else: blackmail made possible only by the existence of air power."[55]

Historians agree that the actual strength of the Luftwaffe was exaggerated, but it was formidable by 1938 standards. Estimates made after the war on the basis of German quartermaster figures as of August 1, 1938, list 643 fighters with 453 combat ready, 1,157 bombers with only 582 ready, and 207 dive bombers with 159 ready. Total combat strength was 2,928 aircraft. Six weeks later, on September 19, British Air Intelligence was more generous and credited Germany with 810 fighters, of which 717 (including 414 late-model Bf 109Ds) were combat ready; 1,235 bombers, with 1,019 ready; and 247 dive bombers, with 227 ready.[56] Opposed to this force, England had only 29 fighter squadrons of 406 aircraft, with 160 fighters in reserves and a monthly production of 35. There were no Spitfires, and only 5 fighter squadrons were equipped with the new Hurricanes. Of England's 640 bombers, only 120 were modern. The French had about 859 bombers, 350 of which were modern. Total aircraft production per month for England was 200 and for France about 70. Both England and Germany accelerated their armament production after the Munich conference, and by the outbreak of war British production, which had increased faster, just about equaled Germany's output of approximately 700 aircraft per month.[57]

Although it is recognized that the Luftwaffe's superiority was a major consideration at Munich, it is less well known what the German leadership made of its position from then until the outbreak of the war. During that time, they were constantly assessing their strength relative to England's and France's. The distinct possibility that England and France would go to war against the Reich once it moved against Poland was implicit in Hitler's decision to order a fivefold increase in the Luftwaffe on October 14. Faced with the dreaded prospect of a two-front war, the Luftwaffe had to be prepared.

The first staff study for operations against England was ordered in the midst of the Czech crisis, on August 23, 1938, to be carried out by General Felmy, commander of Luftwaffe Fleet 2. Felmy had only two wings of bombers stationed in his area of western Germany, but he was ordered to make preparations for three or four more once they were released from duty in Czechoslovakia. Felmy concluded that his ground detachments would have trouble backing these bombers until additional bases were constructed, but at least his units would be able to support retaliation strikes against Paris and London should that be necessary.[58] A full-scale attack on major British industrial and shipping centers was ruled out because of the limited range of German twin-engined bombers.

On September 17, Felmy was named chief of a special staff to study the possibility of war against England. On the twenty-second, scarcely a week before the Munich Conference, he reported that operations against England without advance airfields in the Lowlands would be impossible; German aircraft did not have sufficient range or the crews adequate training in overwater flights and long-range bombing missions. Although

Göring had ordered the development of a long-range fighter to cover England, Felmy knew that the planned Bf 110 formations would lack the necessary range. Twin-engined bombers like the He 111 could, by reducing bomb loads to half a ton, extend their combat range to 400 miles, putting some English targets within their bombsights, but not enough to seriously threaten the country. Felmy concluded, "A decisive war against England appears to be ruled out with the means now available."[59] His staff considered converting four-engined civilian transports such as the FW 200 and Ju 90 into bombers and forming three wings to attack England, but this plan was quickly dropped in favor of using the He 177 as the chief attacker.

When the general staff and the Technical Office began preparations for the "Concentrated Aircraft Program" based on Hitler's plan to increase the Luftwaffe fivefold, the results of Felmy's study were taken into consideration. Jeschonnek's projected Luftwaffe for the fall of 1942 was to have 58 bomber wings equipped with Ju 88s and He 177s (as many He 177s as possible, but at least 4 wings); 16 long-range fighter wings (*Zerstörer*) of Me 210s and Bf 110s (as many Me 210s as possible, but at least 7 or 8 wings); 8 dive-bomber wings of Me 210s (replacing the Ju 87B); 10 army reconnaissance groups equipped with Hs 126s and FW 189s; 10 long-range reconnaissance squadrons for the army equipped with Do 17Ps, Do 17Zs, and FW 189s; 13 long-range reconnaissance squadrons for the Luftwaffe equipped with Ju 88s and He 177s; 1 assault wing of FW 189s; 36 carrier squadrons of Bf 109s, Ju 87Bs, Fi 167s or their replacements such as the Ar 195 or Ar 196; 4 transport wings of Ju 90s (if the full number not available, then its replacement); 16 fighter wings of Bf 109s or a newer model. Jeschonnek figured on 12 aircraft per squadron, except for fighter squadrons, which were to have 18. Included in the 58 bomber wings were 13 so-called Pirate Wings specially equipped to attack shipping with bombs and torpedoes and to lay mines. Another 30 bomber wings were earmarked for strategic attacks against England, while the remaining 15 were for attacks against France.[60]

Beginning in early January 1939, the Luftwaffe concentrated on the possibility of a two-front war. General Felmy's staff was particularly concerned with the problems of a war against England as they related to Luftwaffe Fleet 2. Other staffs were assigned to study the problems of war in Poland and against France. From these efforts came three studies: *Studie Rot* (France), *Studie Grün* (Poland), and *Studie Blau* (England). *Studie Blau*, by far the most important, was a collection of reports done from January to June 1939 under the direction of the Air Intelligence Office (Abteilung Ic-5. Abt. des Luftwaffe Generalstab) under Colonel Beppo Schmidt for Jeschonnek. They were based on lectures by and discussions with a vast array of officials, engineers, military staff officers, academicians, and private citizens held at least once or twice weekly, usually for four or five hours. They spanned the entire spectrum of English life, including government, politics, armed services, trade relations, food supply, vulnerability to air attacks, canal and electric systems, and national character traits. Two of the most important sections of *Studie Blau* were General Felmy's *Planstudie 1939* and Colonel Schmidt's air situation report.

General Felmy's *Planstudie 1939* culminated in extensive three-day maneuvers for the general staff in May. His conclusions reemphasized his pessimistic reports of six months earlier: the lack of navigational equipment, low level of crew proficiency, and short range of the twin-engined bombers meant that an all-out aerial war against England could be launched only after securing forward air bases in the Lowlands or France. The use of Lufthansa aircraft as pathfinders for bomber formations was useless from a military point of view but might be helpful in destroying morale. The handing out of gas masks and digging of slit trenches in England at the time of the Czech crisis indicated a propensity toward war hysteria which such attacks for morale purposes might exploit. The report concluded that if a major war did occur, the Reich would attack London and the rest of England with all possible force. Felmy assumed that strategic operations against England could be launched only in 1942 when Germany had long-range bombers or had captured forward bases. He told Milch that there was not the slightest chance that the Luftwaffe would be ready in 1939 to fight a major war.[61]

At the same time, other Luftwaffe offices were arriving at contradictory conclusions. Schmidt's situation report on relative air power in Europe in 1939 stressed the overwhelming superiority of the Luftwaffe. He argued that air power had helped localize the Ethiopian war and made possible the peaceful solution to the Czech crisis. England and France had had to acquiesce to German demands because of their weakness in the air. Their prestige had sunk considerably, especially among the neutral nations, and their wish to secure an aviation pact with the Soviet Union indicated that the aerial superiority of the Axis powers was the decisive factor in the military and political inferiority of the West. Schmidt estimated British strength at 5,545 aircraft, with only 5,380 in the first- and second-class categories. These were scattered around the empire, with only 3,600 in the motherland—perhaps 20 percent of them first-class. About 200 first-class fighters, chiefly Hurricanes, were stationed at home. The English flak detachments were estimated at 600 heavy guns, 280 light guns, and 3,000 overaged searchlights. The tactics and the training of the RAF and the flak units were classified as "primitive." The RAF bomber fleet of 2,300, with only 500 modern planes and was also overaged. Schmidt doubted that the existing armament program could be fulfilled by 1940, although he did not rule out the possibility of help in an emergency from Canada, Australia, and the United States.

The French Air Force was even more antiquated, consisting of 4,650 aircraft, only 30 percent of which were modern. France had about 400 modern fighters, but her bomber force and flak were overaged and her aircraft industry was always behind the expectations of the government. By mid-1940 the French Air Force would be largely reequipped with modern fighters like the Morane 406 and heavy flak guns equal in quality to the German ones. In short, Schmidt argued that Germany had a decisive advantage for the next year or two until the rapid rearmament programs of the West produced results. He thought that even then the Western powers' bomber fleets would still be outdated and help from America would be too late. For the rest of Europe, Schmidt considered the Italian air fleet overaged, their flak poor, and their industrial capacity unable to sustain their air force. The Soviet Union, with 6,000 aircraft was a major power, but only 2,000 of those planes were first-class. Soviet industry could meet their immediate needs. The rest of the smaller European air forces were dismissed as unimportant. Schmidt's evaluation rested largely on German experiences in Spain. In effect, he was arguing that Germany then enjoyed a brief technological and military advantage which would soon be lost.[62]

On May 12 the Luftwaffe general quartermaster submitted his estimate of Western air power. He though that from April 1, 1939, to April 1, 1940, England would build 3,730 warplanes, France 2,450, the United States 2,700, and Germany 9,192. By the latter date, the RAF and French Air Force would soon have about 6,400 first-class warplanes in their units, including 1,850 fighters and 2,370 multi-engined bombers. That would represent a considerable increase in first-class aircraft and reflect the rapid progress expected under their rearmament programs. Actual first-class aircraft strength as of March 1, 1939, was estimated at only 790 for the RAF and 1,220 for the French Air Force. Implicit in the report was the idea that Germany had a superior force but that the gap between Germany and the West would be narrowed.[63]

On the next day, May 13, the Technical Office issued its even more optimistic estimate of Germany's relative strength in warplanes. German production of first-class warplanes had a decisive advantage over English and French. Production of the highest-quality fighters, bombers, and reconnaissance aircraft had long been under way in Germany and Italy but was just beginning in France and England. The equipment of foreign aircraft—radios, bombsights, and electrical and navigational equipment —was not comparable to the German or Italian, nor was as much produced. Germany also had an advantage in that in previous years a higher percentage of its aircraft production had been used for training than in the Western countries. Now Germany could use most of its production for warplanes while the West devoted a higher percentage of its planes to training. In a series of graphs accompanying the report, the Technical Office estimated that from April 1, 1939, to April 1, 1940, England would build 3,200 warplanes, France 2,000, and the United States 2,700. Monthly production would rise in England from 180 in April 1939 to 310 a year later, and in France from 100 to 200. Udet's office also endorsed a graph of warplane production since 1932 which showed that from the first quarter of 1934 to the fourth quarter of 1938 Germany and Italy had a numerical superiority over the combined totals of England, France, and the United States. The conclusion was obvious again: Germany had an advantage in warplane production which would rapidly dwindle.[64]

In an oral summary (of which no written record was made) of these various reports from *Studie Blau*, Colonel Beppo Schmidt concluded that England had an extraordinary form of government, was "*Völkisch*" sound, and had a strong economy. Her first line of defense was her fleet, followed by the RAF. England was, however, vulnerable on two scores: she needed to import large quantities of food and raw materials, and her air protection was weak. Schmidt thought that given the English toughness and gift for improvisation, it was doubtful that she could be destroyed from the air. The English fleet and air force would have to be destroyed first and then the country occupied. Since the German fleet would be no match for the English, it was clear that the Luftwaffe would have to be the counterbalance. When Chief of Staff Jeschonnek reported the results of *Studie Blau* to Göring, including the comparative armament studies which indicated that Germany would lose its edge in aerial rearmament in 1940, Göring became furious and ordered Jeschonnek to withdraw or destroy such worthless "defeatist appraisals."[65] Whether Hitler ever saw the conclusions of these reports is not clear.

Germany's relative strength vis-à-vis England and France was a concern of the army as well as the Luftwaffe. Colonel Georg Thomas of the army's important Wehrwirtschaftsamt gave a series of speeches in the first half of 1939 which clearly indicated the army's assessment of the situation.[66] He reasoned that Germany's presumed enemies would soon achieve a level of armament that would remove most of Germany's recently acquired advantages. Therefore, timing became all-important. Germany needed a quick and decisive war to maintain her advantage, or she must gird herself for the possibility of a long war by broadening the basis of her rearmament. Thomas concluded that Germany was in a better position at the moment than the other states, but she would soon lose it. Thomas's solution was full-scale rearmament—costly, time-consuming, and, quite possibly in the long run, futile. There was another solution: strike now.

The question remaining from all these deliberations was how much the Luftwaffe's advantage would compensate for the obvious limitations of a weak navy and a newly built army. Would the offensive strength of the Luftwaffe keep in check or, if need be, cancel the overwhelming naval power of England? Would it compensate for the strong defensive position of the French army? German leaders pondered these questions during the summer of 1939.

In June the Luftwaffe conducted its last big maneuver before the war, Generalstabreise 1939, which dealt chiefly with the anticipated attack on Poland. In the critique afterwards, Jeschonnek echoed the main point of the Luftwaffe's war strategy since the mid-1930s: the first strike was vital. "For the first strike, the strength of the strategic air force can never be strong enough," he said.[67] All forces, including training units, were to be used. The enemy's air force must be knocked out in the first hours of combat, and then the Luftwaffe could be released for other missions. Turning to the details of the maneuvers, Jeschonnek remarked that the slow progress of tactical training in some units was caused by the rapid expansion of the Luftwaffe. Major Pohle of the general staff mentioned the limitation of not having a four-engined bomber in operation, but felt that the decision to scrap the first big bomber projects and wait for the development of a superior large bomber was a sound one. The effectiveness of dive bombing and the twin-engine medium bombers was particularly noted. In Jeschonnek's final summary, he stressed confidence in the leadership of the Reich but warned that too much emphasis should not be placed on Germany's momentary technological edge. An advantage in aerial weapons lasted at best only six months before the enemy could match or counter them. Better tactics offered a longer advantage. Jeschonnek felt the Blitzkrieg style of warfare might be hard to counter quickly but hedged on the important question of whether the Luftwaffe was ready to fight a European war. He knew it could handle Poland easily, but he was relying on the political leaders to steer a course that would avoid a multifront war, which the Luftwaffe was not quite ready to fight.[68]

Jeschonnek's warning about overestimating the technological edge in aerial warfare dampened the enthusiasm over the Luftwaffe's superiority among certain circles in aviation. Ever since the Fourth

International Flying Meeting in Zürich in July 1937, Göring and Udet had purposely tried to show off the Luftwaffe. At that meet, Dip. Ing. Karl Francke won the climb and dive competition with a specially built Bf 109V-13, while Major Willy Polte, with Milch as his copilot, won the Alpine Flyaround with a special Do 17MV-1, a twin-engined bomber that was 40 kilometers faster than the single-engined French Dewoitine D 510 fighter. After that the Luftwaffe never missed a chance to impress the world. On November 11, 1937, Dr. Hermann Wurster, Messerschmitt's chief test pilot, flew a Bf 109V-13 at a record-breaking 610.9 km./h. On June 5, 1938, Udet flew an He 100V-1 at 634.7 km./h., establishing a new record. Earlier in the same year Dip. Ing. Ritz of Heinkel had set eight world seaplane speed records in an He 115. In 1939 both Heinkel and Messerschmitt, intent on winning the absolute world speed record, engaged in a bitter duel in which Heinkel went to the extreme of planting a spy in Messerschmitt's racing division.[69] On March 30, 1939, Hans Dieterle established a world record of 746.7 km./h., with the He 100V-8, only to see it broken twenty-seven days later by Fritz Wendel flying an Me 209V-1 at a top speed of 755.1 km./h. The Me 209 was powered by a special DB 601 racing engine which used a water-methanol injection system. Another attempt by Heinkel to top the record was called off by the RLM, which preferred to have the record rest with the company that built the standard fighter for the Luftwaffe. All these specially built record-breaking aircraft were billed as standard equipment by the Luftwaffe leaders.[70]

The Luftwaffe's technological superiority was also exhibited to foreign visitors to the Reich. During the five-day visit of a French Air Force delegation headed by General Joseph Vuillemin in August 1938, a grand bluff was perpetrated as the French moved around the Reich. At the Junkers, Heinkel, and Messerschmitt plants, they saw row after row of new aircraft parked for their inspection. Even when they made short refueling stops, Milch cagily had large numbers of new aircraft flown in from around the Reich to impress them. At the Heinkel plant, when Vuillemin asked Udet how many of the record-breaking He 100s he had, Udet casually answered that there already were three production lines going, when, in fact, fewer than 25 had actually been built. General Vuillemin was duly impressed by the German show. When he returned home at the time of the Czech crisis, he stated that should war break out, the French Air Force would be wiped out in two weeks.[71]

The biggest victims of the Luftwaffe's mania for superiority may have been Göring and Hitler. As they pondered the future of Europe in those hectic days of 1939, the two leaders counted heavily on the technological superiority of their Luftwaffe. The RLM encouraged them, for a report of March 16, 1939, outlining the chief developmental projects with the major firms in the aircraft industry was brimming with enthusiasm. Messerschmitt had the Me 210 and Me 261 under construction, planned for an advanced fighter in 1940, and thought its Me 209 would be ready for serial production by May. Focke-Wulf pinned its hopes on the FW 189 and planned a large transport for the immediate future. Heinkel reported steady progress with its He 177 and had a new fighter in the planning stage. Junkers was working on a new transport, the Ju 252, and was planning a replacement for the Ju 88. Henschel had a battle plane, the Hs 129, and a high-altitude bomber, the Hs 130, in progress, while Arado was working on its new heavy dive bomber, the Ar 240. Dornier, while concentrating on a new sea reconnaissance airplane, was also planning a replacement for the Ju 88.[72]

Even more impressive was the pioneer work being done on new forms of aircraft propulsion. The gasoline piston engine had nearly reached its limits, although there were still contracts out for bigger engines such as the gigantic 6,000-h.p. one BMW had under development. Most engineers were now turning to rocket and jet engines. On June 27, 1939, Heinkel premiered the world's first rocket-engine aircraft, its He 176, for Udet and Milch; and shortly thereafter the first jet-powered airplane, the He 178, was flown. Udet showed little interest in either, however, for there were still innumerable engineering problems to be solved.[73] Messerschmitt had already been given a contract for a new jet fighter and by July 1939 had a mock-up of the Me 262 on display at Rechlin for Hitler. Junkers had the contract for the engine for the Me 262—the Jumo 004, which suffered long delays before its first test run in October 1940.

Hitler and his staff were treated to a spectacular display at the Rechlin experimental station on July 3. The latest weapons of the Luftwaffe were shown: the Ju 88 speed bomber, the Bf 110 destroyer, the record-breaking Me 209 and He 100, and the mock-up of the Me 262. New developments such as an air-to-ground missile; an early-warning radar set; rocket assist take offs; a powerful new 30-mm. airborne cannon, the MK 101; and a pressurized high-altitude cabin were but a few of the innovations shown to the Führer. He was impressed, as the foreign visitors to the Reich had been, with the Luftwaffe's enormous technological achievements. The engineers and officers did not, however, indicate that much of this equipment was only in the experimental stage and might not be ready for distribution to units for years. Several years later, Hitler and Göring bitterly complained that they had been deceived during their July 1939 visit. The promises of newer weapons were not kept as year after year went by. In May 1942, Göring remarked: "The

Führer took some serious steps on account of his inspection visit,''[74] although Milch asserted in 1954 that he warned Hitler at Rechlin not to expect too much from these weapons because it might be five years before they were in the hands of the troops. Political decisions based on what he had seen would be risky and might lead to war. Hitler is purported to have said that he did not want a war. Unlike William II and his advisers, he was no fool; he was only bluffing with what he had.[75] General Josef Schmidt, on the other hand, seems to have heard something entirely different that day. According to Schmidt, Hitler said, "It is not possible for me to achieve my political goals in Europe peacefully. I must forge the Greater Reich with weapons. There will be a war; when, I do not know. This war must under all circumstances be won. If it takes one, two, or ten years, I don't care, but it must be won.''[76]

Göring paid particular attention to what attracted Hitler at Rechlin. On July 20, he ordered Udet to push the MK 101 project and the pressurized high-altitude cabin. He also wanted the high-altitude bomber and fighter developed. The Ju 88 program was to be accelerated to at least 170 per month, even if it meant cutting back production of other aircraft. By April 1, 1943, he wanted at least 5,000 Ju 88s. Ominously he queried Udet about camouflage measures for his beloved Karinhall.[77] If Göring thought Hitler was ready to move against Poland, the fact cannot be established from his talks with Udet on July 20 or his conference with Jeschonnek, Udet, and Milch on August 5. As far as the Luftwaffe leaders were concerned, the master plan still called for completion of general rearmament by 1942 and, for delayed programs such as the Ju 88, by 1943. Göring's own assessment of the Luftwaffe's strength varied considerably in 1939. In April, he told Mussolini and Count Ciano that he thought the next nine months to a year would be the most favorable time for the Axis powers to act, since after that the English and French rearmament would show results. He emphasized, in particular, that the navy would bring two new battleships into service early in 1940 while the Luftwaffe was in the process of changing over to the Ju 88. Göring was very optimistic about the bomber, which he claimed would have the range to bomb England and cut the sea approaches to the island. He expected to have a monthly production of 280 by fall and 300 by the beginning of the year. The Italians' response was guarded; they wanted more time to counsel; war should be avoided at all costs until at least 1942. During the late spring and early summer, Göring operated in his normal manner. He accepted the usual reports of delays with the Ju 88 and He 177, took his summer yachting vacation, and gave no sign of believing war was close at hand. Only in August when Hitler seemed bent on war was Göring stirred to action; he tried to limit the war to the Polish theater. When the war actually came, he complained that his Luftwaffe was not ready for it and was forced to fight the Polish campaign with training cadres.

The rest of the top Luftwaffe leaders—Milch, Udet, Jeschonnek, and Kesselring—were more sanguine than Göring; they believed that Hitler would not move until at least 1942. They had taken at face value his word that there would not be an early war. Their detailed plans were predicted on that assumption, and despite the tense international situation, nothing in the first seven months of the year changed them. There was, however, some uneasiness about what kind of information Göring was giving to Hitler. In early June, for example, Milch and Udet, irked by Göring's reluctance to explain to the Führer the critical shortage of materials, went to Rudolf Hess, Hitler's private secretary, in the hope of gaining a hearing, but to no avail. Particularly troublesome to some of the younger staff officers was the conspiracy of silence surrounding Hitler's fivefold expansion of the Luftwaffe. Did Hitler realize how impossible his plan was and how much the general staff and RLM had cut back the original plans? Did he know how green most of the Luftwaffe units were? Or how short the supply of aircraft parts and fuel was? Did he realize how little had been done to develop a unified war economy? Did he know that despite years of work there still was not a complete mobilization plan for the aircraft industry which included extending its capacity by using the resources of the nonessential industries?[78]

And what of Hitler, that typical twentieth-century man so fascinated by technology? Did he overestimate the Luftwaffe? Granted there were many other factors in his apparent decision to risk a major war in August 1939, but the influence of air power must be ranked as one of the more important. Hitler's utterances during August indicated he counted heavily on air power to destroy Poland quickly and keep the West in check. He thought the threat of the Luftwaffe along with the obvious superiority of the rest of the German rearmament program would be enough to keep England from fulfilling her obligations to Poland. He told Ribbentrop and Ciano on August 12 that although the British were making progress under their aircraft and flak programs, judging from Germany's experience of seven years, it would be another one or two years before they had appreciable results.[79]

In the same vein, Hitler told his military leaders on August 22 that England was vulnerable from the air. He insisted that English rearmament was still in the infant stage, with only three divisions ready, a beginning of an air force, and a bare start on antiaircraft artillery. The

English, French, and Polish air forces with a combined strength of 215,000 men, could not match the 390,000-strong Luftwaffe. Besides, Hitler argued, the English were too sensible to risk endangering their empire at this time for the sake of Poland. As for the French, they had a Maginot Line complex and would not move without the English. The English, Hitler concluded, "will demonstrate, they will protest, they will sign compacts but they will never march. And the French? No, gentlemen, you don't bury yourself twelve years in the Maginot Line and then one day come running against the German West-wall."[80]

Hitler was going to wave his magic wand of air power once again and come up with another Munich, or at least mesmerize the West until he disposed of Poland. He remarked the week before the war: "As neither France nor Britain can achieve any decisive successes in the West, and as Germany, as a result of the agreement with Russia, will have all her forces free in the East after the defeat of Poland, and as air supremacy is undoubtedly on our side, I do not shrink from solving the Eastern question even at the risk of complications in the West."[81] The timing was in his favor; he chose to move.

NOTES

1. The so-called Hossbach Conference has been subjected to various interpretations ranging from A. J. P. Taylor's *The Origins of World War II* (New York: Atheneum, 1961), in which he asserted that Hitler was dreaming aloud and trying to impress his military, to Hugh Trevor-Roper's view in "A. J. P. Taylor, Hitler and the War," *Encounter* 17 (1961): 88-96, that there was a continuity in his thinking since *Mein Kampf.* On the accuracy of Hossbach's reporting, see Walter Bussmann, "Zur Entstehung und Überlieferung der Hossbach-Niedeschrift," *Vierteljahreshefte für Zeitgeschichte* 16 (1968): 373-84.

2. For Göring's involvement in the Blomberg case, see, "Bericht über die Befragung des Generals d.Fl.a.D. W. Kreipe," 22.Nov.1954; General Bodenschatz, 22.Juni 1954, and Paul Körner in Lw 104/3, DZ/MGFA; Suchenwirth, "Hermann Göring", pp. 3-4. Apparently Göring wanted to be named reich chancellor after Hindenburg's death, with Hitler assuming the post of president. After that was rejected, he wanted to be foreign minister in 1938 or, after Blomberg's fall, war minister.

3. Oberst Georg Thomas, "Besprechung bei Generalfeldmarschall Göring am 14.Oktober 1938, 10.00 Uhr im Reichsluftfahrtministerium," *NCA*, 3:901-3, PS 1301.

4. Irving, *Milch*, p. 119.

5. (Vorl. Zusammenstellung) Untersuchung der Durchführbarkeit der von Herrn G.F.M. geforderten Flugzeugmengen, 25.Oktober 1938, Lw 103/65, DZ/MGFA.

6. Völker, *Die Deutsche Luftwaffe*, p. 138; Suchenwirth, *Jeschonnek*, pp. 48-49.

7. C-Amts Anschlussprogramm Nr. 9 (Zweiter Entwurf) LC 1 Nr. 460/38, g.Kdos., 15.Nov. 1938, Lw 103/4, DZ/MGFA.

8. *NCA*, 6:267-70, PS 3575.

9. Irving, *Milch*, pp. 119-20; Suchenwirth, *Turning Points*, p. 24, and *Jeschonnek*, pp. 46-49; Planung für den weiteren Aufbau der Luftwaffe-Auszug aus einem Brief von Gen.A.D. Kammhuber vom 11.10.1954, A/I/2, KDC/M. There is some disagreement over the dates of the conference. Suchenwirth claims it was about January 8, 1939, on the basis of Kammhuber's letter cited above, but Irving gives an earlier date, November 28, 1938, with follow-up conferences the next two days. Irving's date, based on Milch's diary, seems more plausible, especially since there is no substance to Suchenwirth's claim that the RLM divisional chiefs were not officially notified of the new fivefold program until December 6. See, for example, the folder of documents, "Stellungsnahme zum Anschluss-Programm Nr. 9" (2.Entw.) from the divisional chiefs, 29.Nov. and 30.Nov.1938, Lw 103/13, DZ/MGFA, which would agree with Milch's date.

10. LC 1/I, Aufstellungsprogramms 1.4.1942, 6.12.1938, Lw 103/65, DZ/MGFA.

11. These and the subsequent figures are from the von Rohden study, NA Microcopy T-971/26/1150-56; "Vortragsunterlagen für den Vortrag vor dem Herrn Generalfeldmarschall," 13.Dez.1938, Lw 103/48, DZ/MGFA.

12. Suchenwirth, *Turning Points*, pp. 24-25, and *Jeschonnek*, pp. 50-51.

13. C-Amts-Anschlussprogramms Nr. 10 (3.Entwurf), LC 1, Nr. 2/39, g.Kdos. (III Ang.), 24.Jan.1939, Lw 103/5; Flugzeugbeschaffungs-Programm (LC) L.Pr. Nr. 10 vom 1.1.39, Nr. 70/39 g.Kdos., Lw 103/7, DZ/MGFA.

14. GL 1/I, Aktennotiz über Etat 1939, g.Kdos., Berlin, den 10.2.1939, von Rohden document (4406-567), BA/F.

15. GL 1, Nr. 141/39, g.Kdos. 28.Feb.1939, Flugzeugbeschaffungs-Programm Nr. 11 (Generalstab) von Rohden document (4376-936), BA/F.

16. Flugzeugbeschaffungs-Programm (Industrie-Programm), L Pr. Nr. 11, vom 1.4.1939, Nr. 205/39 g.Kdos., Lw 103/7, DZ/MGFA.

17. LC I A, Berlin, den 11.4.1939, Betr: Beschaffungsprogramm Nr. 11, Lw 103/13, DZ/MGFA; and report of April 12, 1939, NA Microcopy T-971/15/447-50, 558-59.

18. Forderungen des Genst. und Gen.Qu., 5.Mai 1939, NA Microcopy T-971/15/394-406.

19. Ibid., frames 450-51; Der Chef des Generalstabes, Nr. 2005/39 g.Kdos., Genst. 6. Abt. III, 5.Mai 1939, Betr: Umrüstung der Verbände, Lw 103/50, DZ/MGFA.

20. Generalquartiermeister, Genst. 6. Abt. III, Nr. 1060/39 g.Kdos., 12.Mai 1939, von Rohden document (4376-1260), BA/F.

21. Meldung über die Beschaffungslage April 1939, GL 1 Az. 65, Nr. 349/39, 1 I B, g.Kdos. 15.Mai 1939, von Rohden document (4376-478), BA/F.

22. Information for June 1939 taken from Meldung über die Beschaffungslage Mai 1939, GL 1 Az. Nr. 439/39, g.Kdos., 1 I B, Berlin, 17.Juni 1939, von Rohden document (4376-478); Flak und Gerätelage, 16.Juni 1939, Gen. Qu. Genst. 6. Abt. (IV A), von Rohden document (4376-1260); Überblick über die Versorgung der Luftwaffe mit Eisen und Stahl, Holz und Zement, GL 2 II, 26.Juni 1939, von Rohden document (4376-1786), BA/F.

23. Aktenvermerk. Haushaltsbedarf 1939/40 nach vorläufiger Schätzung, GL 1 I B, g.Kdos., Berlin, 23.Mai 1939, von Rohden document (4376-1765); Haushalt 1939/40, NA Microcopy T-971/15/573-768; RLM Folder 153, NA Microcopy T-177/12/3696535-40.

24. LC 6 Az. 58, a.10, Nr. 347/39, g.Kdos. (I 1 b) 2.Nov.1938, Stand der Kassenmittel, BA 241, BA/F; Richterliche Überprüfung des Geschäftsbereichs des technischen Amtes nach dem Freitod des Generals Udet, 14.3.1956, Lw 103/25, DZ/MGFA.

25. Genst.Gen.Qu.6.Abt. Nr. 2628/39, g.Kdos. (IV A), 3.Aug.1939 von Rohden document (4406-817); Steigerung des Flakerzeugung, OKW Wa A Nr. 969/39, g.Kdos. Wa.Stab I a, 1.8.1938, von Rohden document (4376-2086); Flak- und Gerätelage, 16.Juni 1939, RO 8/237, Gen.Qu.Genst. 6.Abt. (IV A) von Rohden document (4376-1260) BA/F; RLM Folder 153, NA Microcopy T-177/12/3696535 ff.

26. Irving, *Milch*, p. 131; Generalstab der Luftwaffe, Nr. 2701/39, g.Kdos., Genst.Gen.Qu. 6.Abt., Berlin, den 9.8.1939, Betr: Konsentriertes Flugzeugprogramm, von Rohden document (4376-2413), BA/F.

27. GL 1 Nr. 602/39, g.Kdos., Berlin, 31.Aug.1939, Betr: Industrieplannungs-Grundlagen, von Rohden document (4376-1286), BA/F; Hertel, "Die Flugzeugbeschaffung," Lw 16/2, pp. 70-71, DZ/MGFA.

28. Meldung über die Beschaffungslage Juli 1939, GL 1, Az. 65 Nr. 585/39, g.Kdos. (IIe), 15.August 1939, von Rohden document (4376-478), BA/F.

29. GL 1 Az. 80 a-m Nr. 576/39, g.Kdos., 16.August 1939, Betr: Nachschub für Mob.-Fall; GL 1, Nr. 602/39, g.Kdos., 1.Sept.1939, von Rohden document (4376-8936), BA/F.

30. Generalstab d.L. Gen.Qu., 6.Abt. Nr. 2838/39 g.Kdos., (Ia), 24.August 1939, von Rohden document (4376-2197), BA/F.

31. Z.d.A.b. LC 2/I.B., Gef. Ng 3.8.1939, Rückstand am 31.8.1939, von Rohden document (4376-1701); Meldung an die Beschaffungs, August 1939, GL 1, Az. 65, Nr. 643-39, g.Kdos., 1IE, 13.Sept.1939, von Rohden document (4376-478), BA/F.

32. Der R.d.L.u.Ob.d.Luftwaffe, GL 2 II, Nr. 2418/39, g.Kdos., an Herrn Staatssekretär Körner, 31.August 1939, von Rohden document (4376-2377); GLZ, LC 2 Nr. 632/39, g.Kdos., 12.Sept.1939, von Rohden document (4406-817), BA/F.

33. USSBS, Overall Report (*European War*), p. 11.

34. Norbert Schausberger, "Wirtschaftliche Aspekte des Anschlusses Österreiches an das Deutsche Reich," *Militärgeschichtliche Mitteilungen* 2 (1970): 154-56; Webster and Frankland, *Strategic Air Offense*, pp. 272-74.

35. Abschrift-Die Veränderung der Wirtschaftlichen Verteidigungsstärke durch die Unterwerfung Böhmens, Mährens und der Slowakei, NA Microcopy T-177/234/974942-43.

36. Schnellbrief, Nr. 2560, 16.März 1939, von Rohden document (4376-2883), BA/F.

37. "Abschrift- Die Veränderung," NA Microcopy T-77/234/974945.

38. Luftfahrtindustrie-Statistik, GL 1 Az. 67r Br. Nr. 3438/40 (U) geh., Berlin, 18.Juni 1940, von Rohden document. (4406-601), BA/F.

39. Irving, *Milch*, p. 104; Bericht von Milch, 28.Juli 1945, von Rohden document (4376-463), BA/F.

40. Ibid. Interestingly, Milch does not mention this episode in the memoirs written by Irving.

41. Irving, *Milch*, pp. 109-10; Suchenwirth, *Udet*, pp. 20-24, Nielsen, *German Air Force General Staff*, pp. 33-35.

42. Tagebücher von General Franz Halder, 1937-1939, Lw 106/1, DZ/MGFA.

43. Suchenwirth, *Udet*, p. 35; Irving, *Milch*, p. 120.

44. Bericht von Milch, 28.Juli 1945, von Rohden document (4376-463), BA/F.

45. According to von Seidel, Jeschonnek was a "100% National Socialist," quoted in Suchenwirth, *Turning Points*, p. 127. For his personality, see Suchenwirth's sympathetic portrait, "Jeschonnek: Ein Versuch über Wesen, Wirken und Schicksal des vierten Generalstabschefs der deutschen Luftwaffe," Studiengruppe Karlsruhe, Maxwell Air Force Base, and the interviews of Generals Josef Schmid, Seidel, and Student; Major Pohle; Colonel Torsten; GFM Milch; and Jeschonnek's private secretary, Lotte Kersten, in Lw 104/5, DZ/MGFA.

46. Nielsen, *German Air Force General Staff*, pp. 160-61; Interview of Milch, 2.9.1955, Lw 104/5, DZ/MGFA. Later in Irving, *Milch*, pp. 120-21, this view was modified somewhat.

47. Heinkel, *Stürmisches Leben*, pp. 413-16; Thorwald, *Udet*, p. 167. Only Edgar Petersen, chief of aircraft testing, seems to disagree. In a letter to Prof. Ernst Heinkel dated June 17, 1953, Lw 103/29, DZ/MGFA, he refutes Heinkel's account of the feud, which had just been published. Petersen asserts that Udet never said a word against Milch and Milch never intrigued against Udet.

48. Bericht von Milch, 28.Juli 1945, von Rohden document (4376-463), BA/F; Bericht über eine Befragung des Ministerials-direktor Knipfer, 22.11.1954, Lw 104/3, DZ/MGFA; Suchenwirth, *Turning Points*, p. 4.

49. Irving, *Milch*, p. 90. There was a minor cult of Karl May readers in the Third Reich. Hitler, Göring, Milch, and Himmler were avid fans of the "German Zane Grey."

50. Telford Taylor, *The Breaking Wave: The Second World War in the Summer of 1940* (New York: Simon & Schuster, 1967), p. 96.

51. Das technische Amt der deutschen Luftwaffe, Frhr. Hammerstein, 3.9.1955, Lw 103/25; Technische Luftrüstung, Lw 103/39, DZ/MGFA; Taktik-Technik, von Rohden document (4376-435), BA/F.

52. Gen.Ing.a.D. Reidenbach über Dr. Dr. Koppenberg, am 17.4.1946, Lw 103/51, DZ/MGFA.

53. Emme, "German Air Power," pp. 432-34, 455-56. See also Bernhardt, *Aufrüstung*, pp. 92-124; Webster and Frankland, *Strategic Air Offensive*, pp. 79-81.

54. "Epilogue. Hitler: The Nazi Concept of War," *Makers of Modern Strategy*, ed. Edward Mead Earle (Princeton: Princeton Univ. Press, 1941), p. 516.

55. *Bombs Bursting in Air* (New York: Little Brown, 1939), pp. 80-81; Winston Churchill agreed with this view in *The Gathering Storm* (New York: Bantam Books, 1961), p. 132.

56. For German estimates, see "Strength of German Air Force," Lw 106/7, 106/2, DZ/MGFA; von Rohden document (4376-454), BA/F. For English estimates of the Luftwaffe, see Lw 106/7, DZ/MGFA, "Aus den in England befindlichen Lagekarten."

57. Churchill, *The Gathering Storm*, p. 302; Hanson W. Baldwin, *Battles Lost and Won.* (New York: Discus, 1968), p. 58; Hanfried Schliephake, *Wie die Luftwaffe wirklich entstand* (Stuttgart: Motorbuch, 1972), pp. 76-78; Wood, "Luftwaffe as a factor in British Policy," p. 323; Basil Liddell Hart, *Memoirs: The Later Years,* vol. 2 (New York: G. P. Putnam's Sons, 1965), pp. 190-92; Bernhardt, *Aufrüstung,* pp. 101-2; Basil Collier, *The Defence of the United Kingdom*

(London: H.M.S.O., 1957), pp. 63-70.

58. Völker, *Die Deutsche Luftwaffe*, p. 159; Suchenwirth, *Jeschonnek*, pp. 38-40; Irving, *Milch*, p. 116, *NCA*, 3:282-83, PS 375.

59. Suchenwirth, *Jeschonnek*, Lw 104/5; Luftwaffengruppenkdo. 2, "Planstudie Fall Grün," 22.9.1938, DZ/MGFA.

60. Schliephake, *Wie die Luftwaffe wirklich entstand*, pp. 70-71; Völker, *Die Deutsche Luftwaffe*, pp. 160-61; 170; Genst. d.F.M. 3244138 g.Kdos. 1 Abt. (III), 7.11.1938, Konzentriertes Flugzeugmuster-Programms, Lw 103/65, DZ/MGFA.

61. General Felmy, Schlussbesprechung des Planspieles des Luftflottenkommandos 2. zur Frage der Luftkriegsführung gegen England und über See, Nr. 7093/39 g.Kdos., 13.5.1939, Lw 106/5, DZ/MGFA; Irving, *Milch*, p. 123; Suchenwirth, *Jeschonnek*, p. 39.

62. Die Luftlage in Europa, Dr.d.L. und Ob.d.L. (Chef des Generalstabes) Nr. 700/39, g.Kdos. (5.Abt.I), 2.Mai 1939, von Rohden document (4376-349), BA/F; von Rohden study, NA Microcopy T-971/26/972-76.

63. Gen. Qu. Genst. 6.Abt., Luftrüstungslage Westmächte, 1.4.39 bis 1.11.1940, g. Kdos., Berlin 12.5.1939, von Rohden document (4376-1260), RO 8/237, BA/F.

64. GL 1/III, Nr. 345/39 g.Kdos., 13.Mai 1939, Bemerkungen zur Beurteilung der Erzeugung an Kriegsflugzeugen, von Rohden document (4376-1914), BA/F.

65. General Schmidt, Abteilung Ic (5.Abt. des Luftwaffe Generalstab), von Rohden document (4376-437), BA/F.

66. For Thomas's speeches, see Folder Wi/IF 5.115, NA Microcopy T-77/14/725561-82, for the Cologne address; Berlin Handelsgesellschaft, 27.1.1939, frames 725545-61; Kiel address, 725351-79; to Wehrmacht inspectors, 725323-49; military attachés, 725321-42; Propaganda Ministry, 725282-320; and Stand der Aufrüstung in Deutschland 1939, Vortrag von Generalmajor Thomas, am 24.Mai 1939, Lw 103/21, DZ/MGFA.

67. Schliephake, *Wie die Luftwaffe wirklich entstand*, p. 76; Völker, *Die Deutsche Luftwaffe*, pp. 198-201; Suchenwirth, *Command and Leadership*, pp. 226; Jeschonnek was quoting from "Organisationsvorschlag 2. Abschnitt," (Kammhuber) 2.Abt. Generalstab d.Luftwaffe, 1.Oktober 1937, Lw 101/4, Teil III, DZ/MGFA.

68. Von Rohden study, NA Microcopy T-971/26/970-72.

69. Schmidt, "Grundlagen und Wandlungen," p. 23.

70. On racing competition, see letter from Dr.Ing.Ernst Heinkel to Col. a.D. Greffrath, July 18, 1952, Lw 103/39, DZ/MGFA; Lusar, *Die deutschen Waffen*, pp. 57-58; Heinkel. *Stürmisches Leben*, pp. 378-79; Schmidt, "Grundlagen und Wandlungen," pp. 23-24.

71. Heinkel, *Stürmisches Leben*, pp. 382-83; Irving, *Milch*, pp. 115-16; John Wheeler-Bennett, *Munich: Prologue to Tragedy* (New York: Duell, Sloan & Pearce, 1948), p. 99.

72. LC2/I, Aktenvermerk, Entwicklungsmeldung 16.März 1939, Berlin, von Rohden document (4376-1701), BA/F.

73. Heinkel, *Stürmisches Leben*, pp. 490-94.

74. Irving, *Milch*, p. 128; Gerbert Hübner, "Wehrmacht und Technik," Lw 103/21, DZ/MGFA.

75. Bericht über eine Mitteilung des Gfm Milch über die Rechliner Besichtigung vom 3.7.1939, 2.9.1954, Lw 106/1, DZ/MGFA; a slightly different version

appears in Irving, *Milch*, p. 128.

76. Mundliche Mitteilung des Gllt.a.D. Josef Schmidt, April 1955, Lw 106/1, DZ/MGFA, and quoted in Suchenwirth, *Jeschonnek*, p. 43.

77. GL 1 Aktennotiz: Fragen, die der Gfm anlässlich seiner Besprechung mit Generalleutnant Udet am 20.Juli 1939 berührt hat, Lw 103/50, DZ/MGFA.

78. Felmy, "Führung der Luftwaffe," Lw 21/1, p. 115; Rieckhoff, *Trumpf oder Bluff*, pp. 116, 89; Kesselring, *Soldat*, p. 45; "Der Einfluss der politischen Planung auf die materiellen Kriegsvorbereitungen der deutschen Luftwaffe vor dem II. Weltkrieg," von General d.F.a.D. Paul Deichmann, 1956, Lw 103/51, DZ/MGFA; Bericht über die Befragung des Oberst i.G.a.D. Bernd von Brauchitsch, 5.Nov.1956, Lw 104/3, DZ/MGFA; Suchenwirth, *Göring*, p. 23.

79. *NCA*, 4:508-9, PS 1871.

80. *NCA*, 3:584 ff., PS 798; Winfried Baumgart, "Zur Ansprache Hitlers vor den Führern der Wehrmacht am 22.August 1939—Eine quellenkritische Untersuchung," *Vierteljahrschefte für Zeitgeschichte* 16 (1968): 120-49; Rieckhoff, *Trumpf oder Bluff*, p. 117.

81. *Documents on German Foreign Policy*, ser. D, vol. II (Washington, D.C.; USGPO, 1950), p. 314.

CHAPTER 9

The Balance Sheet

WHAT CONCLUSION may we draw from the history of the German aircraft
industry during the interwar period? In spite of many formidable
obstacles, Germany was able to construct an aircraft industry second to
none by 1939. Allied prohibitions and restrictions imposed in the 1920s
failed to prevent the Germans from laying the groundwork for future
expansion. The chief difference between the Weimar and Nazi periods
was the audacity of the Nazi planning. While the Weimar planners were
timid, hesitant, and circumspect about aerial rearmament, the Nazis were
bold and determined. Keenly aware of the propaganda impact of aerial
rearmament, they organized a program that was part showmanship, part
enthusiasm, and part performance.

There can be little doubt that the Nazis gave preferential treatment
to the Luftwaffe. Göring's status as commander of the Luftwaffe along
with his cabinet position as Air Minister indicated clearly that the
Luftwaffe was the favorite son of the regime.

Spending for the new branch was quick and heavy; what Göring
could not get from the military budget came from his civilian budget as
Minister or later from the Four-Year Plan. The magnitude of Nazi
spending on aerial rearmament before the war is difficult to judge
because the estimates of total defense spending vary widely, depending
on the method of calculation and the political bias of the calculator.
Hitler's celebrated boast that 90 billion RM were spent before the
invasion of Poland seems untenably high in the light of postwar
investigations. Reich Finance Minister Graf Schwerin von Krosigk
pegged defense spending at 63-64 billion, Milch at 63 billion, which
included Autobahn construction, and Schacht at 67.5 billion.[1]
Economists' estimates vary widely, depending on what they have chosen
to include in defense spending. Burton Klein of the USSBS team
estimated 55 billion was spent on strictly military items, while the West
German Heinrich Stuebel places it at 60.7 billion from 1933 to the
outbreak of war.[2] The American Arthur Schweitzer estimated 69.8
billion, including the costs of the Four-Year Plan, close to the East

German Dietrich Eichholtz's estimate of 71.8 billion, which also included spending on paramilitary groups. The dean of East German economic historians, Jürgen Kuczynski, on the other hand, finds Hitler's general figure of 90 billion acceptable by including the Autobahn, Four-Year Plan, subsidies, price guarantees, and quasi-military spending at all levels of government and by the Nazi party.[3]

The exact amount spent on aerial rearmament likewise varies considerably. Two of the more detailed analyses, those of Steubel and Schweitzer, agree substantially on air force expenditures, but the percentage of military spending on aerial rearmament in the two estimates is deceiving. Much of the air industry's expansion, military hardware for the Luftwaffe, and construction costs for both military and civilian aircraft was paid for by Mefo-bills, secret rearmament funds drawn on Metallurgische Forschungs G.m.b.H., the major purpose of which was to conceal both the extent and the type of defense spending. Although the exact breakdown for Mefo-bills spending is not available, it can be surmised that the share for aerial rearmament was considerably larger than the Luftwaffe's average of 34 or 35 percent of the defense budget shown in table 20. The boom years of aircraft plant expansion coincided with the years the Mefo-bills were largely used. Until the 1935 announcement of the new Luftwaffe, the Nazi government maintained the guise that the Reich had no air force, hence it is only logical to assume that most of the aviation expenditures came from Mefo-bills. Once the Mefo-bills were phased out, Göring's Four-Year Plan stepped in and continued to support the aircraft industry and the Luftwaffe. Carroll estimates that nearly one-half of the total military expenditures in those years were for the Luftwaffe, while the von Rohden study more discreetly comments that the Luftwaffe got more than the other branches of the military services, but details are sparse.[4] Colonel Wimmer of the Technical Office mentioned in a report in July 1933 that his office was spending five marks secretly to every one publicly acknowledged.[5] Presumably these secret marks were Mefo-bills. After the war, Milch offered little clarification of this point. He asserted that Schacht and he organized the Mefo-bill system on June 9, 1933, and a day later a special secret account (Kasse L.) was established within the ministry to handle their distribution. While the officially announced budget for the RLM was 78.3 million RM for 1933, rising to 210 for 1934, Milch estimated actual secret spending was many times higher.[6] Until a detailed breakdown of the 12 billion RM worth of Mefo-bills issued can be found, the best that can be assumed is that a large portion of them were channeled into aerial rearmament.

TABLE 20

Two Estimates of Germany's Prewar Military Spending

(in million marks)

Agency	1932	1933	1934	1935	1936	1937	1938	1939[1]	1934-1939[2]	% of Total Budget
Heinrich Stuebel's Estimate										
RKM and OKW[3]	—	—	3	5	128	346	452	258	1,192	2.5
Army	457	478	1,010	1,392	3,020	3,990	9,137	5,611	24,160	50.4
Navy	173	192	339	339	448	679	1,632	2,095	5,491	11.4
Air Force	—	76	642	1,036	2,204	3,258	6,026	3,942	17,128	35.7
Total Budget	630	746	1,952	2,772	5,821	8,273	17,247	11,906	47,971	100.0
Mefo-bills[4]	—	—	2,145	2,715	4,452	2,688	—	—	12,000	
GRAND TOTAL	630	746	4,197	5,487	10,273	10,961	17,247	11,906	59,971	
Arthur Schweitzer's Estimate										
RKM		3.5	5	127	346	452	278		1,211.5	
Army		1,083	1,793	3,449	4,611	9,148	5,614		25,698	
Navy		559	385	491	747	1,633	2,095		5,910	
Air Force		642	1,036	2,224	3,257	6,025	3,941		17,125	
Mefo-Bills		2,145	2,715	4,452	2,688				12,000	
Four-Year Plan (Planned figures only)					2,866	3,067	1,979		7,912	
TOTAL		4,432.5	5,934	10,743	14,515	20,325	13,907		69,856.5	

SOURCE: Dr. Heinrich Stuebel, "Die Finanzierung der Aufrustung im Dritten Reich," *Europa-Archiv* 12 (1951): 4128-36; Arthur Schweitzer, *Big Business in the Third Reich* (Bloomington, Indiana: Indiana University Press, 1964), p. 331.

[1] Only from April 1, 1939, until September 1, 1939.
[2] From April 1, 1934, until September 1, 1939.
[3] Reichskriegministerium und Oberkommande der Wehrmacht (War Minister and Supreme Command of the Armed Forces)
[4] Secret rearmament funds drawn on Metallurgische Forschungs G.m.b.H.

The precise amount of the Reich's financial involvement in the aircraft industry is difficult to determine, since most of the records were destroyed by bombing. Ministerialrat Fritz Müller, division chief of contracts and exports (LF 1) in the Generalluftzeugmeister office, estimated after the war that 5 billion marks were invested by 1945. This sum did not include the many billions paid for bomb damage, time lost because of air raids, dispersal, underground plants, and other extraordinary wartime expenditures.[7]

Karl Hettlage, another RLM official, estimated that the government's participation in financing the airframe industry alone ran approximately 80 percent, while the aeroengine industry with its close connection to the auto companies was financed mostly with private funds. He thought about 1.5-1.75 billion marks had been invested in plant facilities for the airframe industry, including 250 million for construction of new plants, 100 million in direct stock participation, 130 million in the government-owned Junkers Works, 800 million in loans to the industry through the government-controlled Deutsche Luftfahrt Bank, and perhaps another 200-300 million in private loans guaranteed by the RLM. About 2.5 billion had to be invested in the air munitions, repairs, and subsidiary industries, which were virtually built and owned by the government, while another 400-500 million was granted as special subsidies to the aircraft industry for particular wartime requirements.[8]

A rough total of Hettlage's estimate gives 4.48 billion; and assuming that Müller's estimate of 5 billion was correct, that would mean about 600 million was spent in the aircraft engine industry. Partial records of Reich investment in the aircraft industry indicate that 211,000,000 RM was invested in fiscal year 1934-35, 500,000,000 RM in 1935, and 980,000,000 RM in 1936. Assuming a rate of one billion for 1937, 1938, and 1939, it is quite possible that before the war started the Reich had 5 billion RM invested in the industry. Müller's rough figures included the war years, but it is entirely possible that most of the Reich's investment in those years was written off as extraordinary wartime expenditures or that the individual companies were able to retire their debt obligations from ongoing profits. Although the total running balance never went much over 5 billion RM even by the end of the war, it is reasonable to assume that, given the rapidity with which the firms liquidated their bond debts to the Reich, the Reich had already invested 5 billion RM in the industry before the war.

The precise amount of the Reich's investment before the war may never be known because of the lack of adequate records, the government's habit of later declaring loans as subsidies, and the bewildering variety of means used to obscure its actual participation in this key industry. The government not only deliberately followed a policy designed to disguise from foreign observers the extent of its participation in the supposed private air industry, but had compelling reasons to hide it from the less favored segments of its own government, economy, party, and military branches, segments that might have been extremely critical of its massive participation. Nazi Germany was determined to pursue a policy which gave the appearance that the aircraft industry was largely private when, in fact, the opposite was true. The industry was for all practical purposes owned, financed, and controlled by the government, a quasi-public industry with only the façade of private ownership to maintain its respectability.

HOW GOOD WAS NAZI MANAGEMENT?

Given the vast amount of Reich participation, why did not the Nazis nationalize the aircraft industry? It would have been relatively simple to nationalize the bankrupt industry in 1933 when the only foreseeable markets were in rearmament and in commercial needs, already controlled by the nationalized Lufthansa. Some of the Young Turks in the newly founded RLM wanted to nationalize, but the Nazi leadership seems never to have seriously considered this alternative. The blatant takeover of the Junkers and Arado firms certainly indicated that the Nazis had few scruples about nationalization when it suited their purposes. Had they wanted to, they could have nationalized or allowed big business to take over the industry. Instead, the Nazi policy toward ownership was more manipulative than ideological, an outgrowth of the prevailing 1920s view of rationalization. Under this concept, who owned the industry was not as important as how it operated and was controlled. Thus, the Nazis preferred mixed ownership, part Reich (Junkers and Arado), part big business (ATG, Weser, Blohm and Voss, Gothaer, Henschel, MIAG, Focke-Wulf), part older private motor firms (Daimler-Benz, BMW, Opel), part long-time aircraft designer entrepreneurs (Dornier, Messerschmitt, Heinkel, Fieseler, Siebel, Klemm), and even one part local state bank (the Erla firm, held by the Saxony State Bank). And the biggest practitioner of rationalization in the industry was the man who ran it all—Milch.

Milch had been the rationalizer of the commercial airlines during the 1920s, and now military rearmament would be handled in the same "scientific" way but on a much larger scale. The assumed superiority and importance of rationalization was a common ground of agreement between the most diverse groups, including the industrialists, military planners, bureaucracy, bankers, and the Nazis. The German trait of preferring expertise and avoiding conflicts, as indicated so brilliantly by Ralf Dahrendorf,[9] blended beautifully with the modern technological need for greater planning and control. The generals, Nazis, industrialists, and civil servants were thinking on the same frequency.

Milch was considered solid; he knew how to organize business, cooperate with the existing powers, and operate as an exponent of rationalization. His actions in office confirmed these views. His first production plans were based on an industry-wide level, allowed sufficient room for individual initiative, and were balanced carefully to maintain the relative strength between the various firms. They had all the earmarks of the old cartel system of operation so dearly loved by German business. Milch's overall plan of expanding the industry, developing complexes from the firms with technical competence, and generally maintaining a balance between the major complexes helped to contain some of the fierce fighting in the industry. His innovative methods of financing the industry with Reich funds after the conservative banking community's initial lack of investment enthusiasm was particularly welcomed by the firms, but by 1936 the situation had changed. The combination of many things—the death of Wever; the formation of a Luftwaffe general staff and its misgivings about Milch; the growing coolness between Milch and Göring; the appointment of Udet; shortages of money, materials, and labor; and the ascendency of Hitler's favorites like Heinkel, Messerschmitt, and Koppenberg—brought about an intensification of the in-fighting, and control of aerial rearmament slipped away from Milch.

After 1936 the Nazi management of the aviation industry was not centralized. Udet's Technical Office, the general staff, Göring, Milch, and the aircraft designers vied with one another for control of the aviation program, but in the long run none of them managed to gain the control that Milch had had up to 1936. In that authoritarian state which in essence was more an anarchic-impulsive dictatorship, as Heinrich Uhlig so aptly labeled it,[10] there was no one authority, but many. Instead of a uniform, consistent policy toward the aircraft industry, there was confusion and chaos. Each firm tried to build everything from single-engined trainers to multiengined bombers, and every effort of the ministry to squeeze them into specialization was successfully countered.

The general staff's and the Technical Office's constant shifting of specifications and introduction of new industrial programs only compounded the problems of the industry. The inability of the general staff to fashion clear-cut technical objectives for the industry meant an enormous waste of priceless engineering skill, time, and materials. While the General Staff was placing confusing and impossibly high technical demands on the ministry and the industry, it was also insistent on adequate equipment for its rapidly expanding operational units. To meet these heavy demands the Technical Office and the firms resorted to promising more than they could deliver. The Technical Office tried to keep pace with the changing technical specifications of the general staff, but its average of three complete production programs a year from 1933 to 1939 would have played havoc with a bicycle firm, much less an airframe plant with its four- to five-year lead time. Of course, some of the constant jockeying of programs was caused by factors outside the control of the Luftwaffe, for example, materials and foreign exchange shortages in 1936. But much of it was of their own doing. The desire to protect their labor force and maintain steady industrial expansion, coupled with the desire to prove the need for more funding, meant that the ministry did a lot of unnecessary shifting from plant to plant despite the obvious inefficiency involved.

An overall assessment of the way the Nazis managed the aircraft industry would have to be negative. Although the industry expanded rapidly, its full capacity in terms of potential for production and development was never reached in the prewar period.

The pattern of management in the industry was not significant for the rest of German industry. The concept of rationalization had long preceded its application in the aircraft industry, but the experience there had some effect on the organization of the Four-Year Plan. Many of the early Luftwaffe planners such as Loeb moved in 1936 to the Four-Year Plan program, where after some initial success they were displaced by professional rationalizers drawn from industry. The same phenomenon occurred in the aircraft industry, where, by the late 1930s, civilian managers displaced military men, who were frequently rotated into technical posts but whose interests were chiefly in command positions. They were, however, no match for the civilian managers with their technical mastery of the aviation field. Even Milch, who possessed enormous talent and managerial ability, was seriously handicapped in his dealing with civilians because of his lack of technological and engineering competence.

Another pattern in the aircraft industry that was typical of later Nazi managerial style was the rapid evolution from scattered, uncoordinated to highly detailed planning. It was obvious by 1936 that further success in the limited area of arms production could be ensured only by broad economy-wide planning. The political decision to commit so much of the nation's limited economic resources to one sector, armaments, meant that the rest of the economy had to be subjected to more comprehensive planning and control. The leaders of the Third Reich sensed this, but they did not know quite how to achieve it. Without a guiding ideology or even a well-thought-out economic plan, they fell back on what they could do best—improvise. Much of their prewar and wartime rhetoric such as "cannons instead of butter" and "total war" signaled their vague aspirations. Certainly by September 1939, as this study indicates, they were unable to control effectively and plan one industry, much less an entire economy.

AERIAL REARMAMENT: A LITMUS TEST FOR NAZI INTENTIONS?

The course of the aerial rearmament program in the prewar period furnishes a reflection of Nazi intentions in foreign and domestic affairs. The accent from the very beginning was on the offensive force, the bombers. The risk fleet during the camouflage period (1933-35), with heavy emphasis on bombers, was designed to neutralize any threat from the immediate neighbors of the Reich and prevent them from interfering with the general rearmament drive. The risk fleet bought time, but with the public proclamation of the Luftwaffe in March 1935 came a new role, that of the elite branch of the Wehrmacht. The secret threat had become reality.

The Nazis intended the Luftwaffe to become a strategic weapon, but from its inception a series of decisions gradually formed it into something quite different—a superb tactical weapon closely bound to a mobile army. The preponderance of army officers transferred into the Luftwaffe at the command and staff level, the political intentions of the Nazi leadership which stressed continental supremacy, and the conditions in the aircraft industry turned the Luftwaffe toward a more tactical orientation. Granted that the professional military built the kind of air force they thought the political leadership wanted, still it was not a realistic possibility for the industry to build a strategic air force in the 1930s. The low level of engine development; shortages of skilled labor, materials, and factory capacity; and an immature research and development program steered the Luftwaffe into a tactical orientation. Besides, Germany was simply not rich enough in the 1930s to build a strategic air force; that would be a task for the 1940s.

Although Hitler was a master at exploiting the threat of aerial warfare in the thirties, there is little evidence that he seriously planned to use his air force until 1938. After the Austrian crisis and before the Czech crisis, he and Göring apparently decided to freeze model development and begin mass production. The cutbacks that had been planned for 1937-38 were forgotten and conversions to the new twin-engined bombers and the new fighters were given top priority. By far the most decisive indication of Hitler's intentions came only after Munich. The fivefold increase in the Luftwaffe proclaimed by Göring on October 14, 1938, which aimed at full military preparedness by 1942 with the capability of long-range operations against England and Russia, was definitely a "war in sight" program. The Luftwaffe was still only the torso of the force planned. As Karl Bodenschatz, Göring's adjutant said at Nuremberg, "The German Air Force, at the beginning of the Polish campaign, as regards leadership, planning, or material, was not equal to its tasks."[11]

Hitler and Göring were victims of their own propaganda about the Luftwaffe. In the summer of 1939, Hitler apparently came to the conclusion that his Luftwaffe had a decided advantage over his expected opponents but that time was running against him. He mistakenly decided to gamble. His first move at Munich was a brilliant success, but his next gamble of intimidating the West into neutrality while he disposed of Poland failed.[12] The West was cautious as Germany overran Poland, but nonetheless they entered what proved to be a long war. Speaking about Hitler's miscalculation in 1939, Göring observed in 1942, "It was lucky that things went as well as they did at first and the consequences were not any worse."[13]

HOW SUCCESSFUL WAS THE HANDLING OF AERIAL TECHNOLOGY?

One of General Wever's favorite maxims was "Perhaps in no other arm of the service is the interdependence of tactics and technology and their interworking so great as in the Luftwaffe."[14] Nazi Germany found this interdependence as baffling as most other nations. The most publicized technological failures, that of quick employment of the jet fighter and of radar, belong more properly to the period after the war broke out, but responsibility for the failure to develop an operational long-range bomber lies in the prewar years.

The Luftwaffe's decision to halt development of the first generation of heavy bombers and gamble on the much more technically advanced He 177 was a sound one, but its handling of the He 177 program was indecisive. Unclear of its strategic air power concepts, the Luftwaffe failed to push the program with vigor. The results were predictable: the changing of tactical requirements by the military, shifting of building priorities within the ministry and industry, coupled with the countless technological problems of such an advanced aircraft, meant that the He 177 could not possibly meet the original schedule laid down in December 1937.

Critics have suggested that the German failure to push the heavy bomber was a blessing in disguise. The failure of Allied strategic bombing during World War II is cited as evidence that Germany's concentration on tactical air power was the wiser course. This line of thinking does not necessarily apply to the German situation, however. Germany's two major European foes were peculiarly susceptible to strategic bombing. England with her dependence on trade, food, and raw materials from abroad and Russia with her vulnerable transportation, industrial, and electrical power systems presented strategic bombing problems far different from those of a German-dominated continent. The Battle of Britain might have been different had the Luftwaffe possessed a bomber with the range to cover the entire British Isles and the coastal approaches, and the German attacks in the North Atlantic, Polar Sea, Mediterranean, and Russia also lost a valuable dimension by not having strategic bombing.

In general the handling of aerial technology during the period 1933-39 anticipated the flaws of the war years. The enormous political pressure to produce quick results so forced the pace of aircraft and engine development that prototypes were accepted and set into production before they had been properly tested. The constant shifting of specifications and production programs resulted in many abuses, including unwarranted politicization of aircraft selection, intensified personnel feuds, uncontrolled fighting among the aircraft firms, confusion, and waste. The cooperation and coordination between the Luftwaffe, the Air Ministry, and the industry suffered accordingly, and in the case of the He 177 simply broke down. Ironically, the Technical Office, which so conservatively supported the production of standard models, allowed the entire industry to experiment and build all kinds of prototypes. The most rudimentary rule of rational production was ignored. It was only in 1938, under the threat of impending war, that some degree of rationality was applied to aircraft types in the mobilization plan. Göring's insistence on cutting down the plan to one model per aircraft category marked the first halt to what had been a badly proliferated program, but it was not enough. The encrusted mini-empires in the Air Ministry and the industry were far too securely lodged to be swept away by the wave of an absent warlord's hand.

The leaders of the Luftwaffe after 1936—Göring, Milch, Udet, and Jeschonnek—were unable effectively to coordinate, tap, or shape German aerial technology. Limited by their lack of scientific and technical knowledge, they increasingly lacked the ability to anticipate the future technological needs of the Luftwaffe, nor were they able to devise an administrative system that might compensate for their own shortcomings. Although German scientific-technological knowledge was on a par with or superior in most respects to that of the other leading industrial nations, this most fragile and indispensable element in modern civilization was so poorly used by the Luftwaffe leadership that the best they could manage was a slight numerical and weaponry advantage over their European foes by 1939, and their advantages lasted only a short while.

NOTES

1. Graf Schwerin von Krosigk, "Wie Wurde der zweite Weltkrieg Finanziert?" *Bilanz des Zweiten Weltkrieges* (Oldenburg: Gerhard Stalling, 1953), pp. 321-28; Irving, *Milch*, p. 137; for Schacht's estimate, see *IMT*, 12:484.

2. Burton H. Klein, *Germany's Economic Preparations for War* (Cambridge, Mass.: Harvard University Press, 1959), pp. 256-58; Dr. Heinrich Stuebel, "Die Finanzierung der *Aufrüstung im* Dritten Reich," *Europa Archiv* 10 (June 1951): 4128-36.

3. Arthur Schweitzer, *Big Business in the Third Reich* (Bloomington, Indiana: Indiana University Press, 1964), p. 331; Eichholtz, *Kriegswirtschaft*, p. 31; Jürgen Kuczynski, *Studien zur Geschichte des staatsmonopolistischen Kapitalismus in Deutschland 1918 bis 1945* (Berlin: Akademie-Verlag, 1963), pp. 131-33.

4. Carroll, *Design for War*, p. 81; Die Finanzierung der deutschen Luftrüstung, von Rohden document (4376-470), BA/F.

5. Haushaltsplan-Gesamtprogramm 1933, C Nr. 1400/33 R, den 21.7.1933, von Rohden document (4376-680), BA/F.

6. Irving, *Milch*, pp. 407, 421. Milch's estimate for the RLM budget, 1934-39, was exactly the same as the two estimates in table 20; Suchenwirth, *Development of the German Air Force*, pp. 159-60, has a much higher estimate.

7. Statement by Ministerialrat Fritz Müller, September 17, 1945, von Rohden document (4376-463), BA/F.

8. Karl Hettlage Interview, 12 A., August 10, 1945, USSBS, 4d43; Suchenwirth, *Development of the German Air Force*, pp. 158-60, lists the investments for 1933-36 cited in the next paragraph.

9. *Society and Democracy in Germany* (Garden City: Doubleday, 1967), pp. 149-63.

10. Heinrich Uhlig, *Die Warenhäuser im Dritten Reich* (Cologne: DTV, 1956), p. 152.

11. *IMT*, 9:27; Kesselring agreed (*Soldat*, p. 460); Deichmann did too; "Der Einfluss der politischen Planung auf die materiellen Kriegsvorbereitungen der deutschen Luftwaffe vor dem II. Weltkrieg," 1956, LW 103/51, DZ/MGFA.

12. Heinkel, *Stürmisches Leben*, pp. 402-4; Rieckhoff, *Trumpf oder Bluff*, p. 89; Jon Kimche, *The Unfought Battle* (New York: Stein & Day, 1968), pp. 40, 108, 146.

13. Irving, *Milch*, p. 128.

14. Baumbach, *Life and Death*, pp. 6-7.

Bibliographical Note and Selected Bibliography

MOST OF THE ARCHIVES of the Luftwaffe were lost or deliberately destroyed to prevent their falling into Allied hands. What little survived the war has been moved several times and microfilmed in a variety of places. The best-known collection, the von Rohden documents, were originally part of the Luftwaffe archives under Division 8 (Kriegswissenschaftlichen Abteilung) of the general staff. Generalmajor Herhudt von Rohden, the chief of the division, had been ordered to collect the documents necessary for the preparation of an official history of the Luftwaffe. Much of the collection was destroyed or scattered during the last days of the war, but what survived eventually ended up in the British Air Ministry. The British microfilmed large parts of the collection and sent copies, which appear as the T-971 series in this manuscript, to the National Archives in Washington, D.C. In 1955 the West German government opened negotiations for the return of captured German records from the United States and England. After a number of years the von Rohden collection was sent back to Germany to be stored in the Document Center of the Militärgeschichtliches Forschungsamt in Freiburg. In 1968 the Federal Republic began closing the Document Center and shipping its collection to the new Military Archive in Freiburg. At the same time the military records at Koblenz were also shipped to Freiburg.

It was at this point that I became acquainted with the collection. Most of the documents were bundled up with rope and had nothing to identify them except some handwritten von Rohden numbers inked on each bundle. The collection had obviously been much abused. It had been picked over by the Allied intelligence teams, the Nuremberg trial group, and the Bundeswehr. On the basis of a rough index that the British had furnished the National Archives, I began the process of untying the bundles and searching. Fortunately, what was left was very useful for my purposes, although the index was rather unreliable. Much of the collection seemed to have come from the Technical Office, and that shaped the way I wrote my account. Since there was no adequate way to label this material, I decided to cite the von Rohden numbers for my documentation. I knew after seven months of work at Freiburg that it would take some time to restore these vast holdings to an accurate filing system. The documents were piled up in a huge warehouse and Bundesarchivrat Wolf Noack, his assistant, and one typist were beginning the task of restoring them to order. Four years later when I returned to Freiburg, they were still working on the collection, so my decision to cite the documents by von Rohden numbers was a good one.

The original drafts of the von Rohden history and many of the documents appear on the National Archives T-971 series. The differences between the drafts written under the direction of the Allies makes for interesting contemporary history. Von Rohden and a few of his assistants tried to reconstruct the collection and write a history of the Luftwaffe for the British using not only the documents but also their own and British interrogation reports of Luftwaffe leaders and other materials that the British had picked up. Most of these papers are either still in England or have been sent to the Militärgeschichtliches Forschungsamt.

A second large collection of Luftwaffe documents is the Karlsruhe collection picked up by the Americans. In 1953 the United States Air Force organized a German Air Force Monograph Project under Colonel Wendell A. Hammer and Albert F. Simpson with the intention of writing forty monographs about the Luftwaffe's activities. They enlisted the aid of many former Luftwaffe officers, including Kesselring, Deichmann, and the historian Suchenwirth. Only about a quarter of these monographs were finished before the Air Force ran out of money or desire. The documents were then divided and duplicates or microfilm copies were sent back to Germany. Copies of documents along with some general books and special U.S. intelligence reports were then shipped to Maxwell Air Force Base, where they remain. The material sent to Germany first went to the Bundeswehr Leadership Academy in Hamburg and then finally to Freiburg. I used both sets, but found the German set far superior, since it had been kept up to date with additional books and articles, recent interviews, and obituaries. The Maxwell collection was of some particular use as a backstop, since some of the materials in the Freiburg collection were checked out by Bundeswehr personnel the entire time I was there. The emphasis in the Freiburg collection is on operational matters.

The Imperial War Museum in London has a superb pictorial collection of the Luftwaffe and the Milch papers, which have been microfilmed and copies sent to Freiburg. I do not know what has become of the British interrogations of Luftwaffe leaders and the technical papers they found. Most of the technical papers in American possession have been sent to Wright-Patterson for evaluation and then either returned to the original German owners, destroyed, or sent to the new Aerospace Museum in Washington, D.C.

The National Archives's Strategic Bombing Survey materials have a wealth of information about industrial preparations, along with some excellent interviews with the leading aircraft manufacturers. The huge Captured German Document Collection, which is on microfilm, is indispensable for the relationship between the Luftwaffe and the other service branches and the government.

An interesting account of what happened to the Luftwaffe archives as well as what research is being done on German military aviation can be found in the small pamphlet of the Militärgeschichtliches Forschungsamt entitled, *Fünfzig Jahre Luftwaffen- und Luftkriegs-Geschichtsschreibung* (Freiburg, 1970).

PRIMARY SOURCES

Baumbach, Werner. *The Life and Death of the Luftwaffe.* Translated by Frederick Holt. New York: Coward-McCann, 1960.

Bäumker, Adolf. *Zur Geschichte der deutschen Luftfahrtforschung.* Munich: Vogel, 1944.

Baur, Hans. *Mit Mächtigen Zwischen Himmel und Erde.* Oldendorf: K. Schütz, 1971.

Churchill, Winston. *The Gathering Storm.* New York: Bantam, 1961.

Deichmann, General der Flieger a.D. Paul. *German Air Operations in Support of the Army.* U.S. Historical Study No. 163. June 1962.

François-Poncet, André. *The Fateful Years: Memoirs of a French Ambassador in Berlin, 1931-1938.* New York: Fertig, 1972.

Galland, Adolf. *Die Ersten und die Letzten: Die Jagdflieger im zweiten Weltkrieg.* Darmstadt: Franz Schneekluth, 1953.

Gessler, Otto. *Reichswehrpolitik in der Weimarer Zeit.* Stuttgart: Kurt Sendtner, 1958.

Göring, Emmy. *An der Seite Meines Mannes.* Göttingen: K. W. Schütz, 1967.

Göring, Hermann. *Aufbau einer Nation.* Berlin: Eher, 1934.

Guderian, Heinz. *Panzer Leader.* New York: E. P. Dutton, 1952.

Heiber, Helmut. *Hitlers Lagebesprechungen.* Stuttgart: Deutsche Verlags-Anstalt, 1962.

Heinkel, Ernst. *Stürmisches Leben.* Stuttgart: Mundus, 1953.

Hoeppner, General der Kavallerie Ernst von. *Deutschlands Krieg in der Luft: Ein Rückblick auf die Entwicklung und die Leistungen unserer Heeres-Luftstreitkräfte im Weltkriege.* Leipzig: Koehler & Amelang, 1921.

Hoffman, Karl Otto. *Ln-Die Geschichte der Luftnachrichtentruppe.* Vol. 1. *Die Anfange- von 1935-1939.* Neckargemünd: Kurt Vowinckel, 1965.

Hossbach, Friedrich. *Zwischen Wehrmacht und Hitler, 1934-1938.* Wolfenbüttel: Wolfenbütteler Verlag, 1949.

Irving, David. *Die Tragödie der deutschen Luftwaffe: Aus den Akten und Erinnerungen von Feldmarschall Milch.* Frankfurt: Ullstein, 1970.

Kármán, Theodore von, and Lee Edson. *The Wind and Beyond: Theodore von Kármán, Pioneer in Aviation and Pathfinder in Space.* Boston: Little, Brown, 1967.

Kesselring, Generalfeldmarschall a.D. Albert. *Gedanken zum Zweiten Weltkrieg.* Bonn: Athenäum, 1955.

_____. *Soldat bis zum letzten Tag.* Bonn: Athenäum, 1953.

Koch, Horst-Adalbert. *Flak: Die Geschichte der deutschen Flakartillerie und der Einsatz der Luftwaffenhelfer.* Bad Nauheim: Podzun, 1965.

Krosigk, Graf Schwerin von. *Es geschah in Deutschland.* Stuttgart: Rainer Wunderlich, 1951.

Ley, Willy. *Rockets, Missiles, and Space Travel.* New York: Viking, 1954.

Liddell Hart, Basil. *The Liddell Hart Memoirs: The Later Years.* Vol. 2. New York: G. P. Putnam's Sons, 1965.

Manstein, Erich von. *Aus einem Soldatenleben.* Bonn: Athenäum, 1958.

_____. *Verlorene Siege.* Bonn: Athenäum, 1956.

Morgan, J. H. *Assize of Arms: The Disarmament of Germany and Her Rearmament, 1919-1939.* New York: Oxford University Press, 1946.

Morzik, Generalmajor a.D. Fritz. *German Air Force Airlift Operations.* U. S. Historical Division, Study 167, June 1961.

Morzik, Fritz, and Gerhard Hümmelchen. *Die deutschen Transportflieger im Zweiten Weltkrieg: Die Geschichte des "Fussvolkes der Luft."* Frankfurt: Bernard & Graete, 1966.

Nielsen, Generalleutnant Andreas. *The German Air Force General Staff.* USAF Historical Studies, no. 173. June 1959.

Osterkamp, Theo. *Durch Höhen und Tiefen jagt ein Herz.* Heidelberg: Kurt Vowinckel, 1952.

Raeder, Erich. *Mein Leben.* 2 vols. Tübingen: Fritz Schlichtenmayer, 1957.

Reichsgesetzblatt. 1933-39.

Rieckhoff, Generalleutnant Hans J. *Trumpf oder Bluff? 12 Jahre deutsche Luftwaffe.* Zurich: Interavia, 1945.

Schweppenburg, Geyr von. *Erinnerungen eines Militärattachés London 1933 bis 1937.* Stuttgart: Deutsche Verlags-Anstalt, 1949.

Seeckt, Hans von. *Thoughts of a Soldier.* London: E. Benn, 1930.

Speer, Albert. *Inside the Third Reich, Memoirs.* New York: Macmillan, 1970.

Thomas, Georg. *Geschichte der deutschen Wehr- und Rüstungswirtschaft (1918-1943/45).* Edited by Wolfgang Brikenfeld. Schriften des Bundes-Archives, vol. 14. Boppard am Rhein: Boldt, 1966.

Völker, Karl-Heinz. *Dokumente und Dokumentarfotos zur Geschichte der deutschen Luftwaffe.* Beiträge zur Militär- und Kriegsgeschichte, vol. 9. Stuttgart: Deutsche Verlags-Anstalt, 1968.

Weinberg, Gerhard L., ed. *Hitlers zweites Buch.* Stuttgart: Deutsche Verlags-Anstalt, 1961.

SECONDARY SOURCES

Addington, Larry H. *The Blitzkrieg Era and the German General Staff, 1865-1941.* New Brunswick, N.J.: Rutgers University Press, 1972.

Aleff, Eberhard; Walter Tormin; and Friedrich Zipfel. *Das Dritte Reich.* Bremen: Verlag für Literatur und Zeitgeschehen, 1970.

Bartz, Karl. *Als der Himmel brannte: Der Weg der deutschen Luftwaffe.* Hannover: Adolf Sponholtz, 1955.

Bauer, Wolfred. "The Shipment of American Strategic Raw Materials to Nazi Germany: A Study in United States Economic Foreign Policy, 1933-1939." Ph.D. dissertation, University of Washington, 1964.

Bekker, Cajus [pseud.]. *The Luftwaffe War Diaries.* New York: Ballantine, 1968.

Benoist-Mechin, Jacques. *Historie de l'armée allemande.* Vol. 1. Paris: A. Michel, 1936.

Bernhardt, Walter. *Die deutsche Aufrüstung, 1934-1939.* Frankfurt: Bernard & Grafe, 1969.

Bewley, Charles. *Hermann Göring and the Third Reich.* New York: Devin-Adair, 1962.

Bilanz des Zweiten Weltkrieges: Erkenntnisse und Verpflichtunger für die Zukunft. Oldenburg: Gerhard Stalling, 1953.

Birkenfeld, Wolfgang, *Der synthetische Treibstoff, 1933-1945.* Göttingen: Musterschmidt, 1964.

Blunck, Richard. *Hugo Junkers: Ein Leben für Technik und Luftfahrt.* Düsseldorf: Econ Verlag, 1951.

Bracher, Karl Dietrick. *Die Auflösung der Weimarer Republik: Eine Studie zum Problem des Machtverfalls in der Demokratie.* Villingen/Schwarzwald: Ring-Verlag, 1960.

Bracher, Karl Dietrich; Wolfgang Sauer; and Gerhard Schulz. *Die national-sozialistische Machtergreifung.* Schriften des Instituts für Politische Wissenschaft, vol. 14. Cologne: Westdeutscher Verlag, 1960.

Brady, Robert A. *The Rationalization Movement in German Industry.* Berkeley: University of California Press, 1953.

Broszat, Martin. *Der Staat Hitlers: Grundlegung und Entwicklung seiner inneren Verfassung.* DTV-Weltgeschichte des 20 Jahrhunderts, Vol. 9. Munich: DTV, 1969.

Caidin, Martin. *Me 109: Willy Messerschmitt's Peerless Fighter.* New York: Ballantine, 1968.

Carr, Edward Hallett. *The History of the Soviet Russia.* Vol. 3. *The Bolshevik Revolution, 1917-1923.* London: Macmillan, 1953.

Carroll, Berenice A. *Design for Total War: Arms and Economics in the Third Reich.* The Hague: Mouton, 1968.

Carsten, F. L. *The Reichswehr and Politics, 1918 to 1933.* Oxford: Clarendon Press, 1966.

_____. *The Rise of Fascism.* Berkeley: University of California Press, 1967.

Castellan, Georges. *Le Réarmement clandestin du Reich, 1930-1935: Vu par le 2e Bureau de l'Etat-Major Français:* Paris. Librarie Plon, 1954.

Collier, Basil. *The Defence of the United Kingdom.* London: H.M.S.O., 1957.

Conradis, Heinz. *Nerven, Herz und Rechenschieber: Kurt Tank, Flieger, Forscher, Konstrukteur.* Göttingen: Musterschmidt, 1955.

Craig, Gordon A. *The Politics of the Prussian Army, 1640-1945.* Oxford: Clarendon Press, 1955.

Craig, James F. *The Messerschmitt Bf 109.* New York: Arco, 1968.

Czichon, Eberhard. *Wer verhalf Hitler zur Macht? Zum Anteil der deutschen Industrie an der Zerstörung der Weimarer Republik.* Cologne: Westdeutscher, 1967.

Dahrendorf, Ralf. *Society and Democracy in Germany*. Garden City, N.Y.: Doubleday, 1967.

Davies, R. E. G. *A History of the World's Airlines*. New York: Oxford University Press, 1964.

Demeter, Karl. *The German Officer Corps in Society and State, 1650-1945*. New York: Praeger, 1965.

Douhet, Giulio. *Il Dominio del'aria: Probabili aspetti della guerra futura*. Rome: Ferrari, 1921.

Earle, Edward Mead, ed. *Makers of Modern Strategy: Military Thought from Machiavelli to Hitler*. New York: Atheneum, 1967.

Eicholtz, Dietrich. *Geschichte der deutschen Kriegswirtschaft, 1939-1945*. Vol. 1. *1933-1941*. Berlin: Akademie Verlag. 1969.

Eichholtz, Dietrich, and Wolfgang Schumann, eds. *Anatomie des Krieges: Neue Dokumente über die Rolle des deutschen Monopolkapitalismus bei der Vorbereitung und Durchführung des Zweiten Weltkrieges*. Berlin: Deutscher Verlag der Wissenschaften, 1969.

Emme, Eugene. "German Air Power, 1919-1939." Ph.D. dissertation, University of Iowa, 1949.

Erbe, René. *Die nationalsozialistische Wirtschaftspolitik 1933-1939 im Lichte der modernen Theorie*. Zürich: Polygraphischer, 1958.

Erfurt, Waldemar. *Die Geschichte des deutschen Generalstabes von 1918 bis 1945*. Göttingen: Musterschmidt, 1957.

Esenwein-Rothe, Ingeborg. *Die Wirtschaftsverbände von 1933 bis 1945*. Berlin: Duncker & Humblot, 1965.

Eyck, Erich. *Geschichte der Weimarer Republik*. Vol. 2. Zurich: E. Rentsch, 1956.

Fest, Joachim C. *Das Gesicht des Dritten Reiches: Profile einer totalitären Herrschaft*. Munich: R. Piper, 1963.

Feuchter, Georg Werner. *Der Luftkrieg*. Frankfurt: Athenäum, 1962.

Fischer, Wolfram. *Die Wirtschaftspolitik des Nationalsozialismus*. Lüneburg: Peters, 1961.

Förster, Gerhard. *Totaler Krieg und Blitzkrieg: die Theorie des Totalen Krieges und des Blitzkrieges in der Militärdoktrin des Faschistischen Deutschlands am Vorabend des Zweiten Weltkrieges*. Berlin: Deutscher Militärverlag, 1967.

Frischauer, Willi. *The Rise and Fall of Hermann Goering*. Boston: Houghton-Mifflin, 1951.

Gandenberger, Moisy F. von. *Luftkrieg—Zukunftskrieg? Aufbau, Gliederung und Kampfformen von Luftstreitkräften*. Berlin: Zentralverlag, 1935.

Gilles, J. A. *Flugmotoren 1910 bis 1918*. Frankfurt: E. S. Mittler, 1971.

Gordon, Harold J., Jr. *The Reichswehr and the German Republic, 1919-1926*. Princeton, N.J.: Princeton University Press, 1957.

Görlitz, Walter. *History of the German General Staff, 1657-1945*. New York: Praeger, 1953.

Goss, Hilton P. *Civilian Morale under Aerial Bombardment, 1914-1939*. 2 vols. Maxwell Air Force Base, 1948.

Green, William. *Augsburg Eagle*. Garden City, N.Y.: Doubleday, 1971.

————. *War Planes of the Second World War*. 10 vols. London: Macdonald, 1961-68.

Grey, C. G. *The Luftwaffe*. London: Faber & Faber, 1944.

Grimme, Hugo. *Der Reichsluftschutzbund: Aufgaben, Organisation, Tätigkeit*.

Berlin: Junker & Dünnhaupt, 1937.

Guhr, Hans. *Sieben Jahre interalliierte Militär-Kontrolle*. Breslau: Korn, 1927.

Heiden, Konrad. *Der Fuehrer*. Boston: Houghton Mifflin, 1944.

Herlin, Hans. *Udet—eines Mannes Leben und die Geschichte seiner Zeit*. Hamburg: Nannen, 1958.

Hermann, Hauptmann [pseud.]. *The Luftwaffe: Its Rise and Fall*. New York: G. P. Putnam's Sons, 1943.

Heron, S. D. *The Development of Aviation Fuels*. Cambridge: Harvard University Press, 1950.

Higham, Robin. *Air Power: A Concise History*. New York: St. Martins, 1973.

_____. *Armed Forces in Peacetime: Britain, 1918-1940, a Case Study*. Hamden, Conn.: Archon Books, 1962.

_____. *Britain's Imperial Air Routes, 1918-1939: The Story of Britain's Overseas Airlines*. London: G. T. Foulis, 1960.

_____. *The Military Intellectuals in Britain, 1918-1939*. New Brunswick, N.J.: Rutgers University Press, 1966.

Jacobsen, Han-Adolf. *Nationalsozialistische Aussenpolitik 1933-1938*. Frankfurt: Alfred Metzner, 1968.

Killen, John. *A History of the Luftwaffe, 1915-1945*. London: Frederick Muller, 1967.

Klein, Burton H. *Germany's Economic Preparations for War*. Cambridge, Mass.: Harvard University Press, 1959.

Knight-Patterson, W. M. *Germany from Defeat to Conquest*. London: Macmillan, 1945.

Krassin, Lubov. *Leonid Krassin: His Life and Work*. London: Sheffington & Son, 1929.

Kuczyneki, Jürgen. *Studien zur Geschichte des staats-monopolistischen Kapitalismus in Deutschland 1918 bis 1945*. Berlin: Akademie-Verlag, 1963.

Laqueur, Walter. *Russia and Germany: A Century of Conflict*. Boston: Little, Brown, 1965.

Lee, Asher, *Air Power*. New York: Praeger, 1955.

_____. *The German Air Force*. London: Duckworth, 1946.

_____. *Goering, Air Leader*. London: Duckworth, 1972.

Leeb, Emil. *Aus der Rüstung des Dritten Reiches*. Frankfurt: E. S. Mittler, 1958.

Lochner, Louis Paul. *Tycoons and Tyrant: German Industry from Hitler to Adenauer*. Chicago: H. Regnery, 1954.

Lusar, Rudolf. *Die deutschen Waffen und Geheimwaffen des 2. Weltkriegs und ihre Weiterentwicklung*. Munich: J. F. Lehmanns, 1959.

Manvell, Roger, and Heinrich Fraenkel. *Goering*. New York: Simon & Schuster, 1962.

Meinck, Gerhard. *Hitler und die deutsche Aufrüstung 1933-1937*. Wiesbaden: Franz Stein, 1959.

Meir-Welcker, Hans. *Seeckt*. Frankfurt: Bernard & Graefe, 1967.

Mosley, Leonard. *The Reich Marshal: A Biography of Hermann Goering*. Garden City, N.Y.: Doubleday, 1974.

Mueller-Hillebrand, Burkhart. *Das Heer 1933-1945: Entwicklung des organisatorischen Aufbaues*. Vol. 1. *Das Heer bis zum Kriegsbeginn*. Darmstadt: E. S. Mittler, 1954.

O'Neill, Robert John. *The German Army and the Nazi Party, 1933-1939*. New York: Heineman, 1966.

Orlovius, Heinz, and Ernst Schultze. *Die Weltgeltung der deutschen Luftfahrt*. Stuttgart: Fred Enke, 1938.

Peterson, E. N. *Hjalmar Schacht, for and against Hitler: A Political-Economic Study of Germany, 1923-1945*. Boston: Christopher, 1954.

Petzina, Dieter. *Autarkiepolitik im Dritten Reich: Der Nationalsozialistische Vierjahresplan*. Schriften der Vierteljahrshefte für Zeitgeschichte, 16. Stuttgart: Deutsche Verlag-Anstalt, 1968.

Postan, M. M.: D. Hay; and J. D. Scott. *Design and Development of Weapons, Studies in Government and Industrial Organization: History of the Second World War*. London: H.M.S.O., 1964.

Rabenau, Friedrich von. *Seeckt—Aus seinem Leben, 1918-1936*. Vol. 2. Leipzig: Hase & Koehler, 1940.

Rauschning, Hermann. *The Revolution of Nihilism*. New York: Alliance, 1939.

Ries, Karl. *Luftwaffe*. Vol. 1. *Die Maulwürfe, 1919-1935*. Mainz: Dieter Hoffmann, 1970.

Robertson, E. M. *Hitler's Pre-War Policy and Military Plans, 1933-1939*. London: Longmans, 1963.

Robinson, D. F. *Foreign Logistical Organization and Methods: A Report for the Secretary of War*. Washington, D.C., 1947.

Robinson, Douglas H. *Giants in the Sky: A History of the Rigid Airship*. Seattle: University of Washington Press, 1973.

Rosinski, Herbert. *The German Army*. New York: Harcourt, Brace, 1940.

Schlaifer, Robert. *Development of Aircraft Engines*. Boston: Harvard University Press, 1950.

Schliephake, Hanfried. *Wie die Luftwaffe wirklich entstand*. Stuttgart: Motorbuch, 1972.

Schramm, Percy Ernst. *Hitler: The Man and the Military Leader*. Chicago: Quadrangle, 1971.

Schuman, Frederick L. *The Nazi Dictatorship: A Study in Social Pathology and the Politics of Fascism*. New York: Knopf, 1935.

Schweitzer, Arthur. *Big Business in the Third Reich*. Bloomington, Indiana: Indiana University Press, 1964.

Schwipps, Werner. *Kleine Geschichte der deutschen Luftfahrt*. Berlin: Haude & Spenersche, 1968.

Simon, Leslie E. *German Research in World War II: An Analysis of the Conduct of Research*. New York: John Wiley, 1947.

Sörgel, Werner. *Metallindustrie und Nationalsozialismus*. Frankfurt: Europäische Verlagsanstalt, 1965.

Suchenwirth, Richard. *Command and Leadership in the German Air Force*. USAF Historical Studies, No. 174. Air University. 1969.

————. *The Development of the German Air Force, 1919-1939*. USAF Historical Studies, No. 160. Air University. 1968.

————. *Historical Turning Points in the German Air Force War Effort*. USAF Historical Studies, No. 189. Air University. June 1959.

Supf, Peter. *Das Buch der deutschen Fluggeschichte*. Vol. 2. Berlin: Klemm, 1935.

Tantum, W. H., and E. J. Hoffschmidt, eds., RAF. *The Rise and Fall of the German Air Force (1933 to 1945)*. Old Greenwich, Conn.: We Inc., 1969.

Taylor, Telford. *Sword and Swastika*. New York: Simon & Schuster, 1952.

————. *The Breaking Wave: The Second World War in the Summer of 1940*.

New York: Simon & Schuster, 1967.

Tessin, Georg. *Formationsgeschichte der Wehrmacht 1933-1939*. Boppard: Boldt, 1959.

Thoeny, Alan Robert. "Role of Separate Air Force in Nazi Germany." Master's thesis, University of Wisconsin, 1963.

Thorwald, Jürgen. *Ernst Udet: Ein Fliegerleben*. Berlin: Ullstein, 1954.

Turner, P. St. John. *Heinkel: An Aircraft Album*. New York: Arco, 1970.

Uhlig, Heinrich. *Die Warenhäuser im Dritten Reich*. Cologne: Westdeutsche Verlag, 1956.

Völker, Karl-Heinz. *Die Deutsche Luftwaffe 1933-1939*. Beiträge zur Militär-und Kriegsgeschichte, vol. 8. Stuttgart: Deutsche Verlagsanstalt, 1967.

_____. *Die Entwicklung der militärischen Luftfahrt in Deutschland 1920-1933*. Beiträge zur Militär- und Kriegsgeschichte, vol. 3. Stuttgart: Deutsche Verlagsanstalt, 1962.

Webster, Sir Charles, and Noble Frankland. *The Strategic Air Offensive against Germany, 1939-1945*. Vol. 1. London: H.M.S.O., 1961.

Weinberg, Gerhard L. *The Foreign Policy of Hitler's Germany: Diplomatic Revolution in Europe, 1933-1936*. Chicago: University of Chicago Press, 1970.

Westphal, Siegfried. *Heer in Fesseln*. Bonn: Athenäum, 1950.

Weyl, Alfred Richard. *Fokker: The Creative Years*. Totowa, N.J.: Putnam, 1965.

Wheaton, Eliot Barculo. *The Nazi Revolution, 1933-1935: Prelude to Calamity*. Garden City, N.Y.: Doubleday, 1969.

Wheeler-Bennett, John. *Munich: Prologue to Tragedy*. New York: Duell, Sloan & Pearce, 1948.

_____. *The Nemesis of Power: the German Army in Politica, 1918-1945*. New York: St. Martin's, 1954.

Williams, Roger Allan. "The Development of Luftwaffe Aircraft in the Nazi Era." Ph.D. dissertation, University of Minnesota, 1971.

Wood, Derek, and Derek Dempster. *The Narrow Margin*. New York: Paperback Library, 1961.

Wood, John Edwin. "The Luftwaffe as a factor in British Policy, 1935-1939." Ph.D. dissertation, Tulane University, 1965.

Yakovlev, A. S. *Fifty Years of Soviet Aircraft Construction*, U.S. Dept. of Commerce, NASA TTF-627, 1970.

ARTICLES

Baumgart, Winfried. "Zur Ansprache Hitlers vor den Führern der Wehrmacht am 22.August 1939—Eine quellenkritische Untersuchung." *Vierteljahrshefte für Zeitgeschichte* 16 (1968): 120-49.

Blaich, Fritz. "Wirtschaftspolitik und Wirtschaftsverfassung im Dritten Reich." *Das Parlament*. 71:3-18.

Bussman, Walter. "Zur Entstehung und Überlieferung der Hossbach-Niederschrift." *Vierteljahreshefte für Zeitgeschichte* 16 (1968): 373-84.

Carsten, F. L. "The Reichswehr and the Red Army, 1920-1933." *Survey* 44-45 (October 1962): 114-32.

Czichon, Eberhard. "Der Primat der Industrie im Kartell der nationalsozialistischen Macht." *Das Argument* 47(1968): 168-92.

Duisberg, Curt. "Die Einstellung der deutschen Unternehmer zur Wirtschafts-politik des Dritten Reiches." *Tradition* 5 (1968): 243-49.

Eichholtz, Dietrich, and Kurt Gossweiler. "Noch einmal: Politik und Wirtschaft 1933-1945." *Das Argument* 47 (1968): 210-27.

Feuchter, Georg W. "Entwicklung und kriegsentscheidende Bedeutung der Luft-kriegführung in zweiten Weltkrieg." *Flug-Wehr und Technik*, September 1948-December 1949 [15 installments].

Frankfurter Rundschau, May 30, 1970.

Grosser, Dieter. "Die nationalsozialistische Wirtschaft." *Das Argument* 32 (1965): 1-11.

Hallgarten, George W. F. "General Hans von Seeckt and Russia, 1920-1922." *Journal of Modern History* 21 (1949): 28-34.

Heimann, Bernhard, and Joachim Schunke. "Eine geheime Denkschrift zur Luftkriegskonzeption Hitler-Deutschlands vom Mai 1933." *Zeitschrift für Militärgeschichte* 3 (1964): 72-86.

Higham, Robin. "Government, Companies, and National Defense: British Aeronautical Experience, 1918-1945, as the Basis for a Broad Hypothesis." *Business History Review* 39 (1965): 321-47.

————. "Quantity vs. Quality: The Impact of Changing Demand on the British Aircraft Industry, 1900-1960." *Business History Review* 42 (1968): 443-66.

Kühnl, Reinhard. "Probleme der Interpretation des deutschen Faschismus." *Das Argument* 58 (1970): 258-79.

Mason, Tim. "Primat der Industrie? Eine Erwiderung." *Das Argument* 47 (1968): 193-209.

————. "Der Primat der Politik—Politik und Wirtschaft im Nationalsozial-ismus." *Das Argument* 41 (1966): 473-94.

Meinck, Gerhard. "Der Reichsverteidigungsrat." *Wehrwirtschaftliche Rundschau* 8 (1956): 411-22.

Nuss, Karl. "Einige Aspekte der Zusammenarbeit von Heereswaffenamt und Rüstungskonzernen vor dem zweiten Weltkrieg." *Zeitschrift für Militär-geschichte* 4 (1965): 433-43.

Parsons, Talcott. "Democracy and Social Structure in Pre-Nazi Germany." *Journal of Legal and Political Sociology* 1 (1942): 96-114.

Petzina, Dieter. "IG-Farben und Nationalsozialistische Autarkiepolitik." *Tradition* 5 (1968): 250-54.

Riess, Curt. "Die Junkers Tragödie." *Münchner Illustrierte,* July-August, 1955.

Schausberger, Norbert. "Wirtschaftliche Aspekte des Anschlusses Österreiches an das Deutsche Reich." *Militärgeschichtliche Mitteilungen* 2 (1970): 133-165.

Schmidt, Eberhard. "Entwicklung und Versuch in der deutschen Flugindustrie." *Flug-Wehr und Technik*, March 1947, pp. 79-82.

————. "Grundlagen und Wandlungen in der deutschen Flugzeugindustrie in den Jahren 1933-45." *Flugwehr und Flugtechnik* 1 and 2 (January and February 1947).

Schweitzer, Arthur. "Business Policy in a Dictatorship." *Business History Review* 38 (1964): 413-38.

————. "Depression and War: Nazi Phase." *Political Science Quarterly* 62 (1947): 301-53.

_____. "Der ursprüngliche Vierjahresplan." *Jahrbücher für Nationalökonomie und Statistik* 168 (1957): 348-96.

Simpson, Amos E. "The Struggle for Control of the German Economy, 1936-37." *Journal of Modern History* 31 (1959): 37-45.

Speidel, Helm. "Reichswehr und Rote Armee." *Vierteljahreshefte für Zeitgeschichte* 1 (1953): 20-34.

Spetzler, Eberhard. "Der Weg zur Luftschlacht um England in kriegsgerechtlicher Bedeutung." *Wehrwissenschaftliche Rundschau* 6 (1956): 442-55.

Stuebel, Heinrich. "Die Finanzierung der Aufrüstung im Dritten Reich." *Europa Archiv* 6 (1951): 4128-36.

Treue, Wilhelm. "Die Einstellung einiger deutscher Gross-industrieller zu Hitlers Aussenpolitik." *Geschichte in Wissenschaft und Unterricht* 17 (1966): 491-507.

_____. "Hitlers Denkschrift zum Vierjahresplan 1936." *Vierteljahreshefte für Zeitgeschichte* 3 (1955): 188-210.

Trevor-Roper, H. R. "A. J. P. Taylor, Hitler, and the War." *Encounter* 17 (1961): 88-96.

Turner, Henry Ashby, Jr. "Big Business and the Rise of Hitler." *American Historical Review* 75 (1969): 56-70.

Völker, Karl-Heinz. "Die geheime Luftrüstung in der Reichswehr und ihre Auswirkung auf den Flugzeugbestand der Luftwaffe bis zum Beginn des Zweiten Weltkrieges." *Wehrwissenschaftliche Rundschau* 9 1962: 540-49.

Vorwald, Wolfgang. "Die deutsche Luftwaffenrüstung im Rahmen der Gesamtrüstungen." *Wehrtechnische Hefte* 1 (1953): 8-19.

Watt, Donald Cameron. "German Plans for the Reoccupation of the Rhineland: A Note." *Journal of Contemporary History* 1 (1966): 193-99.

Weber, Theo. "Die Luftschlacht um England in historischer Sicht," *Flugwehr und Technik*, 1954, pp. 122-31.

Index

Aachen, 29
Aachen Academic Aviation Club, 14
ABC Program, 77–78, 84–85
Academic Flying Group (Akademischen Fliegergruppen; Akaflieg), 20
Adam, Wilhelm 46–47, 49, 75
Adlershof, 28
Aerial technology, 265–67
Aero (Czech firm), 233
Aerodynamic Research Institute at Göttingen, 210
Aero Sport, 108
Ago, 154, 185, 187
Aircraft, 41, 63, 66, 88, 154; models, 38, 148–50, 154, 160, 163, 170–71, 191, 212–13; selection of, 116–21, 124, 132
Aircraft industry, 1, 3, 24, 31, 62–68, 73, 98, 109, 139, 180–91, 194–95, 261–64. *See also* Industry
Airframe industry, 28, 183, 201, 203, 209–10, 260; employment in, 93, 108–9, 183–85, 189–90; engine plants and, 82–83, 183, 191; plants, 26, 35–36, 82–85, 87, 92–93, 107, 180, 186–87, 240; production of, 78, 224, 228
Airlines, 11–13, 32
Airships, 1, 4
Air Technical Academy, 101
Air War Academy 55, 101
Al 84, 36
Albatros, Blohm and Voss firm, 8–9, 12, 25–26, 31, 35–36
Allegemeine Elektrizität Gesellschaft (AEG), 11, 63, 108
Allegemeine Transportanlagen-Gesellschaft (ATG), 66–68, 108, 153, 181, 185, 187, 203, 261

Allied Aviation Guarantee Committee, 19
Allied Control Commission, 7
Allies, 7, 244; restrictions of, 1–2, 4, 6, 13, 39–40, 82, 257, 266
Altmärker, 20
Aluminum production, 144–46, 225, 228, 230, 232
Ambi-Budd Waggon-und Apparatebau A.G., 66
Ammoniakwerk Merseburg G.m.b.H., 147
Apparatebau Oscherslaben, 108
Ar 64, 26, 36, 80, 83, 105, 107, 150
Ar 65, 21, 26, 36, 80, 105, 107, 150, 155
Ar 66, 115–16
Ar 68, 105, 107, 115–16, 128, 150, 155
Ar 80, 128, 130
Ar 81, 126, 150, 151
Ar 95, 151
Ar 96, 116
Ar 195, 242
Ar 196, 242
Ar 197, 230
Ar 199, 230
Ar 240, 248
Ar SD 1, 25
Arado Flugzeugwerke, 25, 88, 115–16, 192, 199, 202, 224, 261; planes of, 36, 126, 128–29, 131, 203, 248; plants of, 26, 35, 91, 108, 183, 185, 187
Argentina, 207
Argus Motoren Gesellschaft of Berlin, 26–28, 36, 108, 186, 188, 192
Arianization of firms, 191–92, 233
Army, 2, 5, 13, 22–23, 28–29, 34,